T0336069

Applications of Machine Learning and Deep Learning for Privacy and Cybersecurity

Victor Lobo
NOVA Information Management School (NOVA–IMS), NOVA University Lisbon, Portugal & Portuguese Naval Academy, Portugal

Anacleto Correia
CINAV, Portuguese Naval Academy, Portugal

A volume in the Advances in Information Security, Privacy, and Ethics (AISPE) Book Series

Published in the United States of America by
    IGI Global
    Information Science Reference (an imprint of IGI Global)
    701 E. Chocolate Avenue
    Hershey PA, USA 17033
    Tel: 717-533-8845
    Fax: 717-533-8661
    E-mail: cust@igi-global.com
    Web site: http://www.igi-global.com

Library of Congress Cataloging-in-Publication Data

Names: Lobo, Victor, 1965- editor. | Correia, Anacleto, 1961- editor.
Title: Applications of machine learning and deep learning for privacy and
  cybersecurity / Victor Lobo and Anacleto Correia, editors.
Description: Hershey, PA : Information Science Reference, an imprint of IGI
  Global, [2022] | Includes bibliographical references and index. |
  Summary: "This comprehensive and timely book provides an overview of the
  field of Machine and Deep Learning in the areas of cybersecurity and
  privacy, followed by an in-depth view of emerging research exploring the
  theoretical aspects of machine and deep learning, as well as real-world
  implementations"-- Provided by publisher.
Identifiers: LCCN 2021052894 (print) | LCCN 2021052895 (ebook) | ISBN
  9781799894308 (h/c) | ISBN 9781799894315 (s/c) | ISBN 9781799894322
  (ebook)
Subjects: LCSH: Computer networks--Security measures--Data processing. |
  Computer security. | Deep learning (Machine learning)
Classification: LCC TK5105.59 .A67 2022 (print) | LCC TK5105.59 (ebook) |
  DDC 005.8--dc23/eng/20211207
LC record available at https://lccn.loc.gov/2021052894
LC ebook record available at https://lccn.loc.gov/2021052895

This book is published in the IGI Global book series Advances in Information Security, Privacy, and Ethics (AISPE) (ISSN: 1948-9730; eISSN: 1948-9749)

British Cataloguing in Publication Data
A Cataloguing in Publication record for this book is available from the British Library.

All work contributed to this book is new, previously-unpublished material.
The views expressed in this book are those of the authors, but not necessarily of the publisher.

For electronic access to this publication, please contact: eresources@igi-global.com.

Advances in Information Security, Privacy, and Ethics (AISPE) Book Series

Manish Gupta
State University of New York, USA

ISSN:1948-9730
EISSN:1948-9749

MISSION

As digital technologies become more pervasive in everyday life and the Internet is utilized in ever increasing ways by both private and public entities, concern over digital threats becomes more prevalent.

The **Advances in Information Security, Privacy, & Ethics (AISPE) Book Series** provides cutting-edge research on the protection and misuse of information and technology across various industries and settings. Comprised of scholarly research on topics such as identity management, cryptography, system security, authentication, and data protection, this book series is ideal for reference by IT professionals, academicians, and upper-level students.

COVERAGE

- Security Classifications
- Internet Governance
- Information Security Standards
- Cyberethics
- IT Risk
- Device Fingerprinting
- Data Storage of Minors
- Privacy-Enhancing Technologies
- Privacy Issues of Social Networking
- Tracking Cookies

IGI Global is currently accepting manuscripts for publication within this series. To submit a proposal for a volume in this series, please contact our Acquisition Editors at Acquisitions@igi-global.com or visit: http://www.igi-global.com/publish/.

Titles in this Series

For a list of additional titles in this series, please visit: http://www.igi-global.com/book-series/

Cross-Industry Applications of Cyber Security Frameworks
Sukanta Kumar Baral (Indira Gandhi National Tribal University, India) Richa Goel (Amity University, Noida, India) Md Mashiur Rahman (Bank Asia Ltd., Bangladesh) Jahangir Sultan (Bentley University, USA) and Sarkar Jahan (Royal Bank of Canada, Canada)
Information Science Reference • © 2022 • 244pp • H/C (ISBN: 9781668434482) • US $250.00

Cybersecurity Issues and Challenges for Business and FinTech Applications
Saqib Saeed (Imam Abdulrahman Bin Faisal University, Saudi Arabia) Abdullah M. Almuhaideb (Imam Abdulrahman Bin Faisal University, Saudi Arabia) Neeraj Kumar (Thapar Institute of Engineering and Technology, India) Noor Zaman (Taylor's University, Malaysia) and Yousaf Bin Zikria (Yeungnam University, Republic of Korea)
Business Science Reference • © 2022 • 300pp • H/C (ISBN: 9781668452844) • US $270.00

Methods, Implementation, and Application of Cyber Security Intelligence and Analytics
Jena Om Prakash (Ravenshaw University, India) H.L. Gururaj (Vidyavardhaka College of Engineering, India) M.R. Pooja (Vidyavardhaka College of Engineering, India) and S.P. Pavan Kumar (Vidyavardhaka College of Engineering, India)
Information Science Reference • © 2022 • 269pp • H/C (ISBN: 9781668439913) • US $240.00

Information Security Practices for the Internet of Things, 5G, and Next-Generation Wireless Networks
Biswa Mohan Sahoo (Manipal University, Jaipur, India) and Suman Avdhesh Yadav (Amity University, India)
Information Science Reference • © 2022 • 313pp • H/C (ISBN: 9781668439210) • US $250.00

701 East Chocolate Avenue, Hershey, PA 17033, USA
Tel: 717-533-8845 x100 • Fax: 717-533-8661
E-Mail: cust@igi-global.com • www.igi-global.com

Table of Contents

Detailed Table of Contents

Chapter 1

Ioannis Tsimperidis, Democritus University of Thrace, Greece
Avi Arampatzis, Democritus University of Thrace, Greece

The anonymity that users can maintain when connecting to the internet, in addition to the positive effects, such as being able to express their views and ideas freely without fear of retaliation, also carries some risks, such as the fact that it is a significant advantage for malicious users. In order to remove the complete anonymity of internet users, so as to protect unsuspecting users, this work attempts to identify some of their characteristics, namely gender, age, and handedness, using data coming from typing. For this purpose, the rotation forest is used as a classifier, and keystroke dynamics features are selected based on the chi-square feature selection procedure. The final results show that user profiling can be achieved with an accuracy of 88.9% in gender prediction, 86.3% in age prediction, and 94.3% in handedness prediction.

Chapter 2

Ntebogang Dinah Moroke, North West University, South Africa
Katleho Makatjane, Department of Statistics, University of Botswana,
Botswana

Financial fraud remains one of the most discussed topics in literature. The financial scandals of Enron, WorldCom, Qwest, Global Crossing, and Tyco resulted in approximately 460 billion dollars of loss. The detection of financial fraud, therefore, has become a critical task for financial practitioners. Three factors determine the likelihood of fraud occurrence, including pressure, opportunity, and rationalization. The core of these factors lies in people's beliefs and behaviour. Due to the unpredictability and uncertainty in fraudsters' incentives and techniques, fraud detection requires a skill set that encompasses both diligence and judgment. Big data technologies have had a huge impact on a wide variety of industries because they tend to be ubiquitous, starting in the last decade and continuing today.

Swati Jaiswal, Pimpri Chinchwad College of Engineering, Pune, India
Pallavi S. Yevale, Dr. D. Y. Patil Institute of Engineering, Management,
and Research, Pune, India
Anuja R. Jadhav, Pimpri Chinchwad College of Engineering, Pune, India

The automotive industry is developing trends in autonomous driving and connected vehicular systems. These vehicles can access and send the data, download the software updates, connect with other vehicles or other IoT devices via the internet or wireless communication. Autonomous vehicle control urges very strict requirements about the security of the communication channels used by the vehicle to exchange information and the control logic that performs complex driving tasks. So, the increased connectivity results in a heightened risk of a cyber-security attack. For maintaining the advances in safe communication, it is important to establish strong security for connected vehicular systems. For this, existing cybersecurity attacks must be considered to minimize future cybersecurity risks in the connected and autonomous vehicle systems. In this chapter, the authors will emphasize recent works on how autonomous vehicles can ensure strong operation under ongoing cyber security attacks and their possible solutions.

Manoj Jayabalan, Liverpool John Moores University, UK

Authentication is the preliminary security mechanism employed in the information system to identify the legitimacy of the user. With technological advancements, hackers with sophisticated techniques easily crack single-factor authentication (username and password). Therefore, organizations started to deploy multi-factor authentication (MFA) to increase the complexity of the access to the system. Despite the MFA increasing the security of the digital service, the usable security should be given equal importance. The user behavior-based authentication provides a means to analyze the user interaction with the system in a non-intrusive way to identify the user legitimacy. This chapter presents a review of user behavior-based authentication in smartphones and websites. Moreover, the review highlights some of the common features, techniques, and evaluation criteria usually considered in the development of user behavior profiling.

Chapter 5

Banyatsang Mphago, Botswana International University of Science and
    Technology, Botswana
Dimane Mpoeleng, Botswana International University of Science and
    Technology, Botswana
Shedden Masupe, Botswana Institute for Technology Research and
    Innovation, Botswana

The use of deception systems is a viable option in reducing the never-ending tussle between the attackers and the defenders. The deception systems give the defenders an edge over their counterparts since they provide the platform to learn the methods and techniques the attackers use. However, the effectiveness of the deception system is highly dependent on how they truly hide their identity. A deceptive honeypot has the capacity to persuade and change the cognitive behavior of an attacker. An attacker whose cognitive behavior has been altered by the deception capabilities of a honeypot is more likely to reveal his attack methods; hence, the defenders are able to learn how to defend against those future attacks.

Chapter 6

Eduardo Barros, Instituto Superior Técnico, Portugal
Victor Lobo, NOVA Information Management School (NOVA-IMS),
    NOVA University Lisbon, Portugal & Naval Academy, Portugal
Anacleto Correia, CINAV, Portuguese Naval Academy, Portugal

Distributed denial of service (DDoS) attacks are an enormous threat, mainly because of the extension they can reach, the ease of deployment, the losses that it can cause, and the effort it can take to detect and stop this type of attack. Machine learning techniques have been and are widely used to prevent DDoS attacks. As a matter of fact, many gigantic intrusion detection systems (IDS) have been proudly utilising machine learning techniques to help the conventional signature detection system by adding another layer of "intelligent" thinking. This chapter provides a context of the techniques used for detecting DDoS attacks using machine learning, and in demonstrating why the merge of these concepts have huge potential for the defence of a given system. To that matter, some studies that use machine learning approaches for DDoS detection are analysed. Finally, this chapter provides a high-level view of the types of DDoS attacks that are considered a threat, the machine learning approaches to detect these attacks, and why these approaches are cohesive.

Chapter 7

Sivasankari Narasimhan, Mepco Schlenk Engineering College, India

Many types of physical unclonable function (PUF) structures have been proposed in the last decade. The responses generated from the conventional PUF are vulnerable to attack. In this chapter, the transient effect of ring oscillator structure has been used. This works on two loops with complex loops containing NOT gates and NAND gates. Response prediction of these loops is a very difficult task for the adversary. Many machine learning algorithms may produce the responses with higher accuracies. This study provides new masked PUF architectures that are more secure and invulnerable to modeling attacks. Hence, in this chapter, masking-based configurability design on various PUF structures is introduced. This will be helpful for resource-constrained machines. For different sizes of challenge-response pair, machine learning techniques need to be changed, but prediction accuracy by the attacker should be low. By using this kind of masked PUF structure, 54.7% uniqueness can be obtained, and 97.5% reliability can be achieved. Machine learning accuracy is 70.7% with SVM and 63.67% accuracy in LR.

Chapter 8

Katleho Makatjane, Department of Statistics, University of Botswana, Botswana

Ntebogang Dinah Moroke, North West University, South Africa

Artificial intelligence is gradually becoming the standard mechanism underpinning online banking. Users' profiles can be confirmed using a variety of methods, including passcodes, fingerprints, acoustics, and images through this technology. On the other hand, traditional cybersecurity measures are unable to prevent internet-based fraud after the visualisation process has been infiltrated. In light of this, the aim of this chapter is to examine the efficiency of the logistic model tree (LMT) in detecting financial fraudulent transactions in South African banks and, ultimately, to develop a financial fraud early warning system. Web-scraping credit and debit card fraud data from SA are used to acquire daily data. The LMT is constructed utilizing a training set from the LogitBoost algorithm and obtained 17 financial conditioning elements. Overall, an early warning system model has shown to be a good performer with a prediction rate of 99.9%. This appears to be a promising approach for detecting online fraud vulnerabilities.

Chapter 9

Darrell Norman Burrell, Marymount University, USA & Capitol Technology University, USA
Calvin Nobles, Illinois Institute of Technology, USA
Maurice Dawson, Illinois Institute of Technology, USA
Eugene J. M. Lewis, Capitol Technology University, USA
S. Raschid Muller, Capitol Technology University, USA
Kevin Richardson, Edward Waters University, USA
Amalisha S. Aridi, Capitol Technology University, USA

According to the US Federal Bureau of Investigations (FBI) the number of complaints about cyberattacks to their cyber division is up to as many as 4,000 a day. Every year in the U.S., 40,000 jobs for information security analysts go unfilled, and employers are struggling to fill 200,000 other cybersecurity-related roles. Colleges and universities have created certificate, undergraduate, and graduate programs to train professionals in these job roles. The challenge to meeting the cybersecurity workforce shortage through degree programs is intensified by the reality of the limited number of cybersecurity and engineering faculty at colleges and universities. This chapter explores the essential need to develop more doctorate faculty in technology-related areas and explains some unique and non-traditional paths to doctoral completion that allow professionals with significant real-world work experience to complete a doctorate without career interruption and relocation from highly respected and established universities in the US and the UK.

Chapter 10

Chhaya Suryabhan Dule, Dayananda Sagar University, India
Rajasekharaiah K. M., AMC College of Engineering, Visvesvaraya Technological University, India

The methods used to predict, categorize, and recognize complex data like pictures, audio, and texts have been popular in machine learning. These methods are the basis for future AI-driven internet providers because of unparalleled precision in deep learning methodologies. Commercial firms gather large-scale user data and perform machine learning technique. The massive information necessary for machine learning raises privacy problems. The user's personal and extremely sensitive data such as photographs and voice records are gathered and retained forever by these commercial firms and users can not limit the intents of these sensitive information. In addition, centrally stored data is susceptible to legal and extrajudicial monitoring. Many data owners use profound extensive learning by security and confidentiality. This chapter contains a practical approach that allows several parties to learn a precise model of complex systems for a specific purpose without disclosing their data sets. It provides an interesting element in utility and privacy.

Preface

Information is of paramount importance in contemporary economies. The access to information in modern societies is automated by several processes and systems (*e.g.*, financial, health care, government, traffic, and military) supported by a plethora of information technologies. Many users are led to rely on digital transactions since they are, most of the times, the most effective way to access and transfer goods and services.

The information security's mantra of CIA (confidentiality, integrity, and availability) highlights the relevance of aspects such as the trustworthiness of information for users, the privacy of whom interacts or accesses social media platforms, or the security of information stored digitally. However, cyberspace has become a new battlefield with cyberthreats and cyberattacks increasing substantially. Eavesdropping and theft in cyberspace has resulted in losses of hundreds of billions of dollars to businesses. It is estimated that in 2021 cybercrime was the economic activity with the third largest yield in the world, worth around more than € 5.5 billion USD, more than arms and drug trafficking together, just behind the GDP of the economies of the United States and China.

Cyber operations have jeopardized fair elections and instigated social movements, undermining people's confidence in governments, markets, and even military security. As the modern market has become more connected online, cyberthreats have grown more sophisticated and ubiquitous.

In a more insidious way, hacking operations generate distrust in how systems operate by exploiting security flaws in computer systems. For instance, a cyberattack can hack and control a pacemaker, causing harm to the patient using the device; a system's backdoor can allow hackers to access a weapon's control, changing the real target of the weapon; cyberattacks can lead to distrust in the integrity of data or the algorithms that process data, such as in the case of voters distrusting from elections' accuracy, or the military not knowing whether the missile detected by a situational awareness system is a real attack or a fake scenario triggered by malware. Privacy, in a digital world, can also be jeopardized and produce distrust in ownership or control of information to the point that a user can no longer be sure whether its photos remain private, a company's intellectual property was leaked, or nuclear weapons plans have fallen into the rivals' possession. Finally, cyberattacks create distrust by manipulating social networks and relationships and ultimately deteriorating social cohesion. Online trolls, fake bots, and disinformation campaigns sow suspicion among groups and the information conveyed by each other. All these cyberthreats have implications that can erode the foundations on which markets, societies, governments, and the international system were built.

Inability to protect intellectual property from cybertheft has similar ramifications. Hacking into a company's network and collecting sensitive data to steal intellectual property or trade secrets has become a lucrative criminal activity. The more widespread and effective such attacks become, the less firms can trust that their research and development efforts will pay off, eventually destroying knowledge-based economies. Online banking is equally vulnerable to cyberthreats. If people lose faith in the security of their digital data and money, the entire modern financial system could implode.

Schools, courts, and municipal governments, as well as virtual classrooms, judicial records, and local emergency services, have all been victims of ransomware attacks, in which systems are knocked offline or rendered worthless until the victim pays up. The impact of these attacks erodes governance and social functions, leading to the lack of confidence in the integrity of data maintained by governments—whether birth certificates, marriage records, property divisions, or criminal records - thus jeopardizing society's most basic processes.

The possibility of cyber-operations being able to jeopardize military capacity is another concerning factor, given the risk of weapons being made hostages of hackers, due to the fact that military are ever more dependent on smart weaponry, networked sensors, and autonomous platforms in their forces. Hence, as armed forces evolve towards digital transformation, they become more vulnerable to cyberattacks, which can jeopardize the security and facilitate inappropriate access to smart weapon systems. Furthermore, as commanders move further away from the battlefield thanks to remote operation of military systems and delegate responsibility to autonomous systems, this trust becomes even more important, to the point where the military have to have faith that cyberattacks on autonomous systems will not render them ineffective or, worse, cause fratricide or the deaths of civilians.

To date, cyberthreat solutions have primarily centred on preventing, protecting against, and defeating cyberthreats as they attack their targets. However, as cyberattacks are on the rise, as the efficiency of deterrence is uncertain, and as offensive approaches appear to be insufficient to stem the flood of attacks that threaten the world's contemporary digital foundations, this strategy has been only partially successful, if not an actual failure. The key to success in cyberspace over the long term and to find ways to defeat cyberattacks could rely on machine learning and in particular deep learning. Some machine learning and deep learning techniques applied to privacy and cybersecurity are discussed in different chapters in this volume.

In a concise definition, a cyberattack is any activity aggressively taken to affect information systems, networks, and infrastructures. A cyberattack occurs when a system or network weakness is exploited due to security vulnerabilities. The primary aim of a cyberattack is to rob, alter, or erase data, using cyberthreat tool to access confidential data, or compromise systems. Even if the target is unaware of all forms of cyberattacks, it may have a system in place to cope with a few of them.

A taxonomy of cyberthreats includes: (i) download of applications threats (malware, spyware, privacy breaching software, software that exploits zero-day vulnerabilities), (ii) Network and Wi-Fi security threats (network exploiting, wi-fi sniffing, cross platform attacks, and BOYD), (iii) general cybersecurity threats (phishing, social engineering, drive-by-downloads, browser flaws, OS flaws, and data storage flaws), and (iv) physical threats (loss and theft of hardware, or its compromise).

On the other hand, cyberattacks classification include the following types of operations: Malware (ransomware, virus, worms, spyware, adware, and trojan horses), Phishing (deceptive phishing, data theft), Password attacks (brute force, dictionary, keylogger), Man-in-the-Middle, SQL injection, Denial-of-Service (application layer flood, distributed DoS, unintended DoS), DNS tunnelling, Drive-by-Download, Malverting (pop-up Ads, inline frames, Video Ads, Banner, Central Ads, Animated Ads), Rouge software, and Zero-day exploit.

Artificial Intelligence (AI) models can contribute to improving cybersecurity protection and for building solutions to minimise cyberattacks and ensure better information privacy. Machine learning (ML), as a subset of AI, is a data-driven approach that can be used for predictive purposes. ML algorithms generally use supervised or unsupervised learning methods. Unsupervised learning does not require labelled data or user feedback concerning the evaluation of the results while supervised learning relies on labelled data, or feedback by humans concerning the correction of the results. ML methodology usually involves training an algorithm with a set of data so it can identify patterns in new data sets. Reinforcement learning, on the other hand, is a class of ML where the system learns by trial and error, being rewarded or penalized based on the success of its actions.

Some of the machine learning and deep learning techniques, with varied perspectives, are explored in different chapters in this volume. The chapters present a wide variety of applications concerning privacy and cybersecurity. And it is an international perspective, both in terms of the varied geographical points of origin for the research and for the authors' locations. While this book is a comprehensive overview, and the research and thinking presented in these chapters provide solutions to their specific topics, each chapter also raises many additional questions that deserve further scrutiny and exploration.

ORGANIZATION OF THE BOOK

Those who are interested in machine learning and deep learning applied to privacy and cybersecurity should find ample material for study and exploration. The chapters of this book present a variety of topics on machine learning and deep learning applied to privacy and cybersecurity.

In Chapter 1, Ioannis Tsimperidis and Avi Arampatzis explore keystroke dynamics as biometric trait from which information can be extracted by exploiting data that comes from the way a user types on a real or virtual keyboard. Studies in keystroke dynamics have been conducted for about fifty years and their object is mainly user authentication to replace or enhance the authentication method using passwords. Keystroke dynamics were also used to classify users according to an inherent or acquired characteristic, such as gender or age, as well as to assess users' physical and mental conditions, such as whether they were exhausted, if they suffer from depression, or if they suffer from a neurological disease. Many years of experimentation with keystroke dynamics resulted in the development of systems with very good performance in user authentication and user classification. The work of Tsimperidis, *et al.* uses keystroke dynamics to find some characteristics of completely unknown Internet users, to remove complete anonymity and solve some of the existing problems. To achieve this, a machine learning model is used which combines simplicity of operation with efficiency, namely the rotation forest. In this work, user profiling is attempted with data coming from the way users type and with the help of the rotation forest which uses the C4.5 decision tree as the base classifier. Specifically, the gender, the age, and the handedness of unknown Internet users are predicted, and the highest accuracy achieved was 88.9%, 86.3%, and 94.3%, respectively. The results show that the use of rotation forest in keystroke dynamics classification problems is very promising and can be the basis of a machine learning system that will serve as a cybersecurity tool.

In Chapter 2, Ntebogang Moroke and Katleho Makatjane note that machine learning algorithms have previously been employed to analyse authorised transactions and suspicious reports. These reports are investigated by professionals who contact the cardholders to confirm if the transaction was genuine or fraudulent. The investigators then provide feedback to the automated system which is used to train and update the algorithm to eventually improve the fraud detection performance over time. This traditional way of detecting debit or credit card fraud is tedious and takes quite a lot of time when cards are stolen or lost. Hence this chapter contributes to the existing methods by building a Chrome extension that flags *"Fraud/suspicious"* transactions that will help both banks and cardholders to know about the fraudulent transactions made and further develop a *"find my card application.* The *"find my card application"* is a new system that cardholders will be able to install and have an opportunity to trace the whereabouts of their cards if stolen or lost. Cardholders will also be able to stop their usage with the use of their cell phones or computer browsers. Even though detecting financial fraud is considered a high priority for many organisations, recent literature lacks updated and comprehensive in-depth reviews that can help organisations with their decisions for selecting an appropriate data mining method. Therefore, the objective of the chapter is to apply the gradient boosting decision tree (GBDT) under deep learning to extract knowledge about the processing of the credit/debit card data to detect whether a normal transaction of datasets qualified as a novel fraud and finally determine its effectiveness to classify the number of fraudulent transactions.

In Chapter 3, Swati Jaiswal, Pallavi S. Yevale, and Anuja R. Jadhav introduce readers to the realm of autonomous vehicles' security and its applications. These vehicles can access and send the data, download software updates, and connect with other vehicles or other *Internet of Things* (IoT) devices via the internet or wireless communication. Data from various kinds of sensors are combined and used for the detection of obstacles in the vehicle's path, and after due pre-processing, enabling autonomous control of the vehicle, including the braking mechanism and the engine. The list of observed objects provides a vehicle environment model where the present condition is analyzed, and the track to the destination is scheduled. With a sudden increase in wireless communication, the complexity of connected vehicular systems has changed the traditional security in the automotive industry. Autonomous vehicle control urges very strict requirements about the security of the communication channels used by the vehicle to exchange information and the control logic that performs complex driving tasks. So, the increased connectivity results in a heightened risk of a cyber-security attack. For maintaining the advances in safe communication, it is important to establish strong security for connected vehicular systems. To this end, existing and known cybersecurity attack methods must be considered so as to minimize future cybersecurity risks in the connected and autonomous vehicle system. In this chapter, the authors emphasize recent work on how autonomous vehicles can ensure operation under ongoing cyber security attacks and their possible solutions. Results using machine learning algorithms in this field will also be summarized.

In Chapter 4, Manoj Jayabalan focuses on digital authentication, as a mean to provide secure access to digital information using various technologies. There are several methods proposed in the literature to secure data access, such as multifactor authentication, but usability is a concern with most of them. Transparent and continuous authentication provides a better trade-off between security and usability. Employing user behavior-based authentication to the existing multi-factor authentication framework will provide additional security to the system without user intervention. There is a need for continuous authentication to be performed in the industries managing sensitive data, by analyzing the user behavior in the access to their digital services, so as to detect potential threats. The purpose of the chapter is to understand the potential inclusion of user behavior profiling in traditional authentication frameworks. Moreover, the chapter highlights some of the common features, techniques, and evaluation criteria usually considered in the development of user behavior profiling. The scope of the chapter is limited to user behavior-based authentication in smartphones and websites. This chapter is meant to be useful for identifying trends in user behavior profiling that will allow researchers to focus on areas that needs to be improved and new features that could be beneficial to stakeholders.

In Chapter 5, Banyatsang Mphago, Dimane Mpoeleng, and Shedden Masupe write about the use of deception systems as a viable option in reducing the never-ending tussle between the attackers and the defenders. Traditional approaches are firmly based on the premise that the network perimeter is an effective means to protect the information assets within the organization and that employees within the organization can be trusted. In the face of these challenges, some organizations have changed the tactics and employed a 'need-to-know' approach as an effective way to secure their assets. The emergence of deception systems is becoming more and more a viable option to protect computer assets. The use of honeypots in protecting computer and information assets comes from the notion that 'you cannot protect what you don't know'. Therefore, honeypots came as a viable option to understand attackers and their attack methods. Once deployed, a successful honeypot must be able to deceive, lure, and record all the attackers' activities.

In Chapter 6, Eduardo Barros, Victor Lobo, and Anacleto Correia explore the availability pillar of the CIA triad and the threat of Distributed Denial of Service (DDoS) attacks. The way this attack operates is by flooding the target with malicious traffic, depleting its bandwidth and/or computing resources to create total unavailability or some disruption of a network asset. One of the hardest tasks for an Intrusion Detection System (IDS) is to mitigate a DDoS. This type of attack has some peculiarities that makes it hard to defeat, namely: (i) the DDoS might be originated from thousands of legitimate devices; (ii) the requests may not contain any malicious content; (iii) the attacker can exploit a vulnerability in the attacked service but also in an external service to conduct the attack. Unlike most attacks, where only one malicious request is needed for it to be successful, a DDoS generally requires multiple requests, so it might be possible to identify patterns shared by malicious packets. This characteristic is key and allows the use of machine learning for the purposes of identifying recurrent patterns in a DDoS. The aim of the chapter is to demonstrate that the use of machine learning for DDoS detection has potential, and also demonstrate how this can be done, introducing concepts for the creation of a model capable of predicting DDoS requests, and selectively block them.

In Chapter 7, Sivasankari Narasimhan mentions the use of Physical Unclonable Function (PUF) structures for cybersecurity purposes. Since the responses generated from the conventional PUF are vulnerable to attack, in this chapter, the transient effect of ring oscillator structure has been used. This works on two loops with complex loops containing NOT gates and NAND gates. Response prediction of these loops is a very difficult task for the adversary. Many machine learning algorithms may produce the responses with higher accuracies. This work provides new masked PUF architectures that are more secure and invulnerable to modeling attacks. Hence, in this chapter, masking-based configurability design on various PUF structures is introduced. This is helpful for resource-constrained machines. For different sizes of Challenge-Response Pair, machine learning techniques need to be changed, but prediction accuracy by the attacker should be low. By using this kind of Masked PUF structure better results can be attained.

In Chapter 8, Katleho Makatjane and Ntebogang Moroke deal with the identification of financial fraud. Between 2018 and 2019, online transactions increased credit and debit card theft by 20.5 percent. Hackers continue to obtain sensitive and private information from users, allowing them to trade on their accounts without their permission. A good fraud detection solution should be able to correctly categorize and detect fraudulent transactions in real-time transactions. The goal of this chapter is to leverage the Google Flutter platform to crowd-source credit and debit card ratings in order to classify transactions using supervised learning as fraudulent or not. The Logistic Model Tree (LMT) algorithm was used for detecting financial fraudulent transactions and, ultimately, to develop the financial fraud early warning system. Overall, an early warning system model has shown to be a good performer with a prediction rate of 99.9 percent.

In Chapter 9, Darrell Burrell, Calvin Nobles, Maurice Dawson, Eugene Lewis, Raschid Muller, Kevin Richardson, and Amalisha Aridi consider cybersecurity from the point of view of education, given that the number of complaints about cyberattacks to the Cyber Division of the US Federal Bureau of Investigations (FBI), has gone up to as many as 4,000 a day. The chapter explores the essential need to develop more PhD holding faculty in technology related areas and explains some unique and non-traditional paths to doctoral completion that allow professionals with significant real world work experience to complete a doctorate without career interruption and relocation from highly respected and established universities in the US and the UK.

In Chapter 10, Chhaya Dule and Rajasekharaiah K.M. note that the massive gathering of information necessary for machine learning raises very clear privacy problems. The firms that gather the information retain forever the user's personal and extremely sensitive data such as photographs and voice records. Users cannot remove it or limit the intents for which it is utilized. However, centrally stored data is susceptible to legal and extrajudicial monitoring. Many data-owning organizations, for instance professional organizations that desire to use deep learning techniques in clinical records, are hindered from sharing the information and, more generally, from conducting extensive learning with that data by security and confidentiality rules. The chapter contains practical approaches that allow several parties to learn and develop models of complex systems for a specific purpose without disclosing their data sets and violating the security and confidentiality rules. It provides an interesting element in utility and privacy: the respondents (that give away their personal information) retain the privacy of their information while gaining from other users' designs, thereby enhancing the accuracy of learning beyond what can be achieved by their contributions alone.

We hope you find the chapters to follow both interesting and useful.

Victor Lobo
NOVA Information Management School (NOVA-IMS), NOVA University Lisbon,
Portugal & Portuguese Naval Academy, Portugal

Anacleto Correia
CINAV, Portuguese Naval Academy, Portugal

Chapter 1
User Profiling Using Keystroke Dynamics and Rotation Forest

Ioannis Tsimperidis
https://orcid.org/0000-0003-0682-1750
Democritus University of Thrace, Greece

Avi Arampatzis
https://orcid.org/0000-0003-2415-4592
Democritus University of Thrace, Greece

ABSTRACT

The anonymity that users can maintain when connecting to the internet, in addition to the positive effects, such as being able to express their views and ideas freely without fear of retaliation, also carries some risks, such as the fact that it is a significant advantage for malicious users. In order to remove the complete anonymity of internet users, so as to protect unsuspecting users, this work attempts to identify some of their characteristics, namely gender, age, and handedness, using data coming from typing. For this purpose, the rotation forest is used as a classifier, and keystroke dynamics features are selected based on the chi-square feature selection procedure. The final results show that user profiling can be achieved with an accuracy of 88.9% in gender prediction, 86.3% in age prediction, and 94.3% in handedness prediction.

INTRODUCTION

People work, communicate, trade goods and services, are entertained and educated, and much more, in a very different way than a few years ago. Telecommunication and teleconferencing applications, various eShops, online games, courses of any

DOI: 10.4018/978-1-7998-9430-8.ch001

kind, and many more, have made their appearance serving the needs of individuals, companies, and organizations. The cause of all these rapid changes is the evolution and dissemination of the Internet and the services it offers. Today, a user has the ability to connect with other users from anywhere in the world through video calling or instant messaging applications, or through social networks. Also, every user has the opportunity to purchase products or services from the global market, with the same ease that he/she would do in his/her neighborhood, or even easier. It is also possible to find work for or with companies and individuals that may be located thousands of kilometers away.

Many opportunities for personal, national, and global growth and development are offered, but at the same time there are many risks, such as financial frauds, seduction of minors, hacking, anonymous threats, etc. (Degtereva et al., 2020). One of the most important reasons for the existence of these risks is the partial or complete anonymity that a user can maintain when connecting to the Internet. This anonymity, on the one hand, often proves useful as it helps the user to express and freely be creative, but on the other hand may alter his/her behavior by turning him/her into a rude, aggressive, and disrespectful person (Krysowski & Tremewan, 2020). In addition, anonymity or concealment of true identity is one of the major advantages of malicious users in their plans to deceive unsuspecting users and/or carry out cyber-attacks.

Also noteworthy is that the way in which users interact on the Internet is shaped by the fact that although a variety of communication methods are offered, such as voice calls, video calls, file sharing, etc., text is still the dominant form of communication (Nitzburg & Farber, 2019) among users. A variety of instant messaging applications are available and many companies invest significant amounts of money in their development. If we additionally consider the email service, the comments made by users on various social media, and searches carried out in search engines, each of which is primarily in text, a backdrop is formed in which text, or rather text typing, plays a prominent role on the World Wide Web, in user communication, and in computer operations in general.

Keystroke dynamics are a biometric trait from which information can be extracted by exploiting data that comes from the way a user types on a real or virtual keyboard. Studies in keystroke dynamics have been conducted for about fifty years and their object is mainly user authentication (Raul et al., 2020) in order to replace or enhance the authentication method using passwords. Keystroke dynamics were also used to classify users according to an inherent or acquired characteristic, such as gender or age, as well as to assess users' physical and mental condition, such as whether they were exhausted (Ulinskasa et al., 2018), if they suffer from depression (Mastoras et al., 2019), or if they suffer from a neurological disease (Lam et al., 2020). Many years of experimentation with keystroke dynamics resulted in the development of systems with very good performance in user authentication and user classification.

The features used in keystroke dynamics relate to how the users type, not what they type, and can be divided into temporal and non-temporal. The most commonly used temporal features are the keystroke durations which are the time intervals between the push of a button and its release, and the digram latencies which are the time intervals between the uses of two consecutive keys. Digram latency can be expressed in four different ways, firstly, the time elapsed between the pressing of the first key and the pressing of the second key (i.e. the down-down digram latency or DDDL), secondly, the time elapsed between the pressing of the first key and the releasing of the second key (i.e. the down-up diagram latency or DUDL), thirdly, the time elapsed between the releasing of the first and the pressing of the second key (i.e. the up-down diagram latency or UDDL), and fourthly, the time elapsed between the releasing of the first and the releasing of the second key (i.e. the up-up diagram latency or UUDL). Other temporal keystroke dynamics features are trigram latencies, which are similarly defined, tetragram latencies, and generally n-gram latencies, the number and duration of typing pauses, typing speed, etc. Non-temporal features include the percentages of usage of each of the duplicate keys, such as "Shift", "Ctrl", and the number keys, the mode of correction of typing errors (i.e., backspace vs. delete), the application in which typing is performed, and other typing features.

This work uses keystroke dynamics to find some characteristics of completely unknown Internet users, in order to remove complete anonymity and solve some of the problems mentioned. To achieve this, a machine learning model is used which combines simplicity of operation with efficiency, namely the rotation forest. The next section of the chapter provides a review of the literature related to the topic of user classification using keystroke dynamics. Then an analysis is made of the stages of the methodology followed and the results of the experiments conducted are presented. Following are suggestions for exploiting the findings of this chapter and references to possible extensions of this research. Finally, the conclusion of the chapter is presented.

KEYSTROKE ANALYSIS

The reasons for trying to identify certain characteristics of a computer user vary. For example, when a cybercrime is committed and the culprit is sought, it would be a valuable help if some of his/her characteristics were known, such as gender, age, handedness, mother tongue, educational level, etc., in order to reduce the number of suspects. In another application, targeted advertising would benefit, since on the one hand the investment of the companies would have better results and on the other hand the users would not be overwhelmed with many and indifferent advertising messages, but with much less and more targeted ones. Also, knowing some characteristics of the user using a computer enables the user-computer interaction to become much more successful. That is, it would be possible to provide advice and suggestions to the users to visit certain websites, use certain services, and participate in certain groups that are more suitable for them. In addition, by revealing the characteristics of the users, it would be possible to warn unsuspecting users about the possibility of falling victim to some deception. These reasons, and possibly others, are the motivation for many works in the field of keystroke dynamics aimed at identifying certain characteristics of computer and Internet users.

In one such study, Fairhurst and Da Costa-Abreu (2011) focused on the use of social networks by young people and the existence of risks of hiding the real characteristics of users. They used an existing dataset with data from 98 male and 35 female users. They used three simple classifiers, namely k-nearest neighbors, C4.5 decision tree, and naive Bayes, as well as three classifier combination techniques. The best results came from the dynamic classifier selection based on local accuracy class (DCS-LA) (Woods et al., 1997), with an error rate of 3% in gender prediction.

Antal and Nemes (2016) attempted to identify the user gender of a mobile device from data from touchscreen swipes and keystroke dynamics. Thus, they used two datasets, one created by recording touchscreen swipes while answering a questionnaire consisting of 58 questions and one created by recording the typing of a specific password by 42 users, 24 males and 18 females. In terms of keystroke dynamics the features that were extracted were the keystroke durations, the down-down digram latencies, the pressure exerted on the virtual keys, and the surface covered when using the keys. Random forest was used for the classification and the results showed an accuracy of 93.5% in the identification of the user's gender.

Lee et al. (2018) also dealt with mobile devices in their research and aimed to solve the problem of authentication of smartphone users using PIN or pattern drawing, due to the fact that it is very vulnerable to the shoulder surfing attack. They collected data from typing on smartphones and as features, among others, used keystroke durations and all versions of digram latencies. Researchers using distance algorithms have been able to identify an impostor with an equal error rate (EER) of 8%, which is an indicator of system performance. EER is a point where false acceptance rate and false rejection rate intersects, and the lower it is, the more accurate the system. But importantly, they also found that it is easier to identify an impostor when the legal user is of the opposite gender, thus proving that it is possible to separate users according to their gender depending on the way they type, offering another suggestion for implementing gender classification.

Udandarao et al. (2020) examined the effect of various characteristics of the users on the way they type, such as their computer experience, their gender, their height, etc. They used an existing dataset created by recording 117 volunteers, who typed two specific sentences and answered a series of questions. Regarding the gender demographics of the volunteers, 72 were males and 45 were females. The features they used were keystroke durations, all types of digram latencies, as well as features related to whole words. For the gender classification, six machine learning models and four deep learning models were tested, of which the convolutional neural network (CNN) achieved the highest accuracy of 93%.

Identifying the gender of the person we are talking to is a simple process during a face-to-face conversation. Facial characteristics, expressions, and differences imposed by some cultures (such as hairstyle and clothing), are clues for making such an identification. But all these are absent when chatting on the Internet and this is the reason why Buker and Vinciarelli (2021) conducted their research to reveal the gender of the user who communicates via chat applications. They collected data from the discussion of 60 people, in pairs, through a chat application, of which 35 were females and 25 were males. The features extracted were the density of "!", density of "?", density of non-alphabetic characters, typing speed, backspace time, etc. For classification they used a random forest reaching an accuracy of 98.8% and showing what the most important features are for separating users according to their gender, i.e. typing speed, backspace time, and density of "backspaces", among others.

Data similar to those derived from keystrokes were addressed by Van Balet et al. (2016). The reason for their research was that gender is hidden in online conversations often for malicious purposes. Given the differentiation of gestures between males and females, the possibility of separating users according to their gender depending on mouse movements was examined. Data were collected from 94 users (49 women and 45 men) with the two groups having similar statistical characteristics in terms of age and computer experience. Features were extracted from the data such as the time that the left click remains pressed, the maximum speed observed during the movement of the mouse, the total distance traveled by the mouse during an action, etc. The user gender was predicted using logistic regression and the results showed an accuracy approaching 76% in an independent test set and once the outliers have been removed.

Gender is the user characteristic sought in most keystroke dynamics research, mainly because it is a characteristic that is quite distinct compared to others, such as age and educational level, as well as because it seems to be of the greatest commercial interest. Idrus et al. (2014) in their work dealt with other characteristics besides gender and attempted to do user profiling from data coming from keystrokes. For this reason they used two datasets, one created by recording the typing of five short phrases and one by recording free text typing. As a classifier they used a support vector machine

(SVM) with a radial basis function kernel. They performed experiments to find the gender, the age group (<30 and ^{3}30), and the handedness of users. In each group of experiments the datasets were balanced by removing excess instances, so that for example the number of males is equal to the number of females, etc. The results showed accuracy up to 86% in gender classification, up to 78% in age classification, and up to 88% in handedness classification.

Beyond gender, the second most frequently sought characteristic is age. In the studies that involve classification, age groups are defined, and the aim is to find the group to which a user belongs. The segregation of groups in each separate research has been usually done based on the limits set by legislation, such as the age that separates minors from adults, based on the available dataset so that classes with the same number of instances emerge, or based on other criteria, which could also be arbitrary. Thus, Tsimperidis et al. (2021) arbitrarily defined four classes and found the age group that a user belongs to, utilizing data from the typing patterns. A dataset from the typing recording of 118 volunteers was used and keystroke durations and down-down diagram latencies were used as features. Of the five classifiers tested, radial basis function network (RBFN) was the most successful with 90% accuracy.

The dangers of the Internet for children led Uzun et al. (2015) to check how successfully typing data can be used to distinguish children from adults. For the needs of their research, they recorded the typing of users who belonged to two age groups, 10-14 and 18-49 years old. The recording was made on a specific computer with an application created by the researchers in which they invited the volunteers to answer some questions. For the separation between children and adults they used a number of classifiers, of which the linear SVM proved to be the most successful with EER 8.8%.

In their work, Hossain and Haberfeld (2020) attempted to separate children from adult users, again with the aim of protecting minors from the dangers of the Internet. They focused on mobile devices and created an application for recording users, in which volunteers were asked to press six keys, in a specific order, several times. They divided users into three age groups, children (5-12 years old), adolescents (13-17 years old), and adults (18 years old and older). The features that were taken advantage of were keystroke durations, the surface occupied by the finger, and the pressure exerted on each virtual key. For the classification they used linear models, nearest neighbors, and SVMs. The results showed a successful identification of the user's age group with a percentage of about 73% on smartphones and 82% on tablets.

In another work, Vesel et al. (2020) was trying to find out if there are any obvious differences in the way users with mood disorders type. For this purpose, they used keystroke dynamics data in order to diagnose depression, bipolar disorder, anxiety, attention deficit hyperactivity disorder, post-traumatic stress disorder, etc. As features they used inter-key delay (IKD) which are the DDDLs between key types (not between each individual key), typing speed, and pauses during typing. An important finding of their research is the significant differentiation in IKDs between the age groups of individuals close to 20 years, close to 45 years, and close to 70 years, which makes it possible to separate users according to their age depending on the way they type.

User handedness is a characteristic which is rarely explored in research, mainly due to the fact that the datasets that are created are extremely unbalanced and the classification procedure is very difficult. In a study, Roy et al. (2018) attempt to reveal the handedness of a smartphone user, among other characteristics. To create a keystroke dynamic dataset, they developed a web-based application and recorded 92 users typing a particular word seven times. Keystroke durations and all types of digram latencies were used as features. After removing the outliers from their data, they proceeded to classification using the SVM, naive Bayes, random forest, and multinomial nominal log linear model. The best results came from random forest with 81.5% accuracy.

The handedness of an unknown user, among other characteristics, is sought in the work of Tsimperidis et al. (2021). Researchers recorded typing by a number of volunteers during the daily usage of their computers. From the data they collected they extracted 230 keystroke durations and digram latencies, and by testing five different machine learning models they were able to identify the dominant hand of an unknown user with 97% accuracy. While in another study, Earl et al. (2021) tried to show that the combined use of keystroke and mouse dynamics features can bring better results in recognizing some user characteristics. To collect keystroke data 240 volunteers copied a piece of text and answered a question. Digram latencies and the error rates were extracted from the recorded data as features. They followed a feature selection process and tried some combinations of features to achieve the best results. Decision trees, random forest, Gaussian naive-Bayes, SVM, and K-nearest neighbors were used for classification. Finally, experiments showed that a user's handedness can be predicted with 73.5% accuracy taking advantage of keystroke dynamics features.

In addition to the gender, age, and handedness that are sought in this chapter, in the literature there are also studies that aim to find other user characteristics, such as ethnicity, educational level, etc. The bottom line, however, is that more and more efforts are being made in this direction, with new techniques being tested, and there are now quite reliable systems for finding certain characteristics of computer users by exploiting data derived from typing.

METHODOLOGY AND RESULTS

The methodology followed in the present study consists of three steps. Firstly, the keystroke dynamics data collection. Secondly, the extraction of features from the data and the selection of the most appropriate ones for user classification according to the gender, age, and handedness. Thirdly, the use of a machine learning model and finding its appropriate parameters for effective user classification.

Data Acquisition

An appropriate dataset in keystroke dynamics studies is crucial for performing experiments and drawing correct conclusions. The dataset should be accompanied by the appropriate demographics and contain the required data. In some keystroke dynamics research ready-made datasets were used (Giot et al., 2015) while in others new ones had to be created. Creating a keystroke dynamics dataset can be done by recording the typing of users who have been asked to copy a specific piece of text, a task usually performed in a closed environment, or by recording the typing of users who type at will, something that is done either by answering specific questions and performing specific tasks, or by using the computer without any restrictions and instructions. The former way to create a keystroke dynamics dataset is called fixed-text and the latter free-text.

In the data acquisition task of this work, the mode that approaches the normal operation of the computer as close as possible was selected. Specifically, a keylogger was installed on the volunteers' computer which has the ability to record typing actions from any application in a Windows environment. For security and privacy reasons, the volunteers were given the opportunity to enable and disable the keylogger whenever they wished, to monitor the recorded data but without being able to modify it, to leave the process at any time, and to decide whether to deliver or not the log files. In addition, a consent form was signed in which the researchers pledged not to share the data in any way and to use it only for the purposes of the present study. This ensures that personal and/or sensitive data, such as passwords and personal messages are not leaked to other people.

In a period that lasted a little over 18 months, 118 volunteers were recorded and handed over log files. Each of the volunteers submitted 3-4 log files resulting in the creation of a dataset of 387 log files, each of which contains data of approximately 3,500 keystrokes and metadata with the characteristics of the volunteers, among which was the gender, the age, and the handedness of users. In each log file, each record corresponds to an action on the keyboard and consists of four fields, separated by a comma. The first field lists the key on which the action was performed, in the form of a virtual key code, which is a standard encoding by which each key and each mouse action is assigned a number from 1 to 255. With the first 7 codes corresponding to mouse actions the recording concerned codes 8 to 255. The second field records the date on which the action took place. The third field records the exact time that the action took place in the form of an integer that indicates the number of milliseconds that have elapsed since the beginning of the day, i.e., at 12 midnight. Finally, the fourth field lists the type of action, which can be key-press or key-release.

Feature Extraction and Feature Selection

From the data recorded in the dataset it is possible to extract most of the features used in keystroke dynamics studies. For example, subtracting the value in the third field of a record for one keypress from the corresponding value of the next record for the key-release of the same key results in the keystroke duration. Also, subtracting the values of the third field that have two consecutive records for key presses results in DDDL. Moreover, counting the number of records that first field has the value 160, and those that have the value 161, results in the number of times the left and right "Shift" were used, respectively, and therefore the percentage of use of each of these. In similar ways it is possible to extract many other keystroke dynamics features.

The number of available features is in the order of millions and therefore a choice must be made as to which of them will be used. As such, in the present work, the most widely used features in keystroke dynamics studies, i.e., keystroke durations and down-down digaram latencies, were selected. In a log file, each key and each digram has been recorded many times, resulting in many different measurements for the same feature. Finally, the value of the feature is the average of these many measurements. In fact, for reasons of reliable calculation of feature values, when the use of a key in a log file has been recorded less than five times it is not taken into account. Similarly, a digram latency is not considered if the corresponding digram has been recorded less than three times.

Approximately 65,000 features were extracted with this process, which is a very large number and the use of all of them will lead to time consuming systems. For this reason, a feature selection procedure was followed in order to find those features that can best distinguish the users according to gender, age, and handedness.

The Chi-Square feature selection was followed as such procedure. In feature selection, Chi-Square calculates the correlation between a class and a feature. When the resulting value of the Chi-square is small it means that it will be difficult to distinguish the classes only using the feature as class differentiator, and therefore may be rejected. On the contrary, when the value is high then this feature is characterized as capable of separating classes. The problem is that the Chi-Square feature selection procedure can be applied when classes and features are categorical, but the features used in this classification are measured in milliseconds, i.e., they are numerical.

However, if numerical features are suitably discretized, they can also be used in the procedure.

The Chi-Square value for each feature f, which has discretized in v values, in a classification problem with C classes, is given by the formula:

$$\chi^2(f) = \sum_{i=1}^{v} \sum_{j=1}^{C} \frac{\left(O_{ij} - E_{ij}\right)^2}{E_{ij}} \tag{1}$$

O_{ij} is the number of times where feature f is observed to have the i-th value in the j-th class. E_{ij} is the number of times where feature f is expected to have the i-th value in the j-th class. If this procedure, which is also described in the work of Rachburee and Punlumjeak (2015), is followed for each feature in each of the three classification problems, three lists of features are generated, with features ranked by their usefulness (as measured by their Chi-Square values) in separating users according to the characteristics studied.

In Table 1, the first 15 features are ranked with the highest Chi-Square for gender, age, and handedness classification problems, where each of them is represented by the virtual key code(s) of the keys that compose it. So, one number indicates keystroke duration, and two numbers indicate down-down digram latency.

Some observations that can be made from Table 1 are: a) keystroke durations seem to play a more important role than digram latencies in age classification, while digram latencies are more significant in gender classification; b) the "A", "M", "N", and "O" keys, along with the digrams in which they participate, show high correlation with gender; c) the keys "A" and "T", along with the digrams in which they participate, are placed quite high on the list of the most important features in case of handedness classification; d) in case of age classification, Chi-Square values are much higher than the other two classification problems, which means that a feature that is in the two, or all three, lists, in the same ranking position, as for example with the "D" keystroke duration, is more capable of separating users by age than others characteristics. It should be noted that as far as observation (b) is concerned, the keys mentioned are at the left end and at the right end of the character range on the keyboard. This finding needs to be further studied to find out if there is a correlation between the location of the keys on the keyboard and the way they are used by users with different characteristics.

Table 1. Keystroke dynamics features with the highest Chi-Square in gender, age, and handedness classification

#	Gender			Age			Handedness		
	Feat.	Keys	χ^2	Feat.	Keys	χ^2	Feat.	Keys	χ^2
1	80-65	P-A	28.4685	65-32	A-(space)	79.2127	79	O	51.0753
2	77-65	M-A	25.8396	69	E	71.9764	84-65	T-A	39.4705
3	73-78	I-N	24.0143	79	O	50.5387	82-65	R-A	35.2808
4	78-65	N-A	23.8809	65	A	43.8988	71	G	28.8362
5	68	D	22.4733	68	D	41.9577	65	A	28.7747
6	77-79	M-O	21.7047	83	S	40.6108	65-84	A-T	25.2559
7	75-65	K-A	21.4770	32	(space)	40.5972	186	;:	23.4427
8	78-79	N-O	20.5897	87	W	40.4034	83-84	S-T	21.3273
9	76-69	L-E	20.1416	39	(right-arrow)	39.2502	69	E	21.1344
10	79-77	O-M	19.4597	89	Y	36.7346	76-69	L-E	20.3488
11	65	A	19.2735	86	V	36.0397	66	B	19.0795
12	69-73	E-I	18.8601	70	F	35.3603	65-32	A-(space)	17.7110
13	79-78	O-N	18.7485	88	X	33.7660	82	R	16.0820
14	65-83	A-S	18.5307	73-32	I-(space)	33.6719	186-89	;:-Y	15.9355
15	87	W	18.4606	78	N	30.4884	76-73	L-I	14.6795

Rotation Forest

As mentioned in the section "Keystroke Analysis", many classifiers have been used to classify users using keystroke dynamics features. Among them are SVM, random forest, naïve Bayes, RBFN, k-nearest neighbors, C4.5 decision tree, and many others. One classifier that has not been used so far in keystroke dynamics user classification studies, to our knowledge, is the rotation forest. It is a classifier ensemble where each base classifier uses a different training set, and all of them can be trained in parallel.

For each classifier in the ensemble the available feature set, for each of the classification problems, is divided into a number of subsets. These subsets may be disjoint or intersecting, but to achieve greater diversity in the training sets of base classifiers the disjoint subsets are preferred. For each of the feature subsets, half the classes of the problem are randomly selected and only the instances labeled with these classes are retained from the original dataset. Thus, a number of different sub-datasets are created. For each of these sub-datasets a percentage of the remaining instances is randomly removed. Then, principal component analysis (PCA) is performed on the features and the instances of each sub-dataset to calculate the coefficients of principal components and to form a sparse matrix. The columns of this matrix are rearranged to correspond to the original features. Finally, the training set for a base classifier is calculated by multiplying this "rotation" matrix with the initial dataset. When this process is completed s, the training set for each base classifier is created. This algorithm is described in more detail in the work of Rodriguez et al. (2006).

Therefore, the classifier parameters are the number of base classifiers, the number of features that will form a subset (which can be set between two values), and the percentage of instances that are removed from the dataset. It is noted that the C4.5 decision tree is chosen as the base classifier, on the one hand because of its simplicity, and on the other hand because it is sensitive to rotation of the features.

Experiments and Results

The keystroke dynamics feature selection procedure showed 514, 690, and 246 features with a non-zero Chi-Square value for gender, age, and handedness classification problems, respectively. In the experimental procedure that was followed, all these features were used, and a different number of base classifiers were tested. Specifically, experiments were conducted for 10, 20, 30, 40, and 50 base classifiers, and for each different number the best performance of the rotation forest was sought, as measured by the accuracy, the training time (time to build model, TBM), the F-score (F1), and the area under the ROC curve (AUC).

The F1 score is used, as a combined measurement of precision and recall, because accuracy alone cannot fully give the picture of the overall performance of a model when classes are imbalanced, and because the F1 score is a measurement of how balanced the prediction across classes is. For example, assume two cases of a system for a handedness classification problem, where, as expected (Papadatou-Pastou et al., 2020), the ratio of left versus right handers is 1:10. In the first case, the system predicts all users as right-handed. The accuracy is 90%, but it is obvious that the system is not working properly. In the second case, the system correctly predicts the dominant hand of users 9 out of 10 instances, for all classes. The accuracy is again 90%, but this system is more reliable. This greater reliability is reflected in the F-score, where in the latter case is higher.

AUC, which is a common tool for evaluating predictions, e.g., Cook and Ramadas (2020), is also used to form a more complete picture of classifier performance. The receiver operating characteristic (ROC) curve is a plot that presents the recall as a function of probability of false alarm, which is equal to 1 - precision. The ROC curve is limited to the interval [0, 1] in both dimensions, thus AUC, which is an area enclosed between the curve and the false positive rate axis, varies between 0 and 1.

The well-known 10-folds cross-validation was used in the experiments, i.e., the dataset is randomly divided into 10 disjoint parts with approximately equal size and every part is in turn used to test the model induced from the other 9 parts, e.g., Wong and Yang (2017). In this study, where there are 387 log files, each part in which the dataset was divided consists of 38 or 39 files. With the volunteers having delivered 3-4 log files it was easy to include all files of each individual in one of the 10 parts, so that to avoid overfitting in case that one log file from a person could end up in the training set while another one ends up in the testing set.

Gender Classification

In the gender classification problem two classes were defined, "male" and "female", and out of the 118 volunteers who participated in the typing process, 61 were male (51.7% of all volunteers) who submitted 203 log files (52.4% of all log files) and 57 were female (48.3% of all volunteers) who submitted 184 log files (47.6% of all log files). That is, the dataset is gender balanced and reflects global demographics, since men and women are roughly equal in number. Table 2 shows the best performance of the rotation forest for different numbers of base classifiers.

The best performance shown in Table 2 was achieved for the case of 10 base classifiers having subsets between 3 and 12 features and removing 50% of instances, for the case of 20 base classifiers having subsets between 1 and 10 features and removing 25% of instances, for 30 base classifiers the rotation forest parameters were the creation of subsets between 5 and 10 features and the removal of 10% of the instances, in the case of 40 base classifiers the values of respective parameters were 9, 10, and 50%, and finally, for the case of 50 C4.5 decision trees, which is the base classifier, the corresponding values of the rotation forest parameters were 3, 12, and 25%.

Table 2. Performance of the rotation forest in the gender classification problem for different numbers of base classifiers

Base Classifiers	Acc.	TBM (secs)	F1	AUC
10	85.0%	3.27	0.850	0.916
20	88.1%	9.33	0.881	0.936
30	87.9%	14.69	0.879	0.939
40	88.4%	14.19	0.884	0.953
50	88.9%	23.09	0.889	0.950

An obvious conclusion drawn from Table 2 is that performance seems to increase as more base classifiers are used, at a cost of increasing TBM.

Age Classification

Four age classes were defined in the age classification problem, "18-25", "26-35", "36-45", and "46+" years old users. Of the 118 volunteers, 31 belonged to the age group "18-25" (26.2% of all volunteers) who submitted 96 log files (24.8% of all log files), 37 belonged to the age group "26-35" (31.4%) who submitted 129 log files (33.3%), 37 belonged to the age group "36-45" (31.4%) who submitted 117 log files (30.2%), and 13 belonged to the age group "46+" (11.0%) who submitted 45 log files (11.7%). The dataset is balanced in terms of the first three classes, while the fourth class is less represented, although the number of instances is considered sufficient as it is less than three times smaller than that of the other classes. Table 3 shows the best performance of the tested classifier for 10, 20, 30, 40, and 50 C4.5 decision trees.

In Table 3 the best performance of the rotation forest with 10 base classifiers was achieved creating subsets having features between 9 and 10 and removing 50% of instances, while with 20 decision trees was achieved with subsets of 10 to 15 features and removing the 75% of instances, with 30 decision trees with subsets of 9 to 10 features and removing the 75% of instances, with 40 trees with 10 to 15 features in subsets and removing 90% of instances, and finally, in the case of 50 base classifiers the best performance achieved having subsets of 10 to 15 features and removing the 50% of instances.

The conclusion drawn from Table 3 for age classification, similar to that of gender classification in Table 2, is that effectiveness seems to increase as more base classifiers are used, at a cost of increasing TBM.

Table 3. Performance of rotation forest in the age classification problem for different numbers of base classifiers

Base Classifiers	Acc.	TBM (secs)	F1	AUC
10	80.1%	6.14	0.799	0.927
20	83.2%	8.69	0.830	0.953
30	83.5%	12.88	0.833	0.951
40	85.0%	13.60	0.848	0.951
50	86.3%	29.92	0.862	0.963

Handedness Classification

In most keystroke dynamics studies dealing with handedness, two classes were defined, "right-handed" and "left-handed", as shown in the section "Background". But in this research the class "ambidextrous", in which included users who said they use both right and left hand with the same skill, is added. Of the 118 volunteers who participated in the process, 105 were "right-handed" (89.0% of all users) who submitted 343 log files (88.6% of all log files), 10 were "left-handed" (8.5%) who submitted 35 log files (9.0%), and 3 were "ambidextrous" (2.5%) who submitted 9 log files (2.4%). The dataset is as unbalanced as would be expected according to global demographics. Table 4 presents the best performance of rotation forest for different numbers of base classifiers in predicting the dominant hand of users.

The values of rotation forest parameters, and specifically the minimum number of features in each subset, the maximum number of features, and the percentage of instances removed, which lead to the best performance showing in Table 4, are as follows: for 10 base classifiers 1, 10, and 90%, respectively, for 20 base classifiers 3, 20, and 85%, respectively, for 30 base classifiers 5, 10, and 50%, respectively, for 40 base classifiers 1, 10, and 75%, respectively, and finally, for 50 base classifiers 3, 3, and 25%, respectively.

Overall, the number of base classifiers does not seem to impact effectiveness much, so using a small number (e.g., 10) is recommended in order to avoid high costs of TBM.

Table 4. Performance of rotation forest in the handedness classification problem for different numbers of base classifiers

Base Classifiers	Acc.	TBM (secs)	F1	AUC
10	94.1%	1.19	0.930	0.967
20	94.1%	1.47	0.931	0.939
30	94.3%	3.70	0.934	0.964
40	94.3%	5.25	0.935	0.959
50	94.1%	9.43	0.933	0.958

Discussion of the Results

The summary results of the experiments in terms of accuracy in the three classification problems examined are presented in Figure 1.

Figure 1. Accuracy in the three classification problems over different number of base classifiers

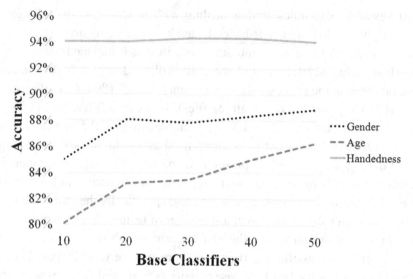

As shown in Figure 1 and Tables 2, 3, and 4, the accuracy in each of the three classification problems far exceeds the baseline. The baseline can be defined as the percentage of instances of the dominant class in the dataset. Thus, the baseline in gender classification case is considered 52.4%, while the highest accuracy that measured is 88.9%. In the case of age classification, the baseline is considered 33.3%, while the highest accuracy is 86.3%. Finally, in the handedness classification the baseline is 88.6% and the highest accuracy is 94.3%.

Regarding the improvement of accuracy in relation to the increase in the number of base classifiers, different behavior is observed in each of the three cases. In the search for user handedness, the accuracy does not seem to increase with the increase of the number of base classifiers and it seems that the 10 C4.5 decision trees are more than enough to achieve the highest accuracy. In the search for gender, there is a significant improvement of accuracy as the number of base classifiers increases from 10 to 20, and then, with the further increase in the number of C4.5 decision trees the accuracy improves at a much lower rate. Finally, in the search of the age group that a user belongs to, there is also a significant improvement of accuracy between 10 and 20 base classifiers, but in contrast to gender classification there is also a significant improvement between 30 and 50 base classifiers. So, a higher accuracy in gender and age classification may be achieved by using more base classifiers. However, this goes beyond the scope of the present study, which is to use the rotation forest for the first time in experiments with keystroke dynamics data and to check whether it has promising results. Therefore, the search for the highest possible accuracy in gender and age classification is shifted to a possible extension of this research.

Also, another important parameter of the operation of the rotation forest during user profiling, which must be taken into account, is the training time required. In gender classification the highest accuracy is 88.9% and is achieved with a training time of 23.09 seconds. With a tradeoff of 0.8% in accuracy the training time is reduced by about 60%, to 9.33 seconds. In age classification the highest accuracy observed is 86.3% which is achieved with training time 29.92 seconds, while with a tradeoff of 1.3%, approximately 55% less time (13.60 seconds) is required. Finally, in the handedness classification the almost highest accuracy, 94.1%, is achieved with training time 1.19 seconds.

The execution of the experiments showed a correlation between the training time and the number of base classifiers. The more base classifiers the longer the training time, since for each additional base classifier an additional iteration is performed in the algorithm. Also, the training time is affected by the percentage of removed instances. The higher the removal rate, the shorter the training time, since a smaller training set is created.

SOLUTIONS AND RECOMMENDATIONS

The rotation forest seems quite promising in creating the profile of completely unknown users utilizing data from the way they type. However, there are two other issues that need to be decided.

Firstly, the keystroke dynamics features to be used in the process. Due to the large number of available features the Chi-Square feature selection procedure was followed and all those features that presented a non-zero Chi-Square value were used. Usually, using more features leads to higher accuracy, but it also leads to systems with longer training time. In the present study it was not tested whether the use of only some of the features that showed non-zero Chi-Square value would lead to the creation of a system with similar, or even higher, accuracy and shorter training time. Also, it was not tested whether the use of features with zero Chi-Square value would lead to the creation of systems with similar, or even shorter, training time and higher accuracy. Those two experiments go beyond the objectives of the present study. In any case, choosing the number of features that will be used, as well as exactly which features will be used, is a decision that depends on how accurate the system must be and how fast it must work.

Secondly, a second tradeoff is again between accuracy and training time, but this time it concerns the number of base classifiers that will be in the ensemble. As stated in the "Discussion of the Results" subsection, it is possible to choose to create an accurate system that runs at a specific time, or a less accurate system that runs faster. The decision to be made will take into account which is the most important criterion, accuracy or training time.

FUTURE RESEARCH DIRECTIONS

In the present study it was shown that rotation forest can be used in user classification using keystroke dynamics data with high accuracy. This research can be extended in different directions.

Firstly, in terms of the performance of the rotation forest, as mentioned above, experiments with a larger number of base classifiers should be conducted in order to check the performance of the model and find the highest accuracy that can be achieved, especially in gender and age classification problems. Moreover, something that has also been mentioned is conducting additional experiments that will use a different set of features than what the Chi-Square feature selection procedure indicated. In addition, although the C4.5 decision tree is proposed to be the base classifier, experiments could be conducted using other base classifiers, such as other decision trees, Bayesian classifiers, k-nearest neighbors, or others.

Secondly, in terms of user attribution, other user characteristics could be sought, such as educational level, mother tongue, height (which is related to the length of the fingers), computer experience, etc. For this purpose, additional data should be collected from a significant number of users so that each defined class is adequately represented. In this direction of extending the research, and if several user characteristics that can be detected with high accuracy are included, the ultimate goal would be to create a system that uses keystroke dynamics features to create the profile of an unknown user so that it can either be used in the case a digital forensics investigation, or to facilitate the use of computers and Internet services, or to be used to protect unsuspecting users. Clearly, there are some issues that need to be addressed. These are, on the one hand, the consent of the users for the recording of their typing, and on the other hand, the way in which the recording will be done in order to avoid the disclosure of sensitive and personal data. One suggestion is to integrate the keylogging application into the operating systems and to perform the extraction of keystroke dynamics features locally. These features will be sent to dedicated servers which will be responsible for evaluating user characteristics, but also for updating databases with labeled data. In this way, data from users whose identity cannot be revealed will be shared, as well as will be used only after the user's choice, except of course in cases of prosecutorial intervention.

Third, since a very large percentage of users connect to the Internet through mobile devices, the research should be extended to seek the characteristics of users of these devices. For this reason, a suitable keylogger should be developed and data from typing on smartphones and tablets should be collected. Although there are differences in the study of typing between portable and non-portable devices, such as the fact that additional features can be utilized, like the pressure exerted on the touch screen, the methodology to be followed will be similar.

Finally, as far as keystroke dynamics studies are concerned, a possible extension is to look for a correlation between user characteristics and how the keys are used depending on their position on the keyboard. That is, for example, to consider whether left-handed users use the left part of the keyboard differently from right-handed users, in terms of the time intervals required to use a key, a digram, etc., or, if males use the keyboard numpad differently than females. Such an extension of the research may lead to the revelation of some hidden patterns that will develop user profiling.

The present research, with the help of machine learning, seems to be able to develop into an important tool of cybersecurity.

CONCLUSION

Rotation forest is an ensemble machine learning model that uses a number of base classifiers, usually decision trees, and can perform classification or regression. Although it was proposed 15 years ago and has shown very good performance in various problems, it has not been used to date in user classification with keystroke dynamics data. In this work, user profiling is attempted with data coming from the way users type and with the help of the rotation forest which uses the C4.5 decision tree as the base classifier. Specifically, the gender, the age, and the handedness of unknown Internet users are predicted, and the highest accuracy achieved was 88.9%, 86.3%, and 94.3%, respectively. The results show that the use of rotation forest in keystroke dynamics classification problems is very promising and can be the basis of a machine learning system that will serve as a cybersecurity tool.

REFERENCES

Antal, M., & Nemes, G. (2016). Gender recognition from mobile biometric data. In *Proceedings of 11th International Symposium on Applied Computational Intelligence and Informatics* (pp. 243-248). Timisoara, Romania: IEEE. 10.1109/SACI.2016.7507379

Buker, A., & Vinciarelli, A. (2021). Who is typing? Automatic gender recognition from interactive textual chats using typing behaviour. In A. E. Hassanien, A. Darwish, S. M. Abd El-Kader, & D. A. Alboaneen (Eds.), *Enabling Machine Learning Applications in Data Science. Algorithms for Intelligent Systems* (pp. 3–15). Springer. doi:10.1007/978-981-33-6129-4_1

Cook, J., & Ramadas, V. (2020). When to consult precision-recall curves. *The Stata Journal, 20*(1), 131–148. doi:10.1177/1536867X20909693

Degtereva, V., Gladkova, S., Makarova, O., & Melkostupov, E. (2020). Forming a mechanism for preventing the violations in cyberspace at the time of digitalization: Common cyber threats and ways to escape them. In *Proceedings of the International Scientific Conference - Digital Transformation on Manufacturing, Infrastructure and Service* (article no.: 55, pp. 1–6). ACM. 10.1145/3446434.3446468

Earl, S., Campbell, J., & Buckley, O. (2021). Identifying soft biometric features from a combination of keystroke and mouse dynamics. In M. Zallio, C. Raymundo Ibañez, & J. H. Hernandez (Eds.), *Advances in Human Factors in Robots, Unmanned Systems and Cybersecurity. Lecture Notes in Networks and Systems* (Vol. 268, pp. 184–190). Springer. doi:10.1007/978-3-030-79997-7_23

Fairhurst, M., & Da Costa-Abreu, M. (2011). Using keystroke dynamics for gender identification in social network environment. In *Proceedings of 4th International Conference on Imaging for Crime Detection and Prevention 2011* (pp. 1-6). London, UK. IET. 10.1049/ic.2011.0124

Giot, R., Dorizzi, B., & Rosenberger, C. (2015). A review on the public benchmark databases for static keystroke dynamics. *Computers & Security, 55*, 46–61. doi:10.1016/j.cose.2015.06.008

Hossain, M. S., & Haberfeld, C. (2020). Touch behavior based age estimation toward enhancing child safety. In *Proceedings of 2020 IEEE International Joint Conference on Biometrics* (pp. 1-8). IEEE. 10.1109/IJCB48548.2020.9304913

Idrus, S. Z. S., Cherrier, E., Rosenberger, C., & Bours, P. (2014). Soft biometrics for keystroke dynamics: Profiling individuals while typing passwords. *Computers & Security, 45*, 147–155. doi:10.1016/j.cose.2014.05.008

Krysowski, E., & Tremewan, J. (2020). Why does anonymity make us misbehave: Different norms or less compliance? *Economic Inquiry, 59*(2), 776–789. doi:10.1111/ecin.12955

Lam, K. H., Meijer, K. A., Loonstra, F. C., Coerver, E. M. E., Twose, J., Redeman, E., Moraal, B., Barkhof, F., de Groot, V., Uitdehaag, B. M. J., & Killestein, J. (2020). Real-world keystroke dynamics are a potentially valid biomarker for clinical disability in multiple sclerosis. *Multiple Sclerosis Journal, 27*(9), 1421–1431. doi:10.1177/1352458520968797 PMID:33150823

Lee, H., Hwang, J. Y., Kim, D. I., Lee, S., Lee, S. H., & Shin, J. S. (2018). Understanding keystroke dynamics for smartphone users authentication and keystroke dynamics on smartphones built-in motion sensors. *Security and Communication Networks, 2018*, 2567463. Advance online publication. doi:10.1155/2018/2567463

Mastoras, R. E., Iakovakis, D., Hadjidimitriou, S., Charisis, V., Kassie, S., Alsaadi, T., Khandoker, A., & Hadjileontiadis, L. J. (2019). Touchscreen typing pattern analysis for remote detection of the depressive tendency. *Scientific Reports, 9*(1), 13414. doi:10.103841598-019-50002-9 PMID:31527640

Nitzburg, G. C., & Farber, B. A. (2019). Patterns of utilization and a case illustration of an interactive text-based psychotherapy delivery system. *Journal of Clinical Psychology, 75*(2), 247–259. doi:10.1002/jclp.22718 PMID:30628062

Papadatou-Pastou, M., Ntolka, E., Schmitz, J., Martin, M., Munafo, M. R., Ocklenburg, S., & Paracchini, S. (2020). Human handedness: A meta-analysis. *Psychological Bulletin, 146*(6), 481–524. doi:10.1037/bul0000229 PMID:32237881

Rachburee, N., & Punlumjeak, W. (2015). A comparison of feature selection approach between greedy, IG-ratio, Chi-square, and mRMR in educational mining. In *Proceedings of 7th International Conference on Information Technology and Electrical Engineering* (pp. 420-424). IEEE. 10.1109/ICITEED.2015.7408983

Raul, N., Shankarmani, R., & Joshi, P. (2020). A comprehensive review of keystroke dynamics-based authentication mechanism. In A. Khanna, D. Gupta, S. Bhattacharyya, V. Snasel, J. Platos, & A. Hassanien (Eds), *International Conference on Innovative Computing and Communications. Advances in Intelligent Systems and Computing* (vol. 1059, pp. 149-162). Springer. 10.1007/978-981-15-0324-5_13

Rodriguez, J. J., Kuncheva, L. I., & Alonso, C. J. (2006). Rotation forest: A new classifier ensemble method. *IEEE Transactions on Pattern Analysis and Machine Intelligence, 28*(10), 1619–1630. doi:10.1109/TPAMI.2006.211 PMID:16986543

Roy, S., Roy, U., & Sinha, D. (2018). Identifying soft biometric traits through typing pattern on touchscreen phone. In J. Mandal & D. Sinha (Eds.), *Social Transformation – Digital Way. Communications in Computer and Information Science* (Vol. 836, pp. 546–561). Springer. doi:10.1007/978-981-13-1343-1_46

Tsimperidis, I., Peikos, G., & Arampatzis, A. (2021). Classifying users through keystroke dynamics. In T. Chadjipadelis, B. Lausen, A. Markos, T. R. Lee, A. Montanari, & R. Nugent (Eds.), Data Analysis and Rationality in a Complex World. Studies in Classification, Data Analysis, and Knowledge Organization (pp. 311-319). Springer. doi:10.1007/978-3-030-60104-1_34

Tsimperidis, I., Rostami, S., Wilson, K., & Katos, V. (2021). User attribution through keystroke dynamics-based author age estimation. In B. Ghita & S. Shiaeles (Eds.), *Selected Papers from the 12th International Networking Conference. Lecture Notes in Networks and Systems* (vol. 180, pp. 47-61). Springer. 10.1007/978-3-030-64758-2_4

Udandarao, V., Agrawal, M., Kumar, R., & Shah, R. R. (2020). On the inference of soft biometrics from typing patterns collected in a multi-device environment. In *Proceedings of 2020 IEEE Sixth International Conference on Multimedia Big Data* (pp. 76-85), IEEE. 10.1109/BigMM50055.2020.00021

Ulinskasa, M., Damaseviciusa, R., Maskeliunasa, R., & Wozniak, M. (2018). Recognition of human daytime fatigue using keystroke data. *Procedia Computer Science, 130*, 947–952. doi:10.1016/j.procs.2018.04.094

Uzun, Y., Bicakci, K., & Uzunay, Y. (2015). *Could we distinguish child users from adults using keystroke dynamics?* https://arxiv.org/abs/1511.05672

Van Balen, N., Ball, C. T., & Wang, H. (2016). A Behavioral biometrics based approach to online gender classification. In R. Deng, J. Weng, K. Ren, & V. Yegneswaran (Eds.), *12th International Conference on Security and Privacy in Communication Networks* (pp. 475-495). Springer International Publishing. 10.1007/978-3-319-59608-2_27

Vesel, C., Rashidisabet, H., Zulueta, J., Stange, J. P., Duffecy, J., Hussain, F., Piscitello, A., Bark, J., Langenecker, S. A., Young, S., Mounts, E., Omberg, L., Nelson, P. C., Moore, R. C., Koziol, D., Bourne, K., Bennett, C. C., Ajilore, O., Demos, A. P., & Leow, A. (2020). Effects of mood and aging on keystroke dynamics metadata and their diurnal patterns in a large open-science sample: A BiAffect iOS study. *Journal of the American Medical Informatics Association, 27*(7), 1007–1018. doi:10.1093/jamia/ocaa057 PMID:32467973

Wong, T. T., & Yang, N. Y. (2017). Dependency analysis of accuracy estimates in k-fold cross validation. *IEEE Transactions on Knowledge and Data Engineering, 29*(11), 2417–2427. doi:10.1109/TKDE.2017.2740926

Woods, K., Kegelmeyer, W. P. J., & Bowyer, K. (1997). Combination of multiple classifiers using local accuracy estimates. *IEEE Transactions on Pattern Analysis and Machine Intelligence, 19*(4), 405–410. doi:10.1109/34.588027

ADDITIONAL READING

Brizan, D. G., Goodkind, A., Koch, P., Balagani, K., Phoha, V. V., & Rosenberg, A. (2015). Utilizing linguistically enhanced keystroke dynamics to predict typist cognition and demographics. *International Journal of Human-Computer Studies*, *82*, 57–68. doi:10.1016/j.ijhcs.2015.04.005

Pentel, A. (2017). High precision handedness detection based on short input keystroke dynamics. In *Proceedings of 8th International Conference on Information, Intelligence, Systems & Applications* (pp. 1-5). IEEE. 10.1109/IISA.2017.8316380

Plank, B. (2018). Predicting authorship and author traits from keystroke dynamics. In *Proceedings of the Second Workshop on Computational Modeling of People's Opinions, Personality, and Emotions in Social Media* (pp. 98-104). The COLING 2016 Organizing Committee. 10.18653/v1/W18-1113

Rodriguez, J. J., Kuncheva, L. I., & Alonso, C. J. (2006). Rotation forest: A new classifier ensemble method. *IEEE Transactions on Pattern Analysis and Machine Intelligence*, *28*(10), 1619–1630. doi:10.1109/TPAMI.2006.211 PMID:16986543

Thaseen, I. S., Kumar, C. A., & Ahmad, A. (2019). Integrated intrusion detection model using Chi-Square feature selection and ensemble of classifiers. *Arabian Journal for Science and Engineering*, *44*(4), 3357–3368. doi:10.100713369-018-3507-5

Tsimperidis, I., & Arampatzis, A. (2020). The keyboard knows about you: Revealing user characteristics via keystroke dynamics. *International Journal of Technoethics*, *11*(2), 34–51. doi:10.4018/IJT.2020070103

Tsimperidis, I., Arampatzis, A., & Karakos, A. (2018). Keystroke dynamics features for gender recognition. *Digital Investigation*, *24*, 4–10. doi:10.1016/j.diin.2018.01.018

KEY TERMS AND DEFINITIONS

Chi-Square Test: The procedure used to examine the differences between categorical variables.

Digital Forensics: The process of uncovering and interpreting electronic data.

Digram Latency: The time elapsed between the pressing or releasing of a key and the pressing or releasing of the next key.

Feature Selection: The process of reducing the number of input variables when developing a predictive model.

Keystroke Duration: The time elapsed between the pressing and the releasing of a key. In the literature it is also found as dwell time, or hold time, or press hold, or key press time.

Keystroke Dynamics: The way a user uses a keyboard, physical or virtual.

User Profiling: The process of identifying some characteristics of a user.

Chapter 2

Predictive Modelling for Financial Fraud Detection Using Data Analytics:
A Gradient-Boosting Decision Tree

Ntebogang Dinah Moroke
iD https://orcid.org/0000-0001-8545-1860
North West University, South Africa

Katleho Makatjane
iD https://orcid.org/0000-0002-3687-4098
Department of Statistics, University of Botswana, Botswana

ABSTRACT

Financial fraud remains one of the most discussed topics in literature. The financial scandals of Enron, WorldCom, Qwest, Global Crossing, and Tyco resulted in approximately 460 billion dollars of loss. The detection of financial fraud, therefore, has become a critical task for financial practitioners. Three factors determine the likelihood of fraud occurrence, including pressure, opportunity, and rationalization. The core of these factors lies in people's beliefs and behaviour. Due to the unpredictability and uncertainty in fraudsters' incentives and techniques, fraud detection requires a skill set that encompasses both diligence and judgment. Big data technologies have had a huge impact on a wide variety of industries because they tend to be ubiquitous, starting in the last decade and continuing today.

DOI: 10.4018/978-1-7998-9430-8.ch002

INTRODUCTION

Financial fraud has been a major concern for many organizations across industries and countries because it causes massive business devastation. Millions of money are lost each year as a result of financial fraud; for example, Bank of America has agreed to pay 16.5 billion US dollars to settle a financial fraud case. According to Ecommerce Fraud Statistics (2021), the fraud management profession is shifting to a risk intelligence model, a field that relies even more heavily on e-commerce fraud statistics and defines itself as a business optimization engine rather than a defensive bulwark. New objectives accompany the new approach. Risk intelligence professionals, on the other hand, work to reduce friction throughout the purchasing process while still protecting the enterprise. The goal of proper fraud management is not to avoid losses but, increasing wins and thereby increase revenue. Hence, modern risk professionals now apply their decisioning skills and technology across the entire buying journey. They optimize revenue and have a clear connection to the enterprise's top line. The new approach to risk intelligence is made possible by advances in technology and fraud prevention strategies. Fraud and consumer abuse prevention that harnesses big data and machine learning allow enterprises to more accurately make split-second decisions on whether an order is legitimate or fraudulent.

Nevertheless, machine learning algorithms have previously been employed to analyse all authorised transactions and report suspicious ones. These reports are investigated by professionals who contact the cardholders to confirm if the transaction was genuine or fraudulent.

The investigators will then provide feedback to the automated system which is used to train and update the algorithm to eventually improve the fraud detection performance over time. Thus far, this is traditional way of detecting debit or credit card fraud is tedious and takes quite a time as some cards are stolen; or lost or users threatened. Hence this chapter contributes to the existing methods by building a Chrome extension that flags *"Fraud/suspicious"* transactions that will help both banks and cardholders to know about the fraudulent transactions made and further develop a *"find my card application.* This is a new system that the cardholders will be able to install the *"find my card application"* and have an opportunity to trace the whereabouts of their cards if stolen or lost and be able to stop their usage with the use of their cell phones or computer browsers. Even though detecting financial fraud is considered a high priority for many organisations, recent literature lacks updated and comprehensive in-depth reviews that can help organisations with their decisions for selecting an appropriate data mining method. Therefore, the objective of this chapter is to apply the gradient boosting decision tree (GBDT) under deep learning to extract knowledge about the processing of the credit/debit card data to detect whether a normal transaction of datasets qualified as a novel fraud and finally determine its effectiveness to classify the number of a fraudulent transaction. This leads to supervised learning alone, not unsupervised learning.

LITERATURE REVIEW

An extensive comprehension of fraud identification technologies can be useful for tackling the issue of credit and debit cards. The empirical analysis by Beigi et al. (2020) proposed combined methods using both data mining and statistical tasks, utilizing feature selection, re-sampling, and cost-sensitive learning for credit card fraud detection. In the first step, useful features are identified using a genetic algorithm. Next, the optimal re-sampling strategy is determined based on the design of experiments (DOE) and response surface methodologies. Finally, the cost-sensitive C4.5 algorithm is used as the base learner in the adaptive boosting (AdaBoost), algorithm. Using a real-time dataset, the results of these authors showed that; applying the proposed method significantly reduces misclassification costs by at least 14% compared with a decision tree, naïve Bayes, Bayesian network, neural network, and artificial immune system.

Behdad et.al. (2012) audited the most well-known sorts of credit card fraud and the existing nature-enlivened detection strategies that are utilized in fraud detection methods. Essentially, there are two types of credit and debit card fraud. These are (1) application fraud and behaviour fraud (Bolton and Hand, 2001). The former is where criminals get new credit cards from issuing companies and produce false data or utilise other authentic cardholders' data. While the latter is when criminals steal the account and password of a card from the genuine cardholder and use them to spend.

Abakarim et al. (2018) focused on one fraud detection system. To have a more accurate and precise fraud detection system, banks and financial institutions are investing more and more today in perfecting the data mining algorithms and data analysis technologies that are used to identify and combat fraud. Mota et al. (2014) proposed an alternative strategy to forestall fraud in online business applications. These authors used a signature-based technique to build up a client's behaviour deviations and thusly detect the potential fraud situations in time. Anyway, they just considered the clickstream is the element of the signature. It is believed that as opposed to utilizing just a single transaction feature includes for fraud recognition, it is better to consider various multiple transaction features. In detecting credit card fraud, Sahinand and Duman (2011) made a comparison of decision trees and support vector machines (SVM). The two authors divided a dataset into three groups with the dissimilar ratio between fraudulent and legitimate transactions. They further develop seven decision trees and SVM based model. Their results revealed that the decision tree-based model is better than the SVM model. However, the accuracy of

SVM-based models could reach the same performance as the decision tree-based models with increasing size of the training dataset.

Wen and Huang, (2020) applied the extreme gradient boosting(XGBoost) model for data mining and analysis, which is inspired by its brilliant reputation in various data mining contests. To filter useless information and preserve useful information, these authors combined kernel principal component analysis (Kernel PCA) with the XGBoost algorithm and proposes a new hybrid unsupervised and supervised learning model, KPXGBoost, and used a grid search to avoid over-fitting and compare the performance of both XGBoost and P-XGBoost and other classical machine learning methods. Their results indicated that P-XGBoost outperforms XGBoost in fraud detection, which provides a new perspective on detecting fraud behaviour while protecting clients' privacy.

Xuan et al. (2018) on the other hand used two kinds of random forests to train the behaviour features of normal and abnormal transactions. These authors compared the two random forests which are different in their base classifiers, and analyse their performance on credit fraud detection data. In addition, Bagga et al. (2020) compared the performance of logistic regression, K-nearest neighbours (KNN), random forest, naïve Bayes, multilayer perception, AdaBoost, quadrant discriminative analysis, pipelining, and ensemble learning on credit cards. To find the most suitable fraud technique, these authors used accuracy, precision, recall, F1 score, and confusion matrix to compare the performance of 9 different techniques they have used and their final results indicated that the performance of Pipelining method is found to be the best.

Karpoff (2021) used the trust triangle and the KleinLeffler model to isolate various factors that trigger fraud and uses them to consider the impact of technology and wealth over time. Some changes, such as increasing anonymity in certain financial transactions, promote new fraud innovations and increase the likelihood of fraud. The COVID-19 pandemic and the ensuing economic shutdown have caused a major disruption in relative demand and organizational capital, which has also increased the potential for fraud in the coming years. Pejić et al. (2019) did a literature review on text mining on big data in the financial sector. The authors aimed to answer "Which techniques are used in the financial sector for textual mining and financial fraud detection, especially in the era of the internet, big data, and social media." These authors have shown that the financial sector generates a vast amount of data like customer data, that is logged from their financial products, transaction data that can be used to support decision making, together with external data, like social media data and data from websites; hence the availability of the top 10 technologies for financial industries, which include among others the rise of application programming interface (API) economy, cloud business enablement, blockchain for banking, and usage of artificial intelligence.

Bao et al. (2022) conducted a study on artificial intelligence and fraud detection. The authors provided a comprehensive overview of the challenges in detecting fraud using machine learning by using a framework (data, method, and evaluation criterion) to review some of the practical considerations that may affect the implementation of machine-learning models to predict fraud. Then, they reviewed selected papers in the academic literature across different disciplines that can help address some of the fraud detection challenges. Finally, they suggested promising future directions for this line of research. Baesens et al. (2021) further proposed several data engineering techniques to improve the performance of an analytical model while retaining the interpretability property. Their data engineering process is decomposed into several feature and instance engineering steps and illustrated the improvement in the performance of these data engineering steps for popular analytical models on a real payment transactions dataset.

METHODS AND PROCEDURES

The proposed system is used to detect frauds on a real-time basis by analysing incoming transactions. The system design consists of two components for fraud detection. These are described or discussed in the next two subsections.

Designing a Framework for Data Pre-processing

This constituent is legally responsible for the usage of big data effectively and bids it to the analytical server for predictive modelling. The configuration of the system mainly consists of the Hadoop network which stores data in Hadoop distributed file system (HDFS) that comes from several sources. The data from Hadoop is read by R/Rstudio unlike in the work of Patil et al (2018) who utilized SAS (here referenced Statistical Analysis System) procedures to read the data and convert it into a raw data file as shown in Figure 1. The fields in a raw data file are separated by a comma delimiter. The raw data file is given to the analytical model for the building of a data model. This makes the system exceptionally versatile and assists with building a solid self-learning analytical model on a real-time basis highly scalable and helps to build a strong self-learning analytical model.

Designing an Analytical Model for Fraud Prediction

The analytical model is used to ensure whether an incoming transaction is legitimate, or it is not. The gradient boosting decision tree machine learning model is implemented for fraud detection. Daily data for the period of 01 Mach 2021 to 31 July 2021, was obtained on the Datarade database using the application programming interface (API). Instead of using team labels to accurately label transactions as fraudulent and non-fraudulent, the authors used a crowd-sourced rating application.

Figure 1. The analytical framework for data pre-processing
Source: https://www.researchgate.net/publication/663203

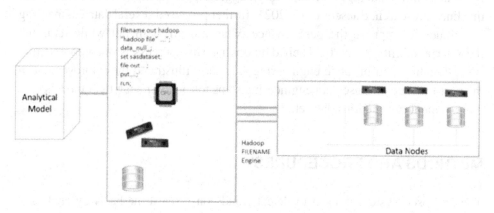

Gradient Boosting Decision Tree

Boosting algorithms were originally introduced by the machine learning community for classification problems. The main approach is to combine iteratively, several simple models; called 'weak learners', to obtain a 'strong learner' with improved prediction accuracy (Touzani et al. 2018). Boosting is an iterative algorithm that combines simple classification rules with 'mediocre' performance in terms of the misclassification error rate to produce a highly accurate classification rule. Stochastic gradient boosting provides an enhancement that incorporates a random mechanism at each boosting step, showing improvement in performance and speed while at the same time generating an ensemble (Culp et al 2016).

As declared by Son et al. (2015), gradient boosting algorithms utilise decision stumps or regression trees as weak classifiers. The weak learners measure the observed error in each node and split the node using the following test function $k : \mathbb{R}^n \rightarrow \mathbb{R}$ with a threshold τ and return values η^l and η^r. To minimise the error after a split, this chapter identifies the following triplet (η^l, η^r, τ) leading to obtaining an optimal split which by Son et al. (2015) it is given by

$$\varepsilon(\tau) = \sum_{i:k(x_i)<\tau} \omega_i^j \left(r_i^j - \eta^l \right)^2 + \sum_{i:k(x_i)\geq\tau} \omega_i^j \left(r_i^j - \eta^r \right)^2 \tag{3}$$

where ω_i^j and r_i^j are the weights and responses of x_i for the jth iteration. Additionally, the error in equation 3 is minimized so that an optimal tiple is obtained by (η^*, η^*, τ^*) over all possible τ's at each nod. Note that $\tau(\eta^l, \eta^r)$ can be found simply by computing the weighted average of r_i^j's over training data that fall on the corresponding side of the split. The training procedure of the gradient boosting decision tree is presented in Algorithm 1.

$$\varepsilon_{t+1}\left(\tau_{(t+1,\rho)}\right) = \sum_{i=1}^{N_{\rho}+1} \omega_{t+1,i}\left(r^i - \eta_{t+1,\rho}\right)^2 . \tag{4}$$

$\eta_{t+1,\rho}$ is firstly optimised because it assumed that $\tau_{(t+1,\rho)}$ is currently known in online learning and $\left\{\left(\omega_{t+1,i}, r_i\right)\right\}_{i=1,\cdots,N_{\rho}}$ is unavailable. For this reason, Touzani et al. (2018) declared that it is therefore impossible to minimise the error directly by adjusting $\tau_{t+1,\rho}$ and also by computing the weighted average of r_i^j. As in the off-line learning. Consequently, Son et al. (2015), updated a weak classifier based on the new classifier as well as the limited information of the present classifier. Note that, equation (5) is obtained by representing the right-hand side of equation (3) by; $\Delta\eta$

$$\varepsilon_{t+1}\left(\tau_{(t+1,\rho)}\right) = \sum_{i=1}^{N_{\rho}+1} \left\{\omega_{t+1,i}\left(r_i - \eta_{t,\rho}\right)^2 + \omega_{t+1,i}\left(-2\left(r_i - \eta_{t,\rho}\right)\Delta\eta + \left(\Delta\eta\right)^2\right)\right\} \tag{5}$$

which helps to minimise the above quadratic function concerning $\Delta\eta$ and obtain the solution in equation (6) as in Son et al. (2015)

$$\Delta\eta\left(\tau_{t+1,\rho}\right) = \begin{cases} \Delta\eta^l\left(\tau_{t+1,\rho}\right), & \text{if } K_\rho\left(x_i\right) < t+1, \rho \\ \Delta\eta^r\left(\tau_{t+1,\rho}\right), & \text{otherwise} \end{cases} \tag{6}$$

where,

$$\Delta\eta^l\left(\tau_{t+1,\rho}\right) = \frac{\sum_{i:K_{\rho(x_i)\geq\tau_{t+1,\rho}}}^{N_{\rho}+1} \omega_{t+1,i}, r_i}{\sum_{i:K_{\rho(x_i)\geq\tau_{t+1,\rho}}}^{N_{\rho}+1} \omega_{t+1,i}} - \eta_{t,\rho}^l$$

and

$$\Delta \eta^r\left(\tau_{t+1,\rho}\right) = \frac{\sum_{i:K_{\rho(x_i)\geq\tau_{t+1,\rho}}}^{N_\rho+1} \omega_{t+1,i}, r_i}{\sum_{i:K_{\rho(x_i)\geq\tau_{t+1,\rho}}}^{N_\rho+1} \omega_{t+1,i},} - \eta_{t,\rho}^r.$$

Employing a recursive procedure to find η, Son et al. (2015) obtained these two models

$$\Delta \eta^l\left(\tau_{t+1,\rho}\right) = \alpha\left(\omega_{t+1,i}N_\rho + 1rN_{\rho+1} - \eta_{t,\rho}^l\right) \tag{7}$$

and

$$\Delta \eta^r\left(\tau_{t+1,\rho}\right) = \alpha\left(\omega_{t+1,i}N_\rho + 1rN_{\rho+1} - \eta_{t,\rho}^r\right). \tag{8}$$

In this case, α denotes a learning rate. Intuitively, the return value η is updated in proportion to the amount of a difference between the weighted response of a new example and a previous return value. For more readings on gradient boosting algorithms (see for instance Touzani et al. 2018, Culp et al.2016, and Son et al. 2015).

Cross-Validation on Classification Problems

Some methods mathematically adjust the training error rate to estimate the test error rate. Since this chapter uses the GBDT with a quantitative response, a class of techniques that estimate the test error rate is deemed by holding out a subset of the training observations from the fitting process and then by applying the statistical learning method to those held out observations. As in the empirical analysis of Magnusso et al. (2020), the authors proceed by using cross-validation on classification procedures. In this setting, instead of using MSE (here referenced mean square error) to quantify the test error, the k-fold cross-validation is employed and a cross-validated estimate of the prediction error is given by

$$\hat{\varepsilon}_{cv} = \frac{1}{n}\sum_{i=1}^{n}\mathcal{L}\left(y_i, \hat{f}_{-k}\left(x_i\right)\right) \tag{9}$$

where $\hat{f}_{-k}$ denote the model that was trained on all but the kth subset of the learning set. The k-fold CV error rate and validation set error rates are defined analogously.

Model Performance

It is worth noting that the obtained dataset for this study is highly imbalanced and for that reason, Zareapoor and Shamsolmoali, (2015) have declared that this is the nature of credit transaction datasets. Because of imbalances in the dataset, some frequent metrics like accuracy and error rate are not considered because they are identified as biased metrics in the case of the imbalanced dataset. Though, in the domain of fraud detection, fraud catching rate and false alarm rate are the most used criteria metrics. For the proposed classification technique in the chapter, its performance is evaluated by the following five classification metrics which are relevant to financial fraud detection, and these are fraud catching rate, false alarm rate, balanced classification rate (BCR), precision, and Matthews correlation coefficient (MCC). Financial fraud is measured as a positive class and legal as a negative class hence the TP (true positive) and TN (true negative) are the numbers of frauds that are correctly classified, and FP (false positive) and FN (false negative) are the numbers of fraud incorrectly classified Hussin et al. (2016).

$$Precision = \frac{TP}{TP+FP} \tag{10}$$

Precision is the ratio of positive predictions to the total number of positive classes predicted. A recall is the ratio of positive predictions to the number of positive class values in the test data. F1 score depicts the balance between precision and recall. Matthews Correlation Coefficient is a balanced measure that uses TP, FP, TN, and FN to measure the performance of a binary classifier if the classes have sizes very different from each other. MCC has values between -1 and 1. -1 value indicates a classifier that is completely wrong while 1 indicated a perfectly correct classifier. As affirmed by Bagga et al (2020) the MCC formula is

$$MCC = \frac{(TP \times TN) - (FP \times FN)}{\sqrt{(TP+FP) \times (TN+FN) \times (FP+TN) \times (TP+FN)}} \tag{11}$$

and BCR (Balanced classification rate) is another metric used for imbalanced datasets. It combines the specificity and sensitivity metrics as follows

$$BCR = \frac{1}{2} \left(\frac{TP}{TP+FN} + \frac{TN}{FP+TN} \right) \tag{12}$$

EMPIRICAL ANALYSIS

This section provides and discusses the empirical analysis of the datasets. To build an analytical model, the South African credit and debit card fraud dataset is taken consisting of 35 attributes out of which 5 are numerical attributes and 30 are categorical and almost 376807 transactions. This is highly skewed data, consisting of 0.157% of fraud cases. This skewed set is justified by a low number of fraudulent transactions. Between the years 2018 and 2019, credit and debit card fraud increased by 20.5% due to online transactions. As per the report of the South African Banking Risk Information Centre Report (2021), the weak state of the country's economy has provided criminals with the impetus, and opportunity to commit financial crimes. The group's data shows that digital banking incidents have increased by 20% in 2019, a number that is set to rise in the future, as criminals continue to use social engineering tactics to extract personal and confidential information from victims; and this enables them to transact on victims' accounts without authority. But, with cybercrime; gross fraud losses on South African issued cards have increased by 20.5%.

Preparation of Training and Validation Datasets

For confidentiality purposes with the obtained dataset, a principal component analysis (PCA) is performed to hide the original features of the dataset and 21 principal components are obtained. Mori et al. (2016) defined PCA as a commonly used descriptive multivariate method for handling quantitative data and can be extended to deal with mixed measurement level data. Table 1 present exploratory data analysis for both identified number of fraudulent and valid transactions. The reported mean for fraudulent transactions indicates South Africans are losing around 122 Rands daily on made online transactions.

Table 1. Exploratory data analysis

	Total No	Mean	Std
Valid Transactions	376215	88.29	250.10
Fraud Transactions	592	122.21	256.68

Financial Conditioning Factors Selection and Model Prediction

To begin the main analysis, a gradient boosting decision tree is first trained with a ratio of 0.8:0.2 training and test sets respectively. The assumption made is that 95%

to 99% of the time, the boosting algorithm will predict or classify every transaction made as a legitimate transaction and this can cost the debit and credit cardholders in South Africa over 211.3 million Rands from the sample period otherwise, the classifier would not be useful. Using a stochastic Gradient Boosting decision tree, the processing scale and centre of the algorithm are set to 30 and re-sampling is cross validated at 5 fold which is repeated 3 times. Tuning parameter 'shrinkage' is held constant at a value of 0.1 while tuning parameter 'n.minobsinnode' is held constant at a value of 10. Reversible jump Markov-chain-Monte-Carlo (RJMCMC), coefficient of determination (R^2) and mean absolute error (MAE) are used to select the optimal model using the smallest value. The final values used for the model are *n.trees*=150, *interaction.depth*=3, *shrinkage*=0.1, and *n.minobsinmode*=10. As recommended by Bui et al. (2016), all the condition factors are removed with null predictive values.

Table 2. Re-sampling results across tuning parameters

interaction.depth	n.trees	RJMCMC	R^2	MAE
1	50	0.026016	0.596929	0.001445
1	100	0.025476	0.612441	0.001404
1	150	0.025186	0.621163	0.001407
2	50	0.022866	0.688353	0.001180
2	100	0.022241	0.704173	0.001129
2	150	0.021967	0.711179	0.001115
3	50	0.022026	0.709232	0.001086
3	100	0.021576	0.720328	0.001054
3	**150**	**0.021346**	**0.726199**	**0.001044**

Evaluation of the Classification Experiment

Financial susceptibility index (FSI) values are calculated using the GBDT model. To reduce variability, a five-fold cross-validation method is used. This method partitions training data into five subsets and averages validation results over five rounds. The five-fold cross-validation method was used. The calculated FSI values were in the range of 0.01 to 0.988. The values of MCC, BCR, F1score, Precision and Recall are presented in Table 3. This model is evaluated using both training and test datasets. The model has high classification performance as indicated by all the performance metrics used. The standard errors are reasonably small for this model. These results indicate a reasonable goodness-of-fit for models with both training and test datasets.

Table 3. Results of cross-validation metrics

Metric	Mean	std	Training data	Test Data
FCR	0.9514	0.0108	0.9510	0.9701
FAR	0.9664	0.0107	0.9645	0.9489
Precision	0.9580	0.0063	0.9577	0.9594
MCC	0.8468	0.0015	0.8489	0.8513
BCR	0.8953	0.0076	0.8909	0.9102

Finally, to compare the significance of the model, the Wilcoxon signed rank and model power tests are used. The former was used in the research that was carried out by Chen et al. (2017) and Bui et al. (2016) while the latter was carried out in the empirical analysis of Makatjane and Moroke (2016). The null hypothesis for this method is that the model is significantly different from zero with the alternative stating otherwise. The results are calculated at a 95% significance level. The z and p-values are further used to evaluate the model significantly. When z values exceed critical values of ($\pm 1{:}96$) and p-values are smaller than the significant level (0:05), the null hypothesis will be rejected and therefore the performance of the model is notably different. The results of the Wilcoxon signed rank and power tests are shown in Table 4. It can be seen that the GBDT model performances are significantly different since (p-value=0.0001, z-value=6.53). Moreover, the model also reveals a high prediction power of over 91%.

Table 4. Pair-wise comparison and power test

Wilcoxon Signed-Rank Test		Model Power Test		
Parameters	GBDT	Data	Mean Difference	Actual Power
z-value	6.53	Training	0.0716	0.9098
p-value	0.001	Validation	0.0348	0.9356

SOLUTIONS AND RECOMMENDATIONS

With an increase in credit card and debit card fraud in the current digitalised economic scenario, financial fraud detection has emerged as a hot topic for academia, research, and industry. The failure of financial institutions' internal auditing systems, particularly banks', to detect financial frauds has necessitated the use of specialized procedures to detect credit and debit card fraud, collectively known as financial forensic. Data mining techniques are greatly assisting in the detection of both credit and debit card fraud, as dealing with large data volumes and the complexities of financial data are significant challenges for financial forensic investigators hence, a substantial amount of planning before throwing machine learning algorithms at it.

Therefore, the statistical input of this chapter lies in employing a gradient boosting decision tree model to detect and correctly classify the gross financial fraud from the online transaction made by the debit and credit cards of South Africans. With the use of gradient boosting algorithm, a real-time detection for online fraud is achieved. This is because, the boosting algorithm uses deep learning to learn the features of the data and detect or predict real-time fraud (i.e fraud that happens in real time.). With this deep learning method, the knowledge about the online fraud will be known well in time and with their extreme timely functionality, the system will notify debit and credit card users about the scam services and goods they would be buying online. On that note, if the fraudster would want to use wrong information to obtain the credit or debit cards from the banks or card issuers, the banks' system shall automatically detect that as fraud. For more effective systems, the authors suggests the establishment of an extreme automated fraud detection. This would be done by developing a probabilistic description and modelling of extreme peak loads using Poison point process. This approach helps in estimating the frequency of occurrence of peak financial frauds in time. Furthermore, adopting the Gaussian process regression coupled with core vector regression of Chandiwana et al. (2021), the short-term hourly global financial fraud will be detected and forecasted with uncertainty.

FUTURE RESEARCH DIRECTIONS

The findings of the GBDT model exhibit reasonably good performance. This is a promising technique for online fraud susceptibility detection. Finally, the results of this chapter may be useful for decision-makers and the financial sector for future use and planning in credit and debit prone areas. A "find my card application" is to be developed in the future and also updating the established crowd-sourcing application and building a Chrome extension that flags "fraud or suspicious transaction" while purchasing goods and services online are recommended. All these recommended procedures will also automatically notify banks of suspicious transactions and automatically train the system without confronting the cardholder if the transaction is fraudulent or not. The main problem with developing these new systems and applications is when the card has been taken from the holder and is being threatened by the perpetrators. However, this can be solved by modifying the ATM (reference here as automatic teller machine) in the way they would request the PIN from the cardholders. Maybe, there should be some personal questions or some one-time password (OTP) numbers to be sent to the cardholders before finalising the transaction.

CONCLUSION

This chapter has developed a deep learning algorithm to detect and classify both debit and credit card fraud in South African context. The data used is a daily data for the period of 01 Mach 2021 to 31 July 2021, which is obtained on the Datarade database using the application programming interface (API) through the execution of Rstudio for windows. To accurately label the data, a method for large machine learning datasets known as crowd-labelling is applied. This approach helps to avoid human biasness in labelling the variables and entries but precisely find the true labels. The results of this chapter showed the established gradient boosting algorithm is the perfect algorithm to detect and classify debit and credit card fraud precisely in real time with the prediction and classification power of 91 percent in a training set and 94 percent in the test sets. This is found to be a promising method with respect to financial detection.

ACKNOWLEDGMENT

The authors are grateful for the anonymous reviewers of this chapter for their positive and constructive comments and suggestions.

REFERENCES

Abakarim, Y., Lahby, M., & Attioui, A. (2018). An efficient real-time model for credit card fraud detection based on deep learning. *Proceedings of the 12th International Conference on Intelligent Systems: Theories and Applications, 30*, 1-7. 10.1145/3289402.3289530

Baesens, B., Höppner, S., & Verdonck, T. J. D. S. S. (2021). Data engineering for fraud detection. *Decision Support Systems*, *150*, 113492. doi:10.1016/j.dss.2021.113492

Bagga, S., Goyal, A., Gupta, N., & Goyal, A. (2020). Credit Card Fraud Detection using Pipeline and Ensemble Learning. *Procedia Computer Science*, *173*, 104–112. doi:10.1016/j.procs.2020.06.014

Bao, Y., Hilary, G., & Ke, B. (2022). Artificial intelligence and fraud detection. Innovative technology at the interface of finance and operations, 11, 223-247.

Behdad, M., Barone, L., Bennamoun, M., & French, T. (2012). Nature-inspired Techniques in the Context of Fraud Detection. *IEEE Transactions on Systems, Man and Cybernetics. Part C, Applications and Reviews*, *42*(6), 1273–1290. doi:10.1109/TSMCC.2012.2215851

Beigi, S., Amin Naseri, M. J. J. A., & Mining, D. (2020). Credit card fraud detection using data mining and statistical methods. *Journal of AI and Data Moning*, *8*(2), 149–160.

Bolton, R. J., & Hand, D. J. (2001). Unsupervised Profiling Methods for Fraud Detection. *Proc Credit Scoring and Credit Control.*, *7*, 5–7.

Bui, D. T., Tuan, T. A., Klempe, H., Pradhan, B., & Revhaug, I. (2016). Spatial Prediction Models for Shallow Landslide Hazards: A Comparative Assessment of the Efficacy of Support Vector Machines, Artificial Neural Networks, Kernel Logistic Regression, and Logistic Model Tree. *Landslides*, *13*(2), 361–378. doi:10.100710346-015-0557-6

Chandiwana, E., Sigauke, C., & Bere, A. (2021). Twenty-Four-Hour Ahead Probabilistic Global Horizontal Irradiance Forecasting Using Gaussian Process Regression. *Algorithms*, *14*(6), 177. doi:10.3390/a14060177

Chen, W., Xie, X., Wang, J., Pradhan, B., Hong, H., Bui, D. T., Duan, Z., & Ma, J. (2017). A Comparative Study Of Logistic Model Tree, Random Forest, and Classification and Regression Tree Models for Spatial Prediction of Landslide Susceptibility. *Catena*, *151*, 147–160. doi:10.1016/j.catena.2016.11.032

Culp, M., Johnson, K., Michailidis, G., & Culp, M. M. (2016). *Package ada*. Available online at URL: https://www.cran. r-project. org/web/packages/ada/index

Ecommerce Fraud Statistics. (2021). Accessed on 08 May 2022 at https://www.nosto.com/ecommerce-statistics/fraud/

Hussin, H. Y., Zumpano, V., Reichenbach, P., Sterlacchini, S., Micu, M., van Westen, C., & Balteanu, D. (2016). Different landslide sampling strategies in a grid-based bivariate statistical susceptibility model. *Geomorphology, 253*, 508–523. doi:10.1016/j.geomorph.2015.10.030

Karpoff, J. M. (2021). The Future of Financial Fraud. *Journal of Corporate Finance, 66*, 101694. doi:10.1016/j.jcorpfin.2020.101694

Makatjane, K. D., & Moroke, N. D. (2016). Comparative study of Holt-Winters Triple Exponential Smoothing and Seasonal ARIMA: Forecasting Short Term Seasonal Car sales in South Africa. *Risk Governance and Control: Financial Markets and Institutions, 6*(1), 71–82.

Mori, Y., Kuroda, M., & Makino, N. (2016). *Nonlinear Principal Component Analysis and Its Applications*. Springer. www.springer.com/series/13497

Mota, G., Fernandes, J., & Belo, O. (2014). Usage signatures analysis as an alternative method for preventing fraud in E-Commerce applications. *International Conference on Data Science and Advanced Analytics*, 203-208. 10.1109/DSAA.2014.7058074

Patil, S., Nemade, V., & Soni, P. K. (2018). Predictive modelling for credit card fraud detection using data analytics. *Procedia Computer Science, 132*, 385–395. doi:10.1016/j.procs.2018.05.199

Pejić, B. M., Krstić, Ž., Seljan, S., & Turulja, L. (2019). Text mining for big data analysis in financial sector: A literature review. *Sustainability, 11*(5), 1277. doi:10.3390u11051277

Sahin, Y., & Duman, E. (2011). Detecting credit card fraud by decision trees and support vector machines. *Lecture Notes in Engineering and Computer Science, 2188*(1). https://hdl.handle.net/11376/2366

Son, J., Jung, I., Park, K., & Han, B. (2015), Tracking-by-segmentation with online gradient boosting decision tree. *Proceedings of the IEEE International Conference on Computer Vision*, 3056–3064. 10.1109/ICCV.2015.350

South African Banking Risk Information Centre Report. (2021). *Annual Crime Stats 2021*. https://www.sabric.co.za/media-and-news/downloads/

Touzani, S., Granderson, J., & Fernandes, S. (2018). Gradient boosting machine for modelling the energy consumption of commercial buildings. *Energy and Building, 158*(1), 1533–1543. doi:10.1016/j.enbuild.2017.11.039

Wen, H., & Huang, F. (2020). Personal loan fraud detection based on hybrid supervised and unsupervised learning. In *2020 5th IEEE international conference on big data analytics (ICBDA)*. IEEE. 10.1109/ICBDA49040.2020.9101277

Xuan, S., Liu, G., Li, Z., Zheng, L., Wang, S., & Jiang, C. (2018). Random forest for credit card fraud detection. In *2018 IEEE 15th International Conference on Networking, Sensing and Control (ICNSC)* (pp. 1-6). IEEE. 10.1109/ICNSC.2018.8361343

Zareapoor, M., & Shamsolmoali, P. (2015). Application of credit card fraud detection: Based on bagging ensemble classifier. *Procedia Computer Science, 48*, 679–685. doi:10.1016/j.procs.2015.04.201

ADDITIONAL READING

Akinje, A. O., & Fuad, A. (2021). Fraudulent Detection Model Using Machine Learning Techniques for Unstructured Supplementary Service Data. *International Journal of Innovative Computing, 11*(2), 51–60. doi:10.11113/ijic.v11n2.299

Al-Hashedi, K. G., & Magalingam, P. (2021). Financial fraud detection applying data mining techniques: A comprehensive review from 2009 to 2019. *Computer Science Review, 40*, 100402. doi:10.1016/j.cosrev.2021.100402

Albashrawi, M. (2016). Detecting financial fraud using data mining techniques: A decade review from 2004 to 2015. *Journal of Data Science: JDS, 14*(3), 553–569. doi:10.6339/JDS.201607_14(3).0010

Albshrawi, M., & Lowell, M. (2016). Detecting Financial Fraud using Data Mining Techniques: A Decade Review from 2004 to 2015. *Journal of Data Science: JDS, 14*(3), 553–569. doi:10.6339/JDS.201607_14(3).0010

Alfaiz, N. S., & Fati, S. M. (2022). Enhanced Credit Card Fraud Detection Model Using Machine Learning. *Electronics (Basel), 11*(4), 662. doi:10.3390/electronics11040662

Bayram, B., Köroğlu, B., & Gönen, M. (2020). Improving fraud detection and concept drift adaptation in credit card transactions using incremental gradient boosting trees. *2020 19th IEEE International Conference on Machine Learning and Applications (ICMLA)*, 545-550. 10.1109/ICMLA51294.2020.00091

Bhowmik, M., Sai Siri Chandana, T., & Rudra, B. (2021). Comparative Study of Machine Learning Algorithms for Fraud Detection in Blockchain. *5th International Conference on Computing Methodologies and Communication (ICCMC)*, 539-541. 10.1109/ICCMC51019.2021.9418470

Botchey, F. E., Qin, Z., & Hughes-Lartey, K. (2020). Mobile Money Fraud Prediction—A Cross-Case Analysis on the Efficiency of Support Vector Machines, Gradient Boosted Decision Trees, and Naïve Bayes Algorithms. *Information (Basel)*, *11*(8), 383. doi:10.3390/info11080383

de Sá, A. G., Pereira, A. C., & Pappa, G. L. (2018). A customized classification algorithm for credit card fraud detection. *Engineering Applications of Artificial Intelligence*, *72*, 21–29. doi:10.1016/j.engappai.2018.03.011

Dhankhad, S., Mohammed, E., & Far, B. (2018, July). *Supervised machine learning algorithms for credit card fraudulent transaction detection: a comparative study. In 2018 IEEE international conference on information reuse and integration.* IRI. doi:10.1109/IRI.2018.00025

Dhieb, N., Ghazzai, H., Besbes, H., & Massoud, Y. (2019). *Extreme gradient boosting machine learning algorithm for safe auto insurance operations. In 2019 IEEE international conference on vehicular electronics and safety.* ICVES. doi:10.1109/ICVES.2019.8906396

Dhieb, N., Ghazzai, H., Besbes, H., & Massoud, Y. (2020). A Secure AI-Driven Architecture for Automated Insurance Systems: Fraud Detection and Risk Measurement. *IEEE Access: Practical Innovations, Open Solutions*, *8*, 58546–58558. doi:10.1109/ACCESS.2020.2983300

Eweoya, I. O., Adebiyi, A. A., Azeta, A. A., & Azeta, A. E. (2019, August). Fraud prediction in bank loan administration using decision tree. *Journal of Physics: Conference Series*, *1299*(1), 012037. https://iopscience.iop.org/article/10.1088/1742-6596/1299/1/012037/meta

Gupta, R. Y., Mudigonda, S. S., Kandala, P. K., & Baruah, P. K. (2019). Implementation of a predictive model for fraud detection in motor insurance using gradient boosting method and validation with actuarial models. *2019 IEEE international conference on clean energy and energy efficient electronics circuit for sustainable development (INCCES)*, 1-6. https://doi.or/10.1109/INCCES47820.2019.9167733

Halvaiee, N. S., & Akbari, M. K. (2014). A novel model for credit card fraud detection using Artificial Immune Systems. *Applied Soft Computing*, *24*, 40–49. doi:10.1016/j.asoc.2014.06.042

Hassani, H., Gheitanchi, S., & Yogini, M. R. (2010). On the Application of Data Mining to Official Data. *Journal of Data Science: JDS*, *8*(1), 75–89. doi:10.6339/JDS.2010.08(1).578

Ileberi, E., Sun, Y., & Wang, Z. (2021). Performance Evaluation of Machine Learning Methods for Credit Card Fraud Detection Using SMOTE and AdaBoost. *IEEE Access: Practical Innovations, Open Solutions, 9,* 165286–165294. doi:10.1109/ACCESS.2021.3134330

Jayakumar, G. D. S., & Thomas, B. J. (2013). A New Procedure of Clustering Based on Multivariate Outlier Detection. *Journal of Data Science: JDS, 11*(1), 69–84. doi:10.6339/JDS.2013.11(1).1091

Khine, A. A., & Khin, H. W. (2020). Credit card fraud detection using online boosting with extremely fast decision tree. *2020 IEEE Conference on Computer Applications (ICCA),* 1-4. 10.1109/ICCA49400.2020.9022843

Kim, E., Lee, J., Shin, H., Yang, H., Cho, S., Nam, S. K., & Kim, J. I. (2019). Champion-challenger analysis for credit card fraud detection: Hybrid ensemble and deep learning. *Expert Systems with Applications, 128,* 214–224. doi:10.1016/j.eswa.2019.03.042

Mijwil, M. M., & Salem, I. E. (2020). Credit Card Fraud Detection in Payment Using Machine Learning Classifiers. *Asian Journal of Computer and Information Systems, 8*(4). Advance online publication. doi:10.24203/ajcis.v8i4.6449

Mishra, A., & Ghorpade, C. (2018). Credit card fraud detection on the skewed data using various classification and ensemble techniques. *2018 IEEE International Students' Conference on Electrical, Electronics and Computer Science (SCEECS),* 1-5. 10.1109/SCEECS.2018.8546939

Nami, S., & Shajari, M. (2018). Cost-sensitive payment card fraud detection based on dynamic random forest and k-nearest neighbors. *Expert Systems with Applications, 110,* 381–392. doi:10.1016/j.eswa.2018.06.011

Reurink, A. (2018). Financial fraud: A literature review. *Journal of Economic Surveys, 32*(5), 1292–1325. doi:10.1111/joes.12294

Roy, A., Sun, J., Mahoney, R., Alonzi, L., Adams, S., & Beling, P. (2018, April). Deep learning detecting fraud in credit card transactions. *2018 Systems and Information Engineering Design Symposium (SIEDS),* 129-134. 10.1109/SIEDS.2018.8374722

Rushin, G., Stancil, C., Sun, M., Adams, S., & Beling, P. (2017). Horse race analysis in credit card fraud—deep learning, logistic regression, and Gradient Boosted Tree. 2017 systems and information engineering design symposium (SIEDS) 117-121. doi:10.1109/SIEDS.2017.7937700

Sadgali, I., Sael, N., & Benabbou, F. (2019). Performance of machine learning techniques in the detection of financial frauds. *Procedia Computer Science, 148*, 45–54. doi:10.1016/j.procs.2019.01.007

Sohony, I., Pratap, R., & Nambiar, U. (2018). Ensemble learning for credit card fraud detection. *Proceedings of the ACM India Joint International Conference on Data Science and Management of Data*, 289-294. 10.1145/3152494.3156815

Tae, C. M., & Hung, P. D. (2019). Comparing ML algorithms on financial fraud detection. *Proceedings of the 2019 2nd International Conference on Data Science and Information Technology*, 25-29. 10.1145/3352411.3352416

Taha, A. A., & Malebary, S. J. (2020). An intelligent approach to credit card fraud detection using an optimized light gradient boosting machine. *IEEE Access: Practical Innovations, Open Solutions, 8*, 25579–25587. doi:10.1109/ACCESS.2020.2971354

Trivedi, N. K., Simaiya, S., Lilhore, U. K., & Sharma, S. K. (2020). An efficient credit card fraud detection model based on machine learning methods. *International Journal of Advanced Science and Technology, 29*(5), 3414–3424. http://sersc.org/journals/index.php/IJAST/article/view/12032

KEY TERMS AND DEFINITIONS

Big Data: Data that is received in high volume and it can be stored in databases, and it comes at a high speed with various data formats.

Credit Card Fraud: An intention to illegally obtain money from a credit card that has been revoked, cancelled, reported lost or stolen to obtain anything of value.

Cross-Validation: A re-sampling technique that uses diverse percentages of a dataset to train and test the model of improved iterations.

Data Mining: The method of extracting inconsistencies, patterns, and relationships within large datasets to predict an outcome.

Deep Learning: This is the branch of machine learning and artificial intelligence that extract knowledge about the processing of the image or quantitative data.

Financial Fraud: It is the unauthorised taking of money in financial institutions such as banks.

Gradient Boosting Decision Tree: A branch of deep learning that uses regression and classification algorithms to produce a prediction model in the arrangement of an ensemble weak prediction.

Supervised Learning: A machine learning method that maps an input to an output based on the input-output pairs of data

APPENDIX

Algorithm 1: Gradient Boosting Decision tree

Initialize: $f_0(X)=0, \eta, d_0=0$

for $j=1,\dots,M$ **do**

$$\omega_i = \exp\left(-y_i f_{j-1}(x_i)\right), \quad i=1,\cdots,N$$

$$r_i = -y, \; i=1,\dots,N$$

$S = \left\{(x_i, \omega_i, r_i)\right\}_{1,\cdots,N}$ and $v = \left\{x \mid x \in \mathbb{R}\right\}$ here, v is a shrinkage factor to training data and the classifier.

$$\mathbf{R} = \text{GROWTREE}(S, v, \eta_0, d_0)$$

$$f_j(x) = f_{j-1}(x) - v\Delta \sum_{k=1}^{|R|} \eta_k \delta\left(x \in \mathfrak{R}_k\right),$$

where $\mathfrak{R}_k, \eta_k \in \mathbf{R}$

end

Procedure SPLITLEARNING(S)

$$(\eta^b, \eta^h, \tau^*) = \arg\min_{\eta^l, \eta^r, \tau} \varepsilon(\tau) \text{ in equation } 3$$

Return (η^b, η^h, τ^*)

Chapter 3
Comprehensive Overview of Autonomous Vehicles and Their Security Against DDoS Attacks

Swati Jaiswal
(iD) https://orcid.org/0000-0001-9671-534X
Pimpri Chinchwad College of Engineering, Pune, India

Pallavi S. Yevale
(iD) https://orcid.org/0000-0001-9366-6810
Dr. D. Y. Patil Institute of Engineering, Management, and Research, Pune, India

Anuja R. Jadhav
Pimpri Chinchwad College of Engineering, Pune, India

ABSTRACT

The automotive industry is developing trends in autonomous driving and connected vehicular systems. These vehicles can access and send the data, download the software updates, connect with other vehicles or other IoT devices via the internet or wireless communication. Autonomous vehicle control urges very strict requirements about the security of the communication channels used by the vehicle to exchange information and the control logic that performs complex driving tasks. So, the increased connectivity results in a heightened risk of a cyber-security attack. For maintaining the advances in safe communication, it is important to establish strong security for connected vehicular systems. For this, existing cybersecurity attacks must be considered to minimize future cybersecurity risks in the connected and autonomous vehicle systems. In this chapter, the authors will emphasize recent works on how autonomous vehicles can ensure strong operation under ongoing cyber security attacks and their possible solutions.

DOI: 10.4018/978-1-7998-9430-8.ch003

INTRODUCTION

In recent years, traffic security has attracted extending thought among trained professionals, organizations, and government affiliations. As demonstrated by a report from the U.S. Division of Transportation, there were 36,560 people were killed due to the car crashes in the U.S. in 2018 (NCSA, 2019) and that suggests there were around 100 deaths reliably. Human mishaps are related with 94 to 96 percent of all motor vehicle crashes. Consequently, the free driving development has been attracting light of an authentic worry for the researchers for quite a while. Beginning from this prolonged stretch of time, further created driver help developments, as electronic constancy control moreover, way departure alerted, were being made to further work on the security and diminish the driver load, which as well prepare to autonomous driving headways. The Society of Automotive Engineers (SAE) has described six particular levels of driver help development types of progress.

The type of technology is explained by established criteria. The automation standard ranges between level 0 and level 5. Level 0 includes all of Porsche's vehicles through 1967 to the new car, completely managed in 2018. The Level 1 automatic control allows the vehicle to decide about how to guide or stop or speed the autonomous driving support system (ADAS) mounted in the car. The functionality of Level 2 comprises of the driving and acceleration ADAS power. The human operator should, nevertheless, remain attentive. Level 2 instances are Audi Traffic Jam Assist, Cadillac Super Cruise, Autopilot, etc. Instances include Both facets of a driving automobile are carried out by level 3 robotics, however the human operator has to assume around when ADAS requires. The human operator must also be careful. In "Audi Traffic Jam Pilot" level 3 of optimization can be obtained. The second stage of autonomy allows the vehicles to execute all the functions as well as to control the world. Although ADAS performs all the tasks during the last stage of automation, people only are the travellers. In Stage 5, the system validates the location in GPS as well as the driver drove the passenger to that same endpoint directly regardless finding the help or knowledge from the person. Automotive industries are now looking for level 3. Tesla argues we are level 3, but Tesla's feedback is automatic level 2. Figure 1. Intelligent vehicle cyber-attack gateways Shows some of the potential cyber-attack gateways mostly on driverless vehicles. The machine is far more susceptible to theft by hackers as the amount of automation rises.

Any network-connected system will perform denial-of-service attack (Jaiswal & Chandra, 2017). IoT that we are using in the everyday lives transmits data on the web, transmits information and is processed in live time but is susceptible to hacking. The intelligent transportation system also communicates in full detail only with networks. The cyberwarfare trend reveals that under this risk the auto sector suffers. In addition, it could influence the rail. The recently installed rail service is connecting with the networks in all the metropolises. The results will be enormously and catastrophically if a Cyber assault were initiated inside a system conducted amongst the railways in the system as well as the data exchanged is changed or postponed. The state-developed public transit system needs massive developments, and this event would not only damage infrastructure, but also damage the confidence of commuters who use it every day to drive to work or school (Desai & Jaiswal, 2021). VANETs allow consumers to improve security problems to traveling ease, to make a safer, healthier, and smarter world possible.

Figure 1. Smart car gateways for cyber-attacks (Mohd et al., 2018)

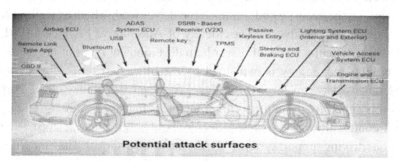

There have been 3 main groups that categorise VANET communications. For such an intelligent vehicle to operate correctly, the authenticity and safety with all 3 kinds of communications must be upheld. In Raya et al., a lag in traffic data by several milliseconds is really to be demonstrated in real-time for generalised protection & responsibility communications. The specific kinds of attacks that can be started in any VANET are misleading info assaults, object detection hacking, ID exposure, previously unknown and service attack refusal. The positioning of an autonomous car is yet other significant aspect that attackers can take advantage of. Customers are given with appropriate localisation-related services (LBS) through their demographics. An intelligent car's position is perhaps the crucial insecure object that attackers can use. The geographical positions of consumers really aren't properly covered given the desired functionality offered by LBS. There has been considerable study into frameworks and principles that can distinguish harmful from benevolent nodes, though not all of them are enough to deter an intrusion. Many studies have been undertaken to create models and definitions that can distinguish between harmful and benevolent networks, but not all of them would be sufficient to deter an attack. Different assessment methods have been suggested and are widely classified into three parts: node-based, messages-based, and mixed methods.

A detection algorithm known as the DDADA algorithm has been proposed on this principle. In addition, a different detection algorithm called the DDAML algorithm was developed to classify the DDoS attack in order to further increase detection performance. The research findings suggest that our optimization methods can help recognise the DDoS attack and have increased detection speeds in relation to current methods. Finally, the test results show that the DDAML algorithm will execute various output tests over the other algorithms. In our future work, the DDADA and the DDAML algorithms will be further improved in the true SDN setting.

Self-service automobile is an environmentally friendly vehicle which navigates regardless of human intervention. Self-vehicles only at greatest order means that certain driver actions can be substituted by an appropriate system. In this case, the automated driving may be seen as a shuttered control unit. The obtained value is a vehicle status defined at the point of destination in which the car can start at a given initial state. The automatic mode of driving impacts other vehicles on the road and other roads such as pedestrians, bikes, animals etc. The sensor set offers information on the car's surroundings in the region specified by its field of vision. This data are used for the detection of obstacles in the vehicle following initial pre-processing. Figure 2 illustrates the normal working of autonomous system using DNS.

Figure 2. Normal process with DNS (Domain network server)

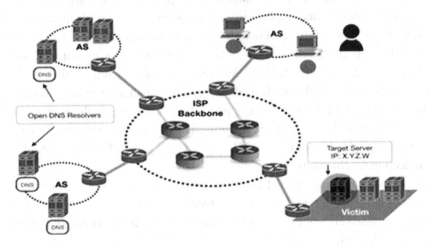

Labels

- DNS- Domain network server
- AS- Application server
- ISP- Information sharing protocol

Data from various kinds of sensors are combined to raise the degree of trust of objects detected in vehicles surrounding. To analyse the present condition and schedule the track to destination the car, the list of observed objects provides a vehicle environmental model. Beside the environmental model for the vehicle, the drivers' model is an essential part of fully automated vehicles, by means of which the characteristics of the actuator can be calculated in a way which enables the driver to manually direct the vehicle as closely as possible to the dynamic. Vehicle movie and dynamic models are important for tuning controls responsible for deciding the trajectory and stability of the vehicle.

As the production of autonomous vehicles is increasing quickly but the protection side of the automotive is not being given proper consideration, which may pose a significant challenge to the safety and acceptance of autonomous cars as many countries attempt to put autonomous vehicles on the road shortly (Tong et al., 2019). Had said that experts would join to make cyber security a priority at design and implementation levels constructive.

Firstly, research article outlines many global security threats on smart connected cars. The attacks are then investigated and summarised and classified into four groups, including cryptography, network security, vulnerability recognition tools, and malware identification. There are more discussions on emerging issues and potential directions to deter attacks on smart vehicle networks.

Over the past decade, the advancement of cyber-physical devices with sophisticated sensors, sub-systems, and clever driving assistance has provided independent decision-making capability for unmanned air and ground vehicles. The autonomy standard depends on the structure and the degree of sensor complexity and the operating applications of the vehicle. As a result, vehicles that drive themselves are seen as a significant challenge. It is also necessary to analyse threats and assaults on auto and ITS vehicles and their appropriate prevention methods to minimise those cyber threats. That is why in recent literature there are a few research articles which draw up possible attacks on VANETs, ITSs, and self-driving vehicles and their detection mechanisms.

Owing to the complexities of the automobile industry, a fully automatic drive would not take place immediately, but as technology progresses. Control systems are now progressively integrated on the market and their functionality is aimed at total vehicle control.

SYSTEM ARCHITECTURE OF AV

Some components of AV make computer close to human intelligence figure 3 and 4 explains the working of AV communication. They are:

- Computer vision- the aim of computer vision is to identify the objects which are near to the vehicles. This phenomenon can be utilized using image classification called Convolution Neural Network.
- Sensor fusion- AV can be equipped with lots of sensors for the proper functioning.
- Localization-This component is used to identify the exact location of the car by using some technology based on mathematical algorithms.
- Path planning- this step is used to plan the journey called as path planning. By using this feature SDC (self-driving vehicles) can take best optimal path from one source to destination.
- Control- Once the path is finalised the next step is to steer the wheel like a human do.

Figure 3. Communication from A to B

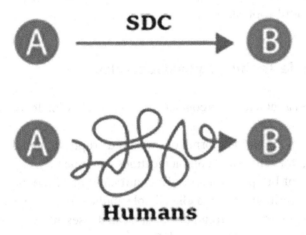

Figure 4. Autonomous car: functional architecture (Hussain, 1275-1313)

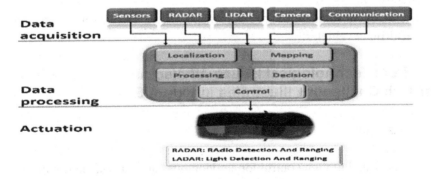

CHALLENGES WITH AUTONOMOUS VEHICLES

Use of automated vehicles provided lots of potential benefits to the community, but it also forces certain challenges also. The impact of AV (automated vehicles) is on automobile industry, health, transport, labour market, traffic, energy and environmental effects, self-parking, parking space, Rescue, emergency response, and military, Telecommunication, Hospitality industry and airlines and privacy. Security challenges in IOT based Auto-VANET applications are

- Secure Communication
- Monitor and detect threat
- Manage devices to the updates
- Authorization and authentication
- Data integrity
- Secure devices
- Secure control applications
- Privacy

Some Possible Technological Obstacles are

1. A device for a vehicle, like a contact machine among vehicles, may theoretically be hacked.
2. Vulnerability to various forms of climate disruption, namely jamming and tampering, for sensor and communications equipment.
3. Prevention of big predator's needs identification and monitoring and Volvo considered caribou, deer and elk-suitable applications unsuccessful.
4. Device programming will entail a sophisticated assessment of product creation as well as the distribution network for modules.
5. In crowded inner city conditions machine learning is now unable to work effectively.
6. The excellent standard of specialist maps will be needed for the operation of self-driving vehicles.

Apart from Technological Issues AV also have Research Challenges Illustrates in Figure 5

They are as follows:

1. Planning and motion control for autonomous car in urban environment.
2. Communication and location privacy in connected and autonomous vehicles.

3. Building long-term maps for different weather environment conditions in autonomous cars.
4. Cyber threats in connected and autonomous cars.
5. Hardware execution of visual perception algorithms in AV.
6. Perception of autonomous cars from users' and pedestrians' perspective.
7. Consumer faith and preferences in AV.
8. Obstacle detection in Autonomous vehicles.
9. Trends in advanced driving support (ADS) and its adaptation in AV.

Figure 5. Current and future challenges (Hussain & Zeadally, 2019)

Parameters Used in Machine Learning

Accuracy

It is the most instinctive exhibition measure and it is just a proportion of accurately anticipated perception to the absolute perceptions. One may feel that, assuming we have high precision, our model is ideal. Indeed, precision is an extraordinary measure however just when you have symmetric datasets where upsides of false positive and false negatives are practically same. In this way, you need to take a gander at different boundaries to assess the exhibition of your model.

$$Accuracy = \frac{TP + TN}{TP + FP + FN + TN} \qquad (1)$$

Precision

Precision is the proportion of accurately anticipated positive perceptions to the all anticipated positive perceptions. High precision identifies with the low false positive rate.

$$\text{Precision} = \frac{\text{TP}}{\text{TP} + \text{FP}} \tag{2}$$

Recall

Recall is the proportion of effectively anticipated positive perceptions to the all perceptions in real class.

$$\text{Recall} = \frac{\text{TP}}{\text{TP} + \text{FN}} \tag{3}$$

F1 Score

F1 score is the weighted normal of Precision and Recall. Accordingly, this score considers both false positives and false negatives. Instinctively it isn't as straightforward as exactness, however F1 is normally more helpful than precision, particularly on the off chance that you have a lopsided class conveyance.

$$F1\ \text{Score} = \frac{2 * (\text{Recall} * \text{Precision})}{(\text{Recall} + \text{Precision})} \tag{4}$$

REVOLUTION TOWARDS AV

It has been determined that by 2040, there will be more than 33 million driverless vehicles out and about, and around 55% of private companies expect that they'll embrace self-driving vehicle innovations in their activities inside the following twenty years. There is still a ton of work and testing to be done to guarantee driverless advances are 100%, you can be certain that driverless vehicles will be surprising the streets not long from now. Some of the companies working on AV's (Betz, 2022) are as follows:

1. **Unity Technologies:** The Company was founded on 2004 in San Francisco CA. The company is working for the development of 3D and visualization technology tools to help public and vehicle for physical navigation. It provides a framework in which an automotive can be checked for VR before entering into real world.

2. **CRUISE:** It is founded in year 2013 in San Francisco CA. The company is working in combining both ride share technology with self-driving to reduce the fuel emission. They merged AI with robotics to ensure that vehicle will observe lanes properly to follow safety rules accurately.

3. **Waymo:** Waymo is a google product which is founded in 2009 in San Francisco to work on AV. It provides a variety of operation to gain mobility for drivers travelling across states.

4. **VOYAGE:** It is founded on 2017 to accelerate the marketing of AV among senior citizens, by providing safe and slow passage among streets for them.

5. **WiTricity**: Company started in 2007 for working in the field of wireless charging stations for AV's. It uses magnetic resonance technology, so that an electric vehicle parked in Witricity parking lot will start its charging immediately.

6. **Zscaler:** Zscaler is working with top-most brands worldwide to provide fast and secure access to the cloud-based services. The organization's Zscaler Internet Access and Zscaler Private Access networks make quick, secure associations among clients and applications on any gadget, area, or organization, making continuous correspondence with self-driving innovation more conceivable than any other time in recent memory.

7. **NODAR:** NODAR makes 3D fringe sensors for driverless vehicles that are worked for significant distance insight and are incorporated with self-adjusting programming to assist with directing their vehicles to objections in a single piece.

8. **HAAS Alert**: HAAS Alert has a dream for self-driving innovation as a method for elevating the administrations of crisis vehicles, giving independent vehicles and other transportation strategies worked to react to outside wellbeing cautions and course the speediest ways to their objections.

9. **Reality AI:** Reality AI founded in 2015 in New York City, makes cloud-based natural recognition advances, worked to be deftly coordinated into previous frameworks and stages.

10. **SEEVA:** SEEVA's group founded in 2016 expects that, lidar and 3D detecting innovation may be improved to react viably to natural changes, there are still

factors like temperature changes and different blocks that can cheapen their responsiveness.

11. **Lumotive:** Lumotive's essential spotlight is on fostering the best lidar framework conceivable so driverless vehicles can precisely foresee and react to episodes out and about without outside input. Their superior natural examining tech is coordinated with pillar controlling frameworks so AI insights can be imparted to vehicle foundations and change courses progressively.

USE OF VARIOUS DETECTION MECHANISM AGAINST DDOS

Use of Intelligent IDS for Autonomous Vehicles

In recent years, the conventional web has extended to incorporate an omnipresent organization which we allude to as Internet-of-Things (IoTs) (Jaiswal & Sarkar, 2018), which highlights Machine to Machine (M2M) communication with the capacity to give a productive network to self-driving vehicles.

Vehicular ad hoc networks (VANETs) are known as remote portable organizations which license self-driving vehicles to effectively trade data like Cooperative Awareness Messages (CAMs) among each other also, street side units (RSUs) in their correspondence region. VANETs are ready to improve street wellbeing and make service agreeable on occupied streets. These organizations have the capacity to trade notice messages, warning messages, control information and CAMs between neighboring vehicles. It is feasible for a noxious assault to be dispatched from any area inside the radio region at any time in such remote organizations as they come up short on a firewalls and doors. Besides, a malignant assault does not need actual admittance to the vehicle, as it would be the situation with wired organizations (Rodge & Jaiswal, 2019).

Providing security to the vehicle Ad-Hoc network has been achieved by using encryption/ decryption and various digital signature algorithms to reduce the potential attack. The use of such algorithms and techniques are considered as the first layer of Defense. For achieving the second layer of defense requires new security measures for self-driving vehicles for autonomous vehicles. The requirements of such systems are developed in such a way that they can identify, and block known and unknown attacks. Such systems required IDS system to achieve security, but they also face some issues like:

1. Developed such a system which provides security to the data which is transferred from one system to another.

2.   Protection and monitoring of each and every message which is conveyed among vehicles and roadside units.

There is a need for such systems which requires to capture whole communication, monitor transfer and examine it, so that no one can attack. This procedure of Thoreau examination is known as audit process full stop the system must be able to detect malicious and benign activity on the basis of the data captured during the audit process.

The IDS consists of three important phases:

1.   First phase is known as the data cleaning and transformation phase. It requires data gathering from multiple sources.
2.   examination and relevance analysis phase
3.   The last phase is also known as response phase or reduction phase.

The author uses a hybrid intrusion detection system that is a combination of anomaly and misuse based detection. The advantage of using this hybrid approach is that it will work fast, provide good accuracy, false rate will be low and the method is able to detect new attacks on the basis of past behavior. This model also utilizes back propagation artificial neural networks with fuzzy sets, which helps to predict any external attack happening to AV.

The data set used here is Kyoto, in which only those data or parameters are considered which have IP addresses. In other words, the main parameter to detect any false user is to find fake or unregistered IP addresses. There are other features also which are utilized to achieve proper efficiency and effectiveness like computation time, memory requirement, accuracy etc. The whole system is bifurcated into four main parts and illustrated in figure 6:

- The first phase is called the data cleaning phase. In some places the space is also known as the data pre-processing phase. This involves three processes known as encoding, normalization and equal distribution of data. Each and every face has its own importance and working, the output data from one phase becomes input for another.
- The encoding phase involves the representation of features with the help of symbols. These symbols are again converted into some integer values for the calculations, because ANN requires numerical values for computation of each of the vectors.
- The next step is to distribute the data uniformly so that the training process of the machine is accurate. From a large data set, three sections are created to identify the traffic which are unknown, known and abnormal. The calculation

is done on the basis of following calculations like if suppose the number of normal behavior or known behavior patterns available are N subsets and the actual data set contains S samples, then there is a probability that there is a chance to find a particular sample in normal class that is S/T. by using this distribution approach each and every subset in a data set is equally and uniformly distributed.

Figure 6. Working architecture

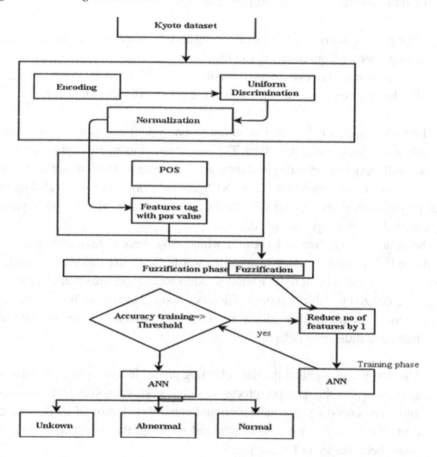

The last process of this phase is called as normalization. Normalization is a process where the data is scaled between 0.0 to 1.0 and -1.0 to 1.0, so that they can fall within a particular specified range. This process is basically used for classification of algorithms that involves neural network, for calculating distance Matrix like nearest neighbor classification and clustering. This process of normalizing each input attribute helps to speed up the learning process during training phase. Three basic type of normalization methods are there known as Min-Max normalization, Z- score normalization and normalization by decimal scaling.

The author uses a Min-Max normalization (Ali et al., 2009) technique for each numerical attribute. Min-max method is basically used to perform linear transformation over data on original data. ANN can perform better with normalized data and also provided better predictions while working.

$$A = \frac{A' - \min}{\max - \min} \tag{5}$$

1. The next phase is the feature selection from the dataset. It is the most important part for any problem solving because the IDS efficiency relies on the number and quality of features. The removal of less required data improves the storage requirement as well as the computation time. It also improves the training process for any data. In this system, thirteen features are taken among all the features to measure the accuracy. For the above, proportional overlapping scores algorithm is used to calculate all the important features from all the available features from the dataset (Alheeti & McDonald-Maier, 2017). For this approach, statistical approach to choose important features which contains high weight and critical effect.

As we all know that, dataset suffers from classification issue, such mechanism is required which overcomes issues and provide a proper solution to above problem is with the use of fuzzy set. This fuzzification process creates a clear boundary among important features among dataset. It clearly identifies normal, known and unknown behavior. The fuzzy set are also called as possibility theory. Following equations have been taken for fuzzification process:

$$F(x,r,s,t)=\max(\min(x-\frac{r}{s})-r, \ t-\frac{x}{t}-s),0) \tag{6}$$

Where x defines the normal value before fuzzification process and r, s, t represents the domain value.

2. Next phase is training phase, in this phase supervised learning with back propagation neural network is used for assuring security. Such system is known as multilayer perceptron model. It uses feed-forward neural network, which uses a collection of non-linear neurons which are connected to one another. This technique is very useful for classification and prediction of data. For calculation

of hidden layers in MLP, cross-validation process is used. Depending upon the operation and experiment k-fold cross-validation process is implemented. With the use of this process, the author obtained a best result for getting a proper set of neurons for the layers of artificial neural network. The training and testing is done with hybrid approach i.e. misuse based and anomaly based IDS system to gain more secure external communication among AV's.

This hybrid approach has the ability to detect malignant behavior for AV. The proposed approach overcomes the conventional security system which does not have the capacity to provide proper security to the external communication with better results among autonomous vehicles.

Malicious Detection in Autonomous Vehicles Using MLA

In Park & Choi (2020) author has proposed a data analysis method based on machine learning for accurately detecting abnormal behaviors occurred because of malware in real time broad-scale self-driving vehicle network traffic. Architecture is defined for intrusion detection module which detects and obstructs malware attempts which affect the self-driving vehicle through a smartphone. An effective algorithm is proposed to detect malicious behavior within a network environment. The proposed algorithm is compared experimentally with different algorithms for cost and detection accuracy.

In Milosevic et al. (2017) many previous cyberattacks malware have been used for crime. Once cyber attacker successfully install malware on some system, then the cyber attacker can be able to install or delete programs, can modify files, and can download sensitive information. Finally, the information can be used to imitate the user of the infected devices and can use the infected system as a source of DDoS attack. Many mobile operating systems were targeted by malicious programs and reported malware were targeting mobile devices. Due to significant processing power of mobile devices attackers can use the devices for DDoS attacks. Attacks using malware creates many user interaction situations which can enter into a self-driving vehicle via smartphone. Many algorithms are available to deal with DDoS attacks. As the autonomous vehicles are connected to other autonomous vehicles for in-vehicle and inter-vehicle communication, the communication is real time communication. So required accurate and fast working mechanism which is suitable for detection of malware in an autonomous vehicle environment.

In-vehicle infotainment systems used to deliver information and entertainment content, enable many applications by using an Android operating system (embedded operating system). If In-vehicle infotainment systems security layout is not taken into consideration in wireless networks, then such interfaces can occur and can be misused as a way for malware to enter the autonomous vehicle network as shown in figure 7.

Figure 7. Head unit connection with mobile device

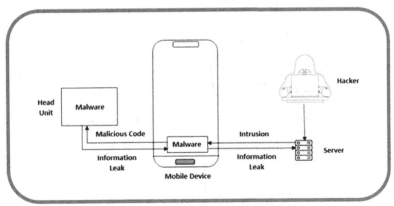

In proposed system, intrusion detection module based on machine learning is installed in the vehicle intrusion detection system. It may detect intrusion in the controller area network or any anomaly. Hence a head unit or electronic controller unit may provide protection from malicious code. The malware behaviors in the autonomous vehicle is monitored by using software-based computing modules. The software can be installed in head unit as an anti-virus agent, or it may be installed as a component in intrusion detection module of the autonomous vehicle. The system evaluates intrusion which is based on learned model as well as which provides intrusion information to control unit or a user. The proposed system can provide improved model's accuracy by analyzing message patterns and malicious behaviors detection rules updated to autonomous vehicle gateway for accurate detection of malicious code as shown in figure 8.

The proposed algorithm (Park & Choi, 2020) works on selected network traffic features for detection of malware. The proposed improved feature selection method finds greedy features and the highest correlation. Classical linear correlation and entropy-based information gain method, these two methods are used for measurement of correlation between two variables. Linear correlation coefficient is derived for two variables using information gain method and correlation-based feature selection method. Information gain method is used for deciding importance of a given attribute in the feature vectors. Highly correlated final features from the dataset and strong relationship between data are determined using these two methods.

Figure 8. Vehicle gateway and intrusion detection system

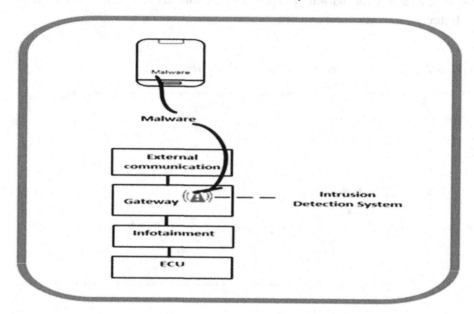

Algorithm

Input: U-universal set including all features.

Output: Ω^*-subset with the selected feature by improved feature selection method.

1. Initialization
   a. $x_n, y_n, z_n \in U$ Where $(1 \leq n \leq N)$
2. Using linear correlation coefficient get all $r(x_n, y_n)$
3. Sort $\left| r_{x_n, y_n} \right|$ values for $(1 \leq n \leq N)$
4. Select m sets for the top x_n with max value of $|r|$ for suitable variable m and $(1 \leq m \leq N)$
5. Obtain combination $x_n, y_n \in C_m$, where $C_m \subset U$ and $n(C_m) = m$
6. Find C_m^*, where max of *F1* score with x_n
7. Using information gain obtain all *H(n)*
8. Get *l* which is related to the highly ranking variable.
9. Select *l* sets for the top z_n with max value of *H(n)*, suitable variable *l* and $(1 \leq l \leq N)$
10. Get elements $z_n \in C_l$, where $C_l \subset U$ and $n(C_l) = lc$
11. Find C_l^*, where the max of *F1* score with z_n
12. Merge $\Omega^* = \left\{ C_m^* \right\} \cup \left\{ C_l^* \right\}$

At correlation-based feature selection, $r(x_n, y_n)$ i.e linear correlation coefficient is derived and final C_m^* calculating highest F1 score which is 0.796. At information gain stage, the information ranking $H(n)$ is derived and final C_I^* calculating highest *F1* score which is 0.806 (Park & Choi, 2020). Final feature selection is calculated by union of information gain features and correlation-based feature selection sets.

By using intrusion detection system, the malware can be detected from network traffic for that nine features are selected using improved feature selection method. Learning from the original data which is having unique characteristics and distributions may be slow or modeling error can be resulted. So that scaling can be performed for data processing which is based on nine selected features. After applying Min Max Scaler and Standard scalers F1 score results 0.813 and 0.810 respectively. Its shows that Min Max scaler is more beneficial for network traffic so Min Max Scaler applied to each algorithm. Malware in Android OS detecting algorithms are analyzed by using six machine learning algorithms. For that dataset used is classified under 3 classes which are benign, adware and malware. The proposed intrusion detection system detects malware for autonomous vehicle as shown in figure 9.

Figure 9. Intrusion detection system in a vehicle network

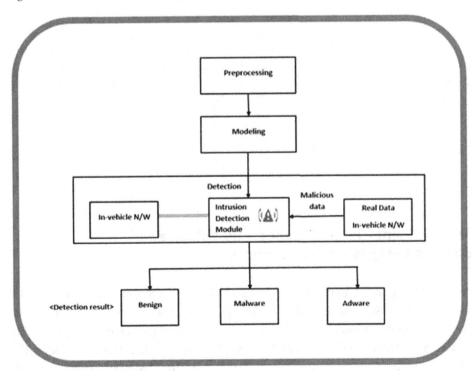

Six machine learning based algorithms are used to analyze which are data random forest (RF), gradient boosting classifier (GB), bagging classifier (BC), k-nearest neighbor's classi.er (KC), decision tree (DT) and extra tree classifier (ET) algorithms. Results of these six algorithms are compared with proposed algorithm. Feature selection process are used to define nine input features. Output is calculated by using two classification situations for analyzing the experimental results. Adware, benign code, and malware are detected accurately in first scenario as shown in figure 10 and second scenario is binary classification in which begin code and adware are detected as shown in figure 11. Accuracy recall and precision are through machine learning uses F1 score. It detects malware in real time on autonomous vehicles. Simulation of proposed algorithm is fast (0.049 s) and highly accurate (92.9%), so that it is suitable to detect real-time malware in autonomous vehicle environment.

Figure 10. Multiclass classification

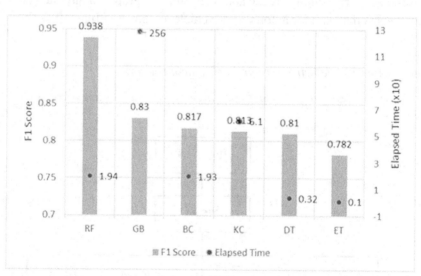

An Intelligent IDs for Autonomous Vehicles Based on Magnetometer Sensors

Proposed Integrated Circuit Metric- Intrusion Detection System (ICMetric-IDS) is based on vehicle sensing scheme. It uses magnetometer sensor in self-driving cars to protect external communication. The system is designed for the training and testing of normal and abnormal (malicious) behavior and also it identifies the vehicle. The emerging security technology known as Integrated Circuit Metric extracts the basic features of a device to generate a unique device identification. Proposed system detects internal as well as external attacks with higher accuracy- rate of detection with low rate of error and false alarm to identify malicious behavior in self driving car (Alheeti & McDonald-Maier, 2017).

The successful implementation of self-driving car concept will reduce the burden on drivers. Also, it will reduce the number of accidents happed due to the human errors. The working of self-driving car is totally dependents on internal and external communication of vehicles as shown in figure 12. Both internal and external communication must be safe as it directly related to passengers' lives. Internal communication is the communication between vehicles called as vehicle to vehicle (V2V) communication and the external communication is the communication between vehicle and Roadside Units called as vehicle to Road Side Unit (V2R) communication. As V2V and V2R communications are wireless communications, the term security must be taken into consideration. So the network of the vehicle must be protected from different types of attacks such as DDoS attack.

Intrusion detection System is used to detect malicious behavior inside the communication network. In proposed system, Integrated Circuit Metric is combined with traditional Intrusion Detection System which provides strong detection system to make external communication of the self-driving car more secure. Integrated Circuit Metric is used to extracts the features of a device to generate a unique device identification. The normalized extracted features are used to determine that they are deterministic and unique. For this reason, the magnetometer sensor is added into system.

Figure 11. Binary classification

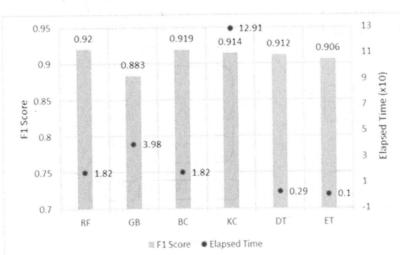

Figure 12. Communication System of autonomous vehicle

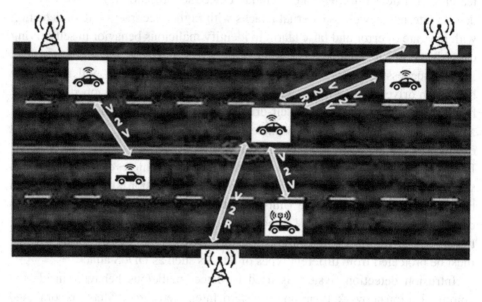

Bias reading is extracted from Magnetometer sensor and provided to ICMetric-IDS for identification of autonomous vehicle. The architecture of proposed system provides six stages detection system as shown in figure 13.

Figure 13. ICMetric-IDS architecture

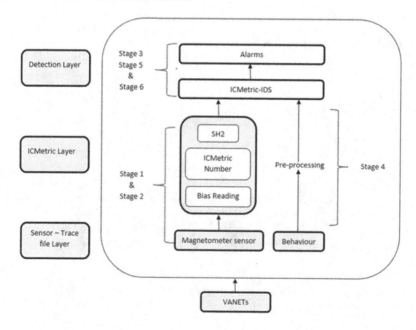

Six stages of detection system are (Alheeti & McDonald-Maier, 2017):

- Stage 1: Generate ICMetric number: The ICMetric number is generated by applying statistical and mathematical functions on readings extracted from magnetometer sensor. The ICMetric number generates hash value.
- Stage 2: Real world: Simulation Urban Mobility and Mobility Vehicles tools are used to generate real world simulation which reflects mobility of vehicle. Files generated from these two tools are provided as input to generate the trace file.
- Stage 3: Feature extraction: Only 16 significant features are utilized by proposed Integrated Circuit Metric- Intrusion Detection System from the complete extracted features space. Due to reduced number of features detection rate is enhanced and decreased false alarms and error rate.
- Stage 4: Prepressing: The significant features need some preprocessing, first, transformation of some letters and symbols in to numbers; second, uniform distribution for balancing normal and abnormal records to improve the efficiency of intrusion detection system and third, the normalized extracted features generated from trace file makes the performance of proposed system more efficient in identification and blocking malicious behavior.
- Stage 5: Training phase: k-NN is used to design the ICMetric-IDS and the system is trained with the extracted dataset produced in stage three.
- Stage 6: Testing phase: The proposed system is tested with the extracted features. Four types of alarms and accuracy rate of detection are calculated in the test phase. Efficiency of k- NN is measured through detection rate, number of false alarms (true positive, true negative, false positive, and false negative), throughput, Packet Delivery Rate (PDR), and End-to-End delay.

Table 1. Performance metrics of ICMetric-IDS system

Performance Metrics	False Alarm	Detection rate		Throughput	Delay	PDR
		Normal	Abnormal			
VANETs with Normal- IDS	12.24%	98.45%	85.02%	-	-	-
VANETs with ICMetric- IDS	1.21%	99.77%	98.78%	-	-	-
VANETs without- IDS	-	-	-	1.02%	0.05%	23.33*ms*
VANETs with Normal-IDS	-	-	-	78.57%	97.86%	1.47ms
VANETs with ICMetric-IDS	-	-	-	80.22%	99.64%	28.71ms

As per the discussion in stage six, the efficiency of k- NN for proposed ICMetric-IDS system is measured through detection rate (normal and abnormal), number of false alarms (true positive, true negative, false positive, and false negative), throughput, Packet Delivery Rate (PDR), and End-to-End delay and results of proposed systems are shown in figure 14, figure 15 and table 1.

Figure 14. Detection Rate and False Alarm

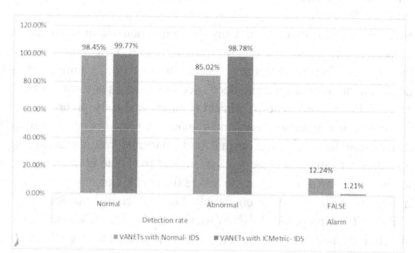

Figure 15. Performance Metrics

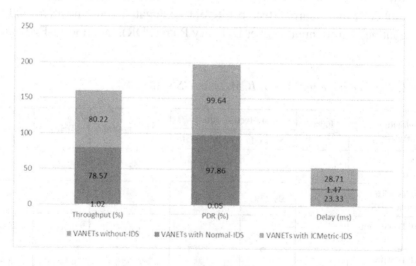

The successful implementation of self-driving car is dependent on secure network environment for external communication. The average error rate of ICMetric –IDS system is 0.72%. The detection rate ranges in between 98.78% and 99.77% with accuracy. The average false alarm rate was 1.21% which is very low. Detection rate of the VANET with normal IDS ranges in between 85.02% and 98.45% where false alarm was 12.24%. ICMetric technology with k-NN is used to improve the detection rate. Therefore, proposed ICMetric-IDS system detects internal as well as external attacks with higher accuracy rate of detection with low rate of error and false alarm to identify malicious behavior in self-driving car.

CONCLUSION

The chapter deals with the working of autonomous vehicles, ongoing cyber security attacks and their possible solutions. Along with that, discussions on various results using machine learning algorithms will also summarize. Certain parameters discussed like accuracy, normalization, precision, and recall based on the algorithm. So along with recent work, the authors will discuss industries involved in the development of autonomous vehicles. As all major companies are investing in developing autonomous vehicles. So, along with recent work, the authors discussed industries involved in the development of autonomous vehicles.

REFERENCES

Alheeti, K. M. A., & McDonald-Maier, K. (2017). An intelligent intrusion detection scheme for self-driving vehicles based on magnetometer sensors. *2016 International Conference for Students on Applied Engineering, ICSAE 2016*. 10.1109/ICSAE.2016.7810164

Ali, K. M., Samawi, V. W., & Al Rababaa, M. S. (2009). The affect of fuzzification on neural networks intrusion detection system. *2009 4th IEEE Conference on Industrial Electronics and Applications*, 1236–1241.

Betz, S. (2022). *25 Top Self Driving Car Companies 2022*. https://builtin.com/transportation-tech/self-driving-car-companies

Desai, M., & Jaiswal, S. (2021). Importance of Information Security and Strategies to Prevent Data Breaches in Mobile Devices. Research Anthology on Securing Mobile Technologies and Applications. doi:10.4018/978-1-7998-8545-0.ch025

Hussain, R., & Zeadally, S. (2019). Autonomous Cars: Research Results, Issues, and Future Challenges. IEEE Communications Surveys and Tutorials. doi:10.1109/COMST.2018.2869360

Jaiswal, S., & Chandra, M. B. (2017). A Survey: Privacy and Security to Internet of Things with Cloud Computing. *International Journal of Control Theory and Applications, 10*(1).

Jaiswal, S., & Sarkar, S. (2018). COT: Evaluation and Analysis of Various Applications With Security for Cloud and IoT. In Examining Cloud Computing Technologies Through the Internet of Things (pp. 251–263). IGI Global.

Milosevic, N., Dehghantanha, A., & Choo, K. K. R. (2017). Machine learning aided Android malware classification. *Computers & Electrical Engineering, 61*, 266–274. Advance online publication. doi:10.1016/j.compeleceng.2017.02.013

Mohd, T. K., Majumdar, S., Mathur, A., & Javaid, A. Y. (2018). Simulation and Analysis of DDoS Attack on Connected Autonomous Vehicular Network using OMNET++. *2018 9th IEEE Annual Ubiquitous Computing, Electronics and Mobile Communication Conference, UEMCON 2018.* 10.1109/UEMCON.2018.8796717

NCSA. (2019). *Early Estimates of Motor Vehicle Traffic Fatalities for the First 9 Months (Jan–Sep) of 2019.* https://crashstats.nhtsa.dot.gov/#!/PublicationList/51

Park, S., & Choi, J. Y. (2020). Malware Detection in Self-Driving Vehicles Using Machine Learning Algorithms. *Journal of Advanced Transportation, 2020*, 1–9. Advance online publication. doi:10.1155/2020/3035741

Rodge, J. & Jaiswal, S. (2019). *Comprehensive Overview of Neural Networks and Its Applications in Autonomous Vehicles.* doi:10.4018/978-1-5225-7955-7.ch007

Tong, W., Hussain, A., Bo, W. X., & Maharjan, S. (2019). Artificial Intelligence for Vehicle-To-Everything: A Survey. *IEEE Access: Practical Innovations, Open Solutions.* Advance online publication. doi:10.1109/ACCESS.2019.2891073

ADDITIONAL READING

Keshavarz, M., Shamsoshoara, A., Afghah, F., & Ashdown, J. (2020). A real-time framework for trust monitoring in a network of unmanned aerial vehicles. *IEEE INFOCOM 2020 - IEEE Conference on Computer Communications Workshops, INFOCOM WKSHPS 2020.* 10.1109/INFOCOMWKSHPS50562.2020.9162761

Mairaj, A., Majumder, S., & Javaid, A. Y. (2019). Game theoretic strategies for an unmanned aerial vehicle network host under DDoS attack. *2019 International Conference on Unmanned Aircraft Systems, ICUAS 2019*. 10.1109/ICUAS.2019.8797939

Malik, S., Bandi, P., & Sun, W. (2021). An Experimental Study of Denial of Service Attack against Platoon of Smart Vehicles. *Proceedings - 2021 4th International Conference on Connected and Autonomous Driving, MetroCAD 2021*. 10.1109/MetroCAD51599.2021.00013

Saglam, E. T., & Bahtiyar, S. (2019). A Survey: Security and Privacy in 5G Vehicular Networks. *UBMK 2019 - Proceedings, 4th International Conference on Computer Science and Engineering*. 10.1109/UBMK.2019.8907026

Saulaiman, M. N. E., Kozlovszky, M., & Csilling, A. (2021). A Survey on Vulnerabilities and Classification of Cyber-Attacks on 5G-V2X. *21st IEEE International Symposium on Computational Intelligence and Informatics, CINTI 2021 - Proceedings*. 10.1109/CINTI53070.2021.9668440

KEY TERMS AND DEFINITIONS

Accuracy: It is the measurement used to determine which model is best at identifying relationships and patterns between variables in a dataset based on the input, or training, data.

Autonomous Vehicle: An autonomous car is a vehicle which can sense its surroundings and operate without human intervention.

Cryptography: It provides a secure communications technique that allow only the sender and intended recipient of a message to view its contents.

DDoS Attack: A DDoS attack occurs when an intruder uses resources from multiple, remote locations to attack an organization's online operations.

Entropy: A high entropy means low information gain, and a low entropy means high information gain.

IDS: An Intrusion Detection System (IDS) is a network security technology originally built for detecting vulnerability exploits against a target application or computer.

Linear Correlation: Correlation is said to be linear if the ratio of change is constant.

Normalization: It is a scaling technique in Machine Learning applied during data preparation to change the values of numeric columns in the dataset to use a common scale.

Precision: It is one of the important performance indicators, which indicates the quality of a positive prediction made by model.

Recall: It measures the model's ability to detect positive samples.

Chapter 4

Application of Machine Learning to User Behavior–Based Authentication in Smartphone and Web

Manoj Jayabalan
iD https://orcid.org/0000-0002-1599-965X
Liverpool John Moores University, UK

ABSTRACT

Authentication is the preliminary security mechanism employed in the information system to identify the legitimacy of the user. With technological advancements, hackers with sophisticated techniques easily crack single-factor authentication (username and password). Therefore, organizations started to deploy multi-factor authentication (MFA) to increase the complexity of the access to the system. Despite the MFA increasing the security of the digital service, the usable security should be given equal importance. The user behavior-based authentication provides a means to analyze the user interaction with the system in a non-intrusive way to identify the user legitimacy. This chapter presents a review of user behavior-based authentication in smartphones and websites. Moreover, the review highlights some of the common features, techniques, and evaluation criteria usually considered in the development of user behavior profiling.

DOI: 10.4018/978-1-7998-9430-8.ch004

INTRODUCTION

Digital authentication provides a means to secure access to digital information through various technologies. It acts as a prime component in the access control system to mitigate the risk of unauthorized access (Grassi et al., 2017; Jayabalan, 2020). The traditional and most widely used approach to identify the legitimacy of the user consists of supplying a username and password, a system known as Single Factor Authentication. The password is the oldest and predominant authentication factor that exists in the information security world. It is the simplest method to implement and inexpensive, but it is prone to vulnerabilities such as users using weak passwords that are easily cracked, phishing attacks, and other common hacker techniques (Raza et al., 2012). The technological advancements plethora the usage of digital service that requires several authentication factors to be implemented to prevent malicious users. As such, there is a need for organizations to employ Multi-Factor Authentication (MFA) where increased complexity such as using a combination of two or more independent authentication factors (smart cards, biometrics, and security tokens) offers extra security protection (Andrean et al., 2020).

Three-factor authentication using the combination of the above factors can offer greater privacy and security, but as it is more complex, and organizations also have to maintain acceptable efficiency levels, it is a greater challenge to implement. There is an increase in biometric authentication systems in several organizations since these grant access only after validating a subject's unique characteristics (Memon, 2017). Biometric authentication is broadly classified into physiological and behavioral. The physiological biometrics are based on the subject physical properties such as iris, fingerprint, face, and palm. Whereas behavioral biometrics measures the subject unique behavior or patterns from voice, keystroke, mouse dynamics, gait, and system usage, which can uniquely identify an individual (Aupy & Clarke, 2005; Ferbrache, 2016; Meng et al., 2015; Vielhauer, 2006).

The behavioral biometric strike the balance between security and usability via monitoring the user behavior throughout the active session. According to Global Opportunity Report 2017,

Behavioral biometrics analyses specific human behavior with intelligent software, adding a new layer of security to verifying identification that is nearly impossible to replicate, without any additional stress for the user. Products and services in this market are moving digital security beyond simple passwords and pin codes, ensuring that as cybercriminals become more advanced, so too do everyday users (DNV GL AS, 2017).

The advancement of Artificial Intelligence provides a venue for the information security experts to make an informed decision through gaining insights from the historical user access logs. Access logs are an integral part of the system that collects traces of event that was executed by an individual entity. The logs are beneficial for experts to identify the deviation that has occurred in the process through monitoring and auditing of the operations. Moreover, logs can be effectively utilized in many ways; process mining is the process of extracting the historical log to identify the cause of business process deviation and to improve the business flow (Claes & Poels, 2014; Jayabalan & Thiruchelvam, 2017). It can be further extended to extract user behavior to perform additional authentication by integrating machine learning algorithms.

The purpose of this chapter is to understand the potential inclusion of user behavior profiling in traditional authentication framework. Moreover, the chapter highlights some of the common features, techniques, and evaluation criteria usually considered in the development of user behavior profiling. The scope of this chapter is limited to user behavior-based authentication in smartphones and websites. This chapter is meant to be useful for identifying trends in user behavior profiling that will allow researchers to focus on areas that needs to be improved and new features that could be beneficial to stakeholders.

At the end of this Chapter, you should be able to:

- Understand the functionality and significance of user behavior authentication.
- Identify the factors that are influencing the utilization of user behavior authentication in the digital information service to protect privacy and security.
- Investigate existing and potential approaches with regards to the application of behavior biometric authentication.
- Determine the possible challenges which might occur while introducing the user behavior authentication in digital service.

ISO 29115:2013

The ISO 29115:2013 provides a detailed framework for entity authentication assurance for the overall process in Information and Communications Technology (ISO, 2013). The standard categories the four authentication factors such as "something you know" (e.g., password, PIN), "something you have" (e.g., smart card, device), "something you are" (e.g., biometric characteristic) and "something you do" (e.g., behavior pattern).

ISO 29115:2013 provides guidance to the four Level of Assurance (LOA) from "control technologies, processes, management activities and assurance criteria for mitigating authentication threats." Each LOA describes the level of confidence in the authentication processes from Level 1 to Level 4 (Low, Medium, High and Very High). The determination of choosing the appropriate LOAs depends on several factors such as risk, authentication errors, misuse of credentials, the resultant harm/impact and the likelihood of occurrence. The user behavior-based authentication is suitable for LOA 3 and LOA 4. The requirements and implementation guidance of the LOAs are given in Table 1.

Table 1. Requirements and implementation guidance of the LOAs

Level	Requirement(s)	Implementation
Level of Assurance 1 (LOA1)	No specific requirement for this level. This level is used when the minimum risk is associated with the data.	- Simple username and password.
Level of Assurance 2 (LOA2)	This level is used when the moderate risk is associated with the data. Necessary steps to be considered for reducing the eavesdropper, online guessing attacks and action on protecting stored credentials.	- Single-factor authentication.
Level of Assurance 3 (LOA3)	This level is used when a substantial risk is associated with the data. No special requirements for the generation of credentials.	- Multi-factor authentication - Cryptography to be applied to the authentication information exchange and rest.
Level of Assurance 4 (LOA4)	This level is used when the high risk is associated with the data. Should follow LOA3 implementation and requirement for in-person identity proofing for human and the storage of cryptographic keys should be secured with the tamper-resistant hardware.	- Multi-factor authentication - Cryptography to be applied to the authentication information exchange and rest. - Digital certificates for all ICT devices.

USER BEHAVIOR PROFILING IN AUTHENTICATION

This section discusses the results obtained from analyzing the existing studies on user behavior profiling based on the application and system usage. Authentication is one of the important factors for any level of digital service that requires validating user legitimacy and ensures user confidentiality. With the gradual surge in the number of security breaches across digital services in diverse industries such as healthcare, banking, military etc., organizations boost their security by using MFA that increases the complexity of the access to the system. The design of usable security should be given equal importance to reduce the hindrance level of users. Usability is one of the key drivers that makes a system good enough to be acceptable to the end-user and other stakeholders (Vasudavan et al., 2016).

Biometric user authentication overcomes the issue of transferability of credentials, in which knowledge and possession of the credential are not belonging naturally to the owner. This means the biometric properties of an individual are distinct from one another and difficult to be transferred to another person. Behavioral biometric authentication considers the properties of an individual pattern captured during the interaction with the information system and use it as a mechanism to identify the legitimacy. Therefore, significant data loss can be avoided through the early detection of unusual behavior. User behavior profiling different from a traditional intrusion detection system in which user behavior is utilized to detect anomalies rather than tracking system or device behavior.

The user behavioral profiling implication is demonstrated in the general Java Authentication and Authorization Service (JAAS) classes that are utilized to securely authenticate the client. It provides a modular framework allowing the applications to remain independent from underlying authentication technologies. Hence, providing a framework to customize based on the organization needs to implement the authentication factors. Figure 1 demonstrates the user behavior profiling in JAAS.

The client-side application acquires user login credentials and environmental conditions as input and sends those parameters to the login module. The web logic server container (for example, RMI, EJB etc.) passes the parameters received from the clients to the web logic server. It sends the parameters to authentication providers to verify the credentials. A meanwhile, the environmental conditions are sent to the decision logic for measuring the similarity of data access and the decision logic decides whether to demand additional authentication based on the organization policy. The patterns are generated by the "behavior profile generator" from the user access log and stored into the "behavior profile data store" for the decision logic to classify the future user behavior.

The below subsection will discuss the most commonly used features in the development of user behavior authentication, machine learning models and evaluation criteria to measure the performance of the model.

Features

The features are the important measures that are required for constructing user behavior profiling, which could identify future user behavior. Text analysis performed on the reviewed articles to identify the most commonly utilized features along with their relationships. Cluster analysis (k = 3) was performed with the extracted keywords to find the Jaccard's coefficient based on the agglomerative order. Figure 2 shows the Dendrogram for the feature, which resulted in two clusters and one single word removed from the cluster.

Figure 1. User Behavior Profiling Mapping in JAAS

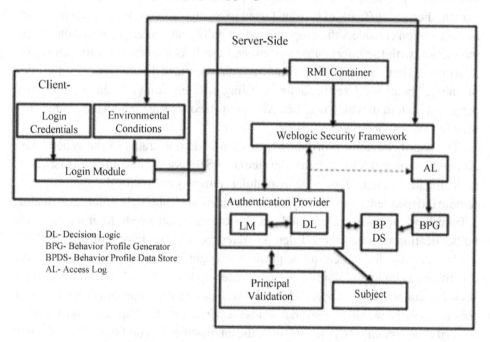

Figure 2. Dendrogram for the keyword Feature

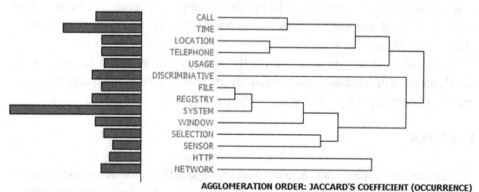

In a typical web-related application, general features such as browsing sequence, time, date, Internet Protocol (IP) address are usually considered in user behavior profiling. The parameter for mobile devices constitutes, the mobile sensor, spatial and the general usage of varied applications are usually considered during the development of profiles. The user call and time are directly linked, and the time parameter has a strong link between the location in which the user accessed (usage) the file and the system.

The user behavior profiling pertaining to the system and application interactions generates an enormous amount of dense data. The significant challenges arise due to an increase in model training time and accuracy in detecting legitimate users. In addition, utilizing the dense data generated from the different sensors and access logs may not produce useful behavior, thus reducing the quality of user profiling. The application of dimensionality reduction techniques over dense data can overcome the issues. Researchers considered the smoothing function to reduce the noise and extract the most usable behavior from the dense data using additive smoothing, moving average which yields better accuracy (Albayram et al., 2013; Li et al., 2014).

User Behavior Learning Methods

User behavior learning is a process of understanding the human interactions with information systems and different means to extract profiles for identifying future user behavior. The dynamic behavior propels the obstructive user authentication in client machines such as mobile devices, desktops, laptops, cloud computing and the Internet of Things (IoT).

The advancement in the mobile device provides a multifaceted approach towards user behavior profiling with the increase in quality of in-built sensors and capabilities to process different applications with ease of access (Ismael et al., 2020). The locking/ unlocking of the mobile device provides inconvenience, thus causing the user not to adopt secure authentication. Therefore, one study has shown the possibility of 3-dimensional sensors in the verification as soon as the unlock event action initiated by the user to detect anomaly (Buriro et al., 2017). For the readers to understand the user behavior perspective of locking/unlocking the smartphone, refer to the article (Mahfouz et al., 2016).

Social network usage is increasing at a rapid rate through the use of a smartphone, leading to utilize them in continuous authentication. TrackMasion is a behaviometric analytics platform to monitor social network usage to identify user behavior and utilize it in mobile authentication (Anjomshoa et al., 2016). Further, Radial Basis Function Neural Network applied on the short messaging service to create a linguistic profile that can be used to determine the user behavior and perform continuous authentication (Saevanee et al., 2011).

One study trained the model using n-gram and utilized the perplexity method to predict the abnormal/normal behavior. The spatial and temporal parameters usage in the construction of user behavior generates a significant number of instances. As such, the additive smoothing method was considered to extract the instances for training (Albayram et al., 2013). In another study, the system-level user behavior model proposed to collect data from the registry, file system, as well as general actions performed in the system such as creation and deletion. The features were selected through the fisher method and multivariate Gaussian mixture were utilized to build the model (Yingbo Song et al., 2013).

Cloud computing offers several benefits to an individual and organization without requiring the user to have any knowledge of the infrastructure used by the service providers. Further, virtualization in cloud computing provides an opportunity to increase or decrease IT resources as needed to meet the demands. However, privacy and security are a major concern in storing the organization sensitive information in the third-party server (Kubbo et al., 2016). Thus, several researchers focus on the incorporation of user behavior analysis for anomaly detection and misuse of the service. The user profiling system using Fuzzy and genetic algorithms to monitor the usage pattern and detect suspicious activity in the system (Sahil et al., 2015). Further, research proposed user behavior analysis for the cloud users through analyzing the application usage and multi-algorithmic approach (Adaptive classifier) implemented for each service to achieve better performance (Al-bayati et al., 2016). In addition, to the general discussion on the different learning methods discussed earlier, this section further introduces three classifications of user behavior learning methods based on their applications.

Steering Behavior

The user behavior profiling generated based on the predefined set of sequences can be effectively utilized in analyzing the behavior such as web page navigation. One study (Alswiti et al., 2016), proposed a k-NN algorithm for building the classifier based on the user navigation historical data. Another study constructed the user profiles based on the unigram Markov model, which allows to construct of a logical sequence. The utilization of the entire web class leads to a higher false-positive rate, thus only the top k/2 web classes are considered along with the browsing time and classes of web pages (Zhao et al., 2016). However, the researchers do not consider a logical relationship between the web pages.

The user interacting with a web application is considered as a web language through which user actions are modeled as words. The n-gram was utilized to predict user behavior based on past usage patterns (Milton & Memon, 2016). It was performing better in binary classification when compared with multi-classification. Moreover, the performance of the model entirely dependent on the keyword abstraction and even a slight change affects the ability to detect the anomaly and requires high performance computing environment. Most of the web browsing sequences reported the need for a greater number of instances to increase the accuracy of the model (Milton & Memon, 2016; Zhao et al., 2016). Interested readers to understand the process involved in weblog mining can refer to this article (Pabarskaite & Raudys, 2007).

Trust Behavior

Trust is an important notion to believe an entity is a legitimate person accessing the system without any malicious intent (Jayabalan, 2020). The trust of a user is calculated using several parameters such as the number of transactions, credibility of feedback, transaction context and community context. The trust vector generated using these criteria are applied with association rule mining to generate user behavior. The obtained patterns are applied with a Bayesian classifier to determine whether the given user access is trustworthy or untrustworthy (D'Angelo et al., 2016). Similarly, (Brosso et al., 2010) proposed continuous authentication through analyzing the user behavior, which is computed using the measure of confidence on the various environmental factors and scores are evaluated using the Neuro-Fuzzy to determine the trust level.

In (Kent & Liebrock, 2013), proposed user authentication for a large-scale enterprise to model the behavior using graphs and the characteristics of the graphs are utilized to build the logistic regression model. The concept of graphs only benefited in providing basic insights into potential credential mixing risks within the network. Another study proposed an adaptive authentication for Malaysia government e-service, which combines multiple applications with single sign-on capabilities (Bakar & Haron, 2014). The user behavior profiling is generated based on the frequency of attribute values and the approach does not find the correlation between them. It lacks predictive capability, high variance in certain attributes, and does not adapt to the most recent changes.

One study proposed the use of an "Interactive Dichotomiser 3" algorithm to characterize the behavior of the user authentication and utilizes the Random Petri network model to analyze the credibility (Lu & Xu, 2014). The credibility degree is computed on normalized user behavior and assigned different levels of trust score to access the data. However, the authenticated users are allowed to directly access the resources based on the roles and user behavior is analyzed at a later stage. This approach needs to compromise on a certain amount of data loss before the anomaly is being identified. There are additional problems in characterizing the user behavior, for instance, only the attributes with the highest entropy are selected and the remaining attributes are not utilized when the instances are correctly classified with fewer attributes, thus, leading to an overfitting problem. Secondly, the approach does not perform better when there are limited instances.

The mobile phone operates with limited resources leads to the computational overhead of processing the trust score within the device considering the entire user behavior activity of different applications with spatial and temporal parameters. Hence, the cloud platform provided an efficient infrastructure to process the trust score using the probability to determine the legitimacy of a user (Chow et al., 2010).

Trial Behavior

Generating a challenge question based on the previous transactions dating back over a decade (B. & Venkataram, 2007). With the recent era of Big Data and its technologies, the possibilities to generate user behavior with the huge volume of data from different sources leads to the prospects of constructing challenge questions in authentication framework (Ibrahim & Ouda, 2016). The knowledge of historical user transactions is the key factor to identify the legitimacy of the user based on the challenge questions.

The questions are usually generated based on the predefined features mapped with the user transactions to measure the frequency of actionable items (Skračić et al., 2017). Notwithstanding, mobile misuse is a major challenge and the researchers' utilized mobile application usage for building the user profiles. The rule-based classifier is used for determining the probability of the event and neural networks for analyzing the call history (Li et al., 2014).

The recommender system analyzes user needs and preferences by finding the correlation between the user, items, rating or reviews. The recommender system has been implemented to identify the top selling items, products, customer demographics, past buying behavior, search history and can also consider social connections of the specific user (Katarya and Verma, 2016; Rana and Jain, 2012; Tarus et al., 2017). Further, the researchers have shown the possibilities of generating user behavior profiles and dynamic challenge questions based on past transactions with the help of collaborative filtering (Ibrahim & Ouda, 2017).

Evaluation Criteria

The models are built on the annotated data should generalize well on future unseen data (Raykar & Saha, 2015). A decent estimate of the model performance is an important characteristic that usually computed through measuring accuracy in order to detect the future predicted behavior. The performance evaluation metrics are broadly classified into the threshold, probability, and ranking metrics. These metrics are the scalar group method that presents the classifier performance in a single score value, thus making it easier to compare and contrast the results with other metrics. In most cases, these types of metrics are employed in three different evaluation applications (Hossin & Sulaiman, 2015).

- **Generalization:** In this evaluation, the metrics were used to measure the generalizability and quality of the summary on the trained classifier. The common metrics utilized for this evaluation consist of accuracy and error.
- **Model Selection:** The best classifier among the different trained classifiers are selected based on the performance of the test set.
- **Discriminator:** The evaluation metrics are employed to discriminate and select the optimum classifier during the validation.

In order to measure the performance of generalization and model selection, all the three discussed evaluation metrics (threshold, probability and ranking) can be employed to measure the effectiveness. However, only certain types of metrics from the three categories utilized for discriminating the classifier such as A Receiver Operating Characteristic Curve (ROC), confusion matrix etc. (Caruana & Niculescu-Mizil, 2004; Han et al., 2012; Marcot, 2012). The commonly used evaluation methods for user behavior profiling are listed below (Pisani et al., 2016).

- **False Acceptance Rate (FAR)** measures how often a classifier falsely identifies an impostor as a genuine user by calculating false matches over total impostor match attempts.
- **False Rejection Rate (FRR)** measures how often a classifier falsely identifies a genuine user as an impostor by calculating false rejection over total genuine match attempts.
- **Equal Error Rate (EER)** measures the threshold point between FAR and FRR.
- Accuracy rate measures correct classification obtained by the classifier in percentage; and
- Integrated error measures the portion of the area resulted by plotting FAR and FRR together.

DISCUSSION AND FUTURE DIRECTION

This section presents the discussion and future directions of user behavior-based authentication. The behavioral biometrics authentication uniquely identifies legitimate users from the adversary based on the behavioral trail. The concept of behavioral biometric dates back to over a century and was even utilized in World War II to uniquely identify the telegraph operators based on the keystroke dynamics. The approach was termed as "Fist of the Sender" to uniquely identify and validate the sender message by analyzing the typing rhythm, pace, and syncopation of the telegraph keys (Banerjee & Woodard, 2012). Behavioral biometrics such as keystrokes and mouse dynamics, which are usually captured under static and controlled conditions. These approaches are vulnerable to replay attacks, human interaction simulation and advanced malware injections. However, the behavioral biometrics are trained as the user operates the system which is difficult to be mimic by the robots due to the invisible challenge and improve security with a cognitive fingerprint of the user (Ferbrache, 2016; Turgeman & Zelazny, 2017).

The researchers' major perseverance to adopt the user behavior analytics in authentication is to detect insider threats, prevent misuse and usable security. The system level attacks are well planned, and several security tools are utilized to monitor and prevent external threats to organization wide networks. Nevertheless, the insider threat and misuse are a major concern to the organizations where co-workers or imposters steal credentials and access the sensitive information, which able to be detected through user behavior profiling (Al-bayati et al., 2016; Li et al., 2014; Yingbo Song et al., 2013). The 2017 Verizon Data Breach Investigations Report says, "Insider misuse is a major issue for the Healthcare industry; in fact, it is the only industry where employees are the predominant threat actors in breaches". Just over half of the incidents with confirmed healthcare data disclosure analyzed were due to privilege misuse and misdelivery (Verizon, 2017).

With the Health Insurance Portability and Accountability Act (HIPAA) and ISO22600-1:2014 requiring healthcare organizations to boost security by using MFA that increases the complexity of the access to the system, the design of usable security should be given equal importance (ISO, 2014; Jayabalan & O'Daniel, 2016; Tipton et al., 2016). As such, healthcare practitioner behavior and the nature of their interaction with security features should be considered as an important characteristic at the design stage (Jayabalan & O'Daniel, 2019; Realpe-Munoz et al., 2016). In studies conducted to identify usability issues in electronic health record authentication, the major concerns among healthcare practitioners were revealed to be efficiency and availability (Ferreira et al., 2011; Wang & Jin, 2008). It was further noted that practitioner acceptance and attitude depend on electronic health records usability (Kaipio et al., 2017).

According to Gartner, "Affiliated physicians are not employees of the healthcare delivery organization but have an elective relationship. Obliging the affiliated physician to use an OTP hardware token may sour and even curtail that relationship. Adopting contextual/analytic and adaptive capabilities can minimize the burden of higher-trust authentication on physicians by limiting its use to only those instances where the level of risk demands it" (Mahdi et al., 2016).

A semi-structured interview for the physiological needs for privacy and security in smartphones resulted in a low response from the participants (Kraus et al., 2017). Since the individual expectations are beyond the need for general authentication. However, this might not be the case for an organization to adapt user behavior profiling. As the behavioral patterns constructed based on the application usage in a continuous manner (intrusive monitoring) to ensure the verification process is carried out in a user-friendly way without any additional efforts from the user.

The trail behavior discussed in the previous section focused on generating the challenge questions based on the historical transactions. It might be suitable for industries such as social networks, e-commerce, banking and finance. However, the information security experts should consider the users' age as an important factor before deciding to adopt this variant. Because older people face age-related impairments which might affect their ability to recall their historical transactions (Vasudavan et al., 2016). The trust behavior variant focuses on calculating the risk associated with user authenticity and applies a mathematical formula to compute a trust score or rank. This method of authentication is more suitable in different areas such as handheld devices, IoT, and dynamic industries. Cloud computing, National Security and Intelligence, military, and healthcare works in a unique operating environment, and high impact of threats that requires additional mechanisms to protect privacy and security (Jayabalan, 2020). For instance, the cloud service provider offers the organization to manage their service which requires dynamic threat assessment (Ehsan Rana et al., 2017). Thus, user behavior profiling through its implementation can assess the user risk and trust using the vulnerability of the current environment, threats and integrity of user with the historical user behavior.

People tend to exhibit certain uniqueness in the level of interaction to the system which can change gradually over the course of time, thus pattern aging is one of the root causes to influence false positives or error rates (Clarke, 2011). Accuracy can be improved by dynamically adopting the most recent changes in user behavior. However, renewing the template might include the illegitimate usage which an imposter might be accepted by the system over time as the genuine user (Al-bayati et al., 2016). One article considers this issue and addressed using the change point detection with the fixed sliding window for the number of instances using time series (Al Solami et al., 2010). Further studies required in identifying illegitimate usage while renewing the template.

Another major challenge to information security experts in user behavior-based authentication is to overcome the cold start problem for the new users, which is not addressed in the existing studies. The new users without having any access trails will most likely not be selected for continuous authentication, which is referred to as "cold start". However, it can be overcome by using the general access templates for individual role-based profiles.

The general hypothesis in authentication factors is "a successfully authenticated subject is a truthful owner accessing the information", thus naïve to authorization mechanism allowing an intruder to take for granted. Further research can consider the access policies (XML, Web Ontology Language) that represent the semantic meaning of every object and its relationships based on the user roles to monitor along with the user behavior (Jayabalan & Oadaniel, 2018). Thus, a combination of authentication mechanisms can be tailored based on the consumption of different sensitive data. For instance, fingerprint authentication is required to access highly sensitive data from certain locations and single factor authentication (username and password) is sufficient to access highly sensitive data from the trusted region and device.

There are two perspectives of privacy risk in user behavior profiling, first order and second order; the leakage of single information is known as first order privacy risk. The second order privacy risk arises due to the user profiling and data mining techniques that are applied to individual data access (Bal et al., 2015). Hence, access confinement and distorting data are methods used to protect sensitive data. At the user data profiling depository phase, encryption techniques such as Identity-Based Encryption and Attribute-Based Encryption are well-known apart to protect while data stored in the cloud vendor or server. The privacy-preserving techniques are mainly acquired in the data processing step of big data analytics. Data anonymization, also known as data masking or data desensitization, is used to obfuscate or conceal any sensitive data about an individual, thus limiting the person's re-identification (Rajendran et al., 2017). Further research needed in virtue of overcoming second order privacy risks through the application of cryptographic and privacy preserving techniques.

CONCLUSION

Authentication is a fundamental security mechanism to protect user privacy and security in digital services. There are several methods proposed in the existing studies to secure data with multifactor authentication and usability is always a concern. Transparent and continuous authentication provide a better tradeoff between security and usability. Employing user behavior-based authentication to the existing multi-factor authentication framework will provide additional security to the system without user intervention. There is a need for continuous authentication to be performed in the industries managing sensitive data through analyzing the user behavior towards their digital services to detect the potential threats.

User behavior-based profiles are created based on the pertinent information from the historical access log. The confidence levels are computed based on the similarity between the real-time factors with the existing patterns to determine the legitimacy of the user. The user behavior-based authentication was demonstrated using the Java Authentication and Authorization Services for the information security experts and developers to understand the implementation details. Further, the taxonomy of the user behavior learning methods was introduced in this chapter such as trail behavior, trust behavior, and steering behavior. The application of machine learning and natural language processing was dominant in trail behavior and steering behavior. Whereas trust behavior is an amalgamation of the aforementioned techniques with probability and statistics. This chapter also presented the most common issues to be dealt with whilst the organizations adopt user behavior-based authentication to protect privacy and security. Moreover, the chapter highlighted some of the research gaps with a lack of empirical studies.

ACKNOWLEDGMENT

I would like to thank Dr. Thomas O'Daniel from Asia Pacific University of Technology and Innovation, Malaysia for sharing his valuable suggestions during the research.

REFERENCES

Al-bayati, B., Clarke, N., & Dowland, P. (2016). Adaptive Behaviroal Profiling for Identity Verification in Cloud Computing: A Model and Preliminary Analysis. *GSTF International Journal on Computing, 5*(1), 21–28. doi:10.5176/2251-3043

Al Solami, E., Boyd, C., Clark, A., & Islam, A. K. (2010). Continuous Biometric Authentication: Can It Be More Practical? *2010 IEEE 12th International Conference on High Performance Computing and Communications (HPCC)*, 647–652. 10.1109/HPCC.2010.65

Albayram, Y., Kentros, S., Jiang, R., & Bamis, A. (2013). A method for improving mobile authentication using human spatio-temporal behavior. *2013 IEEE Symposium on Computers and Communications (ISCC)*, 305–311. 10.1109/ISCC.2013.6754964

Alswiti, W., Alqatawna, J., Al-Shboul, B., Faris, H., & Hakh, H. (2016). Users Profiling Using Clickstream Data Analysis and Classification. *2016 Cybersecurity and Cyberforensics Conference (CCC)*, 96–99. 10.1109/CCC.2016.27

Andrean, A., Jayabalan, M., & Thiruchelvam, V. (2020). Keystroke Dynamics Based User Authentication using Deep Multilayer Perceptron. *International Journal of Machine Learning and Computing, 10*(1), 134–139. doi:10.18178/ijmlc.2020.10.1.910

Anjomshoa, F., Catalfamo, M., Hecker, D., Helgeland, N., Rasch, A., Kantarci, B., Erol-Kantarci, M., & Schuckers, S. (2016). Mobile behaviometric framework for sociability assessment and identification of smartphone users. *2016 IEEE Symposium on Computers and Communication (ISCC), 2016-Augus*, 1084–1089. 10.1109/ISCC.2016.7543880

Aupy, A., & Clarke, N. (2005). User Authentication by Service Utilisation Profiling. *Advances in Network and Communications Engineering, 2*, 18.

B., S. B., & Venkataram, P. (2007). An Authentication Scheme for Personalized Mobile Multimedia Services: A Cognitive Agents Based Approach. *Future Generation Communication and Networking (FGCN 2007)*, 167–172. doi:10.1109/FGCN.2007.57

Bakar, K. A. A., & Haron, G. R. (2014). Adaptive authentication based on analysis of user behavior. *2014 Science and Information Conference*, 601–606. 10.1109/SAI.2014.6918248

Bal, G., Rannenberg, K., & Hong, J. I. (2015). Styx: Privacy risk communication for the Android smartphone platform based on apps' data-access behavior patterns. *Computers & Security, 53*(69), 187–202. doi:10.1016/j.cose.2015.04.004

Banerjee, S. P., & Woodard, D. L. (2012). Biometric Authentication and Identification using Keystroke Dynamics. *Survey (London, England), 7*(1), 116–139. doi:10.13176/11.427

Brosso, I., La Neve, A., Bressan, G., & Ruggiero, W. V. (2010). A Continuous Authentication System Based on User Behavior Analysis. *International Conference on Availability, Reliability, and Security, 2010. ARES '10*, 380–385. 10.1109/ARES.2010.63

Buriro, A., Crispo, B., & Zhauniarovich, Y. (2017). Please hold on: Unobtrusive user authentication using smartphone's built-in sensors. *2017 IEEE International Conference on Identity, Security and Behavior Analysis (ISBA)*, 1–8. 10.1109/ISBA.2017.7947684

Caruana, R., & Niculescu-Mizil, A. (2004). Data mining in metric space: an empirical analysis of supervised learning performance criteria. *Proceedings of the Tenth ACM SIGKDD International Conference on Knowledge Discovery and Data Mining*, 69–78. 10.1145/1014052.1014063

Chow, R., Jakobsson, M., Masuoka, R., Molina, J., Niu, Y., Shi, E., & Song, Z. (2010). Authentication in the clouds. *Proceedings of the 2010 ACM Workshop on Cloud Computing Security Workshop - CCSW '10*, 1. 10.1145/1866835.1866837

Claes, J., & Poels, G. (2014). Merging event logs for process mining: A rule based merging method and rule suggestion algorithm. *Expert Systems with Applications*, *41*(16), 7291–7306. doi:10.1016/j.eswa.2014.06.012

Clarke, N. (2011). Transparent User Authentication. In *Transparent User Authentication*. Springer London. doi:10.1007/978-0-85729-805-8_1

D'Angelo, G., Rampone, S., & Palmieri, F. (2016). Developing a trust model for pervasive computing based on Apriori association rules learning and Bayesian classification. *Soft Computing*. Advance online publication. doi:10.100700500-016-2183-1

DNV GL AS. (2017). *Global Opportunity*. Author.

Ehsan Rana, M., Kubbo, M., & Jayabalan, M. (2017). Privacy and Security Challenges Towards Cloud Based Access Control in Electronic Health Records. *Asian Journal of Information Technology*, *16*(2), 274–281. doi:10.36478/ajit.2017.274.281

Ferbrache, D. (2016). Passwords are broken – the future shape of biometrics. *Biometric Technology Today*, *2016*(3), 5–7. doi:10.1016/S0969-4765(16)30049-2

Ferreira, A., Cruz-Correia, R., & Antunes, L. (2011). Usability of authentication and access control: A case study in healthcare. *Proceedings - International Carnahan Conference on Security Technology*, 1–7. 10.1109/CCST.2011.6095873

Grassi, P. A., Garcia, M. E., & Fenton, J. L. (2017). *Digital identity guidelines: revision 3*. doi:10.6028/NIST.SP.800-63-3

Han, J., Kamber, M., & Pei, J. (2012). *Data mining : Concepts and Techniques* (3rd ed.). Elsevier.

Hossin, M., & Sulaiman, M. N. (2015). A Review on Evaluation Metrics for Data Classification Evaluations. *International Journal of Data Mining & Knowledge Management Process*, *5*(2), 1–11. doi:10.5121/ijdkp.2015.5201

Ibrahim, A., & Ouda, A. (2016). Innovative Data Authentication Model. *2016 IEEE 7th Annual Information Technology, Electronics and Mobile Communication Conference (IEMCON)*, 1–7. 10.1109/IEMCON.2016.7746268

Ibrahim, A., & Ouda, A. (2017). A hybrid-based filtering approach for user authentication. *2017 IEEE 30th Canadian Conference on Electrical and Computer Engineering (CCECE)*, 1–5. 10.1109/CCECE.2017.7946830

Ismael, A. A., Jayabalan, M., & Al-Jumeily, D. (2020). A study on human activity recognition using smartphone. *Journal of Advanced Research in Dynamical and Control Systems, 12*(5), 795–803. doi:10.5373/JARDCS/V12SP5/20201818

ISO. (2013). *BS ISO/IEC 29115:2013: Information technology. Security techniques. Entity authentication assurance framework*. ISO.

ISO. (2014). BS EN ISO 22600-1:2014: Health informatics. Privilege management and access control. Overview and policy management. British Standards Institute.

Jayabalan, M. (2020). Towards an Approach of Risk Analysis in Access Control. *2020 13th International Conference on Developments in eSystems Engineering (DeSE)*, 287–292. 10.1109/DeSE51703.2020.9450772

Jayabalan, M., & O'Daniel, T. (2016). Access control and privilege management in electronic health record: A systematic literature review. *Journal of Medical Systems, 40*(12), 261. doi:10.100710916-016-0589-z PMID:27722981

Jayabalan, M., & O'Daniel, T. (2019). A study on authentication factors in electronic health records. *Journal of Applied Technology and Innovation, 3*(1), 7–14. https://jati.apu.edu.my/

Jayabalan, M., & Oadaniel, T. (2018). Continuous and transparent access control framework for electronic health records: A preliminary study. *Proceedings - 2017 2nd International Conferences on Information Technology, Information Systems and Electrical Engineering, ICITISEE 2017*, 165–170. 10.1109/ICITISEE.2017.8285487

Jayabalan, M., & Thiruchelvam, V. (2017). A design of patients data transparency in electronic health records. *2017 IEEE International Symposium on Consumer Electronics (ISCE)*, 9–10. 10.1109/ISCE.2017.8355532

Kaipio, J., Lääveri, T., Hyppönen, H., Vainiomäki, S., Reponen, J., Kushniruk, A., Borycki, E., & Vänskä, J. (2017). Usability problems do not heal by themselves: National survey on physicians' experiences with EHRs in Finland. *International Journal of Medical Informatics, 97*, 266–281. doi:10.1016/j.ijmedinf.2016.10.010 PMID:27919385

Kent, A. D., & Liebrock, L. M. (2013). Differentiating User Authentication Graphs. *2013 IEEE Security and Privacy Workshops*, 72–75. doi:10.1109/SPW.2013.38

Kraus, L., Wechsung, I., & Möller, S. (2017). Psychological needs as motivators for security and privacy actions on smartphones. *Journal of Information Security and Applications*, *34*(Part 1), 34–45. doi:10.1016/j.jisa.2016.10.002

Kubbo, M., Jayabalan, M., & Rana, M. E. (2016). Privacy and Security Challenges in Cloud Based Electronic Health Record : Towards Access Control Model. *Third International Conference on Digital Security and Forensics (DigitalSec)*, 113–121.

Li, F., Clarke, N., Papadaki, M., & Dowland, P. (2014). Active authentication for mobile devices utilising behaviour profiling. *International Journal of Information Security*, *13*(3), 229–244. doi:10.100710207-013-0209-6

Lu, X., & Xu, Y. (2014). An User Behavior Credibility Authentication Model in Cloud Computing Environment. *2nd International Conference on Information Technology and Electronic Commerce.*, 271–275. 10.1109/ICITEC.2014.7105617

Mahdi, D. A., Ant, A., & Singh, A. (2016). Market Guide for User Authentication. *Gartner Reprint*, (November), 1–15.

Mahfouz, A., Muslukhov, I., & Beznosov, K. (2016). Android users in the wild: Their authentication and usage behavior. *Pervasive and Mobile Computing*, *32*, 50–61. doi:10.1016/j.pmcj.2016.06.017

Marcot, B. G. (2012). Metrics for evaluating performance and uncertainty of Bayesian network models. *Ecological Modelling*, *230*, 50–62. doi:10.1016/j.ecolmodel.2012.01.013

Memon, N. (2017). How Biometric Authentication Poses New Challenges to Our Security and Privacy. *IEEE Signal Processing Magazine*, *34*(4), 196–194. doi:10.1109/MSP.2017.2697179

Meng, W., Wong, D. S., Furnell, S., & Zhou, J. (2015). Surveying the development of biometric user authentication on mobile phones. *IEEE Communications Surveys and Tutorials*, *17*(3), 1268–1293. doi:10.1109/COMST.2014.2386915

Milton, L. C., & Memon, A. (2016). Intruder detector: A continuous authentication tool to model user behavior. *2016 IEEE Conference on Intelligence and Security Informatics (ISI)*, 286–291. 10.1109/ISI.2016.7745492

Pabarskaite, Z., & Raudys, A. (2007). A process of knowledge discovery from web log data: Systematization and critical review. *Journal of Intelligent Information Systems*, *28*(1), 79–104. doi:10.100710844-006-0004-1

Pisani, P. H., Giot, R., de Carvalho, A. C. P. L. F., & Lorena, A. C. (2016). Enhanced template update: Application to keystroke dynamics. *Computers & Security, 60,* 134–153. doi:10.1016/j.cose.2016.04.004

Rajendran, K., Jayabalan, M., & Ehsan Rana, M. (2017). A Study on k-anonymity, l-diversity, and t-closeness Techniques focusing Medical Data. *International Journal of Computer Science and Network Security, 17*(12), 172–177. http://paper.ijcsns. org/07_book/201712/20171225.pdf

Raykar, V. C., & Saha, A. (2015). Data Split Strategiesfor Evolving Predictive Models. In A. Appice, P. P. Rodrigues, V. Santos Costa, C. Soares, J. Gama, & A. Jorge (Eds.), *Machine Learning and Knowledge Discovery in Databases: European Conference, ECMLPKDD 2015, Porto, Portugal, September 7-11, 2015, Proceedings, Part I* (pp. 3–19). Springer International Publishing. 10.1007/978-3-319-23528-8_1

Raza, M., Iqbal, M., Sharif, M., & Haider, W. (2012). A survey of password attacks and comparative analysis on methods for secure authentication. *World Applied Sciences Journal, 19*(4), 439–444. doi:10.5829/idosi.wasj.2012.19.04.1837

Realpe-Munoz, P., Collazos, C. A., Hurtado, J., Granollers, T., & Velasco-Medina, J. (2016). An Integration of Usable Security and User Authentication into the ISO 9241-210 and ISO/IEC 25010:2011. In T. Tryfonas (Ed.), Human Aspects of Information Security, Privacy, and Trust (pp. 65–75). Springer International Publishing Switzerland 2016. doi:10.1007/978-3-319-39381-0

Saevanee, H., Clarke, N., & Furnell, S. (2011). *SMS Linguistic Profiling Authentication on Mobile Device.* Academic Press.

Sahil, S. S., Mehmi, S., & Dogra, S. (2015). Artificial intelligence for designing user profiling system for cloud computing security: Experiment. *2015 International Conference on Advances in Computer Engineering and Applications*, 51–58. 10.1109/ ICACEA.2015.7164645

Skračić, K., Pale, P., & Kostanjčar, Z. (2017). Authentication approach using one-time challenge generation based on user behavior patterns captured in transactional data sets. *Computers & Security, 67,* 107–121. doi:10.1016/j.cose.2017.03.002

Song, Y., Ben Salem, M., Hershkop, S., & Stolfo, S. J. (2013). System Level User Behavior Biometrics using Fisher Features and Gaussian Mixture Models. *2013 IEEE Security and Privacy Workshops*, 52–59. doi:10.1109/SPW.2013.33

Tipton, S. J., Forkey, S., & Choi, Y. B. (2016). Toward Proper Authentication Methods in Electronic Medical Record Access Compliant to HIPAA and C.I.A. Triangle. *Journal of Medical Systems*, *40*(4), 1–8. doi:10.100710916-016-0465-x PMID:26872782

Turgeman, A., & Zelazny, F. (2017). Invisible challenges: The next step in behavioural biometrics? *Biometric Technology Today*, *2017*(6), 5–7. doi:10.1016/S0969-4765(17)30114-5

Vasudavan, H., Jayabalan, M., & Ramiah, S. (2016). A preliminary study on designing tour website for older people. *2015 IEEE Student Conference on Research and Development, SCOReD 2015*. 10.1109/SCORED.2015.7449423

Verizon. (2017). 2017 Data Breach Investigations Report Tips on Getting the Most from This Report. *Verizon Business Journal*, *1*, 1–48. doi:10.1017/CBO9781107415324.004

Vielhauer, C. (2006). *Biometric User Authentication for IT Security* (Vol. 18). Springer-Verlag. doi:10.1007/0-387-28094-4

Wang, Q., & Jin, H. (2008). Usable Authentication for Electronic Healthcare Systems. *Proceedings of the Symposium On Usable Privacy and Security (SOUPS)*.

Zhao, P., Yan, C., & Jiang, C. (2016). Authenticating Web User's Identity through Browsing Sequences Modeling. *2016 IEEE 16th International Conference on Data Mining Workshops (ICDMW)*, 335–342. 10.1109/ICDMW.2016.0054

ADDITIONAL READING

Andrean, A., Jayabalan, M., & Thiruchelvam, V. (2020). Keystroke Dynamics Based User Authentication using Deep Multilayer Perceptron. *International Journal of Machine Learning and Computing*, *10*(1), 134–139. doi:10.18178/ijmlc.2020.10.1.910

Clarke, N. (2011). *Transparent User Authentication*. Springer London. doi:10.1007/978-0-85729-805-8

Ferbrache, D. (2016). Passwords are broken – the future shape of biometrics. *Biometric Technology Today*, *2016*(3), 5–7. doi:10.1016/S0969-4765(16)30049-2

Halunen, K., Häikiö, J., & Vallivaara, V. (2017). Evaluation of user authentication methods in the gadget-free world. *Pervasive and Mobile Computing*, *40*, 220–241. doi:10.1016/j.pmcj.2017.06.017

Jain, A. K., Nandakumar, K., & Ross, A. (2016). 50 years of biometric research: Accomplishments, challenges, and opportunities. *Pattern Recognition Letters*, *79*, 80–105. doi:10.1016/j.patrec.2015.12.013

Jayabalan, M., & O'Daniel, T. (2016). Access control and privilege management in electronic health record: A systematic literature review. *Journal of Medical Systems*, *40*(12), 261. doi:10.100710916-016-0589-z PMID:27722981

Jayabalan, M., & O'Daniel, T. (2017). Continuous and transparent access control framework for electronic health records: A preliminary study. *2017 2nd International Conferences on Information Technology, Information Systems and Electrical Engineering (ICITISEE)*, 165–170. 10.1109/ICITISEE.2017.8285487

Jayabalan, M., & O'Daniel, T. (2019). A study on authentication factors in electronic health records. *Journal of Applied Technology and Innovation*, *3*(1), 7–14. https://jati.apu.edu.my/

Kraus, L., Wechsung, I., & Möller, S. (2017). Psychological needs as motivators for security and privacy actions on smartphones. *Journal of Information Security and Applications*, *34*(Part 1), 34–45. doi:10.1016/j.jisa.2016.10.002

Ring, T., & Wilk, R. (2015). Behavioural analytics: Sifting good users from bad actors. *Biometric Technology Today*, *2015*(11), 8–11. doi:10.1016/S0969-4765(15)30173-9

KEY TERMS AND DEFINITIONS

Access Policy: A list of roles and resources to which the access permissions are defined for an individual role.

Cloud Computing: On demand availability of computing power and data storage capacity.

Continuous Authentication: A verification method aimed to provide identity confirmation and cybersecurity protection on an ongoing basis.

Intruder Detection: A software application or device to monitor the organization network for unusual activity.

Keystroke: The pressing of a single key on a keyword.

Mouse Dynamics: A tiny patterns and variation in the mouse and/or pointer movements while the user interacts with the screen.

Transparent Authentication: A verification method aimed to assess the user behavior in a non-intrusive way to identify the legitimacy.

Usable Security: A process to ensure the security products and services are usable by those who need them.

Chapter 5
The Role of Deception in Securing Our Cyberspace:
Honeypots Are a Viable Option

Banyatsang Mphago

iD https://orcid.org/0000-0002-9451-3119
Botswana International University of Science and Technology, Botswana

Dimane Mpoeleng
Botswana International University of Science and Technology, Botswana

Shedden Masupe
Botswana Institute for Technology Research and Innovation, Botswana

ABSTRACT

The use of deception systems is a viable option in reducing the never-ending tussle between the attackers and the defenders. The deception systems give the defenders an edge over their counterparts since they provide the platform to learn the methods and techniques the attackers use. However, the effectiveness of the deception system is highly dependent on how they truly hide their identity. A deceptive honeypot has the capacity to persuade and change the cognitive behavior of an attacker. An attacker whose cognitive behavior has been altered by the deception capabilities of a honeypot is more likely to reveal his attack methods; hence, the defenders are able to learn how to defend against those future attacks.

DOI: 10.4018/978-1-7998-9430-8.ch005

INTRODUCTION

Computer security has been a concern ever since the inception of computers, hence the never-ending struggle in the status quo requires a shift in mindset. Traditional approaches are firmly based on the premise that the network perimeter is an effective means to protect the information assets within the organization and that employees within the organization can be trusted. In the face of this challenges, some leading enterprises have changed the tactics and employed a 'need-to-know' approach as an effective way to secure their assets. The emergence of deception systems is becoming more and more a viable option to protecting computer assets. The use of honeypots in protecting computer and information assets comes from the notion that 'you cannot protect what you don't know'. Therefore, honeypots came as a viable option to understand attackers and their attack methods. Once deployed, a successful honeypot must be able to deceive, lure, and record all the attackers' activities.

BACKGROUND

Honeypot Definitions

Honeypots are special systems designed to track and trap attackers and learn their attack methods. They are special in the sense that they are not a solution but rather a general technology that do not solve a specific security problem which is continuously changing, and can be involved in many facets of security such as information gathering, detection, and prevention (Verizon, 2019). Security researchers and administrators often use honeypots to unobtrusively track and monitor what *malicious* attackers are doing in order to compromise computer resources. A honeypot is a tool designed to learn the attack methods the adversaries use to query and exploit vulnerabilities in a system. So, a honeypot is a security resource whose value lies in being probed, attacked, or compromised (WhiteHatSecurity, 2016).

Several definitions for the term `honeypot' have been proposed, and below we present some of those definitions:

- **Definition 1**: "a honeypot is a security resource whose value lies in being probed, attacked and compromised" (Spitzner, 2002).
- **Definition 2:** "a honeypot is a computer which has been configured to some extent to seem normal to an attacker, but actually logs and observes what the attacker does" (Gibbens, 1999).

- **Definition 3**: "a honeypot is a general computing resource whose sole task is to be probed, attacked, and compromised, used or accessed in any other unauthorized way" (Grudziecki et al., 2012).

For the purpose of this chapter, we adopt definition 1 mainly because rather than being specific to a particular security resource like the rest, the definition describes a honeypot in a more general sense, of which we believe a general term `honeypot' should be defined.

History of Honeypots

Despite the fact that the word honeypot was not commonly used, honeypots have been around since the 1960s when the first computer viruses and worms were discovered. The most discussions about honeypots only came after Clifford Stoll's successfully venture into capturing a German hacker using a physical honeypot in 1986. Then Stoll wrote a book `The Cuckoo's Egg', recounting his story of successfully capturing a West German hacker using his physical honeypot, and it was only after this book in the early 90s that majority of the security community started to discuss honeypots though with little publications. Its only after Stoll's book in 1991 (Spitzner, 2002), that commercial honeypots products started being introduced into the market. Bill Cheswick also published his first honeypot experiences in 1991 in his famous publication, *An evening with Berferd*, where he discussed an encounter with a hacker who thought had discovered the famous sendmail DEBUG hole in AT&T Bell laboratories' internet gateway computer and attempted to copy their password file. In 1997 another publication by Fred Cohen called the Deception Toolkit followed. In this publication, Cohen discussed how the Deception Toolkit (DTK) was intended to deceive attackers into believing that the system running DTK has a large number of widely known vulnerabilities. Then a series of other publications and honeypot products followed in 1998 when CyberCop Sting, NetFacade, and BackOfficer Friendly were released (Spitzner, 2002). CyberCop brought the concept of multiple virtual systems destined to a single honeypot. BackOfficer Friendly was a simple Windows based honeypot which brought many people to the understanding of honeypots, and Netfacade later introduced the concept of Snort.

The year 1999 found the formation of the Honeynet project, led by Lance Spitzner along with a series of publications of the ``Know your Enemy'' papers. A lot more honeypots products were released by this group. According to Spitzner (2002), the sudden booming of worms in 2000 and 2001 that compromised a lot of production systems brought in a lot more honeypots that were successfully used to capture these worms as was the case in the CodeRed worm and the Sub7 trojan.

Honeypot Classifications

Different sources have classified honeypots differently, and most of those classifications are based on purpose the honeypot serves and level of interaction to the attacker (Baumann & Plattner, 2002; Gibbens, 1999; Mokube & Adams, 2007; Spitzner, 2002; Wagener, 2011). Figure 1 shows a general summary of the most popular honeypots classifications.

Level of Interaction

One characteristic of honeypots is the degree at which it can interact with the attacker. Thus, the level of interaction measures the possibility to interact with the actual operating system or a system mimicking the operating system.

Low Interaction Honeypot emulates only services that can be exploited but cannot lead to total control of the honeypot. In this type of honeypot, there is no actual operating system for the attacker to interact with it, but rather it only emulates services of a particular system (Mokube & Adams, 2007). Since the host operating system does not interact with the attacker, low interaction honeypots are fairly safe to operate. However, this type of honeypots is ineffective where a more complex, interactive environment is needed (Gibbens, 1999). Low interaction honeypots are generally simple to deploy and maintain, and Honeyd is one commercial example of such (Gibbens, 1999).

Figure 1. Honeypots Classifications

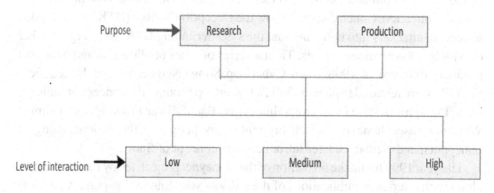

Just like low interaction honeypots, Medium Interaction Honeypot has no operating system installed for the attacker to fingerprint, but rather, the simulated services are more complicated technically and has more services that are closer to that of a real operating system (Baumann & Plattner, 2002; Gibbens, 1999). In medium interaction honeypots, the emulated systems are more complex and have more knowledge about the services they provide. In particular, medium interaction honeypots mimic a collection of software's in order to present a more convincing interaction with the hacker, but still hide the actual operating system to the attacker. It is this emulation of a collection of software's that make it more complex because the deception systems have to show the exact behavior of the real systems but not have the same security holes. Thus, medium interaction honeypots have a better impression to the attacker than low interaction honeypot of an operating system due to its complexity and the amount of interaction it gives the attacker.

High Interaction Honeypots on the other hand are the most advanced honeypots. They do not emulate services but rather they give the attacker the opportunity to interact with the actual operating system along with real instances of programs. The goal of this honeypot is to provide the attacker with real operating system and real programs where nothing is simulated hence log all interactions where the attacker has all the resources at his disposal. Because of the ability of the attacker to interact with the actual operating system, high interaction honeypots have the biggest risk of the system being compromised by the attacker, but also the highest potential of collecting useful information (Baumann & Plattner, 2002; Gibbens, 1999).

Classification on Purpose

Honeypots are generally used in two main purposes: as production honeypots or research honeypots.

Research honeypots are honeypots used by researchers to gain information about attackers and do not add any direct value to an organization. They are generally used for intelligence gathering on the threats the organization may be facing, thereby giving the organization the opportunity to better protect itself (Mokube & Adams, 2007; Shukla et al., 2015). The main objective behind research honeypots is to study the methods, techniques and processes the attacker use to attack computer systems and then pass the knowledge to those who should be protecting the organizations against the threats. Thus, there is little contribution by research honeypots to the direct security of the organization although the lessons learnt can be used to improve the general security of the organization (Mokube & Adams, 2007). Using research honeypots, the security community is trying to establish what the next generation of attacks are and how they are executed (Gibbens, 1999). Research honeypots add value to the research community by providing a platform to study cyber-attacks, and it is their intelligence gathering that makes them unique and exciting characteristics.

Production honeypots on the other hand, are what comes to most people's minds when the word honeypot is mentioned. Production honeypots are honeypots deployed in a particular organization with the main objective as to alert administrators to potential attacks in real time (Gibbens, 1999). These honeypots are generally easy to build and deploy as they don't require complex functionality but rather what the organization wants to protect (Mokube & Adams, 2007; Shukla et al., 2015). Production honeypots often mimic the production network or specific services of an organization deflecting attackers to focus on them rather than the production network while at the same time recording the vulnerabilities available in the network as they are exposed by the attackers. By exposing these vulnerabilities and alerting the administrators on these attacks can provide an early warning of attacks and help reduce the risk of exploiting the production systems.

HOW ATTACKERS DETECT HONEYPOTS

As honeypots are increasingly being deployed within computer networks, adversaries also start to come up with methods to detect and evade these security tools. Attackers do not want their methods observed since this could lead to their attack methods being publicly known. Furthermore, attackers do not want to disclose their methods and exploits, and as such honeypots are a concern to them (Innes & Valli, 2006). As a result, attackers have devised the means to detect honeypots once deployed.

Detecting UML Based Honeypots

User-Mode Linux (UML) give the user a virtual machine that may provide multiple virtual Linux kernels, known as guests, to run on another Linux kernel, known as host kernel or host operating system. Network traffic can be route from the host kernel to the guest kernel or UML, giving an impression that the person connecting to the system is engaging with or inside a live Linux system. As a result, User-Mode Linux has become a popular technique for deploying honeypots designed to run in a Linux environment. However (Innes & Valli, 2006), discovered that UML has various flaws that can alert an attacker that he/she is engaging with a fake system rather than a live one. Since UML lacks physical hard disks, it saves data on virtual devices that point to disk images of an existing file system, which are mounted *as / dev/ubd** on the UML system. The issue with the disk image mount in UML is the major number *98(0x62)*, which is not the same for standard IDE or SCSI systems when identifying the *dev/ubd** devices.

The other discovery with UML based honeypots was by Holz & Raynal (2005b), where they found that a */proc* tree structure of the system has the capabilities to tell that the system on the other side is not a live system but rather a fake one. When UML is used to operate the honeypot, the */proc* tree directory contains hints to the presence of UML. For example, the file */proc/cpuinfo* shown below has model name listed as UML and mode as *tt* for tracing thread. This is because by default UML executes in tracing thread mode. The memory allocation also shows that it has been allocated to a honeypot. Therefore, if the */proc/cpuinfo* file is retrieved from the system, it can be concluded that the system on the other side a honeypot.

Listing 1. Linux CPU Info in UML

```
\$ cat /proc/cpuinfo
Processor               : 0
vendor_id               : User Mode Linux
model name              : UML
mode                    : tt
[ . . . ]\$ egrap "uml honey" /proc/ksysms
a02eb408 uml_physmem
a02ed688 honeypot
```

The second discovery made by Holz & Raynal (2005b), on detecting UML-based honeypots, is that UML was not intended to be hidden when run in its default form. As a result, as shown below, a *dmesg* command would reveal a list of output that is only inherent in UML and not in a live system:

Listing 2. dmesg Command in UML

```
Uml{\textgreater}{\textgreater} dmesg
Linux version 2.6.10-rc2
. . .
Kernel command line: ubd0=[ . . . ]
. . .
Checking that ptrace can change system call numbers . . . OK
Checking syscall emulation patch for ptrace . . . missing
Checking that host ptys support output SIGIO . . . YES
Checking that host ptys support SIGIO on close . . . No,
enabling workaround
Checking for  /dev/anon on the host . . . Not available (open
failed with errno 2)
NET: Registered protocol family 16
mconsole (version 2) initialized on [ . . . ] mconsole
UML Audio Relay (host dsp = /dev/sound/dsp, host mixer = /dev/
sound/mixer)
Netdevice 0: TUN/TAP backend {\textendash}
```

```
divert: allocating divert_blk for eth0
. . .
Initializing software serial port version 1
 /dev/ubd/disc0: unknown partition table
. . .
```

Holz & Raynal (2005b) also discovered that UML-based honeypots can be detected by inspecting the address space of a process in the maps file. The maps file contains information about the memory regions and access permissions that are currently mapped for the current process. The anomaly in this file is the address that indicates the end of a stack. The end of a stack in a live system is usually represented by *0x0000000*, but in a system running as a guest operating system, the end of a stack is represented by *0xbefff000*, which means that each process can access, change, or edit the UML kernel in any way.

Detecting VMware Based Honeypots

Like UML, VMware is another technology that is used to deploy several guest operating systems on virtual machines in one physical machine, and this operating system maps to the physical hardware resources. VMware is one of the most preferred platforms to host honeypots due to their flexibility, cost reduction and due to the fact that if they are compromised the physical resources they are mapping to cannot be damaged. Holz & Raynal, 2005a; Innes & Valli (2006) noted that one of the first step in detecting VMware is to look at its hardware properties which is supposed to emulate. Prior to VMware version 4.5, some of the hardware properties were not configurable in VMware. The hardware, video card, network interface card, hard disk, CD drive, and SCSI controller configurations were all not configurable and they remained at default values that indicated that they for VMware. Another weakness in VMware based honeypots was the MAC address bound to the network card (Holz & Raynal, 2005b; Innes & Valli, 2006). The octet that represents the vendor part (first 3 octets) on a VMware virtual network interface is always one of the following:

Listing 3. VMware MAC Addresses

```
00-05-69-xx-xx-xx
00-0C-29-xx-xx-xx
00-50-56-xx-xx-xx
```

The last weakness on VMware based honeypots which was discussed by Holz & Raynal (2005b) and Innes & Valli (2006), is that of an embedded I/O backdoor known as Agobot that is used for configuring VMware when running. To check whether the system is a VMware, an attacker can try to access Agobot backdoor by either using the known assembly code used for accessing it such as *"mov eax, VMWARE_MAGIC; 0x564D5868"* or run commands that work with the backdoor such as *"04h - Get current mouse cursor position"*. If any of the commands was successful, then the attacker will know that this is a virtual machine and possibly a honeypot.

Detecting chroot and Jails Environment

Despite that the chroot and jails environments were never intended for security, they are frequently used to secure binaries for honeypots. Detecting chroot environments and even bypassing them is not difficult, and the easiest way is to run ls-lia command on the root directory and search for the *inode* of the `.' and `..' directories (Holz & Raynal, 2005b; Innes & Valli, 2006). The *inodes* of the two directories are both 2 in a standard environment.

Listing 4. Displaying File Inode

```
2 drwxr-xr-x 21 root   root    2096 Oct 17 19:47 .
2 drwxr-xr-x 21 root   root    2096 Oct 17 19:47 ..
```

However, when the same command is run under a chroot environment, the inodes of the two directories change, as:

Listing 5. Displaying File Inode

```
1553441 drwxr-xr-x  7 1000 100    2096 Oct 17 19:47 .
1553441 drwxr-xr-x  7 1000 100    2096 Oct 17 19:47 ..
```

Detecting Honeypots Based on Timing Profiles

There is a general expectation that every honeypot should log attacker profiles as the attackers are interact with them. By logging attacker profiles means the computer execute extra instructions. Therefore, when a computer runs extra instructions, the total time taken to execute a process or command can take longer than normal, and this has the ability to cause suspicion to those who understand the protocol well. Honeypots experience a lot of performance degradation if there is many attacking hosts all directed towards the honeypot. This is due to the fact that every instruction sent is logged and the more the instructions sent the more logging the honeypot must do, causing more extended time to complete the instructions. By measuring either the time taken or number of instructions executed, honeypots can be detected (Holz & Raynal, 2005b), and this can be done through the use of execution path analysis (EPA) which is based on a counter for instructions executed. As argued by Jan K. Rutkowski in Phrack magazine (issue 59), the idea behind EPA is to hook the *syscall* handler (*int 80*) and debug exception handler (*int 1*) in the Interrupt Description Table (IDT), and then by setting TF bit (*mask 0x100*) in EFLAGS register the new handlers are able to count each SIGTRAP generated when an instruction is executed.

Sebek, which is one of the data captures used by honeypots to log the attackers' profiles as they interact with them, was designed by The Honeynet Project as a kernel module to be installed mostly in high interaction honeypots for the purpose of collecting extensive data. Sebek record the data accessed by the hacker in an unencrypted way, and it does that by hijacking the *read()* system call. In order to detect Sebek, the attacker can simply measure the execution time of *read()* system call. Systems that use Sebek as a data capture will have their minimal execution time at around 29999 with a scalar product of 0.009930, whereas in a system that doesn't use Sebek the minimal time is 8225 with a scalar product of 0.776282 (Holz & Raynal, 2005b). The reason for the long execution time on a system with Sebek is mainly attributed to the fact that each *read()* operation causes at least one UDP packet to be sent.

VMware based honeypots can also be detected by causing an illegal instruction to system and then measuring the execution time. The time taken to process an illegal instruction is in a live system is 776mms, but for a system that runs on VMware the time taken to process an illegal instruction increases to 2530mms. This is because VMware exception handler checks first whether the exception must be handled by VMware itself or by a particular exception handler in the process that caused illegal instruction (Holz & Raynal, 2005b).

Other Methods of Honeypot Detection

An x86-based processor can be used explicitly as another approach of discovering VMware based honeypots. Instructions need to go through the global descriptor table (GDT) or the local descriptor table (LDT) in order to access the memory if the machine is operating in a protected mode, and these instructions are regularly utilized by the operating framework. This provides advantages that are not available for intel processors that have to utilize a user-land (ring 3) to execute these instructions (Holz & Raynal, 2005a). Therefore, clashes can occur within an intel processor when the same registers need to be accessed simultaneously by a guest system and a host operating system to execute the instructions because it has a single local descriptor table register (LDTR), an interrupt descriptor table register (IDTR) and a global descriptor table register (GDTR). In the event of this, actions performed in the guest operating system can obtain the contents of IDTR by implementing instructions of the SIDT while the host operating system has shifted the IDTR of the guest operating system. As a result, special rights are now not required, and the implementation of instructions will not be implemented by the host operating system. However, the actions of the guest operating systems are assigned the shifted address of the IDT and the resulting internal processes of a virtual machine.

Another honeypot that has demonstrated to be moderately simple for attackers to realize that it is indeed a honeypot is Honeyd. One of the challenges associated with Honeyd is that it usually gives feedback to misdirected packets and as a result, attackers can easily see that it is not a live framework. For example, Honeyd will be unable to differentiate between valid and distorted network packets that allow and disallow communication path instantly (Innes & Valli, 2006). An aggressor in close observation of the network traffic with the use of packet sniffer would be suspicious after picking this inconsistency although this can be disregarded by an attack tool hoping to hear a reaction. Valli (2003) realized that one of the setbacks associated with Honeyd is the way it responds towards operating system fingerprinting when testing its detection characteristics during TCP/IP interactions. It is during this test that Valli tracked down that the TCP/IP stack fingerprint of Honeyd to assess the operating framework of the devices is incompatible and returns false positives and this probably going to raise suspicions if this protocol is fathomable to the attacker.

Valli (2003) also discovered that another problem that makes Honeyd to be easily discoverable is due to its heavy reliant on user configuration when deployed. Some configurations maybe configured incorrectly on the setup file as a result of human mistake. Therefore, arrangements intended to copy a webserver for instance, would likewise be inaccurate and raise doubts to those observing traffic. Lastly, a problem with Honeyd that renders it easy to identify is specifically its service emulations that are generated from basic Perl scripts. Attackers are in position to be alarmed by the dependencies of the scripts that they are possibly inside a honeypot instead of a live system. As an example, the defection of the default route-telnte.pl script that naturally accompanies the honeypot may not yield any output, and this in some instances may be alarming to the attackers.

Wang, Wu, Cunningham, & Zou (2010) devised ways of detecting honeypots in advanced botnets attacks, where their methodology was based on the assumption that *"security professionals deploying honeypots have a liability constraint such that they cannot allow their honeypots to participate in real attacks that could cause damage to others, while on the other side attackers do not need to follow this constraint"*. Through this methodology, attackers can detect honeypots in their botnets by checking which machines can successfully send malicious traffic to other machines. Machines that do not send malicious traffic to other machines might prove to be honeypots due to the liability constraint described above that attacker won't allow their honeypots to infect other computers.

Figure 2. Detecting Honeypots in Advanced Botnets Attacks

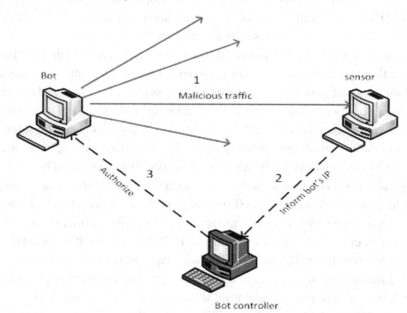

The general belief in botnets environment is that a victim computer would also send malicious traffic to other computers in the botnet. When other computers in the botnet receive real traffic from the victim computers, the victim computer will be regarded as a normal bot rather than a honeypot. Because the honeypot does not know which computers in the botnet are controllers, it cannot verify them without infecting other computers in the botnet. Figure 2 depicts this honeypot detection approach. Wang et al. (2010), suggested that a honeypot can also be discovered by installing bot programs in a freshly infected computer, which is similar to the method described above. The bot programs placed on the computer will then begin to send malicious traffic to other computers, and if the computer is a honeypot, it will not permit malicious traffic to be transmitted from it. If this occurs, the bot-master will be aware that the new machine is a honeypot rather than a legitimate computer.

Fu et al. (2006), discovered a way of detecting Honeyd honeypot when it is deployed to emulate an entire network. I their techniques, they found that by remotely fingerprinting Honeyd and measuring the link latency of the network emulated it can be determined if it's Honeyd or a real network. Fu et al. (2006), found that the problem with virtual honeypots is that a larger portion of the operational nodes such as users, network devices etc. are missing, and emulating their operations requires triggering by time events or signals, and as such the accuracy of event scheduling is dependent on the timing accuracy of the host operating system. In this tests, Fu et al. (2006) studied Honeyd deployed on a Linux x86 computer, and the results of this tests could still be applied to other platforms. It was noted that the kernel parameter HZ of the x86 system defaults to 1000 in Linux kernel 2.6 and 100 in the previous versions of Linux kernel up to 2.4, and this interrupt rates mean that the link latency emulated by Honeyd can only achieve an accuracy of 10ms on Linux kernel 2.4 and an accuracy of 1ms on a linux kernel 2.6. The results shows that the link latency of a virtual network will always be in multiple of 10ms or 1ms. This timing signatures given by Honeyd when emulating virtual network can be a sign to the attackers that the system is a honeypot rather than a legitimate system. Thus, an attacker can measure the link latency of the network, and when he gets the measurements in multiples of 10ms and 1ms, he can conclude that this not a live network but rather a virtual network emulated by Honeyd. This is also made possible by the fact that the link latency of a wired network can barely reach 1ms let alone 10ms (Fu et al., 2006). The diagram below shows how Honeyd can be fingerprinted to get its timing signatures.

Figure 3. Fingerprinting HoneyD

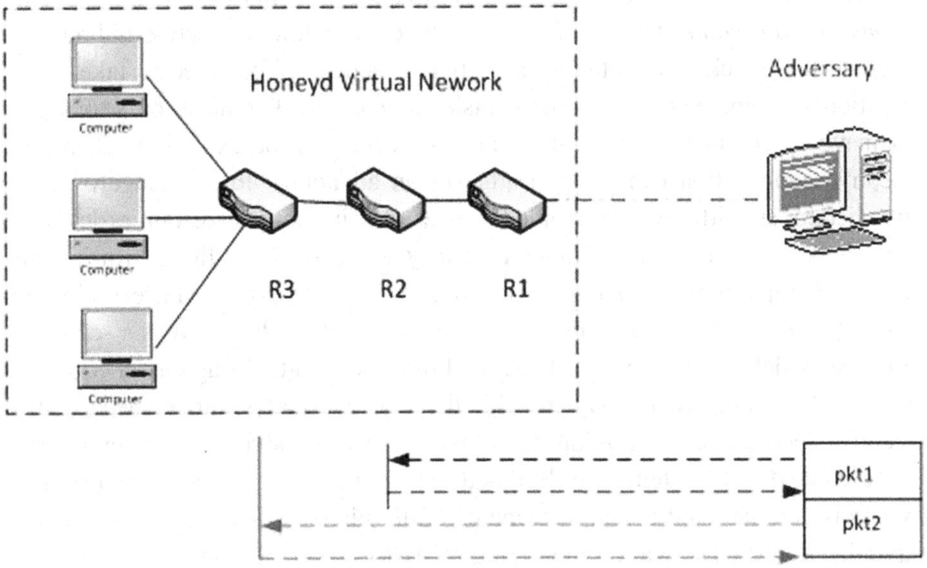

Figure 3 shows how measuring the link latency can be used to determine the timing signatures of Honeyd. To find the link latency of a network connecting two routers, an attacker can send a pair of packets (pkt1 and pkt2) of minimal size, where packet 1 would be addressed to router 2 and packet 3 addressed to router 3. Then the 2-way link latency:

$$= 2*LL_{R1,R2}$$

$$= RTT_{pkt1} - RTT_{pkt1}$$

where RTT_{pktn} is the Return Trip Time of a packet n and $LL_{R1,R2}$ is the one-way link latency between R_2 and R_3.

DECEPTION IN HONEYPOTS

The acts of deceptive attacks are a common occurrence in the cyberspace today to an extent that knowing and understanding deception is quite important in understanding attacks and acting upon them (Rowe & Rrushi, 2016). Cyberspace deception or just cyber deception can be used both offensively to attack targets and defensively to guard against cyber-attacks. Offensively, cyber deception often tends to use a limited number of methods such as impersonation, where defensive deception is more varied.

Yuill et al. (2006) defined cyber security deception as *"the actions taken to deliberately mislead attackers and to thereby cause them to or not to take specific actions that aid computer security"*. The objective behind deceptive hiding is to misguide the attacker from taking a particular action he intended to take. Also, deception in computer security aims at misleading the attacker into a course of action that maybe predictable or not taking an action that can be exploited. Therefore, deceptive actions that can give an attacker an advantage to act dangerously or unpredictably should always be avoided in order to aid in computer resources defenses. As a defensive mechanism in computer security, deception hides things from agents, human or computer, where agents are often referred to as target. De Faveri, Moreira, & Souza (2017) noted that security by deception is often deployed as a second or third line of defense to prevent, detect and respond to attacks against a computer system. Therefore, when coupled with the conventional security mechanisms, deceptive security offers a unique opportunity because adversaries often operate on the context that systems are designed with honesty. However, deception as a process is complex and demands some carefully planned mechanisms in order to maximize the benefits while minimizing the risks. In the next section, we discuss some of the some of the deceptive planning models discussed before and how they aid in the cyber deception process.

Deception Models Applied in Honeypots

Kopp et al. (2018) discussed the four information theoretic models of deception. The paper notes that the four information theoretic models of deception are derived from two important ideas in information theory, especially Shannon's idea of channel capacity and the notion of information theoretic similarity between messages. The four information theoretic models include *Degradation, Corruption, Denial, and Subversion*, where each of these models is a specific form of altering the victim's perception. Two of these models involve manipulation of terms in Shannon's channel capacity equation, one model involves manipulation of similarity, while the other model involves manipulation of internal information processing methods effectively by altering some internal algorithm or process in the victim system. Figure 4 depicts the theoretic deception models and the components of the system they are employed to compromise.

The *Degradation deception model* deals with concealing or hiding information in noise or other background messages, to introduce uncertainty or a false perception in a competing player's belief. This model can be used in both active of passive forms. In the active form, the deceiver produces the noise signal with sufficient magnitude that it prevents the victim from reliably recognizing arriving information but alerting the victim that it is being attacked. In the passive form, the deceiver seeks to make the message indistinguishable from the background noise of the environment. In Shannon's capacity equation, active degradation deception equates to manipulating the noise term such that $N \gg S$ and in turn $C \to 0$, while passive degradation deception equates to manipulating a signal term in Shannon's capacity equation such that $S \ll N$ and in turn $C \to 0$ (Kopp et al., 2018).

The *Corruption deception model* produces a false belief by replacing a real message with a similar but false message, contrived to be very difficult to distinguish from a real message. Thus, the false message mimics a real message. Successful corruption deception model is inherently passive, as the victim remains unaware that the information is misleading. The corruption deception model is equivalent to fabricating a deceptive message enough to look similar to the real message so that the target cannot see the difference, so that $S \to 1$ in the target's cognitive system where S is the information-theoretic similarity (Kopp et al., 2018). Thus, any deception in which a falsehood is contrived to emulate the truth is represented by this model.

Figure 4. Relationship between Deception Models and the Compromised System components

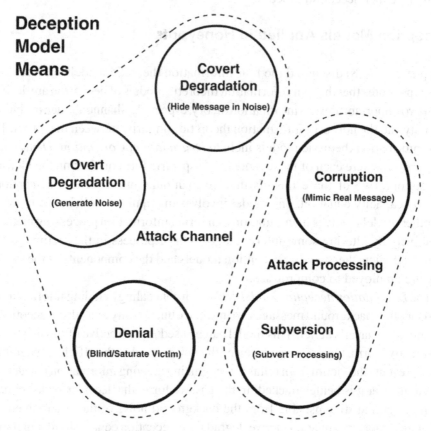

The *Denial deception model* elevates uncertainty by denying the target from collecting information by damaging or preventing the means to use in information collection by the target. This method is often passive as the target is mostly aware that his information collection is being denied either temporarily or persistently. A denial deception model is equivalent to manipulating bandwidth term in Shannon's capacity equation such that $W \rightarrow 0$, yielding in turn $C \circledR 0$ (Kopp et al., 2018).

The last theoretic model of deception is *Subversion,* which involves actions where the target's information processing methods or algorithms are altered to the advantage of the deceiver. Some of the examples of subversion deception model in use is that of political or commercial deceptions using "spin", where the target is encouraged to change the manner in which they interpret a message to the advantage of the deceiver. *Figure 5* depicts the respective relationships between the deception models when deployed to produce deception effects.

Figure 5. Relationship between Deception Models when employed to produce effects

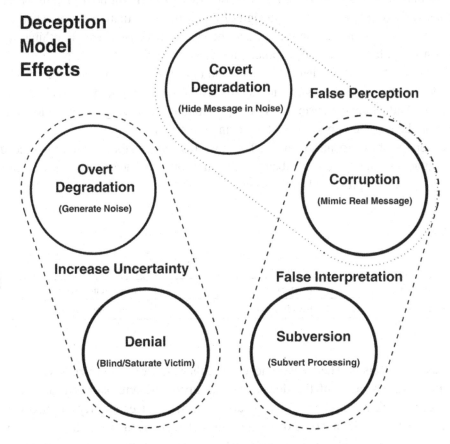

The Role of Deception in the Attacker's Decision Making

Before an attacker makes a decision to attack a system, first he must consider if the system on the other side is worth being attacked. He knows that there is a possibility that the system on the other side is honeypot rather than a legitimate system. Attackers do not want their attack methods exposed as this will enable defenders to harden their systems. To find out if the system on the other side is not a honeypot, the attacker may send some commands and watch what responses comes back. If the attacker notices suspicious responses, he may conclude that the system is fake and decides not to attack it anymore. On the other side, the system administrator wants to know who is likely to attack his systems and how. He therefore installs honeypots in his network. The administrator knows that if honeypots are not deceptive, the attackers are more likely to avoid them. In order to avoid being detected, the system administrator may decide to hide his honeypots within the network. However, attacks knows that there is still a possibility that the honeypots might be available within the network even when there is no sign of them. In that situation, an attacker has a dilemma of whether to continue attack the system because there is nothing that suggest it is a fake system, or he abort the mission because it is still possible that the system is fake even when there is no sign that it is fake. If he goes ahead with the idea of attacking the system, he ran the risk of being exposed. If he aborts the mission of attacking the system, it is still possible that it is a legitimate system and therefore he lost the opportunity of attacking the system.

Given the above scenario, an attacker must make a decision whether to proceed with attacking the system or abandon the mission. The decision matrix of this scenario can be represented as follows:

Table 1.

	Honeypot	Legitimate System
Attack System	Get Exposed	Steal the from System
Avoid System	No Exposure	Loose Opportunity

Based on Decision Theory, an attacker can either choose to minimize or maximize the possible outcomes of the decision made given the alternatives available to him. The attacker can choose to be cautious in his choices and try to maximize the minimal possible outcome of his decisions. This happens when the attacker is not so optimistic about the outcomes of whether to compromise the system or not. Therefore, based on the above scenario, we can say:

The preferences are:
```
    Compromise system, steal from the system
       is better than
    Do not compromise, loose opportunity
       is better than
    Compromise system, get exposed
```

In this case, the security level of not compromising the system would be to stay unknown, hence there will be nothing to get from the system. On the other hand, the security level of compromising the system is getting exposed, but the attacker has the opportunity of getting something from compromising the system. Because compromising the system and stealing something is better than not compromising the system and losing the opportunity to steal, which is also better than compromising the system and getting caught, the attacker is better off not compromising the system at all according to the recommendation of the maximin rule. Subjective values can be assigned to this matrix, based on the background information and the states of nature of the alternatives. For example, in the matrix we can assign *Get Exposed* a value of 0 since it's a bad outcome for the attacker. We can also assign *Steal from the System* a value of 10 since the attacker managed to get benefit from attacking the system. If an attacker avoids compromising the system and the system is a honeypot, we can then assign *No Exposure* a value of 5 since the attacker didn't get anything and he also didn't get exposed. We can also assign *Loose opportunity* a value of 2 since the system was not a honeypot but the attacker opted not to compromise it. This matrix is shown as follows:

Table 2.

	Honeypot	Legitimate System
Attack System	0	10
Avoid System	5	2

Since the security level of not compromising the system is 5 and that of compromising the system is 0, the maximin rule recommends the attacker to avoid compromise the system. The *maximax rule* however recommends the attacker to go ahead attack the system and attempt to steal valuable items from the system. The *maximax rule* represent a situation where the decision maker is too wishful, and this is often seen an irrational decision making by the decision theorists. In this paper, the assumption is that the attacker is an intelligent decision maker who is capable of making rational decisions.

Assuming that the attacker believes that there is a 20% chance that the system he is interacting with is a honeypot. The belief may be based on the fact that the attacker has prior knowledge about legitimate system and therefore, the responses from the deception system causes suspicion to him. The percentage belief would then add to the *Expected Utility* of compromising the system as follows:

$0.2*0 + 0.8*10 = 8$

The expected utility of not compromising the system would be:

$0.2*5 + 0.8*2 = 2.6$

This is therefore, suggesting to the attacker to go ahead and compromise the system as the payoff is larger than not compromising the system.

Now consider an inverse of the above situation where deception is used to hide information away from the decision maker. Assuming that the system on the other side is perfectly deceptive, then the states on nature, alternatives and the occurrence chance would be an inverse of the scenario described above. Therefore, the minimax rule of the Decision Theory would recommend to the attacker to go on and attack the system, hence an ideal situation for the system administrator.

The role played by deception against an attacker when making a decision has also been defined by Greenberg (1982). The author noted that *decision under risk* implies that the probability of each state of nature is known to the decision maker prior to the choice of alternative, and the usual decision criterion is to maximize the expected payoff. Therefore, if q_j is the probability of state S_j then the expected payoff for alternative i is:

$$E_i = \sum_{j=1}^{N} q_j P_{ij}$$

where q_j can be actual probabilities, estimated probabilities, probabilities describing the optimum game-theory mixed strategy, or subjective probabilities. Therefore, it is assumed that the decision-maker is interested in choosing the alternative that yields the largest expectation. The role of deception then is to cause decision-maker to misperceive the true q_j values. Then incorrect probabilities, q_j', are used in place of q_j. Therefore, rather than calculating the true expected value of alternative A_i, the deceived decision-maker calculates a misperceived expectation,

$$E_i' = \sum_{j=1}^{N} q_j' P_{ij}$$

In this case, the decision-maker will choose the alternative that maximizes his E_i' if this alternative differs to the one that maximizes E_i, then the decision-maker will suffer a reduction in the expected payoff caused by the deception.

CONCLUSION

In the previous sections we learnt that the battle between attackers and defenders comes a long way back. The never-ending battle is due to the fact that defenders don't know what they are defending against, and they often put their trust that the traditional network perimeter is enough to fight their battle. However, a switch in mindset on how the defenders approach their security has the potential to aid in winning the battle. By using honeypots in learning the attack methods, defenders have a chance of crafting their defenses better with knowledge of who they are defending against. However, honeypots that are not deceptive run a risk of being identified by the attackers. A honeypot that can't hide its identity is of no use since the attackers would simply avoid it. An effective use of deception in honeypots can persuade and change the cognitive mindset of the attacker, hence make him attack the honeypot. Once attacked, the honeypot can learn the attack methods which may aid in future protection of information assets. Therefore, even though honeypots are deception systems by default, not all honeypots are deceptive. Deception plays a crucial role in the success of honeypots, and honeypots plays a crucial role in the defenses against future attacks.

REFERENCES

Baumann, R., & Plattner, C. (2002). *White Paper: Honeypots*. Academic Press.

Cheswick, B. (1992, January). An Evening with Berferd in which a cracker is Lured, Endured, and Studied. In *Proc. Winter USENIX Conference, San Francisco* (pp. 20-24). Academic Press.

De Faveri, C., Moreira, A., & Souza, E. (2017). Deception planning models for Cyber Security. *2017 17th International Conference on Computational Science and Its Applications (ICCSA)*, 1–8.

Fu, X., Yu, W., Cheng, D., Tan, X., Streff, K., & Graham, S. (2006). On recognizing virtual honeypots and countermeasures. *2006 2nd IEEE International Symposium on Dependable, Autonomic and Secure Computing*, 211–218.

Gibbens, M. (1999). *Honeypots*. Academic Press.

Greenberg, I. (1982). The role of deception in decision theory. *The Journal of Conflict Resolution*, 26(1), 139–156. doi:10.1177/0022002782026001005

Grudziecki, T., Jacewicz, P., Juszczyk, L., Kijewski, P. & Pawlinski, P. (2012). Proactive detection of security incidents honeypots. *European Network and Information Security Agency*.

Holz, T., & Raynal, F. (2005a). *Defeating Honeypots: System Issues, Part 2 | Symantec Connect Community*. Symantec Connect.

Holz, T., & Raynal, F. (2005b). Detecting honeypots and other suspicious environments. *Proceedings from the 6th Annual IEEE System, Man and Cybernetics Information Assurance Workshop, SMC 2005*. 10.1109/IAW.2005.1495930

Innes, S., & Valli, C. (2006). Honeypots: How do you know when you are inside one? *Proceedings of 4th Australian Digital Forensics Conference*.

Kopp, C., Korb, K. B., & Mills, B. I. (2018). Information-theoretic models of deception: Modelling cooperation and diffusion in populations exposed to "fake news." *PLoS One*, *13*(11), e0207383. Advance online publication. doi:10.1371/journal.pone.0207383 PMID:30485356

Mokube, I., & Adams, M. (2007). Honeypots: concepts, approaches, and challenges. *Proceedings of the 45th Annual Southeast Regional Conference*, 321–326. 10.1145/1233341.1233399

Rowe, N. C., & Rrushi, J. (2016). Introduction to cyberdeception. Introduction to Cyberdeception. doi:10.1007/978-3-319-41187-3

Shukla, M., Verma, P. & Scholar, R. (2015). Honeypot: Concepts, Types and Working. *International Journal of Engineering Development and Research*.

Spitzner, L. (2002). Honeypots: Tracking Hackers. Journal of Management.

Valli, C. (2003). *Honeyd-A OS fingerprinting artifice*. Academic Press.

Verizon. (2019). *Data Breach Investigations Report*. https://www.ictsecuritymagazine.com/wp-content/uploads/2017-Data-Breach-Investigations-Report.pdf

Wagener, G. (2011). *Self-adaptive honeypots coercing and assessing attacker behaviour*. Institut National Polytechnique de Lorraine-INPL.

Wang, P., Wu, L., Cunningham, R., & Zou, C. C. (2010). Honeypot detection in advanced botnet attacks. *International Journal of Information and Computer Security*, *4*(1), 30. Advance online publication. doi:10.1504/IJICS.2010.031858

WhiteHatSecurity. (2016). *Web Applications Security Statistics Report 2016*. https://www.whitehatsec.com/resources/web-applications-security-statistics-report-2016/

Yuill, J., Denning, D. & Feer, F. (2006). Using Deception to Hide Things from Hackers: Processes, Principles, and Techniques. *Journal of Information Warfare*.

ADDITIONAL READING

Beham, M., Vlad, M., & Reiser, H. P. (2013). Intrusion detection and honeypots in nested virtualization environments. In *2013 43rd Annual IEEE/IFIP international conference on dependable systems and networks (DSN)* (pp. 1-6). IEEE. 10.1109/DSN.2013.6575329

Bringer, M. L., Chelmecki, C. A., & Fujinoki, H. (2012). A survey: Recent advances and future trends in honeypot research. *International Journal of Computer Network and Information Security*, 4(10), 63–75. doi:10.5815/ijcnis.2012.10.07

Krawetz, N. (2004). Anti-honeypot technology. *IEEE Security and Privacy*, 2(1), 76–79. doi:10.1109/MSECP.2004.1264861

Kreibich, C., & Crowcroft, J. (2004). Honeycomb: Creating intrusion detection signatures using honeypots. *Computer Communication Review*, 34(1), 51–56. doi:10.1145/972374.972384

KEY TERMS AND DEFINITIONS

Decision Theory: A branch of applied probability theory concerned with the theory of making decisions based on assigning probabilities to various factors and assigning numerical consequences to the outcome.

Global Descriptor Table (GDT): A data structure used by Intel x86-family processors starting with the 80286 to define the characteristics of the various memory areas used during program execution, including the base address, the size, and access privileges like executability and writability.

Honeypot: A network-attached system set up as a decoy to lure cyber attackers and detect, deflect and study hacking attempts to gain unauthorized access to information systems.

Local Descriptor Table (LDT): A memory table used in the x86 architecture in protected mode and containing memory segment descriptors: address start in linear memory, size, executability, writability, access privilege, actual presence in memory, etc.

User-Mode Linux: An architectural port of the Linux kernel to its own system call interface, which enables multiple virtual Linux kernel-based operating systems to run as an application within a normal Linux system.

Chapter 6
Holistic View on Detecting DDoS Attacks Using Machine Learning

Eduardo Barros

https://orcid.org/0000-0002-5309-1394
Instituto Superior Técnico, Portugal

Victor Lobo
*NOVA Information Management School (NOVA-IMS), NOVA University Lisbon,
Portugal & Naval Academy, Portugal*

Anacleto Correia

https://orcid.org/0000-0002-7248-4310
CINAV, Portuguese Naval Academy, Portugal

ABSTRACT

Distributed denial of service (DDoS) attacks are an enormous threat, mainly because of the extension they can reach, the ease of deployment, the losses that it can cause, and the effort it can take to detect and stop this type of attack. Machine learning techniques have been and are widely used to prevent DDoS attacks. As a matter of fact, many gigantic intrusion detection systems (IDS) have been proudly utilising machine learning techniques to help the conventional signature detection system by adding another layer of "intelligent" thinking. This chapter provides a context of the techniques used for detecting DDoS attacks using machine learning, and in demonstrating why the merge of these concepts have huge potential for the defence of a given system. To that matter, some studies that use machine learning approaches for DDoS detection are analysed. Finally, this chapter provides a high-level view of the types of DDoS attacks that are considered a threat, the machine learning approaches to detect these attacks, and why these approaches are cohesive.

DOI: 10.4018/978-1-7998-9430-8.ch006

INTRODUCTION

Nowadays, most enterprises depend on the use of technologies, particularly, networked technologies. Not only is this a great opportunity for organisations to leverage and enhance their business, but also for threat agents to achieve their goals by damaging these systems. In order to ensure the security of network services it is essential that, at the very least, the 3 pillars of information security (CIA triad) - integrity, confidentiality and availability -, are met.

This chapter will focus on the *availability* pillar of the CIA triad and its biggest threat, the Distributed Denial of Service (DDoS) attacks. The way this attack operates is by flooding the target with malicious traffic, depleting its bandwidth and/ or computing resources in order to create total unavailability or some disruption of a network asset. One of the hardest tasks for an Intrusion Detection System (IDS) is to mitigate a DDoS. This type of attack has some peculiarities, among other characteristics described in the next section: (i) the DDoS might be originate from thousands of *legitimate* devices; (ii) the requests may not contain any malicious content; (iii) the attacker can exploit a vulnerability in the attacked service but also in an external service to conduct the attack.

Unlike the vast majority of attacks, where only one malicious request is needed for it to be successful, a DDoS generally requires multiple requests, so, it might be possible to identify patterns shared by malicious packets. This characteristic is key and allows the use of machine learning for the purposes of identifying recurrent patterns in a DDoS. The aim of this chapter is to demonstrate that the use of machine learning for DDoS detection has great potentialities, but it is also intended to demonstrate how this can be done, introducing important concepts for the creation of a model capable of predicting DDoS requests.

To accomplish our propose, this chapter was designed as follows: the *Background* section is intended to provide a context to this subject by explaining how modern DDoS attacks work, to briefly introduce what machine learning is, and how it can be applied to detect DDoS attacks. In *Literature Review* section, in order to have an overview of what is currently being done regarding this matter, some studies that use machine learning approaches for DDoS detection are surveyed. The *Results Disussion* section, summarise and discuss the details and procedures of the surveyed articles such as: the types of DDoS attacks used, the machine learning approaches to detect these attacks, and why these approaches are cohesive. Also in this section, we present a high-level detection model based on machine learning that we consider effective. Finally, The *Conclusion* section makes a retrospective of the whole chapter, and draw conclusions about the use of machine learning for DDoS attack detection and the role it is going to play out in the future.

BACKGROUND

Distributed Denial of Service Attacks

A Distributed Denial of Service (DDoS) is a cyberattack that aims at exhausting services by overwhelming the target or its surrounding infrastructure with a flood of traffic. DDoS attacks are a subclass of denial of service (DoS) attacks as they involve multiple devices to replicate an individual DoS. Unlike other kinds of cyberattacks, DDoS may not rely on a vulnerability of its target and do not attempt to breach its security perimeter, the DDoS primary goal is to make a service unavailable to legitimate users. This is possible since services have a finite limit to the number of requests that they can handle and because the channel that connects the server to the internet has a finite bandwidth.

To send many requests to the target, that is, to achieve effectiveness with the DDoS, the cybercriminal will often establish a so-called *botnet*. A botnet is a network of multiple malware compromised systems that permit the attacker to control and manipulate those infected devices. These individual devices are referred to as bots, a group of bots is called a botnet and the server who controls these bots is called the C2 (Command and Control) server. Once a botnet has been established, the attacker is able to direct an attack by sending remote instructions to each bot to perpetuate the DDoS attack.

Regarding the different DDoS attacks, some large and respectful cybersecurity related organisations (Fortinet, 2022; Cloudflare, 2022; University of New Brunswick, 2022) have proposed taxonomies that try to map DDoS with their modus operandis. That being said and knowing the adoption of a single taxonomy is debatable, we believe the classification of DDoS attacks proposed by Cloudflare is consistent and allows for an understanding of how these attacks are triggered.

Based on Cloudflare's taxonomy, there are three types of attack, the application layer attack, the protocol attack and the volumetric attack as Figure 1 illustrates: (i) the *application layer attack*, as the name indicates, is an attack that refers to the seventh layer of the OSI model, this means that the goal of the attack is to exhaust the target's service resources that stand in the application layer using protocols such as HTTP, SSH, TFTP, and many others; (ii) the *protocol attack* focus on exploiting layer 3 and 4 (network and transport layer of the OSI model) weaknesses, causing service disruption by over-consuming server and network resources such as firewalls, load balancers and network monitors; (iii) lastly, the *volumetric attack* attempts to disrupt a service by using a form of amplification, usually, by sending small queries that result in large responses, consequently generating the denial of service.

Figure 1. Cloudflare's taxonomy for DDoS attacks

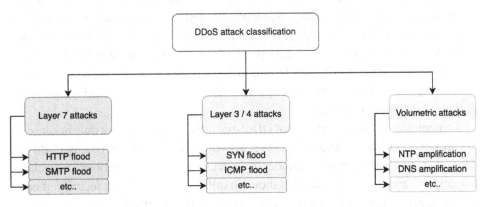

It is important to know that most of these attacks are perpetrated using legitimate devices (botnet) that reflect this traffic to overwhelm the victim with the response packets. This is done by spoofing the victim IP address so that the bots respond to the spoofed IP. Because each bot is a legitimate Internet device, separating the attack traffic from normal traffic can be difficult.

As an example, we will dissect a NTP amplification attack and how it can be mitigated. A NTP amplification is a DDoS in which an attacker exploits a Network Time Protocol (NTP) server functionality to overwhelm a targeted network or server with an amplified amount of UDP traffic. The exploitable functionality is the *monlist* command, which gives the last 600 source IP addresses of requests that have been made to the NTP server and it is a feature that comes by default in older versions of NTP servers. In short, the attacker uses a botnet to send UDP packets with the victim spoofed IP address to a NTP server which has the *monlist* command enabled and will generate a response a lot larger than the initial request as <u>Figure 2</u> represents.

Mitigating this attack is not trivial. Due to the high amount of traffic generated, the ISP may not be able to handle the incoming traffic without blackholing it to the targeted victim's IP address, protecting itself and taking the target's site offline. Additionally, it is not the victim's fault that the NTP servers supported the *monlist* feature and most likely, the victim cannot voluntarily patch the vulnerability.

Considering this, we can still detect and stop a NTP amplification DDoS if the ISP can validate IP spoofing at the network layer, which is usually not done because of the overhead that it takes. Another method is by using an anycast network that scatters all attack traffic to the point where it is no longer disruptive (like Cloudflare's service), however, even using an anycast service, we are always subject to requests being made directly to the background service. Even if these requests are blocked because they do not come from the trusted anycast network, computing power is required to process them, which might cause the unavailability of the service. Both these methods have disadvantages since the detection and mitigation is not in the victim's hands. In contrast with the aforementioned methods, some in-house IDSs may have the ability to identify the abuse of the *monlist* command by signature ruling and can consequently block responses from the NTP servers. Lastly, a more attractive method to handle a NTP amplification attack in our view, consists in identifying features of the malicious packets and, consequently, blocking all off the packets that share these features.

Our opinion is that the problem of DDoS only tends to prevail, not only because of the proven exponential increase in botnet networks in recent years, but also with the entry of 5G that potentiates the number of devices connected to a network, especially IoT devices, and the bandwidth that they can utilise. In parallel, the security of each IoT device does not keep up with the evolution of the 5G itself.

Figure 2. NTP Amplification attack

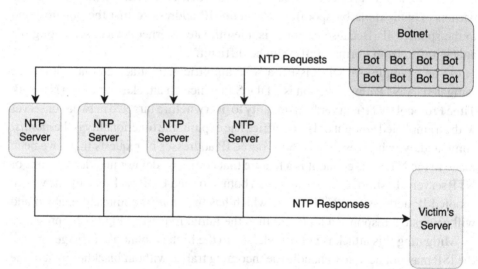

The Role of Machine Learning

Currently, IDSs which only utilise a signature detection approach are not effective. This has to do with the fact that modern attacks do not have easily detectable signatures as attackers build sophisticated malicious requests that originate from compromised machines. Although these requests might bypass the signature-based detection paradigm easily, this does not mean that DDoS traffic does not have patterns, even if these are not easily identifiable.

The concept behind machine learning that is interesting to explore for the purposes of DDoS detection, is to automatically learn from a given set of data if certain patterns tend to be malicious, or benign. If features of DDoS traffic are identifiable, it is theoretically possible to stop the attack before network resources become unavailable. Complementary to this paradigm and an advantage of using machine learning for DDoS detection is that the detection mechanism does not depend on whether the request comes from a blacklisted device, since the method builds its own weights for the characteristics it extracts. This is particularly important since most DDoS attacks come from legit compromised devices.

The available machine learning techniques can be divided into several categories, however, for the sake of practicality and simplicity we will assume the existence of two methods, the supervised and unsupervised learning. In *supervised learning*, each algorithm learns from input variables that serve as a supervisor/teacher to predict the output variables, this means that it is only possible to learn using a pre labelled training dataset. Within supervised learning, there are two types of problems, the classification, and the regression. In classification problems, the output of the classification belongs to two or more *classes*, for example, a given DDoS can be framed within the volumetric, layer 7 or layer 3/4 class. If the classification only considers two classes, for example, a given packet can be malicious or not malicious, then we have a binary classification problem. The other type of problems are the regression problems, where the prediction is of a numerical value and is usually applied to predict, for example, a stock price.

In contrast, the *unsupervised learning* discovers based on its own information, without requiring guidance to discover patterns. The various unsupervised techniques deal with unlabelled data, and they uncover patterns by learning and modelling by themselves (not depending on external information for the classification of data). Bearing in mind that some machine learning algorithms in Figure 3 can belong to several learning types, this figure illustrates and exemplifies the main data mining learning types.

Considering the two learning aforementioned methods there will be two main differences in the way we classify our packets as malicious or benign (binary classification). If we are working with supervised learning, then we need to train, test, and validate our classification model with a dataset containing several DDoS attacks. If we are working with unsupervised learning, then there is no need for this extensive training since we are detecting anomalies within a given set of data.

Regardless of the learning method to use, for the machine learning approach to work and be beneficial, it is necessary to adapt our method to the environment we want to protect and to all his attack surface. If the environment is cloud based, a traditional network, service or application, a Software Defined Network (SDN), or any other kind of environment, the approaches may change accordingly.

Figure 3. Data Mining learning types

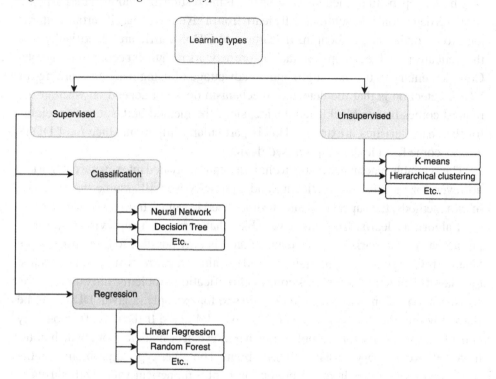

Another concern we must have for the proper functioning of the classification model is to transform the collected raw data in a useful and efficient format, in a so-called data pre-processing phase. To help the mining process, it is necessary to select and construct attributes that might help in the process of DDoS classification. This is an important phase that must carry a lot of thinking as the features used are the key factor for the correct identification of malicious traffic.

Pre-processing data can be done utilising different techniques for different purposes, the most obvious one being the treatment of missing, irrelevant or noisy data, a technique called data cleaning. Another important data pre-processing phase is the data transformation, this method is taken to transform the data in appropriate forms, suitable for the data mining process. This not only means that it is necessary to convert all data (which might be a mix of categorical and numeric data) to a specific type of data, but it also means that it needs to be normalised, that is, data must be in a specified, scaled range in order for the algorithm to calculate distances with proportional values.

Since data mining usually handles huge amounts of data, analysis and processing this data becomes harder in such cases. For this matter, another phase of the mining process that can be worthy of exploring is the data dimensionality reduction phase. Although this step won't be extensively covered in this chapter, in summary, dimensionality reduction reduces the number of variables/features that our machine learning algorithm will be fed and, consequently, the size of data. Nonetheless, despite reducing the data size, it should be noted that using dimensionality reduction techniques may result in information losses.

After all the data is pre-processed in an expected format, we can finally give the final product to the classification model so it can predict if the content is malicious or not. All this flow is compiled and illustrated by Figure 4 for illustration of the normal operation with machine learning methods.

To conclude this subsection, it is important to mention that, after training the model, its decision times and computational resources must be adequate and balanced. We shouldn't forget that, for the model to classify several packets, it has to analyse them all which, by itself, can generate DDoS. Moreover, there are techniques that handle this problem, such as high availability distributed systems, among others.

Figure 4. Stages for binary classification of network traffic

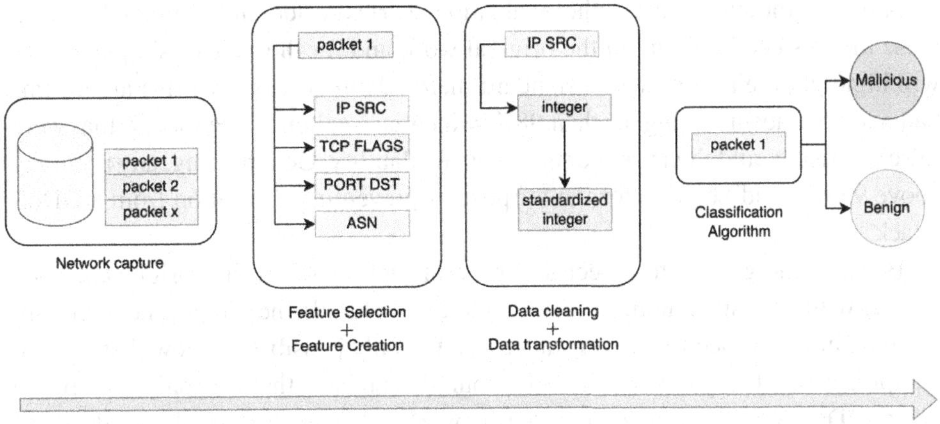

LITERATURE REVIEW

Different types of machine learning algorithms have been proposed as a viable approach for network anomaly detection. That said, it is not surprising that these algorithms are chosen, adapted, and fine-tuned to detect different types of DDoS attacks.

Doshi et al. (2018) proposed a bulk of machine learning methods for DDoS detection focusing on Internet of Things (IoT) network behaviour. The fact that this work only considers IoT-specific behaviours, such as: limited number of endpoints and regular time intervals between packets can result in an accurate and efficient feature selection that consequently results in high accuracy detection rate. Because IoT traffic is usually standardised and a lot of features can be constructed based on the "time" variable, there is real value in building features considering time patterns. This paradigm might not be applied in regular networks since the behaviours differ.

For the construction of the dataset, the authors used an experimental consumer IoT device network based on flood attacks, a type of attack that tries to flood the server by sending large volumes of traffic such as the: SYN flood, UDP flood, and HTTP GET flood attack. In our perspective, using three different flood attacks which does not cover the volumetric type of attacks, does not represent the whole scope of DDoS attacks.

The authors used flows with a limited set of features, which is important for real-time classification as it also restricts computational overhead. Regarding the machine learning classification, the authors tested five different algorithms, K-nearest neighbours (KNN) (Peterson, 2009), Random Forests (Breiman, 2001), Decision Trees (Quinlan, 1986), Support Vector Machines (SVM) (Cristianini & Ricci, 2008), and Deep Neural Networks (DNN) (Wang & Raj, 2017).

Although the authors used other evaluation metrics besides the accuracy, knowing these metrics can be found in the original work and for the sake of simplicity, we will highlight the accuracy as a standard metric from now on. All five algorithms had a test set accuracy higher than 98%, which is excellent since the 2% that were misclassified wouldn't cause the service unavailability. Generalizing, any accuracy above 95% would be good for the purpose of preventing disruption from a DDoS attack.

Because the goal is to detect and prevent DoS attack traffic originated from devices within the smart home Local Area Network (LAN), the adopted methodology is suited in these specific circumstances as it is only possible to know that a given equipment is IoT if you know its behaviour. This means that it is only possible to detect DDoS attacks originated on our network, whether they are destined for the intra or extranet. This is not that interesting. Hereupon, if we have IoT devices in our network, we can easily distinguish benign communication from DDoS traffic effectively using machine learning techniques, otherwise, we need to adopt another approach.

Niyaz et al. (2016) proposed a deep learning-based DDoS detection system for a SDN environment. Although a SDN has its peculiarities that influences the detection methods, it is worth analysing the main deep learning strategy used which utilises a Stacked Auto Encoder (SAE) (Bank et al., 2020), an approach that consists of stacked sparse autoencoders and SoftMax classifier (Bridle, 1989) for unsupervised feature learning and classification, respectively. Naturally, the SAE works as a feature reduction algorithm for the set of features that are going to be analysed and these features are dependent on the transportation protocol that is being utilised for the DDoS attack.

In addition to identifying an individual DDoS attack class (ICMP, UDP or TCP based), this research also focuses on determining whether an incoming request is malicious or benign. That being said, and although the main goal should be the binary classification of packets, classifying the type of the attack can facilitate the choice of the mitigation strategy.

The dataset used consists of data generated by 15 devices (laptops and smartphones) using a home wireless network of which, 5 are victims, and 10 are attackers deploying DDoS attacks using the tool *hping3*. As for the performance indicators, the authors used Accuracy, Precision, Recall, F-Measure and ROC Curve. A list of these evaluation metrics and more can be seen in (Natakarnkitkul, 2019). The SAE system identifies individual DDoS attack classes with an accuracy of 95.65% and classifies the traffic in normal or malicious with an accuracy of 99.82%.

In a more generous way, Pande et al. (2021) proposed a machine learning method utilising random forests to detect, exclusively an ICMP based DDoS, the *ping of death*. Regarding the technologies used for the application of the machine learning method, the authors used Weka to apply Random Forest in a home environment where they deployed the attack using Windows *bash*. Although we found this approach to be poor because of the legacy DDoS attack that was chosen, in its short scope, it has a good accuracy of 99,76%.

Yuan et al. (2017) proposed a deep learning-based DDoS attack detection that aims to automatically extract high-level features from low-level ones and gain powerful representation and inference. For this purpose, the authors designed a recurrent deep neural network to learn patterns from sequences of network traffic. This approach is known as DeepDefense and it leverages different neural network models such as: Convolution Neural Network (CNN) (LeCun, 1989), Recursive Neural Network (RNN) (Rumelhart et al., 1985), Long Short-Term Memory Neural Network (LSTM) (Hochreiter & Schmidhuber, 1997), and Gated Recurrent Unit Neural Network (GRU) (Cho et al., 2014).

The authors are using the UNB ISCX 2012 dataset to train both shallow machine learning models and deep learning models and although this dataset might be outdated and does not contain the newest DDoS attack techniques, the approach itself seems robust and we believe that would also be able to generate good results with newer attacks.

From the experimental results and using a small dataset, the most successful deep learning model reduces the error rate by 39.69% compared with shallow machine learning methods. Using a large dataset, the error rate was reduced from 7.517% to 2.103% which demonstrates that recurrent deep neural networks approaches can handle historical features better than conventional machine learning methods.

Mahajan et al. (2017) proposed four different machine learning algorithms to detect DDoS attacks, namely, Naive Bayes (Hand & Yu, 2001), Decision Trees, Multilayer Perceptron (MLP) (equivalent to previously mentioned DNN), and SVM. Regarding the dataset used, the author decided to create its own dataset by deploying four different DDoS attacks, HTTP Flood, SIDDoS, UDP Flood, and the Smurf attack. This choice was due to the fact that the author wanted a normalised dataset with attacks that, in his opinion, did not belong to any other dataset. The dataset contains 27 features which are well tabled in the document.

The overall accuracy was 96.89%, 98.89% and 98.91%, 92.31% for Naive Bayes, Decision Trees, MLP and SVM correspondingly, being MLP the winner. The proposed work used a custom dataset, which, depending on the environment, on the tools that were used to deploy the attack might affect the quality of the detection and, because of this, does not provide comparison terms with other related work. We find this work to be objective and well-designed allowing a good understanding of the application of machine learning for the detection of DDoS.

Supervised learning methods need large numbers of labelled data and unsupervised learning algorithms have relatively low detection rate and high false positive rate. Gu et al. (2019) proposed a semi-supervised weighted k-means (Macqueen, 1967) detection method that focuses on fighting some of the limitations of both supervised and unsupervised learning.

The authors adopted a different way of selecting the features (compared to the aforementioned documents) which consists in a hybrid feature selection algorithm that finds the most effective feature sets and ensures the best detection results. The authors concluded that this hybrid feature selection method is much better than other feature selection methods.

Regarding the well-known datasets used, the authors resorted to DARPA, CAIDA 2007 and the CICIDS 2017 dataset, additionally, they created a custom real-world dataset using tools to simulate normal and attack traffic.

No accuracy measurement was provided, the evaluation metrics that this article mentions is the Recall and the False Positive Rate (FPR). For the custom real scenario dataset, the proposed machine learning method achieved a recall of 99.75% which is quite good considering DDoS attacks with 0.25% effectiveness would not harm the victim.

RESULTS DISCUSSION

After analysing the articles in the previous section, Table 1 synthetizes the main features of each article: the types of DDoS attacks used, the machine learning algorithms, the datasets, the evaluation metrics, and the top detection accuracy in percentage. This table provides a high-level view about the effectiveness of these approaches for detecting DDoS attacks.

Table 1. Feature summary of the literature reviewed.

References	DDoS attacks	ML algorithms used	Datasets used	Evaluation metrics	Top detection accuracy (%)
(Doshi et al., 2018)	SYN flood, UDP flood, and HTTP GET flood	KNN, Random forests, Decision trees, SVM, and DNN	Custom IoT based	Accuracy, Precision, Recall and F1	99,9
(Niyaz et al., 2016)	TCP, UDP and ICMP based	SAE, Soft-Max and NN	Custom	Accuracy, Precision, Recall, F1 and ROC Curve	99,82
(Pande et al., 2021)	Ping of Death	Random forests	NSL-KDD	Accuracy, Precision, Recall	99,76
(Yuan et al., 2017)	HTTP, TCP, IRC, DNS, ICMP, SMTP and IMAP based	LSTM, 3LSTM, GRU (RNN), CNN	UNB-ISCX Intrusion Detection Evaluation 2012	Error rate, Accuracy, Precision, Recall, F1, AUC	98,41
(Mahajan et al., 2017)	HTTP Flood, SIDDOS, UDP Flood, and Smurf	Naive Bayes, MLP, Decision trees and SVM	Custom	Accuracy, Precision, Recall	98.91
(Gu et al., 2019)	Attacks of the datasets	Weighted K-Means	DARPA, CAIDA 2007, CICIDS 2017 and custom	Recall, FPR	99.75 (recall)

After analysing Table 1 and the top detection accuracy of the machine learning approaches for the respective attacks, it is easily understood by the high accuracy rates that, with proper planning, machine learning strategies can bring benefits to the traditional signature-based detection.

If the approach to be taken is the supervised one, we believe that the planning should focus on building or using a dataset that represents the top notch of DDoS attacks. Additionally, it should focus on extracting and evaluating the features that best serve to distinguish malicious packages from benign. In the case of unsupervised learning, the question of the dataset containing DDoS attacks does not arise, however, the features to be evaluated for the purpose of anomaly detection is still extremely important. For both approaches (supervised and unsupervised), it is key to consider the environment we want to protect, its architecture, and design our machine learning approach to fit our requirements.

We believe that a possible scheme that allows to duly assign the problems of DDoS attacks detection, but not only, is to consider the traditional signature-based detection (IDS) on the front line, followed by a supervised approach that trained with a historical registry of top-notch DDoS attacks and, lastly, followed by an unsupervised approach that aims at identifying anomalies in packets exclusively based on statistics. Despite all the computation and delay problems that this solution may create, we believe that the order of the detection mechanisms is placed concerning the benefits of each one. This scheme is illustrated by Figure 5 where the "Flagged?" differentiates packets catalogued as suspicious or malicious.

Figure 5. Proposed detection system scheme.

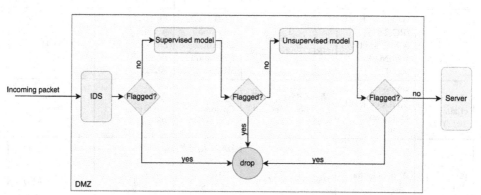

CONCLUSION

Modern DDoS attacks have become much more difficult to detect as attackers build highly sophisticated requests that originate from compromised machines. There are multiple approaches that can be taken in order to detect and block these attacks, however, DDoS attacks continue with an active presence in cyberspace and concerns organisations due to its disruptive power. Considering the already mentioned specifications of a DDoS, for this particular attack vector, we believe that future solutions will heavily rely on machine learning solutions for the detection and later mitigation instead of the traditional signature-based detection.

This chapter served as a context for those who wanted to introduce themselves in detecting DDoS attacks using machine learning by explaining the fundamentals and the different classifications of DDoS attacks, as well as the different machine learning approaches that can serve as security solutions. Moreover, this chapter explained why applying artificial intelligence can bring fine results regarding the defence of networks and proved it by mentioning the accomplishments of already written literature. Finally, as extra, this chapter proposed a defensible architecture employing a traditional signature-based detection system, adding the benefits of both supervised and unsupervised learning.

REFERENCES

BankD.KoenigsteinN.GiryesR. (2020). *Autoencoders*. Retrieved from https://arxiv.org/abs/2003.05991

Breiman, L. (2001). Random forests. *Machine Learning*, *45*(1), 5–32. doi:10.1023/A:1010933404324

Bridle, J. (1989). Training stochastic model recognition algorithms as networks can lead to maximum mutual information estimation of parameters. *Advances in Neural Information Processing Systems*, 2.

Cho, K., van Merrienboer, B., Bahdanau, D., & Bengio, Y. (2014). *On the Properties of Neural Machine Translation: Encoder-Decoder Approaches*. Retrieved from https://arxiv.org/abs/1409.1259

Cloudflare. (2022). *What is a distributed denial-of-service (DDoS) attack?* Retrieved from https://www.cloudflare.com/learning/ddos/what-is-a-ddos-attack/

Cristianini, N., & Ricci, E. (2008). *Support vector machines*. Academic Press.

Doshi, R., Apthorpe, N., & Feamster, N. (2018, May). Machine learning ddos detection for consumer internet of things devices. In *2018 IEEE Security and Privacy Workshops (SPW)* (pp. 29-35). IEEE.

Fortinet. (2022). *What is a DDoS Attack?* Retrieved from https://www.fortinet.com/resources/cyberglossary/ddos-attack

Gu, Y., Li, K., Guo, Z., & Wang, Y. (2019). Semi-supervised K-means DDoS detection method using hybrid feature selection algorithm. *IEEE Access: Practical Innovations, Open Solutions*, *7*, 64351–64365.

Hand, D., & Yu, K. (2001). *Idiot's Bayes: Not So Stupid after All?* Academic Press.

Hochreiter, S., & Schmidhuber, J. (1997). *Long short-term memory*. Retrieved from Institute of Bioinformatics, Johannes Kepler University Linz: https://www.bioinf.jku.at/publications/older/2604.pdf

LeCun, Y. (1989). *Backpropagation applied to handwritten zip code recognition*. Retrieved from http://yann.lecun.com/exdb/publis/pdf/lecun-89e.pdf

MacQueen, J. (1967, June). Some methods for classification and analysis of multivariate observations. In *Proceedings of the fifth Berkeley symposium on mathematical statistics and probability* (Vol. *1*, No. 14, pp. 281-297). Academic Press.

Mahajan, A., Sofi, I., & Mansotra, V. (2017). *Machine Learning Techniques used for the Detection and Analysis of Modern Types of DDoS Attacks Framework to Detect and Analyze Compromised Hosts on network View project Machine Learning Techniques used for the Detection and Analysis of Modern Types of DD*. *International Research Journal of Engineering and Technology*.

Natakarnkitkul, S. (2019). *Evaluation Metrics: Reference Guides*. Retrieved from https://medium.com/@net_satsawat/evaluation-metrics-reference-guides-7c3a2a055351

Niyaz, Q., Sun, W., & Javaid, A. (2016). *A Deep Learning Based DDoS Detection System in Software-Defined Networking (SDN)*. Retrieved from https://arxiv.org/abs/1611.07400

Pande, S., Khamparia, A., Gupta, D., & Thanh, D. N. (2021). DDOS detection using machine learning technique. In *Recent Studies on Computational Intelligence* (pp. 59–68). Springer.

Peterson, L. (2009). *K-nearest neighbor*. Retrieved from http://www.scholarpedia.org/article/K-nearest_neighbor

Quinlan, J. R. (1986). Induction of decision trees. *Machine Learning*, *1*(1), 81–106. doi:10.1007/BF00116251

Rumelhart, D. E., Hinton, G. E., & Williams, R. J. (1985). *Learning internal representations by error propagation*. California Univ San Diego La Jolla Inst for Cognitive Science. doi:10.21236/ADA164453

University of New Brunswick. (2022). *DDoS 2019 | Datasets | Research | Canadian Institute for Cybersecurity | UNB*. Retrieved from https://www.unb.ca/cic/datasets/ddos-2019.html

Wang, H., & Raj, B. (2017). *On the Origin of Deep Learning*. Retrieved from https://arxiv.org/abs/1702.07800

Yuan, X., Li, C., & Li, X. (2017, May). DeepDefense: identifying DDoS attack via deep learning. In *2017 IEEE International Conference on Smart Computing (SMARTCOMP)* (pp. 1-8). IEEE.

ADDITIONAL READING

Chockwanich, N., & Visoottiviseth, V. (2019, February). Intrusion detection by deep learning with tensorflow. In *2019 21st international conference on advanced communication technology (ICACT)* (pp. 654-659). IEEE.

Clarence Chio, D. F. (2018). *Machine Learning and Security O'Reilly Media, Inc.* O'Reilly Media, Inc.

Paffenroth, R. C., & Zhou, C. (2019). Modern machine learning for cyber-defense and distributed denial-of-service attacks. *IEEE Engineering Management Review*, *47*(4), 80–85. doi:10.1109/EMR.2019.2950183

Soma Halder, S. O. (2018). *Hands-On Machine Learning for Cybersecurity*. Packt Publishing.

KEY TERMS AND DEFINITIONS

CNN: Convolution Neural Network. Supervised method used for classification and regression problems, a class of neural networks that specializes in processing data that is organized as a grid, such as an image.

Decision Trees: Supervised method used for classification and regression problems, that simulates a tree diagram and in which the branches represent choices with associated costs, results, or probabilities.

DNN: Deep Neural Networks. Supervised method used for classification and regression problems, built to simulate the activity of the human brain by feeding input data through several layers of simulated neural connections.

K-Means: Unsupervised method used for classification and regression problems, that groups data by assigning all data points to the closest clusters, then determining the cluster means.

KNN: K-Nearest Neighbours. Supervised method used for classification and regression problems, that attempts to determine what group a data point is in by looking at the data points around it.

LSTM: Long Short-Term Memory Neural Network. Supervised method used for classification and regression problems, a type of RNN that is mainly used for learning sequential data prediction problems by discarding information which is not required for further prediction and by holding required information for that matter.

Naïve Bayes: Supervised method used for classification and regression problems, which utilizes Bayes' theorem with the assumption that attributes are conditionally independent for the purposes of object classification.

Random Forests: Supervised method used for classification and regression problems, that builds decision trees on different samples and takes their average in case of regression and majority vote for classification.

RNN: Recursive Neural Network. Supervised method used for classification and regression problems, a class of neural networks that applies the same set of weights recursively over a structured input.

SVM: Support Vector Machines. Supervised method used for classification and regression problems, that determine which category a new data point belongs in by outputting a map of the sorted data with the margins between the two as far apart as possible.

Chapter 7
Masked Transient Effect Ring Oscillator Physical Unclonable Function Against Machine Learning Attacks

Sivasankari Narasimhan
Mepco Schlenk Engineering College, India

ABSTRACT

Many types of physical unclonable function (PUF) structures have been proposed in the last decade. The responses generated from the conventional PUF are vulnerable to attack. In this chapter, the transient effect of ring oscillator structure has been used. This works on two loops with complex loops containing NOT gates and NAND gates. Response prediction of these loops is a very difficult task for the adversary. Many machine learning algorithms may produce the responses with higher accuracies. This study provides new masked PUF architectures that are more secure and invulnerable to modeling attacks. Hence, in this chapter, masking-based configurability design on various PUF structures is introduced. This will be helpful for resource-constrained machines. For different sizes of challenge-response pair, machine learning techniques need to be changed, but prediction accuracy by the attacker should be low. By using this kind of masked PUF structure, 54.7% uniqueness can be obtained, and 97.5% reliability can be achieved. Machine learning accuracy is 70.7% with SVM and 63.67% accuracy in LR.

DOI: 10.4018/978-1-7998-9430-8.ch007

INTRODUCTION

The evolvement of the Machine Learning (ML) combined with advances in computational and storage capacities creates a lot of fruitful things. For example, ML-based algorithms altered the practice of disease findings, stock market analysis and cricket score prediction. But the ML techniques also capture the security domain, by monitoring bait machines, and extracting actionable information that in the past would have been impossible. Hence some vulnerabilities inherent with ML techniques are included with the security set-up. Currently, there are more advanced techniques to mitigate the ML attacks protecting the security set-ups. Such techniques may be smelled by hackers. Effort has been made to rectify the errors in security set-up. Several research sectors are developed for this, still this domain is in vulnerable position. These loopholes also create another focus for research and produce the new solutions for security threats. In this chapter, a unified hardware/software approach is developed as a solution for security issues.

In security and privacy domain, maintaining confidentiality, integrity, and authentication are more essential. Hence, after 2000s, there is a proposal to introduce hardware security modules. Attacks on confidentiality attempt to expose the model structure or parameters (which may be highly valuable intellectual property) or the data used to train it, e.g., patient data, stock market data, continuously monitored information. But when a hardware entity is used, its unclonability nature avoids the data hacking problem and provides confidentiality to both communicating parties. On the other side, the main advantage of a PUF compared to the current classical cryptographic solutions is its compatibility with IoT devices with limited computational resources. Each node can be leveraged as an authentication mechanism to detect tamper. Several papers and works were developed in the last two decades. One simple category of PUF is shown in Figure 1.

Despite the several advantages that PUF brings for safety, there are several concerns and issues which need to be solved before it is incorporated in cyber physical devices. First, in PUF the devices are noisy (i.e., the device response is not the same in all environments). Due to temperature or fluctuations in it, the responses may get 5% deviations. It is quite natural that monitoring and maintenance of every PUF CRP pair is not a simple task. Second, the threshold level introduced for allowing the authorized user may also permit the wrong intruders. Third, when it is implemented in IoT devices, the centralized server may become a fraudulent one. The details from one device may be shifted to another device if they convince the server / trusted third party. Fourth, the details may be modelled by a clever intruder. This work focuses on how to reduce the fourth threat and find the solution.

Figure 1. Categories of PUF on fabrication methodology

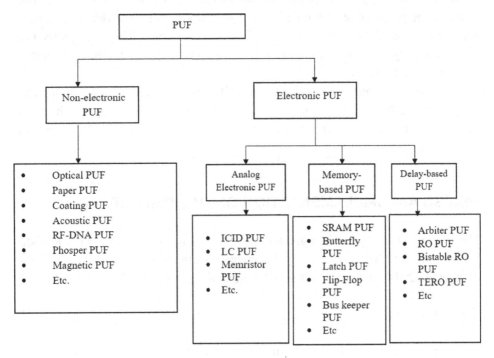

The remaining sections are arranged as follows: Section *Related Work* gives some of the machine learning algorithm related works used for modelling the challenge-response pair. Section *Design and Implementation of Masked PUF* provides the proposed work on PUF with masking. Section *Results and Discussion* provides the results and discussions followed by *Conclusion*.

RELATED WORK

Usually, the attacks are intended to know the communication messages or to know the shared secret key between the authorized users. The attacks can be chosen over plaintext attack or chosen over ciphertext attack. The ways of attack include side channel analysis, linear and differential power analysis attacks. In this way, some known mathematical ways of modelling attacks are now getting popular. The model of any of the communicating parties are designed with the known challenge-response pairs. The attacker snoops the challenge-response behaviour of the secret key generating device (i.e., PUF. Then they try to construct a mathematical form of that CRP behaviour).

Most of the key generating devices are vulnerable, because the response from them can be predictable. If the device is constructed strong enough against these mathematical modelling attacks, then it is a reliable device. The main motivation of hardware cryptographic engineers is focused on finding a mathematically strong PUF against all attacks.

The major drawback to construct such PUF is that no PUF is strong enough for longer. The hackers are also able to model the strong device responses. Then they can be cloned and no longer secure. Some of the prediction ML algorithms are listed in Table 1:

DESIGN AND IMPLEMENTATION OF MASKED PUF

The original challenge is first given to the 64-bit Linear Feedback Shift Register (LFSR). Some LFSR based Strong PUF creation methods are discussed in reference (Hou et al., 2019). The irreducible polynomial used in this work is

$$x^5 + x^4 + x^3 + x^2 + 1 \qquad (1)$$

The most significant bits are accumulated in a register. After it reaches 64 bits, the LFSR results are XORed bitwise with the original challenge. Now the obtained results from XOR PUF are given to the PUF structure. Challenge for the PUF is mapped to a modified challenge. This is given to PUF structure and converted into unique response as shown in Figure 2. In this work, Transient Effect Ring Oscillator PUF structure is used for PUF. As depicted in Figure. 2, a 64-bit TERO-PUF is utilized for this design, which is composed of 64 stages. The TERO-PUF should exploit the mean number of oscillations of the output signal of the TERO loop. When the cell is initialized (rising edge of the signal 'init"), two events start their propagation inside the TERO cell and start the oscillating state. Depending on the delays mismatch between the two branches of the TERO cell which is due to the CMOS process variations, these two events move inside it until they collide and stop the oscillating state. This behaviour results in a finite number of oscillations of the TERO cell output. To accumulate the PUF structure, additional 8-bit accumulators and shift registers are used. In theory, if all gates and all connections inside the TERO cell are perfectly identical, the cell would oscillate indefinitely but due to manufacturing process variations, this is an extremely rare case.

Table 1. Various machine learning algorithm (Sivasankari & Kumari, 2022)

References	Machine Learning algorithm	Description	Equation
(Bishop & Nasrabadi, 2006; Riedmiller & Braun, 1993)	Logistic Regression: supervised machine learning framework	The decision function f determines a decision boundary of equal output probabilities.	Logistic sigmoid function $\sigma(x) = (1 + e\text{-}x)^{-1}$ Parametrized as $$P\left(c,r \mid \breve{w}\right) = r\sigma\left(f\right) + \left(1-r\right)\left(1-\sigma\left(f\right)\right)$$
(Beyer, 2007; Galletly, 1998; Schwefel, 1993)	Evolutionary Strategies- Nature inspired direct search	Adopted from environmental fitness function.	$\forall l = 1,2,\ldots,\lambda:$ $$a_l = \{\sigma_l \leftarrow \sigma e^{TN_l(0,1)}$$ $\{y_l \leftarrow y + \sigma_l N_l(0,1)\}$ $F_L \leftarrow F(y_l)$ $N_l(0,1)$ - Normally distributed random scalars and vectors respectively. Mutated strategy parameter σl controls the strength of the object parameter mutation
(Burges, 1998)	Support Vector Machine	Many Kernel functions for classification have been introduced. Each of them having its own advantages	Generalized Kernel function is $K<>$ Gaussian Kernel: $$K\left(x,z\right) = \exp\left(-\frac{x-z^2}{2\sigma^2}\right)$$
(Zhang et al., 2004)			Wavelet Kernel function $K\left(x,z\right) = j$ $$= 1m\left(\cos\left(1.75\frac{x_i - z_j}{a}\right) exp\left(-\frac{x_i - z_j^2}{2a^2}\right)\right)$$
(Bossuet et al., 2014; Ozer et al., 2011)			Chebyshev Kernel function: $$K\left(x,z\right) = \frac{1+c+\left(2a-1\right)\left(2b-1\right)}{\sqrt{m-c}}$$ $$+\frac{c\left(4a-3\right)\left(4b-3\right)}{\sqrt{m-c}} + \frac{\left(8a^2-8a+1\right)\left(8b^2-8b+1\right)}{\sqrt{m-c}}$$ where a =<x, x>; b =<Z, Z> and C=<x,z>.
(Wen & Lao, 2017)	Linear SVM ((i)Sensitive bits grouping (ii)Different delay differencing	Two-step verification. Strengthening the reliability of PUF response by machine learning method	Algorithm discussed in literature.

Figure 2. Masked PUF

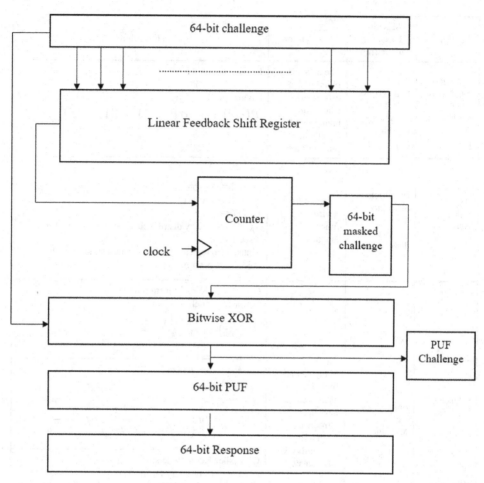

As shown in Figure 3, The control signal 'Enable' is given at the same time for all 64-bit TERO PUF circuit. From each PUF, 1- bit accumulator is connected. All the outputs are saved and transferred immediately for the next stage. For each clock pulse different responses are created and used for authentication purposes. As shown in Figure 4, 1-bit accumulator set collects the response and 64 bit parallel-in parallel out shift register has been used with particular delay as one variable parameter.

Figure 3. TERO PUF basic primitive structure

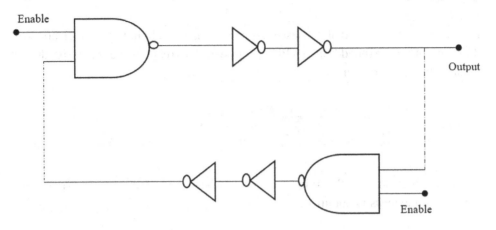

Figure 4. Response generation from PUF structure

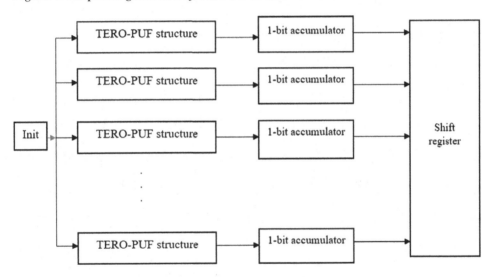

RESULTS AND DISCUSSION

In this algorithm, some masking concepts are utilized to reduce the machine learning based modelling attacks. But the analysis is done with normal PUF metrics. First, the circuit is implemented in the board XC5VLX50T.

Uniqueness

PUF(x) is the response that possesses some information about the identification of the physical entity embedding that PUF (Figure 5). This response cannot be produced by any other physical entity.

$$Uniquenss = \frac{2}{k(k-1)} \sum_{i=1}^{k-1} \sum_{j=i+1}^{n} \frac{HD(R_i, R_j)}{n} X100 \qquad (2)$$

For the ideal circuit, the uniqueness should be close to 50%. In this experiment a 52.3% uniqueness is obtained.

Figure 5. Uniqueness graph for (a) 64 bits (b) 128 bits (c) 256 bits (d) 512 bits

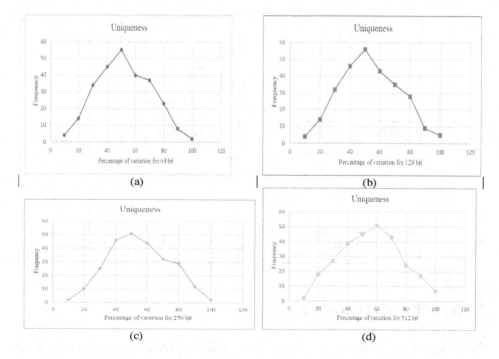

Reliability

It is a measure that shows how efficiently the chip is reproducing the same response under different environmental situations (different temperatures, different voltages and so on). To perform this, the PUF response (Ri) under normal temperature is determined. At different temperatures, the same instance PUF response (Rj') is calculated up to m times. HD between the responses is calculated using the formula

$$HD_{INTRA} = \frac{1}{M} \sum_{i=1}^{m} \frac{HD(R_i, R_i')}{n} X100 \qquad (3)$$

then the reliability is calculated by

$$\text{Reliability} = 100\text{-}HD_{INTRA} \qquad (4)$$

HD $_{INTRA}$ indicates the mean number of unreliable/noisy PUF response bits. The value of HD $_{INTRA}$ should be low, and the value of reliability should be high for a particular instance of a chip. For the proposed PUF design, 97.5 reliability has been achieved.

Table 2. Machine learning works on PUF

References	Type of PUF to overcome Machine learning attack	Specification about PUF	Accuracy				
		ML Techniques	LR (%)	ANN (%)	ML (%)	ES	SVM
(Rührmair et al., 2010)	Conventional arbiter PUF	64 stages & 128-bit arbiter PUFs	99	-	-	-	-
	XOR arbiter PUF (4,5,6 XORs)	64 stages & 128-bit arbiter PUFs	99	-	-	-	-
	Lightweight PUF	64 stages & 128-bit arbiter PUFs	99	-	-	-	-
	Feed forward arbiter PUF (10 Flip flops)	64 stage PUF with 8 flip flop Loops	95.46		-	97	-
(El-Hajj et al., 2021)	Arbiter PUF	With bent function	-	-	-	-	93
(Wang et al., 2018)	Dual-mode PUF	(32,1)	0.9851	0.9933	-	-	-
(Pang et al., 2017)	Cross over RO-PUF	(4,3) row x column	99.1	-	99.1	-	-
Proposed PUF	Masked TERO PUF	64 bits	63.61	-	-	-	70.77

Uniformity

A PUF is said to have good uniformity, when the n bit response contains an equal number of 0' s and 1 s. For ideal case it should be 50%. For experiment set up, n bit responses have been collected. They are matched with subsequent patterns. 10 different board responses were collected. For this proposed PUF design, 1's probability is 51.2% and 0's probability is 49.8%.

Comparison with Machine Learning Studies

As already explained in section 2, some machine learning algorithms results are compared with the proposed design.

From the Table 2, it is inferred that, the proposed Masking-PUF is more resilient against machine learning attacks.

CONCLUSION

The main outcome of this chapter is Masked TERO-PUF structure which is designed against machine learning attacks. The Masked-TERO PUF secret is used for the attestation mechanism to uniquely authenticate each processor chip. This work can be extended to more electronic circuits metastability states to produce non-deterministic random numbers. A reconfigurable PUF configuration has been described as the identity for every user. An almost stable output has been attained. In future, it can be combined with lightweight encryption algorithms and other types of PUF suitable for applications.

REFERENCES

Beyer, H.-G. (2007). Evolution strategies. *Scholarpedia*, *2*(8), 1965. doi:10.4249cholarpedia.1965

Bishop, C. M., & Nasrabadi, N. M. (2006). Pattern recognition and machine learning (Vol. 4). Springer.

Bossuet, L., Ngo, X. T., Cherif, Z., & Fischer, V. (2014). A PUF based on a transient effect ring oscillator and insensitive to locking phenomenon. *IEEE Transactions on Emerging Topics in Computing*, *2*(1), 30–36. Advance online publication. doi:10.1109/TETC.2013.2287182

Burges, C. J. C. (1998). A tutorial on support vector machines for pattern recognition. *Data Mining and Knowledge Discovery*, 2(2), 121–167. Advance online publication. doi:10.1023/A:1009715923555

El-Hajj, M., Fadlallah, A., Chamoun, M., & Serhrouchni, A. (2021). A taxonomy of PUF Schemes with a novel Arbiter-based PUF resisting machine learning attacks. Computer Networks. doi:10.1016/j.comnet.2021.108133

Galletly, J. (1998). Evolutionary algorithms in theory and practice: Evolution strategies, evolutionary programming, genetic algorithms. Kybernetes. doi:10.1108/k.1998.27.8.979.4

Hou, S., Guo, Y., & Li, S. (2019). *A lightweight LFSR-Based strong physical unclonable function design on FPGA*. IEEE. doi:10.1109/ACCESS.2019.2917259

Ozer, S., Chen, C. H., & Cirpan, H. A. (2011). A set of new Chebyshev kernel functions for support vector machine pattern classification. *Pattern Recognition*, 44(7), 1435–1447. Advance online publication. doi:10.1016/j.patcog.2010.12.017

Pang, Z., Zhang, J., Zhou, Q., Gong, S., Qian, X., & Tang, B. (2017). Crossover Ring Oscillator PUF. *Proceedings - International Symposium on Quality Electronic Design, ISQED*. 10.1109/ISQED.2017.7918322

Riedmiller, M., & Braun, H. (1993). Direct adaptive method for faster backpropagation learning: The RPROP algorithm. *1993 IEEE International Conference on Neural Networks*. 10.1109/ICNN.1993.298623

Rührmair, U., Sehnke, F., Sölter, J., Dror, G., Devadas, S., & Schmidhuber, J. (2010). Modeling attacks on physical unclonable functions. *Proceedings of the ACM Conference on Computer and Communications Security*. 10.1145/1866307.1866335

Schwefel, H.-P. P. (1993). *Evolution and optimum seeking: the sixth generation*. John Wiley & Sons, Inc.

Sivasankari, N., & Kumari, R. S. S. (2022). Reliable set of random number generation using Astable Multivibrator PUF. *Analog Integrated Circuits and Signal Processing*, 112(1), 29–48. doi:10.100710470-022-02027-w

Wang, Q., Gao, M., & Qu, G. (2018). A machine learning attack resistant dual-mode PUF. *Proceedings of the ACM Great Lakes Symposium on VLSI, GLSVLSI*. 10.1145/3194554.3194590

Wen, Y., & Lao, Y. (2017). Enhancing PUF reliability by machine learning. *Proceedings - IEEE International Symposium on Circuits and Systems*. 10.1109/ISCAS.2017.8050672

Zhang, L., Zhou, W., & Jiao, L. (2004). Wavelet Support Vector Machine. *IEEE Transactions on Systems, Man, and Cybernetics. Part B, Cybernetics, 34*(1), 34–39. Advance online publication. doi:10.1109/TSMCB.2003.811113 PMID:15369048

ADDITIONAL READING

Arppe, R., & Sørensen, T. J. (2017). Physical unclonable functions generated through chemical methods for anti-counterfeiting. *Nature Reviews. Chemistry, 1*(4), 1–13. doi:10.103841570-017-0031

Gao, Y., Al-Sarawi, S. F., & Abbott, D. (2020). Physical unclonable functions. *Nature Electronics, 3*(2), 81–91. doi:10.103841928-020-0372-5

Herder, C., Yu, M. D., Koushanfar, F., & Devadas, S. (2014). Physical unclonable functions and applications: A tutorial. *Proceedings of the IEEE, 102*(8), 1126–1141. doi:10.1109/JPROC.2014.2320516

Maiti, A., Gunreddy, V., & Schaumont, P. (2013). A systematic method to evaluate and compare the performance of physical unclonable functions. In *Embedded systems design with FPGAs* (pp. 245–267). Springer. doi:10.1007/978-1-4614-1362-2_11

Maiti, A., & Schaumont, P. (2009). Improving the quality of a physical unclonable function using configurable ring oscillators. In *2009 International Conference on Field Programmable Logic and Applications* (pp. 703-707). IEEE. 10.1109/FPL.2009.5272361

Marchand, C., Bossuet, L., Mureddu, U., Bochard, N., Cherkaoui, A., & Fischer, V. (2017). Implementation and characterization of a physical unclonable function for IoT: A case study with the TERO-PUF. *IEEE Transactions on Computer-Aided Design of Integrated Circuits and Systems, 37*(1), 97–109. doi:10.1109/TCAD.2017.2702607

Shamsoshoara, A., Korenda, A., Afghah, F., & Zeadally, S. (2020). A survey on physical unclonable function (PUF)-based security solutions for Internet of Things. *Computer Networks, 183*, 107593. doi:10.1016/j.comnet.2020.107593

KEY TERMS AND DEFINITIONS

Challenge-Response Pair: A family of protocols in which one party presents a question ("challenge") and another party must provide a valid answer ("response") to be authenticated.

Linear Feedback Shift Register (LFSR): A shift register whose input bit is a linear function of its previous state. The most commonly used linear function of single bits is exclusive-or (XOR). Thus, an LFSR is most often a shift register whose input bit is driven by the XOR of some bits of the overall shift register value. The initial value of the LFSR is called the seed, and because the operation of the register is deterministic, the stream of values produced by the register is completely determined by its current (or previous) state. Likewise, because the register has a finite number of possible states, it must eventually enter a repeating cycle. However, an LFSR with a well-chosen feedback function can produce a sequence of bits that appears random and has a very long cycle. Applications of LFSRs include generating pseudo-random numbers, pseudo-noise sequences, fast digital counters, and whitening sequences. Both hardware and software implementations of LFSRs are common.

Logic Gate: An idealized or physical device implementing a Boolean function, a logical operation performed on one or more binary inputs that produces a single binary output. Depending on the context, the term may refer to an ideal logic gate, one that has for instance zero rise time and unlimited fan-out, or it may refer to a non-ideal physical device (see Ideal and real op-amps for comparison).

Masking: A bit field (bitwise) operation. Using masking, multiple bits can be set either on or off, or inverted from on to off (or vice versa) in a single bitwise operation. An additional use of masking involves predication in vector processing, where the bitmask is used to select which element operations in the vector are to be executed (mask bit is enabled) and which are not (mask bit is clear).

Physical Unclonable Function (PUF): A physical unclonable function, or PUF, is a physical object that for a given input and conditions, provides a physically defined "digital fingerprint" output that serves as a unique identifier, most often for a semiconductor device such as a microprocessor.

Resource-Constrained Machine: Devices that by design have limited processing and storage capabilities to provide a maximal data output possible with a minimal power input while remaining cost-effective.

Ring Oscillator: A device composed of an odd number of NOT gates in a ring, whose output oscillates between two voltage levels, representing true and false. The NOT gates, or inverters, are attached in a chain and the output of the last inverter is fed back into the first.

Chapter 8
Detecting Bank Financial Fraud in South Africa Using a Logistic Model Tree

Katleho Makatjane

iD https://orcid.org/0000-0002-3687-4098

Department of Statistics, University of Botswana, Botswana

Ntebogang Dinah Moroke

iD https://orcid.org/0000-0001-8545-1860

North West University, South Africa

ABSTRACT

Artificial intelligence is gradually becoming the standard mechanism underpinning online banking. Users' profiles can be confirmed using a variety of methods, including passcodes, fingerprints, acoustics, and images through this technology. On the other hand, traditional cybersecurity measures are unable to prevent internet-based fraud after the visualisation process has been infiltrated. In light of this, the aim of this chapter is to examine the efficiency of the logistic model tree (LMT) in detecting financial fraudulent transactions in South African banks and, ultimately, to develop a financial fraud early warning system. Web-scraping credit and debit card fraud data from SA are used to acquire daily data. The LMT is constructed utilizing a training set from the LogitBoost algorithm and obtained 17 financial conditioning elements. Overall, an early warning system model has shown to be a good performer with a prediction rate of 99.9%. This appears to be a promising approach for detecting online fraud vulnerabilities.

DOI: 10.4018/978-1-7998-9430-8.ch008

INTRODUCTION

The identification of financial fraud has grown to become a global topic. Fraud detection systems in financial institutions must be smart and effective. Between 2018 and 2019, online transactions increased credit and debit card theft by 20.5 percent. According to the South African Banking Risk Information Centre Report (2019), the country's failing economy has given hackers the impetus and opportunity to commit financial crimes, with digital banking incidents increasing by 20% in 2019. This number is sure to rise as hackers continue to obtain sensitive and private information from users, allowing them to trade on their accounts without their permission. Unfortunately, cybercrime has led to an increase in total fraudulent transactions on South African-issued cards. This premise is illustrated in Figure 1. Electronic technology, such as PayPal and fraud detectives, are helpful in thwarting ever-changing fraud schemes. According to Abdallah et al (2016), the percentage of fraud loss order channels in online stores is currently at 74 percent, with 49 percent in mobile channels. However, according to Cybersource (2021), the online store has recorded 80 percent of payment fraud and mobile commerce has tracked 68 percent. This suggests that there has been an upsurge in both online and mobile commerce fraud worldwide since 2016. The moral, based on these figures, is to manage discrepancies between different types of fraud deeds that have changed over time. A good fraud detection solution should be able to correctly categorise and detect fraudulent transactions in real-time transactions. According to Seyedhossein and Hashemi (2010), fraud detection is classified into two categories: (1) detecting fraud using AI (Artificial Intelligence) and (2) detecting fraud manually. Data analysts construct algorithms to spot abnormalities and trends using the former. This is accomplished by either creating models and training AI or acquiring "off-the-shelf" fraud detection technologies. A system that involves screening applicants and using training models to discover aspects that humans cannot constructed with the help of experts and AI. The latter, on the other hand, relies on the human eye to detect irregularities in a document's text style, alignment, spacing, and color. Unfortunately, this is not easy to do without a trained eye.

Financial crime has long been a source of concern for businesses and organisations across a wide range of industries. According to Budhram (2012), credit card theft caused financial losses in South Africa to increase by 53% between 2019 and 2021. As a result, the South African Financial Risk Intelligence Centre (SABRIC) has confirmed two events that have occurred in the banking system of South Africa (SA) in recent years. In 2019, the industry generated R403,15 million in revenue. This is an increase of R263,8 million over the previous year (SABRIC Report, 2019). Card fraud is a major concern for businesses that accept credit cards, the financial system, and, most crucially, individual users. The use of debit and credit cards for online purchases has expanded rapidly as e-commerce has intensified and accelerated, resulting in a high number of frauds involving both debit and credit cards. In today's digital economy, the ability to recognize both debit and credit card scams is crucial.

Figure 1. Gross fraud (credit and debit)
source https://www.sabric.co.za

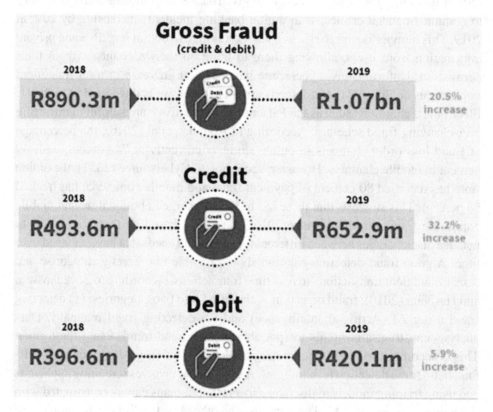

Fraud detection systems have been introduced to the market to combat this problem and provide reliable business solutions. "Fraud is frequently caught using an outlier detection technique supported by data mining tools, in which hidden trends, correlations, and patterns are identified in a large database, and crucial information is also uncovered" (Albshrawi & Lowell, 2016; Jayakumar & Thomas, 2013; Hassani et al., 2010). As a result, the authors developed an automated extreme early warning system for financial fraud, which complements existing approaches. "The benefits of this system include real-time detection of suspicious activity before it causes business damage. More fraud scenarios are detected with greater accuracy, uncovering fraudster rings with global device reputation, and extended fingerprinting detection of cross-organizational money laundering scenarios via the Google Flutter system and Chrome extension for Android" (PSD2, Open Banking and APIS, 2019. As a result, the goal of this chapter is to leverage the Google Flutter platform to crowd-source credit and debit card ratings in order to classify transactions as fraudulent or not. This is supervised learning, as opposed to unsupervised learning, in which the logistic model tree is trained to predict the possibility of debit and credit card financial fraud. The suggested Google Flutter is shown in Figure 2. The domain https://flutter.dev/ was used to create this Google Flutter.

Figure 2. Flutter in android studio
https://flutter.dev/

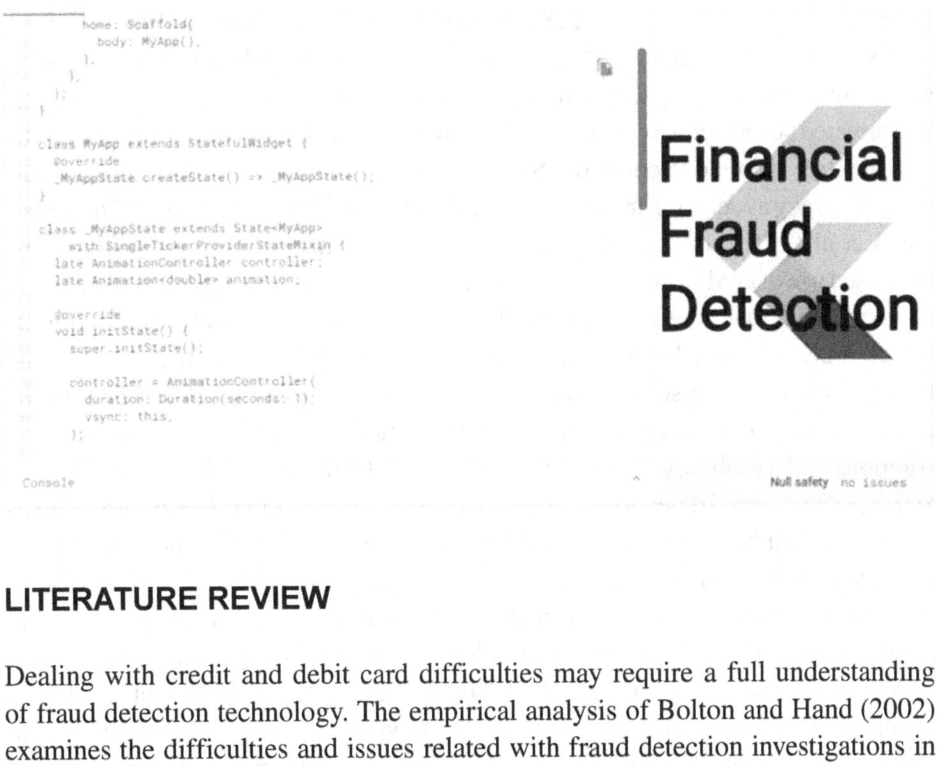

```
        home: Scaffold(
            body: MyApp(),
        ),
    },
    );
}

class MyApp extends StatefulWidget {
    @override
    _MyAppState createState() => _MyAppState();
}

class _MyAppState extends State<MyApp>
    with SingleTickerProviderStateMixin {
    late AnimationController controller;
    late Animation<double> animation;

    @override
    void initState() {
        super.initState();

        controller = AnimationController(
            duration: Duration(seconds: 1),
            vsync: this,
        );

Console
```

Financial Fraud Detection

Null safety no issues

LITERATURE REVIEW

Dealing with credit and debit card difficulties may require a full understanding of fraud detection technology. The empirical analysis of Bolton and Hand (2002) examines the difficulties and issues related with fraud detection investigations in depth. The authors present an empirical review of a wide range of challenges and issues in fraud detection inquiry. Behdad et al. (2012) investigated the most basic forms of credit card fraud as well as current nature-inspired monitoring solutions. "Application fraud and behavior fraud are the two types of credit and debit card fraud" (Bolton & Hand, 2001)." When thieves obtain new credit cards from issuing institutions, they commit fraud by giving false information or using the information of other approved cardholders" (Ileberi et al., 2022). Criminals steal the genuine cardholder's username and password and use them to make purchases of goods and services. Srivastava et al. (2008) demonstrated the efficacy of a hidden Markov model (HMM) in fraud detection by replicating the sequence of transactional features in credit card transaction processing. An HMM is trained using the cardholder's frequent behavior. If the trained HMM does not recognize the present transaction with a high probability, it is considered fraudulent. Mota et al. (2014) developed an innovative approach to preventing fraudulent online business application submissions. These researchers developed a signature-based method for gathering a client's behavioral anomalies and, as a result, detecting potentially fraudulent circumstances in real time. They only regard the clickstream to be a signature element in any case. "It is assumed that considering a variety of numerous transaction attributes rather than depending on a single transaction feature is superior for fraud detection" (Gee, 2015). In order to detect credit card fraud, Sahin and Duman (2011) contrasted decision trees with support vector machines (SVM). A dataset was separated into three categories, each with a different proportion of fraudulent vs lawful transactions. Following that, they created seven decision trees and SVM models. According to their findings, the decision tree model outscored the SVM model. SVM-based models may reach the same accuracy as decision tree-based models as the number of training sets increases. Xuan et al (2018), on the other hand, used a random forest as a classifier. The increased use of credit cards for both online and offline payments has also resulted in an increase in fraud rates. As a result, detecting fraudulent transactions has become increasingly difficult. Traditional and automated detection procedures are not only time-consuming but also inaccurate, rendering them ineffectual. As a result of the introduction of data analytics, financial institutions are now employing creative solutions to the problem. The two types of fraud detection systems are unsupervised and supervised fraud detection systems." Unsupervised learning flags transactions as potentially fraudulent, but supervised learning evaluates the type of new transaction using both fraudulent and valid data" (Domingues, 2015). Several investigations using diverse approaches have been attempted to overcome this challenge." Neural networks, Intelligent Decision Engines, Meta-learning agents, Bayesian networks, Support Vector Machines, and Adaptive Learning are just a few of the methodologies available. The credit card's performance was evaluated using logistic regression, K-nearest neighbors, random forest, naive Bayes, multilayer perception, quadrant discriminative analysis, pipelining, and ensemble learning" (Bagga et al., 2020). Zhang et al. (2018) introduced a convolutional neural network-based online transaction fraud detection model that produces an input feature sequencing layer that reconfigures raw activity features to produce distinct convolutional patterns. These authors opined that when different feature combinations are input into the convolution kernel, this model yields distinct derivative features. This model offers the advantage of employing non-derivative, low-dimensional online transaction data as input." A feature processing layer, four convolutions and pooling layers, as well as a fully linked layer, make up the network. The experimental findings revealed that the model delivers excellent fraud detection performance without the use of derived features when tested against electronic payment data from a financial institution. When compared to the current CNN for fraud detection, its precision and recall may be stabilised at around 91 percent and 94 percent, respectively, a 26 percent and 2 percent increase" (Zhang et al., 2018).

Dai et al. (2016) proposed a general process for identifying online credit card fraud that takes into account the majority of current financial fraud detection system design ideas. The authors built a new framework with four layers such as a shared storage layer, a batch training layer, a key-value sharing layer, and a streaming detection layer. These authors were able to handle massive trade data storage, effective model training, rapid model data transfer, and real-time online fraud detection using these four layers. Mubalaike and Adali (2018) investigated how deep learning (DL) models could be used to accurately detect fraudulent transactions. The authors employed an ensemble of decision trees (EDT), deep learning techniques such as stacked auto-encoders (SAE), and Restricted Boltzmann Machines (RBM) classifiers on a dataset acquired from one month of actual financial records from an African mobile financial service provider. Several model diagnostic tools were used to assess the performance of the created classifier models. The restricted Boltzmann machine clearly surpasses the other approaches based on the observed optimal accuracy findings. A logistic model is another type of regression and classification tree. "This approach combines decision tree learning methods with logistic regression (LR)" (Bui et al. (2016, Fayaz et al., 2022). For a variety of reasons, tree-based models are favoured over rival models for risk mitigation. The first point is that, unlike other models like logistic regression, tree-based models do not require as much supervised learning, making them easier to handle. Tree-based models, in contrast to regression models, are stronger at handling categories of data. "The LMT is an aggregation model that has better accuracy and coverage than single decision trees" (Colkesen & Kavzoglu, 2017; Ghosh & Kumar, 2013; Widodo et al., 2013). This is due to the fact that ensemble models need the production of numerous models rather than just one. Combining the models into a single generalised model has a smaller impact on outliers in the training data.

METHODS AND PROCEDURES

The researchers' major goal was to employ deep learning technology to detect and classify financial crime in South African banking institutions, as previously mentioned. A LTM is applied to accurately identify and categorise fraudulent transactions from non-fraudulent transactions in order to achieve this goal. Although classifiers are complicated, Tsangaratos and Ilia (2016) propose that the size of the training set be considered when completing this assignment. For a d-dimensional classification problem with C categories, a minimum of 10 d C training samples should be used. "The higher the d-dimensions of the dataset, the more complex the model becomes, and bigger training sets are required. The model's complexity, however, is proportional to (1) the number of variables used in its creation and (2) the size of the training set. The latter is more important in terms of learning. These two traits are related in some way, and their combination presents an excellent scenario for the existing model" (Tsangaratos & Ilia, 2016; Costanzo et al., 2012).

The Logistic Model Tree

A LogitBoost approach is utilized to generate a logistic regression model at each tree node, as described by Chen et al. (2017). The tree is then trimmed using the categorization and regression tree (CART) technique of Breiman et al. (1984)." The LMT uses cross-validation to identify numerous LogitBoost rounds to avoid over-fitting the training set" (Chen et al., 2017). This study takes a fresh look at the combination of tree induction and logistic regression by employing the LogitBoost algorithm. The iterative fitting of basic linear regression is interleaved with data splits. "LogitBoost creates a logistic model by iterative refinement, gradually adding further variables, when new linear models $L_M(X)$ are added to the committee of X_i" (Landwehr et al., 2003). In a recursive manner, the purpose is to divide the iterative fitting technique into branches that correspond to subsets of the data. As a result of partitioning, a tree structure can be constructed automatically.

The LogitBoost algorithm, according to Doetsch et al. (2009), employs cumulative least-squares estimates from the logistic regression on each M_i class. The LMT model is estimated according to the author as:

$$L_M(X) = \sum_{i=1}^{n} \beta_0 \beta_i X_i, \tag{1}$$

Who defined β_i as the coefficient of the ith component of vector x, and n is the number of factors. "Linear logistic regression is estimated to produce and compute posterior probabilities of leaf nodes in the LM (Fayaz et al., 2021).

Agresti (2018) and Stokes et al. (2012) calculated posterior probability as follows:

$$P(M \mid X) = \frac{\exp\left(L_M\left(X\right)\right)}{\sum_{M'=1}^{D} \exp\left(L_{M'}\left(X\right)\right)}, \tag{2}$$

with D representing the number of classes. See, for example, Pham and Prakash (2019), Pourghasemi et al. (2018), and Kamarudin et al. (2017) for more information on the LogitBoost algorithm.

Cross-Validation

A weird link exists between the test error rate and the training error rate. "The test error rate is the average error that arises when a statistical learning technique is used to estimate the response on a new observation" (James et al., 2013). That is, it is a metric that is not considered throughout the training. A thorough statistical learning technique is justified if the test error is minimal. If a specified test set is provided, the test error can be simply established. Unfortunately, this is a common occurrence. On the other hand, the training error may be easily measured using the statistical learning approach and the training observations. According to James et al. (2013), the training and test error rates are significantly different. The former frequently underestimates the latter Unavailability of a substantial predetermined test set from which to directly measure the test error rate, multiple methods for projecting it using a preexisting training set are accessible. In order to estimate the test error rate, various ways use math concepts to adjust the training error rate. The authors apply a Bayesian Leave-One-Out Cross-Validation (LOOCV) method, similar to that used by Magnusso et al. (2020) in their empirical analysis. "LOOCV is a cross-validation technique in which each observation acts as a validation set and the remaining n-1 observations serve as a training set. LOOCV uses a single set of observational validations to fit models and make predictions. As an affirmation set, the process is repeated N times per observation. After one observation is eliminated, this technique builds the LMT on the rest of the dataset. The model is then evaluated against the missing data point, and the prediction's test error is recorded. The total prediction error is calculated by averaging the test error estimates for all data points" (Kaplan, 2021). The model is estimated, and the measured values are predicted. The number of folds in this form of K-fold cross-validation is directly proportional to the number of observations ($K=N$). "By decreasing bias and unpredictability, the LOOCV approach aims to minimize the mean squared error rate (MSER) and prevent overfitting" (Bürkner et al., 2020). This strategy, like the validation set strategy, separates the dataset into two sections. Bürkner et al. (2020) added that the set is verified by a single observation (x_1, y_1), whereas the training set is composed of the remaining observations $\{(x_2, y_2), \ldots, (x_n, y_n)\}$. A deep learning procedure fits $n-1$

training observations, and predictions $\hat{y}_1$ are formed using that value x_1 on omitted observations. Because the fitting process did not entail (x_1,y_1); A single observation (x_1,y_1), verifies the set, while the remaining observations $\{(x_2,y_2), ..., (x_n,y_n)\}$ from the training set. A deep learning process fits $n-1$ training observations, and omitted observations x_1 are used to produce predictions $\hat{y}_1$. Because (x_1,y_1) was not included in the fitting process;

$$MSER_1 = \left(y_1 - \hat{y}_1\right)^2, \tag{3}$$

provides a somewhat accurate measure of test error. Despite being neutral for the test error, $MSER_1$ is an insufficient estimate because it is dependent on a single observation (x_1,y_1) and has great diversity. This is remedied by repeating the method n times, yielding n squared errors like $MSER_1, ..., MSER_n$.

The aggregate of these n test error estimates, as per James et al. (2013), is the LOOCV estimate for the test MSER;

$$CV_n = \frac{1}{n}\sum_{i=1}^{n} MSER_i \tag{4}$$

Bürkner et al. (2020) obtained the MSE (Mean squared error) by fitting the entire dataset;

$$CV_n = \frac{1}{n}\sum_{i=1}^{n}\left(\frac{y_i - \hat{y}_i}{1 - h_i}\right)^2, \tag{5}$$

"where $\hat{y}_i$ is defined as the ith fitted value from the original least-squares fit, and h_i represents the amount of influence an observation has on its fit, ranging from 0 to 1 punishing the residual because it divides by a tiny integer and h_i raises the residual value" (Bürkner et al., 2020).

Evaluation of the Performance of the Logit-Based EWS Model

"One of the most useful methods for evaluating the performance of the proposed classifier is the receiver operating characteristic (ROC) curve. With varying cut-off criteria, the ROC curve is formed by sensitivity on the Y-axis and 1-specificity on the X-axis" (Chen et al., 2017). The area under the ROC curve indicates how well the model can predict fraud (AUC). "AUC 1 indicates that the estimated classifier is flawless in all other respects, while 0 implies that the classifier is non-informative" (Bui et al., 2016). According to Khattak (2017), quoted by Ileberi et al. (2022), the correlation between accuracy rate and AUC can be categorised as excellent (0.9-1), very good (0.8-0.9), good (0.7-0.8), moderate (0.6-0.7), and mediocre (0.6-0.7). (0.5-0.6). The current study uses the AUC standard errors. Hussin et al. (2016) asserts that the classifier fares better when the expected standard error is minimal. In addition, predictive accuracy (ACC) has been routinely utilized to assess model forecasting accuracy. The ACC represents the percentage of fraud and non-fraud correctly classified by the classifiers. The "Confusion or Contingency Matrix" shown in Table 1 is used to complete this activity.

Table 1. Probabilities of correct and incorrect predicted daily frauds

	Frauds	No Frauds
Signal Issued	P(1, 1) Correct call of fraud [A]	P(1, 2) Type II Error or Wrong Signal [B]
No Signal Issued	P(2, 1) Type I error or Missing Signal [C]	P(2, 2) Correct call for non-event [D]

In Table 1, event A denotes the occurrence of an online scam when the model predicts it. Occasion B describes a condition in which a model's sign is not followed by a fraud event, i.e. a false sign. It's also possible that the model misses a fraud (due to a low assessed likelihood), but one happens nevertheless, e.g., missing sign, event C. Finally, Occasion D shows what happens when the model fails to forecast fraud and there is no fraud. A 50% threshold is used in this chapter to determine if the probabilities can now be decoded as financial fraud signals. The accompanying presentation standards proposed by Kaminsky et al. (1998) are used to evaluate the early warning system model's performance. Probability of frauds correctly called (PFCC): $\dfrac{A}{B+C}$

1. Probability of non-frauds correctly called (PNFCC): $\dfrac{D}{B+D}$

2. Probability of observations correctly called (POCC): $\dfrac{A}{A+B+C+D}$

3. Probability of an event of fraud given a signal (PRGS): $\dfrac{A}{B+A}$

4. Probability of an event of fraud given no signal (PRGNS): $\dfrac{C}{D+C}$

5. Probability of false frauds to total fraud (PFF): $\dfrac{B}{B+A}$

EMPIRICAL ANALYSIS

In this section, the empirical analysis of the data sets is provided and discussed. Using crowd-labeled and Webb-scraped credit and debit cards used in South Africa, the logistic model tree is trained to rate the reliability of online transaction content. As presented in Table 2, the dataset is considerably skewed, with 792 frauds out of 154653. This means that in South Africa, only 0.512 percent of fraud cases are recorded. The skewed distribution is further justified by the reduced rate of fraudulent transactions.

Preparation of Training and Validation Datasets

The obtained dataset is subjected to a principal component analysis for security reasons, yielding 31 principal components. The dataset contains 154653 observations with 35 characteristics, such as the cardholder's gender, age, and type of online transaction. Table 2 displays the findings of an exploratory data analysis, including the number of fraudulent and legitimate transactions discovered. According to the estimated mean for fraudulent transactions, South Africans lose approximately R646 per day as a direct consequence of online and mobile transactions.

Table 2. Exploratory data analysis

	Total No	Mean	Std
Valid Transactions	153861	88.29	250.10
Fraud Transactions	792	646.21	256.68

The Logistic Model Tree

To begin the investigation, a logistic model tree is created, assuming that every transaction is legitimate and that the LogitBoost algorithm is correct 95 percent to 99 percent of the time, costing South African debit and credit cardholders approximately 211.3 million Rands over the sample period of this chapter; otherwise, the classifiers would be useless. A backward stepwise selection approach is also used, as described by James et al. (2013). This method is a well-organised alternative for selecting the most important subset. Backward stepwise selection, in contrast to forward stepwise selection, begins with a full least squares model with all p predictors and then eliminates the less significant predictors one by one. Algorithm 2 contains more information. Table 8 in the appendix contains the findings of this technique, which includes 17 major components as factors reflecting important predictors of financial fraud in South African banking institutions. An LMT is used to classify the possibility of a fraudulent or non-fraudulent credit or debit card transaction. Appendix Table 8 contains additional information.

The Performance Evaluation of the Logistic Model Tree EWS Model

The key findings of the logistic model tree are summarised in Table 3. According to the results, the model has some EWS potential. Based on the training set estimates, the model can correctly predict 65 percent of credit and debit card frauds and 0.1 percent of credit and debit card no-frauds. The proportion of frauds in the training sample is 0.42 percent, while it is 3.03 percent in the validation sample. Table 4 shows that the percentage of false frauds is low, with 0.10 percent in the training set and 0.68 percent in the validation data.

Table 3. Probabilities of correct and incorrect predicted daily financial fraud.

In-sample Forecasts	Frauds			Non-frauds		Total
Predicted	**Frauds**	645	(65%)	153508		154153
	Non-Frauds	353		147	(0.10%)	500
Total		998		153655		154653
Out-of-sample Forecasts	Frauds			Non-frauds		Total
Predicted	**Frauds**	400	(79%)	12809		13209
	Non-Frauds	105		87	(0.68%)	192
Total		505		12896		13401

The first set of numbers represents counts while figures in parentheses represent percentages of correctly predicted financial frauds.

According to Table 4, there is a 79% chance of fraudulent transactions in the next ten years, which is 14% higher than the current situation. This is not an unusual observation, as the novel coronavirus (COVID-19) emerged and threatened physical and mental health, causing individuals, organizations, and institutions all over the world to change their behavior and decision-making processes. According to Ma and McKinnon (2021), as a result, numerous services have moved online, while others are still moving to the digital economy and others will be online in the future. According to the authors, cyber fraud is also on the rise as a result of the COVID-19 pandemic. However, the findings indicate that future investment losses in the countries' financial markets are possible. The PFF to total alarm ratio is predicted to be 0.68 percent, which is 0.58 percent higher than the in-sample estimates. The percentage of correctly called non-frauds out of sample is 0.68 percent, which is 0.58 percent higher than the in-sample projections. Financial fraud, after all, may become more common in the future. As a result, to reduce the frequency of financial scams, a comprehensive fraud detection system is required.

Table 4. Performance of the EWS

	In-sample Forecasts	Out-of-sample Forecast
PFCC	65%	79%
PNFCC	0.01%	0.68
POCC	0.42%	2,98%
PRGS	0.42%	3.03%
PRGNS	29%	55%
PFF	0.10%	0.68%

Evaluation of the Classification Experiment

To reduce variability, a leave-one-out cross-validation approach is used. The overall validation set error rate is 19.52399 as a result of the cross-validation approach used, with an average accuracy score of 83 percent. Table 5 displays the model's ACC and AUC values derived from a training set and validation data. In terms of ACC and AUC, the LMT-based EWS model performs well, with values of 0.9995 and 0.9875, respectively. For more information, see Table 5 and Figure 3. The three statistics that were observed were the Standard Error (Std. Error), the 95 percent confidence interval (CI), and the observed probability (p). The observed confidence intervals (CIs) are narrow, with small standard errors and ps. The model with a training set has a satisfactory goodness-of-fit, according to these findings. As a result, the LMT approach appears to be effective and has demonstrated good prediction ability, as evidenced by the highest observed ACC score of 0.999 and AUC score of 0.9885 in the validation data.

Table 5. Performance of the LMT

Parameters	Training set	Validation data
ACC	0.9995	0.9990
AUC	0.9875	0.9885
Error Rate		19.52399%

Finally, the statistical significance of the model is determined by performing a pair-wise comparison on training and validation data using the Wilcoxon signed-rank and model power test procedures. Chen et al. (2017) and Bui et al. (2016) used the former, while Makatjane and Moroke used the latter (2016). At a 95% confidence level, the null hypothesis states that the model is not statistically different from zero. The model's significance is also evaluated using z and p-values. In terms of the model's true prediction capacity, a mean difference is calculated and used to complete this assignment. The null hypothesis is rejected when z values exceed the critical value of (± 1.96) and p-values are less than the significant threshold of (0.05), indicating that the model worked well. The results of the Wilcoxon signed-rank and power tests are shown in Table 6. The model differs significantly from zero (p-value=0.0001, z-value=6.53), indicating a good fit for the logistic model tree-based EWS model. This model's AUC and ACC are both high, indicating that it correctly identified financial fraud transactions in South African financial data. The model passes the power test with a score of 92.41 percent, indicating that it matches the data well.

Figure 3. Sensitivity and specificity curves of the logistic model tree

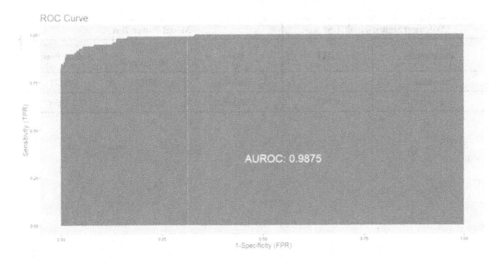

Sensitivity and Detection Rate Analysis

In an ideal world, the computed probabilities for all correctly classified (also known as ones) should be greater than the estimated probabilities for all negatives for the same model (also known as zeros). Concordance and discordance can be used to quantify this phenomenon. Concordance is simply the percentage of 1-0 pair combinations in which the actual positives outperform the actual negatives (actual). For a perfect model, this will be 100 percent; as a result, the higher the concordance, the higher the model's quality. The estimated EWS model is a good model for uncovering financial fraud in South Africa, with an AUC of 98.75 percent on a training set and 98.85 percent on a validation set, as well as a Concordance of 88.89 percent on a training set and 87.90 percent on a validation set. Finally, a training set has a true detection rate of 98.56 percent, while a validation set has a true detection rate of 99.36 percent. The detection prevalence obtained for both the training and validation sets is over 97 percent. This means that the estimated model is the most accurate predictor of financial fraud in South Africa. According to the confusion matrix in Table 3, only 500 incorrect predictions were made, with 353 false positives and 147 false negatives. Although increasing the number of incorrect answers from 353 to 500 is not a significant performance improvement, the importance of sensitivity and specificity in real-world applications is considered, as shown in Table 7. Are the ramifications of a false negative more severe than those of a false positive? Lenders cannot operate if they classify every transaction as fraudulent. Before deciding whether or not to approve the applications, a brief overview must be completed. It may be impossible to do so because the prices would be prohibitively high.

Table 6. Pair-wise comparison and power test

Wilcoxon Signed-Rank Test		Model Power Test		
Parameters	**LMT**	**Data**	**Mean Difference**	**Actual Power**
z-value	6.53	**Training**	-0.0194	0.9241
p-value	0.001	**Validation**	0.0298	0.8956

Table 7. Sensitivity performance

Parameters	Training Set	Validation Set
AUC	0.9875	0.9885
ACC	0.9995	0.9990
Accuracy	0.9891	0.9991
Sensitivity	0.9888	0.9810
Specificity	0.8530	0.8628
Concordance	0.8889	0.8790
Prevalence	0.9776	0.9967
Detection Rate	0.9856	0.9936
Detection Prevalence	0.9872	0.9959
Balanced Accuracy	0.9168	0.9056

DISCUSSION AND RECOMMENDATIONS

Credit and debit card fraud is the fraudulent use of a payment card, such as a credit card or a debit card. It could be to receive goods or services, or it could be to make a payment to a criminally controlled account. The Payment Card Industry Data Security Standard (PCI DSS) is a data security standard designed to assist financial institutions in handling card payments more securely while reducing fraud. When a legitimate customer makes a payment to a criminally controlled account, this is considered authorized credit card fraud, whereas unauthorised credit card fraud occurs when the account holder does not provide authorization for the payment to proceed, and the transaction is completed by a third party. This study used a LMT to calculate the chance of future occurrence of credit and debit card fraud to supplement the financial sectors' current toolbox in the evaluation and detection of the financial fraud environment and the risk of credit and debit card perspective. As presented in literature, the LogitbBoost method is used to build the early warning system model, which employs the LMT to identify the main predictors of financial fraud in South African banks. To the best of the authors' knowledge, only a few studies in South Africa have attempted to detect financial fraud efficiently and develop a map of the likelihood of early warning indicators for fraudulent financial behavior in the banking system.

The analysis made use of 17 different financial conditioning elements, including slope. The authors used ACC values, ROC curves, AUC values, standard error, 95 percent confidence interval, and significance level to evaluate model performance. The EWS paradigm appears to perform admirably in this case study. This model has the highest predictive capacity in this regard, with success and prediction rates of 99.95 percent and 99.9 percent, respectively. This is a useful method for detecting vulnerability to internet scams before they occur. According to Credit card fraud consumer action (2022), approximately half of all Americans have experienced a fraudulent transaction on their credit or debit card, and more than one in every three credit or debit cardholders has been a victim of fraud multiple times. This equates to 127 million Americans who have experienced credit card fraud at least once. This is significant in light of the study's findings, which predict an increase in fraudulent transactions in South Africa over the next ten years based on out-of-sample warning indicators indicating a high risk of fraud in both credit and debit card users. According to Table 4, the risk of fraud is 55% when there is no signal. To avoid such a massive loss, fraud detection systems should be kept up to date at all times, as this will have an impact on the South African banking sector. Makatjane and Tsoku (2022) recommend that linked risk factors be included when developing risk and fraud algorithms.

SOLUTIONS AND RECOMMENDATIONS

Fraud detection is a challenging problem that requires substantial planning before using machine learning or artificial intelligence solutions. Regardless, the utilization of data science and machine learning to assure the safety and security of a customer's assets is noteworthy. Financial risk mitigation and management planning are crucial in today's financial society and economy. To overcome these concerns, a highly automated early warning system for online transactions, as well as Google Flutter devices for people who would use them, should be built. However, a Chrome plugin for individuals and banks will be created. Cardholders will be able to track down lost or stolen cards and prevent transactions without having to contact their bank or card issuer. These proposed systems will also automatically notify banks of suspicious transactions and train the system in real time, eliminating the need for the cardholder to validate whether or not the transaction was fraudulent. The authors do, however, recommend that banks change the way their ATMs (also known as automatic teller machines) request the personal identification numbers from their cards (PINs). According to the research, before processing the transaction, the bank should ask cardholders personal questions or provide one-time pin (OTP) numbers. Finally, the conclusions of this chapter may be useful to South African financial decision-makers in terms of future use and planning in credit and debit-prone locations.

CONCLUSION

South Africa's financial commerce is a significant source of revenue. A good trade balance benefits South Africa's financials, but credit and debit card fraud harms the economy and banking industry. Global financial fraud has increased for South Africa in absolute terms. However, as the EWS model results show, the significance of financial fraud as a contributor to a digitalized economy has grown dramatically in recent years. With the positive COVID-19 pandemic and e-commerce, South Africa will see an increase in credit and debit card usage. South Africa's economy is evolving from a traditional method of trading with the rest of the world to a more sophisticated digital economy that relies heavily on online transactions. This deception contributes nothing to economic growth, which raises living standards in the financial sector and other sectors of the economy. Credit and debit cardholders need more training and awareness about financial fraud and how to avoid it, as well as instructions on how to use the EWS application that will be developed using the algorithms in this chapter.

ACKNOWLEDGMENT

The authors are crateful for the anonymous reviewers of this chapter for their positive and constructive comments and suggestions.

REFERENCES

Abdallah, A., Maarof, M. A., & Zainal, A. (2016). Fraud Detection System: A survey. *Journal of Network and Computer Applications*, *68*, 90–113. doi:10.1016/j.jnca.2016.04.007

Agresti, A. (2018). *An Introduction to Categorical Data Analysis* (3rd ed.). John Wiley and Sons. https://www.wiley.com/ en-us/ An + Introduction +to+ Categorical + Data + Analysis %2C +3rd+ Edition -p- 9781 1194 05283

Albshrawi, M., & Lowell, M. (2016). Detecting Financial Fraud using Data Mining Techniques: A Decade Review from 2004 to 2015. *Journal of Data Science: JDS*, *14*(3), 553–569. doi:10.6339/JDS.201607_14(3).0010

Bagga, S., Goyal, A., Gupta, N., & Goyal, A. (2020). Credit Card Fraud Detection using Pipeling and Ensemble Learning. *International Conference on Smart Sustainable Intelligent Computing and Applications under ICITETM2020. Procedia Computer Science, 173*, 104–112. doi:10.1016/j.procs.2020.06.014

Behdad, M., Barone, L., Bennamoun, M., & French, T. (2012). Nature-inspired Techniques in the Context of Fraud Detection. *IEEE Transactions on Systems, Man and Cybernetics. Part C, Applications and Reviews, 42*(6), 1273–1290. doi:10.1109/TSMCC.2012.2215851

Bolton, R. J., & Hand, D. J. (2001). Unsupervised Profiling Methods for Fraud Detection. *Proc Credit Scoring and Credit Control, 7*, 5–7. http://citeseerx.ist.psu.edu/viewdoc/summary?doi=10.1.1.24.5743

Bolton, R. J., & Hand, D. J. (2002). Statistical Fraud Detection: A Review. *Statistical Science, 17*(3), 235–249. doi:10.1214/ss/1042727940

Breiman, L., Friedman, J. H., Ohlsen, R., & Stone, C. J. (1984). *Classiðcation and Regression Trees*. Chapman and Hall/CRC.

Budhram, T. (2012). Lost, stolen, or skimmed: Overcoming Credit Card Fraud in South Africa. *South African Crime Quarterly, 40*(40), 31–37. doi:10.17159/2413-3108/2012/v0i40a843

Bui, D. T., Tuan, T. A., Klempe, H., Pradhan, B., & Revhaug, I. (2016). Spatial Prediction Model for shallow Landslide Hazards: A Comparative Assessment of the Efficacy of Support Vector Machines, Artificial Neural Networks, Kernel Logistic Regression, and Logistic Model Tree. *Landslides, 13*(2), 361–378. doi:10.100710346-015-0557-6

Bürkner, P. C., Gabry, J., & Vehtari, A. (2020). Approximate leave-future-out cross-validation for Bayesian time series models. *Journal of Statistical Computation and Simulation, 90*(14), 2499–2523. doi:10.1080/00949655.2020.1783262

Chen, W., Xie, X., Wang, J., Pradhan, B., Hong, H., Bui, D. T., Duan, Z., & Ma, J. (2017). A Comparative Study of Logistic Model Tree, Random Forest, and Classification and Regression Tree Models for Spatial Prediction of Landslide Susceptibility. *Catena, 151*, 147–160. doi:10.1016/j.catena.2016.11.032

Colkesen, I., & Kavzoglu, T. (2017). The Use of Logistic Model Tree (LMT) for Pixel-and-Object-Based Classifications Using High-Resolution WorldView-2 Imagery. *Geocarto International, 32*(1), 71–86. doi:10.1080/10106049.2015.1128486

Costanzo, D., Rotigliano, E., Irigaray-Fernández, C., Jiménez-Perálvarez, J. D., & Chacón Montero, J. (2012). Factors Selection in Landslide Susceptibility Modelling on Large Scale following the GIS Matrix Method: Application to the River Beirobasin (Spain). *Natural Hazards and Earth System Sciences, 12*(2), 327–340. doi:10.5194/nhess-12-327-2012

Credit Card Fraud Consumer Action. (2022). *Consumer Action Report.* Retrieved 13 May 2022 at https://www.consumer-action.org/

Cybersource. (2021). *2021 Global Fraud Report.* https://www.cybersource.com/content/ dam/ documents/ campaign/ global-fraud-report-2021.pdf

Dai, Y., Yan, J., Tang, X., Zhao, H., & Guo, M. (2016). August. Online Credit Card Fraud Detection: A Hybrid Framework with big data technologies. 2016 IEEE Trustcom/BigDataSE/ISPApp, 1644-1651. doi:10.1109/TrustCom.2016.0253

Doetsch, P., Buck, C., Golik, P., Hoppe, N., Kramp, M., Laudenberg, J., Oberdörfer, C., Steingrube, P., Forster, J., & Mauser, A. (2009). Logistic Model Trees with AUCSPLIT CRITERION for the KDDCup2009 Small Challenge. *KDD-Cup 2009 Competition,* 77–88. https://proceedings.mlr.press/v7/doetsch09.html

Domingues, R. (2015). *Machine Learning for Unsupervised Fraud Detection* [Thesis]. Royal Institute of Technology. Retrieved from http://urn.kb.se/ resolve ?urn= urn:nbn :se: kth:diva -181027

Fayaz, S. A., Zaman, M., & Butt, M. A. (2021). An application of logistic model tree (LMT) algorithm to ameliorate Prediction accuracy of meteorological data. *International Journal of Advanced Technology and Engineering Exploration, 8*(84), 1424–1440. doi:10.19101/IJATEE.2021.874586

Fayaz, S. A., Zaman, M., & Butt, M. A. (2022). Is Deep Learning on Tabular Data Enough? An Assessment. *International Journal of Advanced Computer Science and Applications, 13*(4), 466–473. doi:10.14569/IJACSA.2022.0130454

Gee, S. (2015). Fraud and Fraud Detection, A data analytics approach. John Wiley and Sons, Inc.

Ghosh, S., & Kumar, S. (2013). Comparative Analysis of K-Means and Fuzzy C-Means Algorithms. *International Journal of Advanced Computer Science and Applications, 4*(4), 35–39. doi:10.14569/IJACSA.2013.040406

Hassani, H., Gheitanchi, S., & Yogini, M. R. (2010). On the Application of Data Mining to Official Data. *Journal of Data Science: JDS, 8*(1), 75–89. doi:10.6339/JDS.2010.08(1).578

Hussin, H. Y., Zumpano, V., Reichenbach, P., Sterlacchini, S., Micu, M., van Westen, C., & Balteanu, D. (2016). 'Different Landslide Sampling Strategies in a Grid-based Bi-variate Statistical Susceptibility Model. *Geomorphology, 253*(15), 508–523. doi:10.1016/j.geomorph.2015.10.030

Ileberi, E., Sun, Y., & Wang, Z. (2022). A machine learning-based credit card fraud detection using the ga algorithm for feature selection. *Journal of Big Data, 9*(1), 24. doi:10.118640537-022-00573-8

James, G., Witten, D., Hastie, T., & Tibshirani, R. (2013). *An Introduction to Statistical Learning.* Springer. doi:10.1007/978-1-4614-7138-7

Jayakumar, G. D. S., & Thomas, B. J. (2013). A New Procedure of Clustering Based on Multivariate Outlier Detection. *Journal of Data Science: JDS, 11*(1), 69–84. doi:10.6339/JDS.2013.11(1).1091

Kamarudin, M. H., Maple, C., Watson, T., & Safa, N. S. (2017). A LogitBoost-based Algorithm for Detecting Known and unknown Web Attacks. *IEEE Access: Practical Innovations, Open Solutions, 5*, 26190–26200. doi:10.1109/ACCESS.2017.2766844

Kaminsky, G., Lizondo, S., & Reinhart, C. M. (1998). Leading Indicators of Currency Crises. *Staff Papers, 45*(1), 1–48. doi:10.2307/3867328

Kaplan, D. (2021). On the Quantification of Model Uncertainty: A Bayesian Perspective. *Psychometrika, 86*(1), 215–238. doi:10.100711336-021-09754-5 PMID:33721184

Khattak, F. K. (2017). *Toward a Robust and Universal Crowd Labeling Framework* [Doctoral dissertation]. Columbia University. doi:10.7916/D8Q24BJ2

Landwehr, N., Hall, M., & Frank, E. (2003). Logistic Model Trees. In N. Lavrač, D. Gamberger, H. Blockeel, & L. Todorovski (Eds.), Lecture Notes in Computer Science: Vol. 2837. *Machine Learning: ECML 2003. ECML 2003.* Springer. doi:10.1007/978-3-540-39857-8_23

Ma, K. W. F., & McKinnon, T. (2021). COVID-19 and cyber fraud: Emerging threats during the pandemic. *Journal of Financial Crime, 29*(2), 433–446. doi:10.1108/JFC-01-2021-0016

Magnusson, M., Vehtari, A., Jonasson, J., & Andersen, M. (2020). Leave-one-out cross-validation for Bayesian model comparison in large data. *International Conference on Artificial Intelligence and Statistics.* 341-351. http://proceedings.mlr.press/v108/magnusson20a.html

Makatjane, K., & Tsoku, T. (2022). Bootstrapping Time-Varying Uncertainty Intervals for Extreme Daily Return Periods. *International Journal of Financial Studies, 10*(1), 10. doi:10.3390/ijfs10010010

Makatjane, K. D., & Moroke, N. D. (2016), Comparative study of Holt-Winters Triple Exponential Smoothing and Seasonal ARIMA: Forecasting Short-Term Seasonal Car Sales in South Africa. *Risk Governance and Control: Financial Markets and Institutions, 6*(1), 71–82. https://virtusinterpress.org/-2016-Issue-1-.html

Mori, Y., Kuroda, M., & Makino, N. (2016). *Nonlinear Principal Component Analysis and Its Applications.* Springer. www.springer.com/series/13497

Mota, G., Fernandes, J., & Belo, O. (2014). Usage signatures analysis is an alternative method for preventing fraud in E-Commerce applications. *International Conference on Data Science and Advanced Analytics,* 203-208. 10.1109/DSAA.2014.7058074

Mubalaike, A. M., & Adali, E. (2018). Deep Learning Approach for Intelligent Financial Fraud detection system. *2018 3rd International Conference on Computer Science and Engineering (UBMK),* 598-603. 10.1109/UBMK.2018.8566574

Pham, B. T., & Prakash, I. (2019). Evaluation and Comparison of LogitBoost Ensemble, Fisher's Linear Discriminant Analysis, Logistic Regression and Support Vector Machines Methods for Landslide Susceptibility Mapping. *Geocarto International, 34*(3), 316–333. doi:10.1080/10106049.2017.1404141

Pourghasemi, H. R., Gayen, A., Park, S., Lee, C. W., & Lee, S. (2018). 'Assessment of Landslide-prone Areas and their Zonation using Logistic Regression, LogitBoost, and Naïve Bayes Machine-learning Algorithms. *Sustainability, 10*(10), 3697. doi:10.3390u10103697

Pranckevicius, T., & Marcinkevicius, V. (2017). Comparison of Naïve Bayes, Random Forest, Decision Tree, Support Vector Machines, and Logistic Regression Classifiers for Text Reviews Classification'. *Baltic Journal of Modern Computing, 5*(2), 221. doi:10.22364/bjmc.2017.5.2.05

Sahin, Y., & Duman, E. (2011). Detecting Credit Card Fraud by Decision Trees and Support Vector Machines. *Lecture Notes in Engineering and Computer Science, 2188*(1). https://hdl.handle.net/11376/2366

Seyedhossein, L., & Hashemi, M. R. (2010), Mining Information from Credit Card Time Series for Timelier Fraud Detection. *5th International Symposium on Telecommunications (IST'2010).* 10.1109/ISTEL.2010.5734099

South African Banking Risk Information Centre Report. (2019). *Annual Crime Stats 2019*. https://www.sabric.co.za/media-and-news/downloads/

Srivastava, A., Kundu, A., Sural, S., & Majumdar, A. (2008). Credit Card Fraud Detection using Hidden Markov Model. *IEEE Transactions on Dependable and Secure Computing*, *5*(1), 37–48. doi:10.1109/TDSC.2007.70228

Stokes, M. E., Davis, C. S., & Koch, G. G. (2012). *Categorical data analysis using SAS* (3rd ed.). https://www.amazon.com/ Categorical – Data – Analysis – Using - Third/dp/ 1607646641

Tsangaratos, P., & Ilia, I. (2016). Comparison of a Logistic Regression and Naïve Bayes Classifier in Landslide Susceptibility Assessments: The Influence of Models Complexity and Training sets Size. *Catena*, *145*, 164–179. doi:10.1016/j. catena.2016.06.004

Widodo, P. P., Handayanto, R. T., & Herlawati, H. (2013). Penerapan Data Mining Dengan Matlab. *Informatika*. https://elibrary.bsi.ac.id/ readbook/ 200622/ penerapan – data – mining – dengan - matlab

Xuan, S., Liu, G., Li, Z., Zheng, L., Wang, S., & Jiang, C. (2018). Random Forest for Credit Card Fraud Detection. In *2018 IEEE 15th International Conference on Networking, Sensing and Control (ICNSC)*. IEEE. 10.1109/ICNSC.2018.8361343

Zhang, Z., Zhou, X., Zhang, X., Wang, L., & Wang, P. (2018). A Model-based on Convolutional Neural Network for Online Transaction Fraud Detection. *Security and Communication Networks*, *2018*, 1–9. Advance online publication. doi:10.1155/2018/5680264

ADDITIONAL READING

Akinje, A. O., & Fuad, A. (2021). Fraudulent Detection Model Using Machine Learning Techniques for Unstructured Supplementary Service Data. *International Journal of Innovative Computing*, *11*(2), 51–60. doi:10.11113/ijic.v11n2.299

Al-Hashedi, K. G., & Magalingam, P. (2021). Financial fraud detection applying data mining techniques: A comprehensive review from 2009 to 2019. *Computer Science Review*, *40*, 100402. doi:10.1016/j.cosrev.2021.100402

Albashrawi, M. (2016). Detecting financial fraud using data mining techniques: A decade review from 2004 to 2015. *Journal of Data Science: JDS*, *14*(3), 553–569. doi:10.6339/JDS.201607_14(3).0010

Alfaiz, N. S., & Fati, S. M. (2022). Enhanced Credit Card Fraud Detection Model Using Machine Learning. *Electronics (Basel)*, *11*(4), 662. doi:10.3390/electronics11040662

Bhowmik, M., Sai Siri Chandana, T., & Rudra, B. (2021. Comparative Study of Machine Learning Algorithms for Fraud Detection in Blockchain. *5th International Conference on Computing Methodologies and Communication (ICCMC)*, 539-541. 10.1109/ICCMC51019.2021.9418470

Ileberi, E., Sun, Y., & Wang, Z. (2021). Performance Evaluation of Machine Learning Methods for Credit Card Fraud Detection Using SMOTE and AdaBoost. *IEEE Access: Practical Innovations, Open Solutions*, *9*, 165286–165294. doi:10.1109/ACCESS.2021.3134330

Mijwil, M. M., & Salem, I. E. (2020). Credit Card Fraud Detection in Payment Using Machine Learning Classifiers. *Asian Journal of Computer and Information Systems*, *8*(4). Advance online publication. https://orcid.org/0000-0002-2884-2504. doi:10.24203/ajcis.v8i4.6449

Reurink, A. (2018). Financial fraud: A literature review. *Journal of Economic Surveys*, *32*(5), 1292–1325. doi:10.1111/joes.12294

Sohony, I., Pratap, R., & Nambiar, U. (2018). Ensemble learning for credit card fraud detection. *Proceedings of the ACM India Joint International Conference on Data Science and Management of Data*, 289-294. 10.1145/3152494.3156815

Tae, C. M., & Hung, P. D. (2019). Comparing ML algorithms on financial fraud detection. *Proceedings of the 2019 2nd International Conference on Data Science and Information Technology*, 25-29. 10.1145/3352411.3352416

KEY TERMS AND DEFINITIONS

Area Under the Roc Curve: This is the measure of performance across all classification thresholds.

Classification: The established criteria or procedure to categorise or group together elements that are similar or dissimilar.

Crowd Labelling: A method that is applied to a large machine learning dataset to accurately find true labels.

Decision Trees: These are classification and regression supervised learning procedures based on a non-parametric approach.

Early Warning System: This is an adaptive measure that uses an integrated communication system to help in the preparation of hazardous climate-related events.

Fraud Detection: Procedures engaged with the aim to prevent money or proposer from being obtained through pretenses.

Logistic Model Trees: A family of discrete classification models that combines a logistic regression model and decision tree models.

LogitBoost: A branch of machine learning classification that applies the cost function of logistic regression.

Web Scraping: The procedure to obtain or extract data from websites.

APPENDIX

Algorithm 1: LogitBoost (*J* classes)

----

1. Start with weights $\omega_{ij} = \dfrac{1}{n}$, $i=1,\ldots,n$; $j=1,\ldots,J$; $F_j(x)=0$ and $p_j(x)=1/J \forall_j$

2. Repeat for $m=1,\ldots,M$:
   a) Repeat for $j=1,\ldots,J$:
      i. Compute working responses and weights in the jth class

$$z_{ij} = \frac{y_{ij}^{*} - P_{j(x_j)}}{P_{j(x_j)}\left(1-P_{j(x_j)}\right)}$$

$$\omega_{ij} = P_{j(x_j)}\left(1-P_{j(x_j)}\right)$$

      ii. Fit the function $f_{mj}(x)$ by a weighted least-squares regression of z_{ij} to X_i with weights ω_{ij}.
   b) Set

$$f_{mj}(x) \leftarrow \frac{J-1}{J}\left(f_{mj}(x) - \frac{1}{J}\sum_{k=1}^{J}f_{mj}(x)\right), F_j(x) \leftarrow F_j(x) + F_j(x)$$

   c) Update $p_j(x) = \dfrac{expF_j(x)}{\sum_{k=1}^{J}\exp F_k(x)}$

3. Output the classifier $F_j(x)$

Algorithm 2: Backward Stepwise Selection

----

1. Let M_p denote the full model, which contains all p predictors.
2. For $k=p, p-1,\ldots,1$:
   a) Consider all k models that contain all but one of the predictors in M_k, for a total of $k-1$ predictors.
   b) Choose the *best* among these k models, and call it M_{k-1}. Here *best* is defined as having the smallest RSS or highest R^2

3. Select a single best model from among $M_0, \ldots, M_p$ using cross-validated prediction error, C_p, AIC, BIC, or adjusted R^2.

Table 8. Logistic Model Tree Estimates

	Estimate	Std. Error	z value	Pr (>|z|)
Intercept	-11.59297	0.56359	-20.570	0.001
P2	0.97034	0.16135	6.014	0.001
P4	2.5051	0.26667	9.394	0.001
P5	1.17946	0.14110	8.359	0.001
P7	1.09164	0.13649	7.998	0.001
P8	-0.39848	0.04979	-8.003	0.001
P9	2.28317	0.34641	6.591	0.001
P10	-2.15369	0.23206	-9.281	0.001
P12	1.30902	0.30054	4.356	0.001
P13	-0.61980	0.18975	-3.266	0.02
P15	0.80611	0.19968	4.037	0.001
P16	-2.34563	0.36838	-6.367	0.001
P17	-1.36377	0.22136	-6.161	0.001
P18	1.99701	0.35711	5.592	0.001
P19	-1.17852	0.26091	-4.517	0.001
P20	-0.39459	0.18683	-2.112	0.05
P22	-0.88614	0.32182	-2.754	0.02
P26	1.60504	0.57022	2.815	0.02

Chapter 9
Innovative Legitimate Non-Traditional Doctorate Programs in Cybersecurity, Engineering, and Technology

Darrell Norman Burrell
ⓘD https://orcid.org/0000-0002-4675-9544
Marymount University, USA & Capitol Technology University, USA

Calvin Nobles
ⓘD https://orcid.org/0000-0003-4002-1108
Illinois Institute of Technology, USA

Maurice Dawson
ⓘD https://orcid.org/0000-0003-4609-3444
Illinois Institute of Technology, USA

Eugene J. M. Lewis
ⓘD https://orcid.org/0000-0002-2956-0760
Capitol Technology University, USA

S. Raschid Muller
ⓘD https://orcid.org/0000-0002-1742-7575
Capitol Technology University, USA

Kevin Richardson
Edward Waters University, USA

Amalisha S. Aridi
Capitol Technology University, USA

DOI: 10.4018/978-1-7998-9430-8.ch009

ABSTRACT

According to the US Federal Bureau of Investigations (FBI) the number of complaints about cyberattacks to their cyber division is up to as many as 4,000 a day. Every year in the U.S., 40,000 jobs for information security analysts go unfilled, and employers are struggling to fill 200,000 other cybersecurity-related roles. Colleges and universities have created certificate, undergraduate, and graduate programs to train professionals in these job roles. The challenge to meeting the cybersecurity workforce shortage through degree programs is intensified by the reality of the limited number of cybersecurity and engineering faculty at colleges and universities. This chapter explores the essential need to develop more doctorate faculty in technology-related areas and explains some unique and non-traditional paths to doctoral completion that allow professionals with significant real-world work experience to complete a doctorate without career interruption and relocation from highly respected and established universities in the US and the UK.

INTRODUCTION

According to the US Federal Bureau of Investigations ([FBI] 2021) the number of complaints about cyberattacks to their Cyber Division is up to as many as 4,000 a day. That represents 400% increase (FBI, 2021). The hack that took down the largest fuel pipeline in the U.S. and led to shortages across the East Coast was the result of a single compromised password, according to a cybersecurity consultant who responded to the attack (FBI, 2021). According to Newman (2016), the cybersecurity threat landscape is continually evolving as malicious cyber actors pursue new vectors to target and capitalize on newly discovered or known vulnerabilities. In 2017 a hacking group known as the Shadow Brokers, claiming to have breached the NSA-linked operation known as the Equation Group. The Shadow Brokers provided samples of the stolen data and attempted to auction off other stolen data (Newman, 2017).

In May of 2017, a strain ransomware virus call WannaCry attacked a series of public and private organizations including temporarily crippling technology-driven operations of several hospitals and medical facilities in the United Kingdom (Newman, 2017). In 2017 there where new revelations about hacking vulnerabilities cell phones, Windows, and the ability to turn some smart TVs into listening devices (Newman, 2017). The top industries targeted by cybercriminals are (1) healthcare, (2) manufacturing, (3) financial services, (4) government, and (5) transportation (Morgan, 2016). These industries are targeted for sensitive information primarily in the healthcare and financial services sectors. Researchers are forecasting the global cost of cybercrime in 2019 to reach over 2 trillion dollars (Morgan, 2016).

The global cybersecurity workforce will have more than 1.5 million unfilled positions by 2020 (Van- Zadelhoff, 2016). Every year in the U.S., 40,000 jobs for information security analysts go unfilled, and employers are struggling to fill 200,000 other cyber-security related roles (Kauflin, 2017). Threats of cyber-attacks have spurred global interest in protecting digital property from external intrusions. The identified risks to American private and public entities were part of an ongoing scenario that placed specific importance on secure, internal, cyber information (Pierce, 2016; Stevenson, 2017). This importance came about because many in the business market had echoed the need for a skilled workforce within cybersecurity, and numerous efforts were made to address those concerns (Pierce, 2016; Stevenson, 2017).

The need for cybersecurity was spearheaded by the rise in cybercrime (Pierce, 2016; Stevenson, 2017). Newman (2017) described cybercrime as the use of communication and information technologies to carry on illegal activity. Cybercrime activity was conducted with the utilization of devices including television, cellular phones, radios, computers, networks, or communication application (Newman, 2017). Newman (2017) noted that cybercrime was widespread and was not limited to petty and small crimes. Morgan (2016) and Newman (2017) indicated that cyber-attacks and malicious hackers have increased with multiple large corporations becoming victims of data breaches. Morgan (2016) noted firms were growing more dependent on cyber connectivity to remain relevant in an increasingly global market, and this has left many of them vulnerable. American organizations made changes to their IT infrastructure to deflect the onset of external threats from cybercriminals as they continued to grow (Van- Zadelhoff, 2016). Newman (2017) identified the cyber-attacks came from multiple sources with a variety of agendas. Newman (2017) noted the cyber threats were distinguished by intent and motivation of the attacker.

LITERATURE REVIEW

The onslaught of cyber-attacks enhanced the need to fill positions focused on the prevention of data breaches (Pierce, 2016; Stevenson, 2017). Besides, the shortage of skilled personnel provided a new dynamic to finding qualified workers that understood the complexities of cybersecurity, and that could contribute significantly to the overall needs of the company (Pierce, 2016; Stevenson, 2017).

Information technology related positions required consistent training to remain on top of constant changes in the field (Andre 2016). With a good understanding of the threats that a professional cybersecurity face, the academic community was the first to attempt to fill the gap in knowledge for practitioners (Van- Zadelhoff, 2016). The field of computing before 1990 was very straightforward (Force, 2001). The

1968 Association for Computing Machinery (ACM) report was the first of its kind to describe the guidelines of computing (Force, 2001). The 1978 ACM report provided details on course descriptions with specific bibliographic references (Force, 2001). In 1983, IEEECS and the Association for Computing Machinery jointly published a more in-depth course description of specific topic areas for both computer science and engineering (Tucker et al., 1991).

The events of September 11, 2001 created new areas of focus including homeland security and cybersecurity. The ACM acknowledges that the scope of what is called computing has drastically changed as of the filing of the 2001 ACM report (Curricula, 2001). Information systems had to address many new challenges with the growth of computing power. Information technology programs began to appear (Force, 2001). Besides, security and cryptography are explicitly listed as reasons why the curriculum of the computing field needed revision (Force, 2001).

The 2004 ACM identifies the differences and similarities of the five major computing disciplines (Shackelford et al., 2006). The options were computer science, electrical engineering, or information systems. The focus of computer science is on programming software, and electrical engineering is on hardware. The focus of information systems is on using hardware and software to meet organizational goals (Shackelford et al., 2006). The only change before 1990 in the computing field was the introduction of computer engineering, which was a specialization of electrical engineering due to the opening of the microprocessors (Shackelford et al., 2006). In 2005, an ACM report identified dramatic growth has been seen in some computing disciplines (Shackelford et al., 2006).

A hindrance to growth in the cybersecurity field is clearly defined paths of professional development. Experience and training seem not to be a typical discussion within the cybersecurity community. Most professionals who attend training or obtain experience do so by job-hopping or by attending training at the expense of the cybersecurity professional (Li & Daugherty, 2015). Others seek academic degrees in cybersecurity and information security. As such, it is easy to see with the shortages of professionals in both the entry and higher complexity roles that the burden falls on the existing cybersecurity professionals to develop the needed skills (Andre, 2016).

An additional hindrance to the developing more professionals falls on universities that do not offer programs in cybersecurity that can re-train older workers interested in career changes and can develop new ones. One factor that increases the number of older workers in the workforce is the improvement in health care and resultant life expectancy (Cappelli & Novelli, 2010). Therefore, leveraging the experience of older workers is of vital importance to engage and help develop the existing workforce (Cappelli & Novelli, 2010). Currently, a large percentage of knowledge is lost due to the unrealized value of this portion of the workforce. Information

Technology, Computer Engineering, and Cybersecurity careers are offering high salaries in industry, thus making it unattractive for professionals in the field to leave the income gained from working to attend a doctoral program for 3 to 7 years. As a result, routes to doctoral study have changed (Peacock, 2017).

THE EVOLUTION OF DOCTORAL PROGRAMS

Walker et al. (2008) delineates the results of The Carnegie Initiative on the Doctorate, a five-year project to develop approaches for transforming doctoral programs. The purpose is one of the central themes in Walker et al.'s (2008) account of how doctoral education needs to improve. At the national level, debates about purpose have centered on two central questions: First, what is the intent of a doctoral degree or doctoral study? Is it preparation for a particular career, or is it for knowledge and understanding? Second, what are the ideal types of students that should be in doctoral programs? Should anyone be allowed to get a doctorate? According to Walker et al. (2008), a recurring concern has been the proliferation of doctorates granted by too many universities and that many of those universities are "sham graduate schools" (p. 36.). Doctoral education is at a place where purpose must be continually reconsidered. There are new challenges facing graduate education today, and there will be new challenges in the coming decades. The need, then, is for faculty and students to objectively examine the purposes of doctoral education to improve the discipline. Walker et al. (2008) refers to this assessment as serving as a good "steward" of the discipline. The word "steward" is used intentionally by Walker et al. (2008) "to convey a sense of purpose for doctoral education that is larger than the individual and implies action" (p. 12). When academic programs directors and faculty members examine their programs to assess if their doctoral programs were student-friendly, relevant, innovative, and employer-friendly, they function as good stewards of the discipline. The five-year study done by The Carnegie Initiative on the Doctorate sheds light on many promising practices in numerous doctoral programs. Walker et al. (2008) makes many suggestions for improvement based on those insights. Two suggestions that were particularly relevant to this study were integrative dissertations and the reconsideration of apprenticeship.

The debate about the usefulness of dissertations has gone on for years. Many faculty members complain that poorly written dissertations are passed to appease colleagues and that the standards used to judge dissertations are unclear to students (Lovitts, 2007). According to Olson and Drew (1998), the dissertation has become an unfocused debate about dissertations' unuseful for years. Many faculty members complain that poorly written dissertations are simply passed to appease colleagues and that the standards used to judge dissertations are unclear to students (Lovitts,

2007). According to literature reviews and uses ambiguous and verbose language exhaustive reviews of literature and uses language that is ambiguous and verbose. Regardless, the dissertation is still the most widely used program completion experience. Walker, et al. (2008) write that the dissertation is an important formative experience, *requiring students to put theory into action, consider multiple lines of evidence, and display a comprehensive understanding of previous scholarship in the field; it is strongly linked to the development of research skills and content area mastery* (p. 80).

Furthermore, Walker et al. (2008) proposes that the dissertation be made a stronger site for integrating the multiple domains of stewardship. To this end, they suggest that dissertations integrate across disciplines and connect students' experiences at multiple levels. Finally, Walker et al. (2008) argues for a shift in the apprenticeship model, from one in which students are apprenticed to a faculty mentor to one in which they apprentice with many mentors. Today's diverse students, having diverse skills and interests, are best served by multiple intellectual mentors.

Traditional vs. Non-Traditional Doctoral Programs

Although the concept of traditional and non-traditional degree programs is often discussed, what differentiates the two can sometimes be difficult to assess (Amorosino, 2017). The archetypical traditional doctoral degree program is "a full-time, residential, four-five-year, research focused graduate program in the sciences or humanities culminating in a dissertation and a PhD" (Archbald, 2011, p. 16). Such programs tend to attract younger students just beginning a career and often provide the student some level of funding (especially in science fields) in exchange for full-time commitment to study and research. These students, upon graduation, often teach and continue to do research at the graduate level (Archbald, 2011).

The term non-traditional as it relates to a doctoral degree is multi-faceted and may include the program design, limited residency at the university, pedagogical underpinnings, as well as what the attainment of the degree can provide the student and their working environment (Amorosino, 2017). All of these dynamics and their differing permutations combine to create a flexible description of non-traditional doctoral programs (Amorosino, 2017). Pappas and Jerman (2011) define a non-traditional degree as having one or more of four characteristics: (a) the students participating are usually not full-time students, nor full-time residents of the university and may have family and social responsibilities that prohibit the full-time engagement expected in traditional programs; (b) the program itself is provided in a compressed, online, hybrid, or other format; (c) the degree itself may not be a PhD, but may serve the needs of the practitioner, employee, or practitioner with particular applied needs—also known as a professional degree; and (d) the degree does not necessarily lead to a life in academe but serves the needs of the practitioner (Pappas & Jerman, 2011, p. 2).

The Development of Non-Traditional Online Doctoral Programs

Several accredited US universities have had success developing non-traditional doctoral programs that offer limited face to face teaching residencies and online learning. Students attempting to pursue a doctorate in this manner have self-directed. These programs allow students from all over the world to complete a doctoral degree in Information Technology, Engineering and Cybersecurity while working full time and not having to move or relocate to complete their degrees. These are all brick-and-mortar universities that are leveraging their campus resources to engage professionals with significant work experience in the field, which with a doctorate degree, could become effective faculty members in the future. These programs have several similar characteristics like either online or limited residency offerings. These programs also offer no distinction or indication on your diploma or transcripts that the degree was completed on-line versus, those students that completed the degree on campus. These programs have coursework combined with dissertation research. These schools include:

1. The George Washington University in Ashburn VA, USA offers an on-line Doctor of Engineering that can be finished remotely in Cybersecurity and Technology Management
2. Old Dominion University in Norfolk, VA, US offers an on-line PhD in engineering management and systems engineering and a Doctor of Engineering.
3. Dakota State University in Madison, South Dakota, USA has an online Ph.D. in Information Security.
4. The University of the Cumberlands in Williamsburg, KY, USA has an online PhD in Information Technology with options to study Blockchain Technology on the graduate level on-line.
5. Mississippi State University in Starkville, MS, USA has an on-line PhD in Systems and Industrial Engineering.
6. Marymount University in Arlington, VA, US has a 2-year on-line Doctor of Science in Cybersecurity that offers an applied dissertation.
7. Purdue Polytechnic Institute in West Lafayette, IN, USA offers an innovative on-line Doctor of Technology.
8. Colorado State University in Fort Carson, CO, USA offers an on-line Doctor of Engineering.

U.S. Research Only PhD Program

Normally the US approach to doctoral student includes academic coursework and then dissertation research but one university in the US, Capitol Technology University, in Laurel Maryland, USA which is an ABET accredited engineering school has a doctoral approach like many European universities where students just engage in their own independent research. This program also allows students that have completed doctoral credits at other universities but failed to complete their doctorate degree to transfer their credits and complete their doctorate in an accelerated format. They offer PhD programs in Cybersecurity Leadership, Cyber-psychology, Healthcare Cybersecurity, Financial Cybersecurity, Artificial Intelligence, Critical Infrastructure, Counterterrorism, Human Factors, Unmanned Systems Applications, Manufacturing, and Technology.

PhD by Published Research or PhD by Publication

The PhD by Published Research or PhD by Published Works emerged as an option in 1966 at Cambridge University in the UK and has grown to become a viable path for doctoral degree completion in the UK and Australia (Peacock, 2017). The PhD by published works was initially conceived to allow practitioners such as creative writers, artists, and accomplished executive to obtain an earned doctorate that would afford them the ability to take their knowledge, experiences, and accomplishments along with a doctorate degree in the university classroom (Peacock, 2017).

The PhD by published works program works by the students submitting a collection of prior peer reviewed published research and works all from the matching field for examination (Peacock, 2017). The portfolio submission can include peer-reviewed full paper conference proceedings, peer reviewed academic articles, and peer reviewed book chapters. Included with the submission of published works is critical content analysis as an evaluated equivalent to fulfilling requirements for a doctoral degree (Peacock, 2017). The critical content analysis explains relevance, impact, and unifying significance of the publications in the academic field of study (Peacock, 2017). Often these publications need to be those that are peer reviewed usually in journals indexed in SCOPUS, The Institute of Electrical and Electronics Engineers (IEEE), The Association for Computing Machinery (ACM), the Association of Business Schools Journals list, or a publication in a journal that is listed on the Australian Business Deans Council Journal Quality list. Journal articles published in journals not listed on one of these lists could have challenges as being accepted.

Universities offering these programs include:
1. Middlesex University in the UK offers a Doctor of Professional Studies by published works.
2. London Metropolitan University in the UK offers a PhD by published works.
3. Technical University of Dublin offers a PhD by published works.
4. These universities with flexible doctoral programs geared towards working professionals and executives in the Cybersecurity, Engineering, and fields to bring their expertise to universities that are challenged to meet new workforce demands in Technology, Engineering, and Cybersecurity.

There are several books that are critical for success in these kinds of programs:

- Getting What You Came For: The Smart Student's Guide to Earning an M.A. or a Ph.D by Robert Peters: ISBN-13: 978-0374524777 (Peters, 1997).
- The Only Academic Phrasebook You'll Ever Need: 600 Examples of Academic Language by Luiz Otavio Barros: ISBN-13: 978-1539527756 (Barros, 2016).
- Grad School Essentials: A Crash Course in Scholarly Skills by Z. Shore: ISBN-13: 978-0520288300 (Shore, 2016).
- Becoming an Academic Writer: 50 Exercises for Paced, Productive, and Powerful Writing by Patricia Goodson: ISBN-13: 978-1483376257. (Goodson, 2016).
- Writing Your Journal Article in Twelve Weeks, Second Edition: A Guide to Academic Publishing Success by Wendy Laura Belcher: ISBN-13: 978-0226499918. (Belcher, 2019).
- Full Speed Ahead: Surviving to Thriving as an Online Doctoral Student: ISBN-13: 978-1456300678. (Doctors Publishing Group, 2010).
- The Dissertation Warrior: The Ultimate Guide to Being the Kind of Person Who Finishes a Doctoral Dissertation or Thesis by Dr. Guy White: ISBN-13: 978-0984089512. (White, 2017).
- The Dissertation Journey: A Practical and Comprehensive Guide to Planning, Writing, and Defending Your Dissertation by Carol Roberts: ISBN ISBN-13: 978-1506373317. (Roberts, 2010).
- The Literature Review: Six Steps to Success by Lawrence A. Machi: ISBN-13: 978-1506336244. (Machi and McEvoy, 2021).
- Writing Literature Reviews: A Guide for Students of the Social and Behavioral Sciences by Jose L. Galvan: ISBN-13: 978-0415315746. (Galvan and Galvan, 2017).
- The Professor Is in: The Essential Guide to Turning Your Ph.D. Into a Job by Karen Kelsky: ISBN-13: 978-0553419429. (Kelskey, 2015).

CONCLUSION

This chapter explored the essential need to develop more doctorate faculty in technology related areas and explains some unique and non-traditional paths to doctoral completion that allow professionals with significant real world work experience to complete a doctorate without career interruption and relocation from highly respected and established universities in the US and the UK.

REFERENCES

Amorosino, S. C. (2017). *Was it worth it? women's satisfaction with earning the online education doctorate* (Order No. 10266971). Available from ProQuest Central; ProQuest Dissertations & Theses Global. (1926748370)

Andre, P. (2016). A phenomenological study of frontline hiring professionals that recruit in a cybersecurity world (Order No. 10250990). Available from ProQuest Dissertations & Theses Global. (1868414289)

Archbald, D. (2011). The emergence of the nontraditional doctorate: An historical overview. In J. P. Pappas & J. Jerman (Eds.), *Meeting adult learner needs through the nontraditional doctoral degree*. Jossey-Bass. doi:10.1002/ace.396

Barros, L. O. (2016). *The Only Academic Phrasebook You'll Ever Need: 600 Examples of Academic Language*. Createspace Independent Publishing Platform.

Belcher, W. L. (2019). Writing Your Journal Article in Twelve Weeks, Second Edition: A Guide to Academic Publishing Success. University of Chicago Press. doi:10.7208/chicago/9780226500089.001.0001

Cappelli, P. (2008). Talent management for the twenty-first century. *Harvard Business Review*, *86*(3), 74. PMID:18411966

Cappelli, P., & Novelli, W. D. (2010). *Managing the Older Worker: How to Prepare for the New Organizational Order*. Harvard Business Press.

Curricula, C. (2001). *Computer Science. IEEE CS*. ACM Joint Task Force on Computing Curricula.

Doctors Publishing Group. (2010). *Full Speed Ahead: Surviving to Thriving as an Online Doctoral Student*. CreateSpace Independent Publishing Platform.

Force, J. T. (2001). *Computing curricula 2001: Computer science*. Retrieved from https://www.acm.org/education/curric_vols/cc2001.pdf

Galvan, J. L., & Galvan, M. C. (2017). *Writing literature reviews: A guide for students of the social and behavioral sciences.* Routledge. doi:10.4324/9781315229386

Goodson, P. (2016). *Becoming an academic writer: 50 exercises for paced, productive, and powerful writing.* Sage Publications.

Kauflin, J. (2017, March 16). The Fast-Growing Job with A Huge Skills Gap: Cyber Security. *Forbes.*

Kelsky, K. (2015). *The professor is in: The essential guide to turning your Ph. D. into a job.* Crown.

Li, J., & Daugherty, L. (2015). *Training cyber warriors: What can be learned from defense language training?* RAND National Defense Research Institute. doi:10.7249/RR476

Lovitts, B. E. (2007). *Making the implicit explicit: Creating performance expectations for the dissertation.* Stylus Publishing, LLC.

Machi, L. A., & McEvoy, B. T. (2021). *The literature review: Six steps to success.* Academic Press.

Morgan, S. (2016, May 13). Top 5 industries at risk of cyber-attacks. Retrieved on February 17, 2018, from https://www.forbes.com/sites/stevemorgan/2016/05/13/list-of-the-5-most-cyber-attacked-industries/#1edfc762715e

Newman, L. (2017, July 1) The biggest cybersecurity disasters of 2017 so far. Wired.

Olson, G. A., & Drew, J. (1998). Reenvisioning the dissertation in English studies. College English, 61(1), 56-66.

Pappas, J. P., & Jerman, J. (Eds.). (2011). *Meeting adult learner needs through the nontraditional doctoral degree.* Jossey-Bass.

Peacock, S. (2017). The PhD by publication. *International Journal of Doctoral Studies, 12,* 123–134. doi:10.28945/3781

Peters, R. L. (1997). *Getting what you came for: the smart student's guide to earning a master's or a Ph. D.* Farrar, Straus and Giroux.

Pierce, A. O. (2016). *Exploring the cybersecurity hiring gap* (Order No. 10250186). Available from ProQuest Dissertations & Theses Global. (1848667353)

Roberts, C. M. (2010). *The dissertation journey: A practical and comprehensive guide to planning, writing, and defending your dissertation.* Corwin Press.

Shackelford, R., Lunt, B., McGettrick, A., Sloan, R., Topi, H., Davies, G., & Lunt, B. (2006). Computing curricula 2005: The overview report. *ACM SIGCSE, 38*(1), 456–457. doi:10.1145/1124706.1121482

Shore, Z. (2016). Grad School Essentials. In *Grad School Essentials*. University of California Press. doi:10.1525/9780520963269

Stevenson, G. V. (2017). *Cybersecurity implications for industry, academia, and parents: A qualitative case study in NSF STEM education* (Order No. 10624075). Available from ProQuest Dissertations & Theses Global. (1958945736)

Tucker, A. B., Aiken, R. M., Barker, K., Bruce, K. B., & Cain, J. T. (1991). *Computing curricula 1991: Report of the ACM/IEEE-CS Joint Curriculum Task Force.* Association for Computing Machinery Press/IEEE Press. doi:10.1145/103701.103710

US Federal Bureau of Investigations. (2021). Retrieved from: https://www.fbi.gov/about

Van-Zadelhoff, M. (2016, September). The Biggest Cybersecurity Threats are Inside Your Company. *Harvard Business Review.*

Walker, G. E., Golde, C. M., Jones, L., Bueschel, A. C., & Hutchings, P. (2008). *The formation of scholars: Rethinking doctoral education for the twenty-first century.* Jossey-Bass.

White, G. E. (2017). *The dissertation warrior: The ultimate guide to being the kind of person who finishes a doctoral dissertation or thesis.* Triumphant Heart International.

ADDITIONAL READING

Burrell, D., & Nobles, C. (2018). Recommendations to Develop and Hire More Highly Qualified Women and Minority Cybersecurity Professionals. Proceedings of ICCWS 2018 13th International Conference on Cyber Warfare and Security. Academic Conferences International Limited.

Clancy, M. (2012). *Improving faculty professional development in higher education high-tech programs: An action science research study of self-directed professional development (Order No. 3542028).* Available from ProQuest Dissertations & Theses Global.

Delia, C. (2015). Exploring the social and organizational factors of the shortage of women in information technology: A multiple case study (Order No. 3732277). Available from ProQuest Dissertations & Theses Global. (1746623174).

Demirbag, J. R. (2015). Gifts of the doctoral process. *Educational Journal of Living Theories*, *8*(1), 67–74.

Di Pierro, M. (2007). Excellence in doctoral education: Defining best practices. *College Student Journal*, *41*(2), 368–376.

Fuller, C. R. (2016). Shortening the skills gap: An exploratory study of cybersecurity professional experience (Order No. 10250901). Available from ProQuest Dissertations & Theses Global. (1868417653).

Gill, P., & Burnard, P. (2008). The student-supervisor relationship in the PhD/ Doctoral process. *British Journal of Nursing (Mark Allen Publishing)*, *17*(10), 668–671. doi:10.12968/bjon.2008.17.10.29484 PMID:18563010

Herling, L. (2011). Hispanic women overcoming deterrents to computer science: A phenomenological study (Order No. 3505844). Available from ProQuest Dissertations & Theses Global. (1013441827).

McClurg, J. D. (2015). Cybersecurity in higher education: Oversight and due diligence (Order No. 10291072). Available from ProQuest Dissertations & Theses Global. (1846958719). Retrieved from https://search-proquest-com.contentproxy. phoenix.edu/docview/1846958719?accountid=35812

Palmer, R. T., Maramba, D. C., & Gasman, M. (Eds.). (2013). *Fostering Success of Ethnic and Racial Minorities in STEM: The Role of Minority Serving Institutions*. Routledge. doi:10.4324/9780203181034

President's Council of Advisors on Science and Technology. (2012). Report to the president: Engage to excel: Producing one million additional college graduates with degrees in science, technology, engineering, and mathematics. Retrieved from https://www.whitehouse.gov/sites/default/files/microsites/ostp/pcast-engageto-excel-final_2-25-12.pdf

Rockinson-Szapkiw, A. J., & Spaulding, L. S. (2014). *Navigating the doctoral journey: A handbook of strategies for success*. Rowman & Littlefield.

Strayhorn, T. L. (2010). Undergraduate research participation and STEM graduate degree aspirations among students of color. *New Directions for Institutional Research*, *2010*(148), 85–93. doi:10.1002/ir.364

Sweem, S. L. (2009). Leveraging employee engagement through a talent management strategy: Optimizing human capital through human resources and organization development strategy in a field study (Order No. 3349408). Available from ProQuest Dissertations & Theses Global. (305162419).

Tinkler, P., & Jackson, C. (2004). *The doctoral examination process*. McGraw-Hill Education.

KEY TERMS AND DEFINITIONS

All but Dissertation (ABD): High-quality doctorate programs require the completion of a dissertation to earn your doctoral degree. ABD means you have completed all the necessary doctorate coursework but have not written and defended your dissertation. ABD doesn't hold academic weight, and you can't be called a doctor until you finish your dissertation. According to the Council of Graduate Schools, almost 50% of students who start a Ph.D. program don't complete their degree. However, Ph.D. programs only represent one type of doctoral degree. Completion stats vary widely between universities and doctoral degree programs. The most significant difference in completing a doctoral degree is often the university and program a student chooses. If you're ABD, you need to find a student-centered program designed to meet the needs of ABD students.

Dissertation Chair: A dissertation chair is a judge, an assessor of your work who ensures that a student meets personal, departmental, university, and even universal standards. The chair provides feedback on the research approach and dissertation chapters as the study are developed.

Time to Completion: European Ph.D. programs are shorter than those in the US. For example, it takes three years to complete a Ph.D. in France, Norway, the UK, and Germany. Across Europe, a three-to-four-year Ph.D. is standard. To be successful in a European style Ph.D., you must have a firm understanding of various research methods and how to execute them in a study. In comparison, six years is the average time to degree in the US because US doctoral programs often require 12 to 16 courses with classmates that include teaching students research methods and then dissertation research. In contrast, European doctorates require a research proposal course and then independent research on the dissertation as the doctoral experience.

Chapter 10
Privacy Preservation of Image Data With Machine Learning

Chhaya Suryabhan Dule
Dayananda Sagar University, India

Rajasekharaiah K. M.
AMC College of Engineering, Visvesvaraya Technological University, India

ABSTRACT

The methods used to predict, categorize, and recognize complex data like pictures, audio, and texts have been popular in machine learning. These methods are the basis for future AI-driven internet providers because of unparalleled precision in deep learning methodologies. Commercial firms gather large-scale user data and perform machine learning technique. The massive information necessary for machine learning raises privacy problems. The user's personal and extremely sensitive data such as photographs and voice records are gathered and retained forever by these commercial firms and users can not limit the intents of these sensitive information. In addition, centrally stored data is susceptible to legal and extrajudicial monitoring. Many data owners use profound extensive learning by security and confidentiality. This chapter contains a practical approach that allows several parties to learn a precise model of complex systems for a specific purpose without disclosing their data sets. It provides an interesting element in utility and privacy.

DOI: 10.4018/978-1-7998-9430-8.ch010

INTRODUCTION

Privacy Preserving Machine Learning for Image Data

Machine learning (ML) is an intelligence branch that consistently uses algorithms to synthesize the links between knowledge and information (Pannu & Student, 2008). For illustration, ML systems on automated speech processing may be developed to translate acoustic information into the conceptual system, which consists of a collection of words in a series of spoken data. An Internet search, ad insertion, credit assessment, financial sector prognosis, DNA sequence analytics, comportment analyses, intelligent coupons, medication research, weather prediction, huge data assessment, and many more apps are already standard in machine training. ML will decisively develop a variety of user-centred technologies. The advancement of machine learning means that fundamental linkages are characterized in wide-ranging information so that big data analysis, behaviour pattern identification, and information development solve issues. In order to represent changes in operational behaviour, machine learning methods may also be trained to categories the changing conditions of a procedure. As security features influence innovative concepts and capabilities, machine learning techniques may recognize interruptions, re-design the latest systems, and educate them to adjust and co-develop new information (Mulla, 2013; Sharma, 2017).

Supervised Learning

Supervised learning (Figure 1) is a set of learning approaches that uncover links between independent characteristics and a chosen dependency characteristic (the label). Learning supervised utilizes a training dataset to create predictive models by using input data and output values. A database can be used to forecast the output values. The effectiveness of supervised learning models depends on how large and varying the training data is so that new datasets can be more generic and more predictive. The majority of induction algorithms come within the area of supervised learning (Kshirsagar et al., 2016b).

Unsupervised Learning

Unsupervised learning includes techniques of learning which group instances lacking a particular property. In general, this method includes learning organized data patterns by eliminating pure unstructured noise. Algorithms for clustering and reduction of dimensionality are typically uncontrolled (Singh & Mishra, 2021).

Figure 1. Supervised Learning

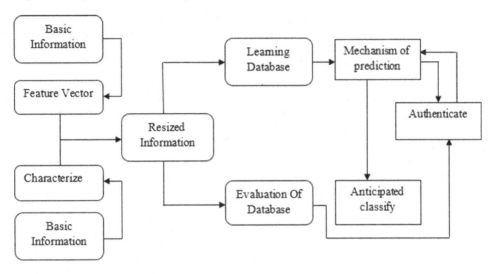

Privacy-Preserving Machine Learning

Many approaches for improving privacy focused on enabling many inputs to train ML models in cooperation without disclosing their private data in its original form. Privacy protection was usually done with the use of cryptographic methods or the publication of unequal private information. In avoiding member inference attacks, differential privacy is very useful. The success of the inversion modelling and inferences assaults on individuals can be reduced by restricting the model prediction performance (Vitale et al., 2017).

Cryptographic Approaches

If a specific machine learning application needs information from several inputs, cryptographic methods may carry out machine learning's / encrypted information validation. In many of these approaches, it is necessary to achieve greater efficiency if data owners donate their encrypted information to computing servers, reducing the problem to a safe 2/3-part computing configuration. Besides increasing productivity, the benefits of such techniques include that the input parties do not need to stay online. Most of these techniques deal with data divided horizontally: the identical set of characteristics for various data items were gathered by each data owner (Shokri & Shmatikov, 2015).

Figure 2. Privacy preserving ML for image data

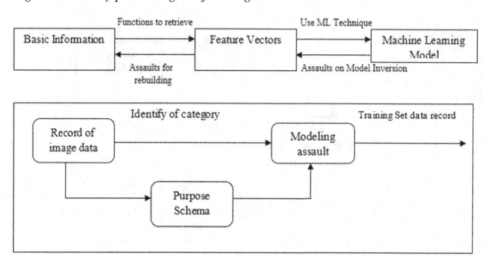

Homomorphic Encryption

Fully homomorphic encryption (Yonetani et al., 2017) makes it possible to compute encrypted data, utilizing operations like adding and multiplying as the basis of more complex arbitrary functions. As the bootstrapping of encrypted text is sometimes quite expensive, additive homomorphic encryption methods were primarily utilized in privacy-preserving machine learning. These methods allow just the addition of encrypted data activities and a plaintext multiplied.

The difficulty with the production of a machine learning model is that the model's behavior might reveal sensitive data from the training samples if exposed to new data. In this part, several techniques are developed to retrieve this confidential material from machine learning models.

A summary of the various risks or assaults is shown in Figure 2. The various attacks demand varying amounts of design and learning information. The justification behind the discussion of several threats is that the remedies proposed under this concept should cover as much protection as feasible.

PRINCIPAL AND PRIVACY FOR PRESERVATION TECHNIQUES

In a traditional setting, privacy will imply that others can only access data about themselves under own choices. That is, the public is not disclosed with unwanted files on a person.

Privacy-Preserving Machine Learning Model

In general, the machine learning system contains four attack sites requiring protection of personal data (Xu & Yi, 2011; Yuan et al., 2012), as illustrated in Figure 3.

- Some machine learning systems include confidential data for training. Legal concerns have overlooked the collection and dissemination of sensitive data utilizing algorithms for machine learning.
- Owing to public architecture methods, several machine-learning designs have been provided to the community in the latest days. The learning models of the machine may be considered secret, as the datasets they are educated on may reveal information. In particular, the hacker may accurately identify whether a given document is in the system's training set. A system can also keep some of its training samples accidentally and unintentionally.
- A person who wishes to forecast using a trained model might be sensitive to the new instance.
- To safeguard data protection used for model development.
- To safeguard the confidentiality of the learning model of machines.
- To safeguard the simulation model private.

Figure 3. Privacy-preserving machine learning technique

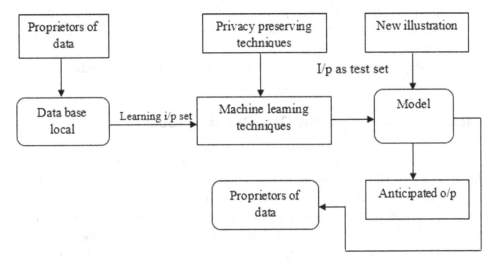

Security Properties

The privacy characteristics of the implementation of machine training that safeguards privacy are (Kshirsagar et al., 2020; Singh et al., 2014; Tramèr et al., 2016; Wang et al., 2012):

- **Strong Anonymity:** The training set should be adequately anonymized so that no one can recognize a person based on a specific record.
- **Confidentiality:** During the model training, no system administrator can understand the database system of other owners. Furthermore, the proprietor of the system cannot identify the owner for any training inputs.
- **Privacy:** No member must acquire much more than the authorized performance. In particular, the sole information regarding other parties' inputs might be drawn from the output itself. The model owners, for example, only get the learned model without understanding any person's entire record.
- **Correctness:** The classification method of machine training is ensured to be accurate for each party. To proceed with the instance of illness forecast training, this means that clinics (data owners) may assure that their local databases are used in learning. In this case, the data owner may utilize any record to forecast expected output modifications for specific input modifications.
- **Guaranteed output delivery:** Totally corrupt entities must not be able to impede the receipt of honest parties. In other words, by conducting a "denial of service" assault, the opponent should not be able to overwhelm the calculation.
- **Non-Repudiation:** By changing the training set input, no system administrator may modify his or her opinion.

Parameter Mapping in the Data Privacy Process

Data confidentiality procedure is carried out by mapping and categorizing all different factors. The mapping of data protection variables is to know which variables are present in the overall data response phase. If they are correctly tuned, it will impact the data protection results, the classifying errors, and the overall data utility results. Secondly, planners, engineers, and architects will improve their work in data protection engineering. By separating these characteristics into three groups, this work provides a distinction (P. Kshirsagar & Akojwar, 2017; Manoharan et al., 2020; Tramèr et al., 2016).

First Category of Parameters

The first group of variables concerns the general objective of the privatized data collection, as the user of that privatized dataset determines or needs. A user of the private data collection defines the first group of parameters and will vary case by case. To reach the satisfaction of such standards, however, would entail total usefulness and, as a result, absolutely no privacy. Thus, trade-offs must be made with these categories of factors. Accuracy, validity, and thoroughness are the initial categories of parameters.

Second Category of Parameters

We assess data privacy methods in the second group of parameters. These are the methods and procedures for data privacy measures. The noise levels are, for example, the parameter we want to regulate and smooth out when utilizing the noise addition approach. The process measures in the second category are examined for this study:

- Deletion: what is the deletion level for the data utility defined by the user?
- Sweeping generalization: what should the DGH be about the consumer data functionality?
- Data exchange: How many ways does data need to be exchanged in order to create a UI?
- Addition of noise: what is the ring level for a data utility determined by users?
- Multiplicative noise added - what noise level should be given a data utility defined by the user?
- Logarithmic noise adding: what degree of noise should the user specify the data utility?
- Differential confidentiality: what noise level should be given a user-defined data utility (the μ epsilon value)?

Third Category of Parameters

In the third class of variables, the parameters are calculated in the classifiers of machine learning. This group of characteristics is not important because the two preceding categories are of relevance. In this research, a study is carried out to determine if the characteristics of the machine learning classifications will influence data usefulness levels.

Figure 4. Mapping out parameters in the data privacy process

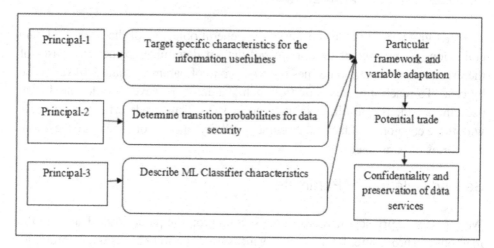

A mixture of different parameters in the multiple categories has been finished and empirical data collected to identify the degrees of modification for the informational usefulness set by the user. In order to implement a degree of appropriate privacy and utility, the classification and mapping of all data privacy factors is essential (Figure 4).

The SIED Data Privacy Engineering Framework

The conceptual framework for data privacy (SIED) – specification, implementation, evaluation, and dissemination -, a novel method to data privacy and utilitarian engineering, is holistic in the form of information data protection. The SIED architecture includes specification, execution, assessment, and ultimately dissemination of the private datasets.

The SIED architecture is motivated by the creation of a number of systems for data privacy and utility processes. Given any original X data collection, the production of a Y privatized data server should include a set of data privacy and utility engineering phases from beginning to conclusion. A few data confidentiality scheme models were proposed; however, most frameworks focus on implementing a data protection method for a particular algorithm and dataset. A comprehensive strategy that data protection engineers could apply is proposed in this work as a contribution (Figure 5). The foundation for SIED's privacy encompasses and draws approaches from the fundamentals of software engineering (Batra & Alam, 2012).

Specifications

During this phase, data protection engineers collect data privacy and utility needs from the customer. The SIED framework is strongly affected by the examination of the requirements. Data privacy rules are further improved and updated for future usage in every succeeding step.

Implementation

The corresponding data privacy algorithms on the relevant data type are designed and implemented.

Evaluation

At this phase, both original and privatized data are evaluated statistically. The privatized data sets are tested using machine learning to guarantee user-defined data utility demands are met. Compensation in the evaluation phase is also being established at this point.

The four main phases of the SIED data privacy and utility framework are as follows:

Figure 5. The SIED framework heavily influenced by specifications analysis

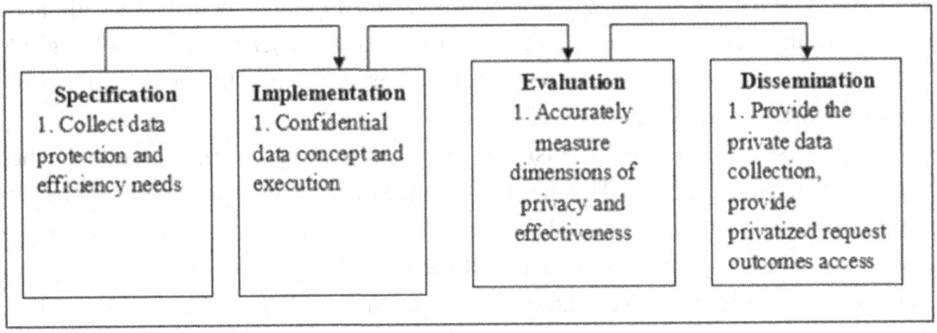

Specification 1. Collect data protection and efficiency needs	**Implementation** 1. Confidential data concept and execution	**Evaluation** 1. Accurately measure dimensions of privacy and effectiveness	**Dissemination** 1. Provide the private data collection, provide privatized request outcomes access

Dissemination

The dissemination of the private dataset takes place at this stage of the procedure. Data Privacy Engineers consider publishing using privatized required data or by micro or macro data of privatized data based on customer needs.

REAL WORLD USE OF TECHNIQUES FOR IMAGE PROCESSING

Digital imaging processing is a digital computer processing method for the modification of digital pictures. The use of signal processing techniques in the field of images — two-dimensional signals like pictures or video. In addition to other methods of extracting data from pictures, image processing generally involves filtering or improving an image using different functions. Adobe Photoshop is the most frequent example. It is one of the most common applications to digital pictures processing. It also requires the computer to analyze and manipulate pictures (Joshi, 2018; Wetcher-Hendricks, 2011).

Three phases are carried out for the image processing (Figure 6): First, import pictures from a scanner, camera, or digital processing using optical devices. Second, somehow alter or evaluate the pictures. This stage might comprise an improved image and a summary of data, or the images are processed to identify the rules which human eyes cannot perceive. For instance, meteorologists examine satellite pictures using this technique. Finally, output the picture treatment result. The result might be a modification in the picture or a report based on the analysis or image result (Akojwar et al., 2014).

Digital image processing within computer science is a widely popular and fast-developing field of application. Its development is driven by technical breakthroughs in digital imagery, computer technology, and mass storage. For their edibility and cost, fields that typically use analog imagery are now switched into digital systems. Medicine, video creation, photography, remote sensing, and security surveillance are important examples. These sources provide a significant amount of digital picture information every day, which may be inspected manually more than before (Sundaramurthy et al., 2020; et al., 2020).

The processing of a two-dimensional image by a computer may essentially be characterized as processing. The output of image processing might be a picture or result as a number of image-related properties or attributes. Most methods of image processing consider a picture as a two-dimensional signal and use basic signal processing technologies. Some major uses in science include computer vision and remote sensing, feature extracting, face identification, prediction, identification of optically made images, fingerprints, optical sorting, argumentation reality, microscope imaging, path departure precaution system. The analysis procedure may be split into many steps utilizing digital image processing. Figure 6 displays the block diagram of a digital image processing system (Phan et al., 2016; Quellec et al., 2012; Xiao et al., 2011).

The overall operation of the block phases is explained as follows:

Image Acquisition

It is the initial or essential stage in the synthesis of digital images. The picture is supplied in the electronic medium under images acquired. In principle, pre-treatment, such as resizing, etc., is part of this step of picture acquisition. Some scanners, camcorders, or overhead cameras may enter a picture. This image ought to be a top-quality, higher-resolution image that supports the proper analysis of images.

Pre-Processing

Certain pre-processing actions on the input picture are necessary. The pre-processing approaches enhance the image data to eliminate undesirable distortion and improve certain input picture characteristics. The picture dimension should be decreased during large photos since it takes longer to prepare high-resolution images. Then it becomes grey when the color image is transformed, as less information is required for each pixel. Indeed, the grey color has the same intensities in the red, blue, and green components; a single intensity level value for each pixel thus must be specified.

Feature Extraction and Fragmentation

Under edge detection, specific places should be detected to detect numerous major alterations and activities in the picture characteristics. For the categorization of the image, the image is identified in many components. The picture in the form of these sections is more comprehensible and easier to understand. Separation takes place by a pixel picture scanner and then labels every pixel based on whether the grey level is up or down the cut off amount.

Image Restoration

Image restoration is a region that improves the look of an image. Image restore approaches are based on math or probabilistic picture analysis. Different filters are available or can be created to restore and improve survival.

Figure 6. Block diagram of image processing

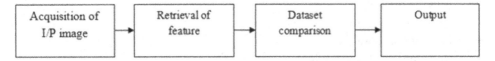

Output Image

The item of interest from that picture can be retrieved after many image processing techniques followed by a feature extraction on a digital image.

Techniques

Corner Detection

Corner recognition is a method used to detect a specific image feature with valuable information in the corners. Corner recognition is a type of point detection of interest and maybe segregated into three groups:

1.   Direct detection of corners.
2.   Corner detection-based template.
3.   Corner detection based on contour.

Corner detection has numerous ways with various mathematical procedures in each method:

- Harris detector of the corner.
- Detectors for Susan Corner.
- The detection algorithm for the Moravec corner.
- The corner detector Forester.
- Robust corner detector for Fuzzy Rule.

Field-Programmable Gate Array (FPGA)

FPGA is an IC that allows us to re-program after fabrication like a read-only (PROM) programmed storage device. It may efficiently be used in real-time image processing applications since it incorporates parallel programming technologies such as real-time video smoothing. Many filters and methods are employed in the FPGA implementation as:

- Average filter.
- Module Sorting.
- Expanded.
- Filter for smoothing.
- Recognition of Sobel edge.
- Movement Flash.

- Filter Emboss.

Focal Plane

The method is a circuit where the space kernels are programmable to their size, configuration, and coefficients. There are two kinds:

- SIMD focal plane: can support real-time results with sustainable operating output of between 500 and 1500 Giga.
- MIMD focal plane: The device uses the Multiple Instructions Multiple Data Architecture (MIMD) architecture, providing five simultaneous pictures processed spatially.

Cloud

Take use of cloud computing capabilities while processing images in real-time where they become less expensive, better stored, and faster to analyze, particularly in real-time. Image processing apps can be placed in the Cloud that we use on the internet and other applications.

For example, We may place image processing and cellular analysis machine vision apps in the Cloud (server), and it can be used from the fix shop (client).

Image Segmentation

We analyze the picture by dividing it into separate objects or component pieces in the image segmentation. The spotted pixel within the object is examined to verify the pixel within the object.

The division into the following groups can be divided:

Region-Based Segmentation

An area consists of a set of pixels with comparable characteristics. Regional Segmentation is a method through which an image is divided into areas. Regions are utilized for picture interpretation. A specific thing or distinct portions of an object may match an area. Furthermore, region-based picture segmentation may be regarded as a pixel-based approach. Methods of regional Segmentation are: Splitting and Merging region.

Pixel-Based Segmentation

The image segmentation depends on the intensity of the image. In this approach, the picture is split into areas based on the features, and each local region has a distinct threshold. We will transform the image into a binary image after setting the suitable threshold. We may utilize Histogram thresholds to display the segmented image. As visual processing, Edge Maximization Technique, Histogram depending methods, Pilot method, and Mean method, we may utilize post-processing techniques for threshold segmentation.

Applications

Computer Vision

Computer vision is a type of automated monitoring dog that incorporates science as well as technology. As a subject from science, the philosophy of design for artificial systems that obtain information from pictures is linked to computer vision. The picture input might be in a vast range of forms, for example, a video signal sequence or many views from separate cameras. Events such as video sequences or numbering of individuals; information organization for indexing digital image bases or pattern of images and modeling objects or ecosystems, such as industrial inspections, medical imaging analyses or topologies include examples in the application of computer vision systems such as an industrial robot or autonomy vehicles.

Face Detection

Important face characteristics are recognized and disregarded in this technique. Face detection is an object class detection and aims to discover the characteristics of faces and the dimensions of a known number of faces. It also aims to tackle difficulties with multiple vision detection that are more broad and challenging.

Digital Video Processing

Image retrieval is a distinctive and vital image analysis facility in several sectors of technology and computer.

Video files or streaming videos are input and output for video processing. The video processing techniques are applied on TV, VCR, DVD, Multimedia codecs, media players, and other equipment.

Ex: Many companies create different visual processing methods and ways with television sets.

Remote Sensing

Distance sensing is essentially the collection by employing different real-time embedded sensors that are portable or not in physical or direct touch with the item of big or median information signals from an object or event (such as aircraft, spacecraft, satellite, or ship). Remotely sensed data is multiple data signals that collect information about a given item or region utilizing various instruments. Examples of remote sensing are parolee surveillance using an ultrasonic identification device, Magnetic Resonance Imaging (MRI), Positron Emission Tomography (PET).

Biomedical Image Enhancement and Analysis

Enhancing the biological image is highly essential for diagnosing the biomedical image. This field aims to improve biomedical pictures. In addition to digital techniques, such as Computed Tomography (CT) or Magnetic Resonance Imaging (MRI), analog images are currently provided with digital capabilities in conventional applications such as endoscopy or radiography. Digital pictures are made of pixels to which discreet luminance or various color values are expressed. They may be effectively processed and objectively assessed after biological image improvement and appropriate analysis.

Biometric Verification

It refers to the automated identification or recognition of human beings by their behavior. Identification and access control of Biometrics is such an efficient kind of identification. It may also be utilized in gatherings which are under surveillance to recognize people. The goal of such a technology is to ensure that only a legitimate user and no one else may access the supplied services. A biometric system is a pattern detection system based on an individual's acquisition of biometric data. The working concept is based on the extraction of certain characteristics from the data obtained and the comparison to the template established in the database. A biometric system may function in verification mode or in verification mode dependent on the kind and method of application.

Signature Recognition

In order to determine if a sign corresponds to a particular signature on the basis of a signature image and a few sample pictures of the initial signatures, the signature verification and reconnaissance are also a major request. Handwritten signatures are not always crisp in nature, lines are not precisely straight, and curves are not necessarily smooth. In addition, in contrast to handwriting generally thought to be written in a fixed position on a baseline, the typefaces can be designed in various sizes and direction. A strong handwritten identification system consequently has to take all these variables into account

Underwater Image Restoration and Enhancement

The underlying physics of light diffusion in the water medium is extinct in the processing of the underwater image. When the light enters water, the deepening of the water level attenuates exponentially, thereby affecting the visibility distance and limiting it. Images from underwater suffer from many issues including blurring, homogeneous illumination, noise, low contrast and so on. The repair and improvement of subsea pictures is therefore a crucial research topic. In enhancing the picture quality, many filters are employed to reduce noise, conserve the edges of an image, and to smooth the image.

Character Recognition

Character recognition sometimes referred to as the recognition of optical character or shortened as OCR. The conversion of manuscript or printed text pictures (typically taken by a scanner) into edible text by machine is mechanical or digital. It is a large field for patterns, artificial intelligence and machine vision researchers. Recognition system is the most economical and quickest option available for many documents entry jobs.

Medical Palmistry

Palmistry is a science that looks at human palms in various ways and draws inferences about the person's nature. Many civilizations, such as Indians, Chinois, Persians, Egyptians, Romans and Greeks, have been employed from ancient times to get direction through palmistry for both their present and future. It covers human qualities, such as health, mental health, intelligence, lifestyle and associated elements. A medical palm tree might be regarded as one of the palm tree branches. Probable sickness may be diagnosed by examining symbols on human palm such Iceland, cross, grill, place, star, quadrangle, and circle utilizing this medical palmistry. In such decision-making processes for diagnosis of illnesses both palm and finger forms play a very essential part.

CURRENT MACHINE LEARNING PRIVACY CHALLENGES

The main obstacle to the safety of machine learning systems is the external role of information in protecting machine learning systems. It makes safeguarding learning systems much more challenging. In most situations, data sets learned by a machine learning system are 60% risk, whereas learning algorithms and source codes are 40% risk. That is why companies must rely on architecture assessment for their energies. Architectural risk analysis is, according to research, a major first step to protecting the learning systems of organizations. More than 70 dangers connected with learning machines are highlighted in the research. It is another major problem to protect data that has become an essential element of a learning model (Kshirsagar et al., 2020).

Fooling the System

One of the most prevalent assaults on machine learning systems is to deceive through malicious input to make incorrect predictions. They are just visual illusions for computers, showing them an image that does not exist in the actual world and forcing them to make judgments on this basis. Fooling the system provides attention to the safety hazards of machine learning. This sort of assault is generally aimed towards machine models.

Data Poisoning

For learning purposes, machine learning systems are dependent on data. Therefore the dependability, integrity, and security of these data are crucial for enterprises to obtain incorrect forecasts. Hackers are familiar with this and aim to attack machine learning system's data. They alter this data, distort them and poison them such that the entire learning mechanism of the computer is lowered down. Businesses should be cautious, and danger should be reduced. Experts on machine learning should avoid harm by reducing the volume and scope of training for cyber data thieves. What is worse is that all data sources must be protected, as attackers can alter any data source to train the system.

Manipulation of Online Systems

The Internet is connected to most machine learning systems, mainly when used in business as it continues to learn. It offers a chance for attackers to take advantage. By supplying false system information or worse, cyber-criminals might mislead machine learning systems in the wrong direction and progressively re-exercise it to follow its order and perform the wrong thing. It is not easy to manipulate an online system for learning, but it is so subtle that the victim even notices that the system is in the hands of others. Engineers who use the correct algorithm, keep data ownership records, and streamline and secure system operations may deal with this problem.

Transfer Learning Attack

Most machine learning systems use a framework that's previously learned. By giving tailored training, that general machine learning model is adapted to specific aims. It is when a learning attack on transmission can be fatal. If the users are popular with the model, attackers might start an attack to insult the machine model. Take a look at the suspicious and unexpected behavior of machine learning to identify such assaults. Because machine learning algorithms are deliberately employed in transfers, this raises the danger, particularly when the transfer is not planned. Group posting models are best chosen since they clearly describe what their processes are doing and how they will control the risk.

Data Privacy and Confidentiality

Machine learning algorithms employ learning and development data. It is essential to guarantee the privacy and security of this data, mainly if they are included in the learning model. Data extraction assaults that might slip under the radar can be launched by hackers, which may endanger the entire system. In addition to making less funds and time, malicious hackers may also execute another kind of assault, such as adversary assaults by malicious input, even when the assaults fail, and may start smaller sub-Symbolic exploitation attacks. That not only involves protecting machine learning systems against assaults on extracting data but also preventing attacks on functional extraction.

Computing Power

Most developers can avoid the amount of power these powerful algorithms consume. The founding stones of modern Artificial Intelligence are machine learning and profound learning and need an ever-growing number of cores and GPUs to operate effectively. We can develop profound learning frameworks in different fields, such as meteorite monitoring, implementation in the healthcare system, cosmic organ tracking, etc. It would help if you had computer power from a computer, and sure, quantum computers are not inexpensive. Even if Cloud Computing is available and developers of massively parallel technologies work more efficiently on AI systems, they are priced. Not everybody can afford that with the influx of unheard-of data and complicated algorithms rising quickly.

Trust Deficit

The critical aspects of AI, how deep learning model forecast output is uncertain. It is difficult for a non-specialist to understand which combination of input provides a solution for diverse issues. Many individuals worldwide do not even realize how artificial intelligence is used or exists and how it is interwoven into everyday things like smartphones, Smart TVs, banking, and even vehicles.

Limited Knowledge

Although we may utilize machine learning as superior to conventional methods in many locations in the industry, machine learning competence is the actual difficulty. With technology fans, college students, and researchers, the possibility of machine learning is known to only a small number of persons.

Human-Level

Human-level is one of the most critical difficulties in the field of machine learning. Specialists in corporations and small firms have been maintained on top of machine learning services. These firms may be over 90 percent accurate, yet in all these instances, humans can do better. Let us anticipate, for instance, if the image is a dog or a cat. The human being can forecast the right results almost every time, thereby achieving a remarkable precision of over 99%.

Data Privacy and Security

The major element relies on the collection of resources and resources to train all deep and machinery model learning models. Yes, we have information, but since millions of people worldwide create the data, this data may likely be misused.

For instance, let us assume that a medical care provider provides services to 1 million individuals in the city, and because of a cyber-assault, all 1 million consumers are personally handled by the Dark Web. These data contain information about illnesses, issues with health, medical history, and much more. We are dealing today with statistics on the planet's size to make matters worse. With this amount of information coming from every corner, some incidents of data leakage would certainly occur. Several firms have already launched innovative efforts to overcome these obstacles. It trains information on intelligent devices and hence is not returned to servers. Only the trained model is returned to the organization.

Data Scarcity

Different nations like India are applying strict IT regulations to limit flow, with large firms like Google, Facebook, and Apple facing penalties for the illegal use of customer data. Therefore, these firms are confronted with the challenge of utilizing local information to build global applications, resulting in prejudices. Data are highly essential for the learning of computers, and marked data are used to train machines for learning and prediction. Some firms strive to create new techniques and focus on creating machine learning models that, despite the data shortage, produce reliable results. The overall structure might be faulty with incomplete information.

FUTURE MACHINE LEARNING PRIVACY CHALLENGES

Client privacy and data security problems are urgently involved, many of them probably being reworked by ML and other data technology (Kumar & Gupta, 2016; Sridhar, 2019). The primary issue is that companies' risk to user privacy and data safety is not properly responsible. In order to restore complete responsibility, three barriers must be overcome, i.e.

- The challenge of compliance with the real activity of companies in the collection, stocking, and use of data.
- The difficulty in quantifying the effect of data practice, in particular before unlikely bad outcomes occur.
- The problem of establishing a causal relationship between a company's data practice and its effects.

In addition, accessibility can, in some circumstances, impede public organizations from fulfilling their tasks or contravene the privacy requirements of the data controller for the personal information of information assets other than those seeking access. A solution aimed at revealing the rationale of algorithms could be the preferable alternative for such reasons. Nevertheless, it can be more or less narrowly construed. Data on the type of user input and the expected performance, explanations of the variables and their weight, or brilliant light on the analytical architecture are several forms of visibility in relation to ML algorithms' logic. Complex analysis processes challenge the idea of transparency when describing algorithm logic and making it challenging to offer thorough information about the rationale behind the data acquisition through decision-making utilizing analytical and non-deterministic systems (Dewangan, 2015; Gurav et al., 2020; Pravin Kshirsagar & Akojwar, 2016a; Quellec et al., 2012).

Transparency

In the context of ML, there may be multiple definitions for transparency. ML applications utilized a description of their logic and access to the structure of the ML algorithms, and the data sets used to train the algorithms if appropriate. Moreover, for data-focused decision-making, openness may be either an ex-ante or an ex-postage necessity. While openness is essential if a computerized decision-making model is to be examined publicly, a generic declaration on the usage of ML offers little to address the issue of unfair or unjustified use of information. On the other side, it can be feasible to discover potential bias by examining the algorithm structure. Nevertheless, IP rights and competitive problems may restrict access, and even if such obstacles do not exist, a key difficulty for human cognition may be the sophistication of the accepted models.

In addition, in contrast to the static character of transparency, the dynamic nature of many algorithms. Algorithms are updated and altered continually, but an algorithm of transparency concerns just the algorithm employed at a particular time. Finally, it does not suffice to access ML algorithms to detect potential biases. This type of analysis also takes funding in terms of effort and talents.

Risk Assessment

Data privacy rules progressively emphasize the importance of risk assessments given the constraints of openness and human self-determination. Data controller risk assessment and a safe ML ecosystem may significantly increase the confidence and readiness of users to utilize ML technologies. Users' preferences might be based not just on marketing champagnes or product quality but on efficient risk assessments and steps to reduce the dangers. The employment of algorithms by current techniques for data processing and the move towards data-intensive technology-led certain people to adopt a more general perspective of the potential negative results of data processing. The influence of data usage on fundamental rights and collective social and ethical values has been examined by experts and researchers beyond the usual area of data protection. Evaluating conformity with ethical and social principles is more difficult than the usual evaluation of data privacy. For instance, although the values underpinning data security and management are technically based and may thus be applied to other social settings, the situation is different in terms of social and ethical values. These are inevitably contextual and differ from community to community, making it more challenging to define a baseline for this type of risk assessment.

CONCLUSION

The development of intelligent, high-technology robots built exclusively by researchers in many countries worldwide is part of the future of digital image processing. It contains advances in various applications for digital image processing. In the course of a few decades, millions of robots will exist globally to alter the management of the world by innovating image processing and other associated technologies. Advance experiment on image recognition and computer vision involves voice recognition, predicting govt information requirements, language translation, recognition and ability to track things and people, diagnostic health conditions, operational activities, and processes, modulating human DNA defectors and automatic transportation in all formats.

The exponential development and broad digital data accessibility have led to an increase in the research effort in the machine learning field. In order to improve the quality of the machine learning output, extensive data gathering is typically needed. Such information often included very sensitive information, like medical records or financial records. Thus, issues about privacy in today's learning systems have been eclipsed by other issues. A key challenge in machine learning that protects patients' rights is how to trade privacy with its usefulness. Firstly, the machine learning solution which safeguards privacy should not allow for the appropriate recovery of the source database files. On the other hand, it has to enable the system to learn the model tightly linked to the model learned by the original information. This chapter examines many emerging innovations that may be utilized in machine learning systems to safeguard privacy.

In order to contribute to the problem of confidentiality, a summary view of SIED was provided of a data protection engineering framework for the systemic data privacy formulation and construction. While SIED may also be adapted for self-supported data protection processing as a paradigm for data privacy engineering. The fundamental purpose of the SIED framework is to request and analyze complete information protection needs, which may subsequently be utilized for the proper deployment of data protection and autonomous data protection agents. However, appropriate mapping of data privacy characteristics is required to assess data confidentiality demands during the data confidentiality process properly. Smart agent-based architectures might provide autonomous intelligent data protection solutions. The complexity of agent-based data protection engineering has to be addressed through a deconstruction method for future projects.

REFERENCES

Akojwar, D. S., Kshirsagar, P., & Pai, V. (2014). Feature extraction of EEG signals using wavelet and principal component analysis. *National Conference on Research Trends In Electronics, Computer Science & Information Technology and Doctoral Research Meet.*

Batra, G., & Alam, M. A. (2012). Preserving privacy in data mining using SEMMA methodology. *International Journal on Computer Science and Engineering, 4*(5), 853.

Dewangan, S. K. (2015). Human authentication using biometric recognition. *International Journal of Computer Science and Engineering Technology, 6*(4), 240–245.

Gurav, Y., Bhagat, P., Jadhav, R., & Sinha, S. (2020). Devanagari handwritten character recognition using convolutional neural networks. *2020 International Conference on Electrical, Communication, and Computer Engineering (ICECCE)*, 1–6. 10.1109/ICECCE49384.2020.9179193

Joshi, M. A. (2018). *Digital image processing: An algorithmic approach*. PHI Learning Pvt. Ltd.

Kshirsagar, P. & Akojwar, S. (2016b). Novel approach for classification and prediction of non linear chaotic databases. *International Conference on Electrical, Electronics, and Optimization Techniques, ICEEOT 2016.* 10.1109/ICEEOT.2016.7755667

Kshirsagar, P., & Akojwar, S. (2016a, July 15). Hybrid Heuristic Optimization for Benchmark Datasets. *International Journal of Computers and Applications, 146*(7), 11–16. Advance online publication. doi:10.5120/ijca2016910853

Kshirsagar, P. & Akojwar, S. (2017). *Optimization of BPNN parameters using PSO for EEG signals.* doi:10.2991/iccasp-16.2017.59

Kshirsagar, P., Balakrishnan, N., & Yadav, A. D. (2020). Modelling of optimised neural network for classification and prediction of benchmark datasets. *Computer Methods in Biomechanics and Biomedical Engineering. Imaging & Visualization, 8*(4), 426–435. Advance online publication. doi:10.1080/21681163.2019.1711457

Kshirsagar, P. R., Manoharan, H., Al-Turjman, F., & Kumar, K. (2020). Design and testing of automated smoke monitoring sensors in vehicles. *IEEE Sensors Journal,* 1. Advance online publication. doi:10.1109/JSEN.2020.3044604

Kumar, N., & Gupta, S. (2016). Offline handwritten Gurmukhi character recognition: A review. International Journal of Software Engineering and its Applications. doi:10.14257/ijseia.2016.10.5.08

Manoharan, H., Teekaraman, Y., Kshirsagar, P. R., Sundaramurthy, S., & Manoharan, A. (2020). Examining the effect of aquaculture using sensor-based technology with machine learning algorithm. *Aquaculture Research, 51*(11), 4748–4758. Advance online publication. doi:10.1111/are.14821

Mulla, D. J. (2013). Twenty five years of remote sensing in precision agriculture: Key advances and remaining knowledge gaps. Biosystems Engineering. doi:10.1016/j.biosystemseng.2012.08.009

Pannu, A., & Student, M. T. (2008). *Artificial Intelligence and its Application in Different Areas. Certified International Journal of Engineering and Innovative Technology.*

Phan, N. H., Wang, Y., Wu, X., & Dou, D. (2016). Differential privacy preservation for deep auto-encoders: An application of human behavior prediction. *30th AAAI Conference on Artificial Intelligence, AAAI 2016.* 10.1609/aaai.v30i1.10165

Quellec, G., Lamard, M., Cazuguel, G., Cochener, B., & Roux, C. (2012). Fast wavelet-based image characterization for highly adaptive image retrieval. *IEEE Transactions on Image Processing, 21*(4), 1613–1623. Advance online publication. doi:10.1109/TIP.2011.2180915 PMID:22194244

Sharma, D. (2017). Challenges Involved in Big Data Processing & Methods to Solve Big Data Processing Problems. *International Journal for Research in Applied Science and Engineering Technology, V*(VIII), 841–844. Advance online publication. doi:10.22214/ijraset.2017.8118

Shokri, R., & Shmatikov, V. (2015). Privacy-preserving deep learning. *Proceedings of the ACM Conference on Computer and Communications Security.* 10.1145/2810103.2813687

Singh, S., Kumar, N., & Kaur, N. (2014). Design and development of RFID Basedb intelligent security system. *International Journal of Advanced Research in Computer Engineering and Technology, 3.*

Singh, T. & Mishra, J. (2021). Learning with artificial intelligence systems: application, challenges, and opportunities. *Impact of AI Technologies on Teaching, Learning, and Research in Higher Education*, 236–253.

Sridhar, B. (2019). Cross-Layered Embedding of Watermark on Image for High Authentication. *Pattern Recognition and Image Analysis*, 29(1), 194–199. Advance online publication. doi:10.1134/S105466181901022X

Sundaramurthy, S., Saravanabhavan, C., & Kshirsagar, P. (2020). Prediction and Classification of Rheumatoid Arthritis using Ensemble Machine Learning Approaches. *2020 International Conference on Decision Aid Sciences and Application, DASA 2020*. 10.1109/DASA51403.2020.9317253

Thippeswamy, G., & Shilpa, B. (2020). Classification of ECG Signal using Artificial Neural Network. *International Journal of Recent Technology and Engineering*. doi:10.35940/ijrte.E6867.038620

Tramèr, F., Zhang, F., Juels, A., Reiter, M. K., & Ristenpart, T. (2016). Stealing machine learning models via prediction APIs. *Proceedings of the 25th USENIX Security Symposium*.

Vitale, J., Tonkin, M., Ojha, S., Williams, M. A., Wang, X., & Judge, W. (2017). Privacy by design in machine learning data collection: A user experience experimentation. *AAAI Spring Symposium - Technical Report*.

Wang, Q., Xu, C., & Sun, M. (2012). Protecting privacy by multi-dimensional k-anonymity. *Journal of Software*, 7(8). Advance online publication. doi:10.4304/jsw.7.8.1873-1880

Wetcher-Hendricks, D. (2011). *Analyzing quantitative data: An introduction for social researchers*. John Wiley & Sons.

Xiao, X., Wang, G., & Gehrke, J. (2011). Differential Privacy via Wavelet Transforms. *IEEE Transactions on Knowledge and Data Engineering*, 23(8), 1200–1214. Advance online publication. doi:10.1109/TKDE.2010.247

Xu, Z., & Yi, X. (2011). Classification of Privacy-preserving Distributed Data Mining protocols. *2011 6th International Conference on Digital Information Management, ICDIM 2011*. 10.1109/ICDIM.2011.6093356

Yonetani, R., Boddeti, V. N., Kitani, K. M., & Sato, Y. (2017). Privacy-Preserving Visual Learning Using Doubly Permuted Homomorphic Encryption. *Proceedings of the IEEE International Conference on Computer Vision*. 10.1109/ICCV.2017.225

Yuan, M., Chen, L., Rao, W., & Mei, H. (2012). A general framework for publishing privacy protected and utility preserved graph. *Proceedings - IEEE International Conference on Data Mining, ICDM.* 10.1109/ICDM.2012.62

ADDITIONAL READING

Magkos, E. (2012). Cryptographic approaches for privacy preservation in location-based services: a survey. *Systems approach applications for developments in information technology*, 273-297.

Wahlstrom, K., Roddick, J. F., Sarre, R., Estivill-Castro, V., & de Vries, D. (2009). Legal and technical issues of privacy preservation in data mining. In *Encyclopedia of Data Warehousing and Mining* (2nd ed., pp. 1158–1163). IGI Global. doi:10.4018/978-1-60566-010-3.ch180

KEY TERMS AND DEFINITIONS

Accuracy: Rate of valid model predictions using a dataset. Accuracy is generally assessed using an independent test set that was not used throughout the study procedure at any point. Cross-validation and bootstrapping, particularly with a small number of datasets, are often employed alongside more complicated precision estimations approaches.

Classifier: It is a process that accepts a new input as an unspecified case of observation or function and determines a class to which it belongs. Many classificatory are used to categories the best label for a given example with inferential statistics.

Confusion Matrix: A matrix that visualizes classification algorithm effectiveness using the information in the matrix. It analyses the projected categorization in the form of true positive, false positive, true negative, and false negative information against the data used for the classification.

Cross-Validation: A check approaches evaluating the capacity of a system to generalize an independent dataset. It provides a database used to evaluate the learned model for fitting throughout the training phase. The effectiveness of individual prediction functions may also be evaluated via cross-validation. The training samples will be randomly divided into k mutually exclusive sub-samples of fixed size in k-fold cross-validation. The model is trained k times, in which one of the k subsamples is used for each iteration, while the other k-1 subsamples are employed to exercise the system. Cross-validation findings are combined to assess the exactness as a single estimate.

Dataset: Data gathering that complies with a scheme without ordering constraints. Each column in a typical dataset is a function, and each row is a part of the dataset.

Feature Vector: An explanatory n-dimensional number vector represents an example of an item, which aids pre-processing and data methods. Feature vectors are frequently weighted to build a predictive function to measure the prediction's quality or fitness. Various feature reduction approaches, such as main component analysis, multi-liner subspace decrease, iso maps and latent semantic analysis, can lower the dimension of a feature vector. Functional space is frequently referred to as vector space.

Model: A structure summarizing a description or prediction of dataset. The unique demands of an application may be tailored to each design. Big-data applications contain enormous datasets with many predictions and characteristics which are too complicated to extract relevant information from a basic functional form. The learning process synthesizes a model from a given collection of attributes and features. Models may usually be classified as parametric or not parametric. Simple and flexible non-parameter models are less assumptive; however, more datasets are needed to arrive at correct results.

Privacy Preservation: A concept in data mining related to data transfer or communication between different parties making compulsory to provide security to that data so that other parties do not know what data is communicated between original parties.

Compilation of References

Abdallah, A., Maarof, M. A., & Zainal, A. (2016). Fraud Detection System: A survey. *Journal of Network and Computer Applications, 68*, 90–113. doi:10.1016/j.jnca.2016.04.007

Agresti, A. (2018). *An Introduction to Categorical Data Analysis* (3rd ed.). John Wiley and Sons. https://www.wiley.com/en-us/An + Introduction +to+ Categorical + Data + Analysis %2C +3rd+ Edition-p-9781119405283

Akojwar, D. S., Kshirsagar, P., & Pai, V. (2014). Feature extraction of EEG signals using wavelet and principal component analysis. *National Conference on Research Trends In Electronics, Computer Science & Information Technology and Doctoral Research Meet.*

Al Solami, E., Boyd, C., Clark, A., & Islam, A. K. (2010). Continuous Biometric Authentication: Can It Be More Practical? *2010 IEEE 12th International Conference on High Performance Computing and Communications (HPCC)*, 647–652. 10.1109/HPCC.2010.65

Al-bayati, B., Clarke, N., & Dowland, P. (2016). Adaptive Behaviroal Profiling for Identity Verification in Cloud Computing: A Model and Preliminary Analysis. *GSTF International Journal on Computing, 5*(1), 21–28. doi:10.5176/2251-3043

Albayram, Y., Kentros, S., Jiang, R., & Bamis, A. (2013). A method for improving mobile authentication using human spatio-temporal behavior. *2013 IEEE Symposium on Computers and Communications (ISCC)*, 305–311. 10.1109/ISCC.2013.6754964

Albshrawi, M., & Lowell, M. (2016). Detecting Financial Fraud using Data Mining Techniques: A Decade Review from 2004 to 2015. *Journal of Data Science: JDS, 14*(3), 553–569. doi:10.6339/JDS.201607_14(3).0010

Alheeti, K. M. A., & McDonald-Maier, K. (2017). An intelligent intrusion detection scheme for self-driving vehicles based on magnetometer sensors. *2016 International Conference for Students on Applied Engineering, ICSAE 2016*. 10.1109/ICSAE.2016.7810164

Ali, K. M., Samawi, V. W., & Al Rababaa, M. S. (2009). The affect of fuzzification on neural networks intrusion detection system. *2009 4th IEEE Conference on Industrial Electronics and Applications*, 1236–1241.

Alswiti, W., Alqatawna, J., Al-Shboul, B., Faris, H., & Hakh, H. (2016). Users Profiling Using Clickstream Data Analysis and Classification. *2016 Cybersecurity and Cyberforensics Conference (CCC)*, 96–99. 10.1109/CCC.2016.27

Amorosino, S. C. (2017). *Was it worth it? women's satisfaction with earning the online education doctorate* (Order No. 10266971). Available from ProQuest Central; ProQuest Dissertations & Theses Global. (1926748370)

Andre, P. (2016). A phenomenological study of frontline hiring professionals that recruit in a cybersecurity world (Order No. 10250990). Available from ProQuest Dissertations & Theses Global. (1868414289)

Andrean, A., Jayabalan, M., & Thiruchelvam, V. (2020). Keystroke Dynamics Based User Authentication using Deep Multilayer Perceptron. *International Journal of Machine Learning and Computing*, *10*(1), 134–139. doi:10.18178/ijmlc.2020.10.1.910

Anjomshoa, F., Catalfamo, M., Hecker, D., Helgeland, N., Rasch, A., Kantarci, B., Erol-Kantarci, M., & Schuckers, S. (2016). Mobile behaviometric framework for sociability assessment and identification of smartphone users. *2016 IEEE Symposium on Computers and Communication (ISCC)*, *2016-Augus*, 1084–1089. 10.1109/ISCC.2016.7543880

Antal, M., & Nemes, G. (2016). Gender recognition from mobile biometric data. In *Proceedings of 11th International Symposium on Applied Computational Intelligence and Informatics* (pp. 243-248). Timisoara, Romania: IEEE. 10.1109/SACI.2016.7507379

Archbald, D. (2011). The emergence of the nontraditional doctorate: An historical overview. In J. P. Pappas & J. Jerman (Eds.), *Meeting adult learner needs through the nontraditional doctoral degree*. Jossey-Bass. doi:10.1002/ace.396

Aupy, A., & Clarke, N. (2005). User Authentication by Service Utilisation Profiling. *Advances in Network and Communications Engineering*, *2*, 18.

B., S. B., & Venkataram, P. (2007). An Authentication Scheme for Personalized Mobile Multimedia Services: A Cognitive Agents Based Approach. *Future Generation Communication and Networking (FGCN 2007)*, 167–172. doi:10.1109/FGCN.2007.57

Bagga, S., Goyal, A., Gupta, N., & Goyal, A. (2020). Credit Card Fraud Detection using Pipeling and Ensemble Learning. *International Conference on Smart Sustainable Intelligent Computing and Applications under ICITETM2020. Procedia Computer Science*, *173*, 104–112. doi:10.1016/j.procs.2020.06.014

Bakar, K. A. A., & Haron, G. R. (2014). Adaptive authentication based on analysis of user behavior. *2014 Science and Information Conference*, 601–606. 10.1109/SAI.2014.6918248

Bal, G., Rannenberg, K., & Hong, J. I. (2015). Styx: Privacy risk communication for the Android smartphone platform based on apps' data-access behavior patterns. *Computers & Security*, *53*(69), 187–202. doi:10.1016/j.cose.2015.04.004

Banerjee, S. P., & Woodard, D. L. (2012). Biometric Authentication and Identification using Keystroke Dynamics. *Survey (London, England)*, *7*(1), 116–139. doi:10.13176/11.427

BankD.KoenigsteinN.GiryesR. (2020). *Autoencoders*. Retrieved from https://arxiv.org/abs/2003.05991

Barros, L. O. (2016). *The Only Academic Phrasebook You'll Ever Need: 600 Examples of Academic Language*. Createspace Independent Publishing Platform.

Batra, G., & Alam, M. A. (2012). Preserving privacy in data mining using SEMMA methodology. *International Journal on Computer Science and Engineering*, *4*(5), 853.

Baumann, R., & Plattner, C. (2002). *White Paper: Honeypots*. Academic Press.

Behdad, M., Barone, L., Bennamoun, M., & French, T. (2012). Nature-inspired Techniques in the Context of Fraud Detection. *IEEE Transactions on Systems, Man and Cybernetics. Part C, Applications and Reviews*, *42*(6), 1273–1290. doi:10.1109/TSMCC.2012.2215851

Belcher, W. L. (2019). Writing Your Journal Article in Twelve Weeks, Second Edition: A Guide to Academic Publishing Success. University of Chicago Press. doi:10.7208/chicago/9780226500089.001.0001

Betz, S. (2022). *25 Top Self Driving Car Companies 2022*. https://builtin.com/transportation-tech/self-driving-car-companies

Beyer, H.-G. (2007). Evolution strategies. *Scholarpedia*, *2*(8), 1965. doi:10.4249cholarpedia.1965

Bishop, C. M., & Nasrabadi, N. M. (2006). Pattern recognition and machine learning (Vol. 4). Springer.

Bolton, R. J., & Hand, D. J. (2001). Unsupervised Profiling Methods for Fraud Detection. *Proc Credit Scoring and Credit Control*, *7*, 5–7. http://citeseerx.ist.psu.edu/viewdoc/summary?doi=10.1.1.24.5743

Bolton, R. J., & Hand, D. J. (2002). Statistical Fraud Detection: A Review. *Statistical Science*, *17*(3), 235–249. doi:10.1214/ss/1042727940

Bossuet, L., Ngo, X. T., Cherif, Z., & Fischer, V. (2014). A PUF based on a transient effect ring oscillator and insensitive to locking phenomenon. *IEEE Transactions on Emerging Topics in Computing*, *2*(1), 30–36. Advance online publication. doi:10.1109/TETC.2013.2287182

Breiman, L. (2001). Random forests. *Machine Learning*, *45*(1), 5–32. doi:10.1023/A:1010933404324

Breiman, L., Friedman, J. H., Ohlsen, R., & Stone, C. J. (1984). *Classiðcation and Regression Trees*. Chapman and Hall/CRC.

Bridle, J. (1989). Training stochastic model recognition algorithms as networks can lead to maximum mutual information estimation of parameters. *Advances in Neural Information Processing Systems*, 2.

Brosso, I., La Neve, A., Bressan, G., & Ruggiero, W. V. (2010). A Continuous Authentication System Based on User Behavior Analysis. *International Conference on Availability, Reliability, and Security, 2010. ARES '10*, 380–385. 10.1109/ARES.2010.63

Budhram, T. (2012). Lost, stolen, or skimmed: Overcoming Credit Card Fraud in South Africa. *South African Crime Quarterly, 40*(40), 31–37. doi:10.17159/2413-3108/2012/v0i40a843

Bui, D. T., Tuan, T. A., Klempe, H., Pradhan, B., & Revhaug, I. (2016). Spatial Prediction Model for shallow Landslide Hazards: A Comparative Assessment of the Efficacy of Support Vector Machines, Artificial Neural Networks, Kernel Logistic Regression, and Logistic Model Tree. *Landslides, 13*(2), 361–378. doi:10.100710346-015-0557-6

Buker, A., & Vinciarelli, A. (2021). Who is typing? Automatic gender recognition from interactive textual chats using typing behaviour. In A. E. Hassanien, A. Darwish, S. M. Abd El-Kader, & D. A. Alboaneen (Eds.), *Enabling Machine Learning Applications in Data Science. Algorithms for Intelligent Systems* (pp. 3–15). Springer. doi:10.1007/978-981-33-6129-4_1

Burges, C. J. C. (1998). A tutorial on support vector machines for pattern recognition. *Data Mining and Knowledge Discovery, 2*(2), 121–167. Advance online publication. doi:10.1023/A:1009715923555

Buriro, A., Crispo, B., & Zhauniarovich, Y. (2017). Please hold on: Unobtrusive user authentication using smartphone's built-in sensors. *2017 IEEE International Conference on Identity, Security and Behavior Analysis (ISBA)*, 1–8. 10.1109/ISBA.2017.7947684

Bürkner, P. C., Gabry, J., & Vehtari, A. (2020). Approximate leave-future-out cross-validation for Bayesian time series models. *Journal of Statistical Computation and Simulation, 90*(14), 2499–2523. doi:10.1080/00949655.2020.1783262

Cappelli, P. (2008). Talent management for the twenty-first century. *Harvard Business Review, 86*(3), 74. PMID:18411966

Cappelli, P., & Novelli, W. D. (2010). *Managing the Older Worker: How to Prepare for the New Organizational Order*. Harvard Business Press.

Caruana, R., & Niculescu-Mizil, A. (2004). Data mining in metric space: an empirical analysis of supervised learning performance criteria. *Proceedings of the Tenth ACM SIGKDD International Conference on Knowledge Discovery and Data Mining*, 69–78. 10.1145/1014052.1014063

Chen, W., Xie, X., Wang, J., Pradhan, B., Hong, H., Bui, D. T., Duan, Z., & Ma, J. (2017). A Comparative Study of Logistic Model Tree, Random Forest, and Classification and Regression Tree Models for Spatial Prediction of Landslide Susceptibility. *Catena, 151*, 147–160. doi:10.1016/j.catena.2016.11.032

Cheswick, B. (1992, January). An Evening with Berferd in which a cracker is Lured, Endured, and Studied. In *Proc. Winter USENIX Conference, San Francisco* (pp. 20-24). Academic Press.

Cho, K., van Merrienboer, B., Bahdanau, D., & Bengio, Y. (2014). *On the Properties of Neural Machine Translation: Encoder-Decoder Approaches*. Retrieved from https://arxiv.org/abs/1409.1259

Chow, R., Jakobsson, M., Masuoka, R., Molina, J., Niu, Y., Shi, E., & Song, Z. (2010). Authentication in the clouds. *Proceedings of the 2010 ACM Workshop on Cloud Computing Security Workshop - CCSW '10*, 1. 10.1145/1866835.1866837

Claes, J., & Poels, G. (2014). Merging event logs for process mining: A rule based merging method and rule suggestion algorithm. *Expert Systems with Applications*, *41*(16), 7291–7306. doi:10.1016/j.eswa.2014.06.012

Clarke, N. (2011). Transparent User Authentication. In *Transparent User Authentication*. Springer London. doi:10.1007/978-0-85729-805-8_1

Cloudflare. (2022). *What is a distributed denial-of-service (DDoS) attack?* Retrieved from https://www.cloudflare.com/learning/ddos/what-is-a-ddos-attack/

Colkesen, I., & Kavzoglu, T. (2017). The Use of Logistic Model Tree (LMT) for Pixel-and-Object-Based Classifications Using High-Resolution WorldView-2 Imagery. *Geocarto International*, *32*(1), 71–86. doi:10.1080/10106049.2015.1128486

Cook, J., & Ramadas, V. (2020). When to consult precision-recall curves. *The Stata Journal*, *20*(1), 131–148. doi:10.1177/1536867X20909693

Costanzo, D., Rotigliano, E., Irigaray-Fernández, C., Jiménez-Perálvarez, J. D., & Chacón Montero, J. (2012). Factors Selection in Landslide Susceptibility Modelling on Large Scale following the GIS Matrix Method: Application to the River Beirobasin (Spain). *Natural Hazards and Earth System Sciences*, *12*(2), 327–340. doi:10.5194/nhess-12-327-2012

Credit Card Fraud Consumer Action. (2022). *Consumer Action Report*. Retrieved 13 May 2022 at https://www.consumer-action.org/

Cristianini, N., & Ricci, E. (2008). *Support vector machines*. Academic Press.

Curricula, C. (2001). *Computer Science. IEEE CS*. ACM Joint Task Force on Computing Curricula.

Cybersource. (2021). *2021 Global Fraud Report*. https://www.cybersource.com/content/dam/documents/campaign/global-fraud-report-2021.pdf

D'Angelo, G., Rampone, S., & Palmieri, F. (2016). Developing a trust model for pervasive computing based on Apriori association rules learning and Bayesian classification. *Soft Computing*. Advance online publication. doi:10.100700500-016-2183-1

Dai, Y., Yan, J., Tang, X., Zhao, H., & Guo, M. (2016). August. Online Credit Card Fraud Detection: A Hybrid Framework with big data technologies. 2016 IEEE Trustcom/BigDataSE/ISPApp, 1644-1651. doi:10.1109/TrustCom.2016.0253

De Faveri, C., Moreira, A., & Souza, E. (2017). Deception planning models for Cyber Security. *2017 17th International Conference on Computational Science and Its Applications (ICCSA)*, 1–8.

Degtereva, V., Gladkova, S., Makarova, O., & Melkostupov, E. (2020). Forming a mechanism for preventing the violations in cyberspace at the time of digitalization: Common cyber threats and ways to escape them. In *Proceedings of the International Scientific Conference - Digital Transformation on Manufacturing, Infrastructure and Service* (article no.: 55, pp. 1–6). ACM. 10.1145/3446434.3446468

Desai, M., & Jaiswal, S. (2021). Importance of Information Security and Strategies to Prevent Data Breaches in Mobile Devices. Research Anthology on Securing Mobile Technologies and Applications. doi:10.4018/978-1-7998-8545-0.ch025

Dewangan, S. K. (2015). Human authentication using biometric recognition. *International Journal of Computer Science and Engineering Technology, 6*(4), 240–245.

DNV GL AS. (2017). *Global Opportunity*. Author.

Doctors Publishing Group. (2010). *Full Speed Ahead: Surviving to Thriving as an Online Doctoral Student*. CreateSpace Independent Publishing Platform.

Doetsch, P., Buck, C., Golik, P., Hoppe, N., Kramp, M., Laudenberg, J., Oberdörfer, C., Steingrube, P., Forster, J., & Mauser, A. (2009). Logistic Model Trees with AUCSPLIT CRITERION for the KDDCup2009 Small Challenge. *KDD-Cup 2009 Competition,* 77–88. https://proceedings.mlr.press/v7/doetsch09.html

Domingues, R. (2015). *Machine Learning for Unsupervised Fraud Detection* [Thesis]. Royal Institute of Technology. Retrieved from http://urn.kb.se/resolve?urn=urn:nbn:se:kth:diva-181027

Doshi, R., Apthorpe, N., & Feamster, N. (2018, May). Machine learning ddos detection for consumer internet of things devices. In *2018 IEEE Security and Privacy Workshops (SPW)* (pp. 29-35). IEEE.

Earl, S., Campbell, J., & Buckley, O. (2021). Identifying soft biometric features from a combination of keystroke and mouse dynamics. In M. Zallio, C. Raymundo Ibañez, & J. H. Hernandez (Eds.), *Advances in Human Factors in Robots, Unmanned Systems and Cybersecurity. Lecture Notes in Networks and Systems* (Vol. 268, pp. 184–190). Springer. doi:10.1007/978-3-030-79997-7_23

Ehsan Rana, M., Kubbo, M., & Jayabalan, M. (2017). Privacy and Security Challenges Towards Cloud Based Access Control in Electronic Health Records. *Asian Journal of Information Technology, 16*(2), 274–281. doi:10.36478/ajit.2017.274.281

El-Hajj, M., Fadlallah, A., Chamoun, M., & Serhrouchni, A. (2021). A taxonomy of PUF Schemes with a novel Arbiter-based PUF resisting machine learning attacks. Computer Networks. doi:10.1016/j.comnet.2021.108133

Fairhurst, M., & Da Costa-Abreu, M. (2011). Using keystroke dynamics for gender identification in social network environment. In *Proceedings of 4th International Conference on Imaging for Crime Detection and Prevention 2011* (pp. 1-6). London, UK. IET. 10.1049/ic.2011.0124

Fayaz, S. A., Zaman, M., & Butt, M. A. (2021). An application of logistic model tree (LMT) algorithm to ameliorate Prediction accuracy of meteorological data. *International Journal of Advanced Technology and Engineering Exploration*, 8(84), 1424–1440. doi:10.19101/IJATEE.2021.874586

Fayaz, S. A., Zaman, M., & Butt, M. A. (2022). Is Deep Learning on Tabular Data Enough? An Assessment. *International Journal of Advanced Computer Science and Applications*, 13(4), 466–473. doi:10.14569/IJACSA.2022.0130454

Ferbrache, D. (2016). Passwords are broken – the future shape of biometrics. *Biometric Technology Today*, 2016(3), 5–7. doi:10.1016/S0969-4765(16)30049-2

Ferreira, A., Cruz-Correia, R., & Antunes, L. (2011). Usability of authentication and access control: A case study in healthcare. *Proceedings - International Carnahan Conference on Security Technology*, 1–7. 10.1109/CCST.2011.6095873

Force, J. T. (2001). *Computing curricula 2001: Computer science*. Retrieved from https://www.acm.org/education/curric_vols/cc2001.pdf

Fortinet. (2022). *What is a DDoS Attack?* Retrieved from https://www.fortinet.com/resources/cyberglossary/ddos-attack

Fu, X., Yu, W., Cheng, D., Tan, X., Streff, K., & Graham, S. (2006). On recognizing virtual honeypots and countermeasures. *2006 2nd IEEE International Symposium on Dependable, Autonomic and Secure Computing*, 211–218.

Galletly, J. (1998). Evolutionary algorithms in theory and practice: Evolution strategies, evolutionary programming, genetic algorithms. Kybernetes. doi:10.1108/k.1998.27.8.979.4

Galvan, J. L., & Galvan, M. C. (2017). *Writing literature reviews: A guide for students of the social and behavioral sciences*. Routledge. doi:10.4324/9781315229386

Gee, S. (2015). Fraud and Fraud Detection, A data analytics approach. John Wiley and Sons, Inc.

Ghosh, S., & Kumar, S. (2013). Comparative Analysis of K-Means and Fuzzy C-Means Algorithms. *International Journal of Advanced Computer Science and Applications*, 4(4), 35–39. doi:10.14569/IJACSA.2013.040406

Gibbens, M. (1999). *Honeypots*. Academic Press.

Giot, R., Dorizzi, B., & Rosenberger, C. (2015). A review on the public benchmark databases for static keystroke dynamics. *Computers & Security*, 55, 46–61. doi:10.1016/j.cose.2015.06.008

Goodson, P. (2016). *Becoming an academic writer: 50 exercises for paced, productive, and powerful writing*. Sage Publications.

Grassi, P. A., Garcia, M. E., & Fenton, J. L. (2017). *Digital identity guidelines: revision 3*. doi:10.6028/NIST.SP.800-63-3

Greenberg, I. (1982). The role of deception in decision theory. *The Journal of Conflict Resolution*, *26*(1), 139–156. doi:10.1177/0022002782026001005

Grudziecki, T., Jacewicz, P., Juszczyk, L., Kijewski, P. & Pawlinski, P. (2012). Proactive detection of security incidents honeypots. *European Network and Information Security Agency*.

Gurav, Y., Bhagat, P., Jadhav, R., & Sinha, S. (2020). Devanagari handwritten character recognition using convolutional neural networks. *2020 International Conference on Electrical, Communication, and Computer Engineering (ICECCE)*, 1–6. 10.1109/ICECCE49384.2020.9179193

Gu, Y., Li, K., Guo, Z., & Wang, Y. (2019). Semi-supervised K-means DDoS detection method using hybrid feature selection algorithm. *IEEE Access: Practical Innovations, Open Solutions*, *7*, 64351–64365.

Hand, D., & Yu, K. (2001). *Idiot's Bayes: Not So Stupid after All?* Academic Press.

Han, J., Kamber, M., & Pei, J. (2012). *Data mining : Concepts and Techniques* (3rd ed.). Elsevier.

Hassani, H., Gheitanchi, S., & Yogini, M. R. (2010). On the Application of Data Mining to Official Data. *Journal of Data Science: JDS*, *8*(1), 75–89. doi:10.6339/JDS.2010.08(1).578

Hochreiter, S., & Schmidhuber, J. (1997). *Long short-term memory.* Retrieved from Institute of Bioinformatics, Johannes Kepler University Linz: https://www.bioinf.jku.at/publications/older/2604.pdf

Holz, T., & Raynal, F. (2005b). Detecting honeypots and other suspicious environments. *Proceedings from the 6th Annual IEEE System, Man and Cybernetics Information Assurance Workshop, SMC 2005.* 10.1109/IAW.2005.1495930

Holz, T., & Raynal, F. (2005a). *Defeating Honeypots: System Issues, Part 2 | Symantec Connect Community.* Symantec Connect.

Hossain, M. S., & Haberfeld, C. (2020). Touch behavior based age estimation toward enhancing child safety. In *Proceedings of 2020 IEEE International Joint Conference on Biometrics* (pp. 1-8). IEEE. 10.1109/IJCB48548.2020.9304913

Hossin, M., & Sulaiman, M. N. (2015). A Review on Evaluation Metrics for Data Classification Evaluations. *International Journal of Data Mining & Knowledge Management Process*, *5*(2), 1–11. doi:10.5121/ijdkp.2015.5201

Hou, S., Guo, Y., & Li, S. (2019). *A lightweight LFSR-Based strong physical unclonable function design on FPGA.* IEEE. doi:10.1109/ACCESS.2019.2917259

Hussain, R., & Zeadally, S. (2019). Autonomous Cars: Research Results, Issues, and Future Challenges. IEEE Communications Surveys and Tutorials. doi:10.1109/COMST.2018.2869360

Hussin, H. Y., Zumpano, V., Reichenbach, P., Sterlacchini, S., Micu, M., van Westen, C., & Balteanu, D. (2016). 'Different Landslide Sampling Strategies in a Grid-based Bi-variate Statistical Susceptibility Model. *Geomorphology*, *253*(15), 508–523. doi:10.1016/j.geomorph.2015.10.030

Ibrahim, A., & Ouda, A. (2017). A hybrid-based filtering approach for user authentication. *2017 IEEE 30th Canadian Conference on Electrical and Computer Engineering (CCECE)*, 1–5. 10.1109/CCECE.2017.7946830

Ibrahim, A., & Ouda, A. (2016). Innovative Data Authentication Model. *2016 IEEE 7th Annual Information Technology, Electronics and Mobile Communication Conference (IEMCON)*, 1–7. 10.1109/IEMCON.2016.7746268

Idrus, S. Z. S., Cherrier, E., Rosenberger, C., & Bours, P. (2014). Soft biometrics for keystroke dynamics: Profiling individuals while typing passwords. *Computers & Security, 45*, 147–155. doi:10.1016/j.cose.2014.05.008

Ileberi, E., Sun, Y., & Wang, Z. (2022). A machine learning-based credit card fraud detection using the ga algorithm for feature selection. *Journal of Big Data, 9*(1), 24. doi:10.118640537-022-00573-8

Innes, S., & Valli, C. (2006). Honeypots: How do you know when you are inside one? *Proceedings of 4th Australian Digital Forensics Conference.*

Ismael, A. A., Jayabalan, M., & Al-Jumeily, D. (2020). A study on human activity recognition using smartphone. *Journal of Advanced Research in Dynamical and Control Systems, 12*(5), 795–803. doi:10.5373/JARDCS/V12SP5/20201818

ISO. (2013). *BS ISO/IEC 29115:2013: Information technology. Security techniques. Entity authentication assurance framework.* ISO.

ISO. (2014). BS EN ISO 22600-1:2014: Health informatics. Privilege management and access control. Overview and policy management. British Standards Institute.

Jaiswal, S., & Sarkar, S. (2018). COT: Evaluation and Analysis of Various Applications With Security for Cloud and IoT. In Examining Cloud Computing Technologies Through the Internet of Things (pp. 251–263). IGI Global.

Jaiswal, S., & Chandra, M. B. (2017). A Survey: Privacy and Security to Internet of Things with Cloud Computing. *International Journal of Control Theory and Applications, 10*(1).

James, G., Witten, D., Hastie, T., & Tibshirani, R. (2013). *An Introduction to Statistical Learning.* Springer. doi:10.1007/978-1-4614-7138-7

Jayabalan, M. (2020). Towards an Approach of Risk Analysis in Access Control. *2020 13th International Conference on Developments in eSystems Engineering (DeSE)*, 287–292. 10.1109/DeSE51703.2020.9450772

Jayabalan, M., & Oadaniel, T. (2018). Continuous and transparent access control framework for electronic health records: A preliminary study. *Proceedings - 2017 2nd International Conferences on Information Technology, Information Systems and Electrical Engineering, ICITISEE 2017*, 165–170. 10.1109/ICITISEE.2017.8285487

Jayabalan, M., & O'Daniel, T. (2016). Access control and privilege management in electronic health record: A systematic literature review. *Journal of Medical Systems*, *40*(12), 261. doi:10.100710916-016-0589-z PMID:27722981

Jayabalan, M., & O'Daniel, T. (2019). A study on authentication factors in electronic health records. *Journal of Applied Technology and Innovation*, *3*(1), 7–14. https://jati.apu.edu.my/

Jayabalan, M., & Thiruchelvam, V. (2017). A design of patients data transparency in electronic health records. *2017 IEEE International Symposium on Consumer Electronics (ISCE)*, 9–10. 10.1109/ISCE.2017.8355532

Jayakumar, G. D. S., & Thomas, B. J. (2013). A New Procedure of Clustering Based on Multivariate Outlier Detection. *Journal of Data Science: JDS*, *11*(1), 69–84. doi:10.6339/JDS.2013.11(1).1091

Joshi, M. A. (2018). *Digital image processing: An algorithmic approach*. PHI Learning Pvt. Ltd.

Kaipio, J., Lääveri, T., Hyppönen, H., Vainiomäki, S., Reponen, J., Kushniruk, A., Borycki, E., & Vänskä, J. (2017). Usability problems do not heal by themselves: National survey on physicians' experiences with EHRs in Finland. *International Journal of Medical Informatics*, *97*, 266–281. doi:10.1016/j.ijmedinf.2016.10.010 PMID:27919385

Kamarudin, M. H., Maple, C., Watson, T., & Safa, N. S. (2017). A LogitBoost-based Algorithm for Detecting Known and unknown Web Attacks. *IEEE Access: Practical Innovations, Open Solutions*, *5*, 26190–26200. doi:10.1109/ACCESS.2017.2766844

Kaminsky, G., Lizondo, S., & Reinhart, C. M. (1998). Leading Indicators of Currency Crises. *Staff Papers*, *45*(1), 1–48. doi:10.2307/3867328

Kaplan, D. (2021). On the Quantification of Model Uncertainty: A Bayesian Perspective. *Psychometrika*, *86*(1), 215–238. doi:10.100711336-021-09754-5 PMID:33721184

Kauflin, J. (2017, March 16). The Fast-Growing Job with A Huge Skills Gap: Cyber Security. *Forbes*.

Kelsky, K. (2015). *The professor is in: The essential guide to turning your Ph. D. into a job*. Crown.

Kent, A. D., & Liebrock, L. M. (2013). Differentiating User Authentication Graphs. *2013 IEEE Security and Privacy Workshops*, 72–75. doi:10.1109/SPW.2013.38

Khattak, F. K. (2017). *Toward a Robust and Universal Crowd Labeling Framework* [Doctoral dissertation]. Columbia University. doi:10.7916/D8Q24BJ2

Kopp, C., Korb, K. B., & Mills, B. I. (2018). Information-theoretic models of deception: Modelling cooperation and diffusion in populations exposed to "fake news." *PLoS One*, *13*(11), e0207383. Advance online publication. doi:10.1371/journal.pone.0207383 PMID:30485356

Kraus, L., Wechsung, I., & Möller, S. (2017). Psychological needs as motivators for security and privacy actions on smartphones. *Journal of Information Security and Applications*, *34*(Part 1), 34–45. doi:10.1016/j.jisa.2016.10.002

Krysowski, E., & Tremewan, J. (2020). Why does anonymity make us misbehave: Different norms or less compliance? *Economic Inquiry*, *59*(2), 776–789. doi:10.1111/ecin.12955

Kshirsagar, P. & Akojwar, S. (2016b). Novel approach for classification and prediction of non linear chaotic databases. *International Conference on Electrical, Electronics, and Optimization Techniques, ICEEOT 2016*. 10.1109/ICEEOT.2016.7755667

Kshirsagar, P. & Akojwar, S. (2017). *Optimization of BPNN parameters using PSO for EEG signals*. doi:10.2991/iccasp-16.2017.59

Kshirsagar, P. R., Manoharan, H., Al-Turjman, F., & Kumar, K. (2020). Design and testing of automated smoke monitoring sensors in vehicles. *IEEE Sensors Journal*, 1. Advance online publication. doi:10.1109/JSEN.2020.3044604

Kshirsagar, P., & Akojwar, S. (2016a, July 15). Hybrid Heuristic Optimization for Benchmark Datasets. *International Journal of Computers and Applications*, *146*(7), 11–16. Advance online publication. doi:10.5120/ijca2016910853

Kshirsagar, P., Balakrishnan, N., & Yadav, A. D. (2020). Modelling of optimised neural network for classification and prediction of benchmark datasets. *Computer Methods in Biomechanics and Biomedical Engineering. Imaging & Visualization*, *8*(4), 426–435. Advance online publication. doi:10.1080/21681163.2019.1711457

Kubbo, M., Jayabalan, M., & Rana, M. E. (2016). Privacy and Security Challenges in Cloud Based Electronic Health Record : Towards Access Control Model. *Third International Conference on Digital Security and Forensics (DigitalSec)*, 113–121.

Kumar, N., & Gupta, S. (2016). Offline handwritten Gurmukhi character recognition: A review. International Journal of Software Engineering and its Applications. doi:10.14257/ijseia.2016.10.5.08

Lam, K. H., Meijer, K. A., Loonstra, F. C., Coerver, E. M. E., Twose, J., Redeman, E., Moraal, B., Barkhof, F., de Groot, V., Uitdehaag, B. M. J., & Killestein, J. (2020). Real-world keystroke dynamics are a potentially valid biomarker for clinical disability in multiple sclerosis. *Multiple Sclerosis Journal*, *27*(9), 1421–1431. doi:10.1177/1352458520968797 PMID:33150823

Landwehr, N., Hall, M., & Frank, E. (2003). Logistic Model Trees. In N. Lavrač, D. Gamberger, H. Blockeel, & L. Todorovski (Eds.), Lecture Notes in Computer Science: Vol. 2837. *Machine Learning: ECML 2003. ECML 2003*. Springer. doi:10.1007/978-3-540-39857-8_23

LeCun, Y. (1989). *Backpropagation applied to handwritten zip code recognition*. Retrieved from http://yann.lecun.com/exdb/publis/pdf/lecun-89e.pdf

Lee, H., Hwang, J. Y., Kim, D. I., Lee, S., Lee, S. H., & Shin, J. S. (2018). Understanding keystroke dynamics for smartphone users authentication and keystroke dynamics on smartphones built-in motion sensors. *Security and Communication Networks*, *2018*, 2567463. Advance online publication. doi:10.1155/2018/2567463

Li, F., Clarke, N., Papadaki, M., & Dowland, P. (2014). Active authentication for mobile devices utilising behaviour profiling. *International Journal of Information Security*, *13*(3), 229–244. doi:10.100710207-013-0209-6

Li, J., & Daugherty, L. (2015). *Training cyber warriors: What can be learned from defense language training?* RAND National Defense Research Institute. doi:10.7249/RR476

Lovitts, B. E. (2007). *Making the implicit explicit: Creating performance expectations for the dissertation*. Stylus Publishing, LLC.

Lu, X., & Xu, Y. (2014). An User Behavior Credibility Authentication Model in Cloud Computing Environment. *2nd International Conference on Information Technology and Electronic Commerce.*, 271–275. 10.1109/ICITEC.2014.7105617

Machi, L. A., & McEvoy, B. T. (2021). *The literature review: Six steps to success*. Academic Press.

MacQueen, J. (1967, June). Some methods for classification and analysis of multivariate observations. In *Proceedings of the fifth Berkeley symposium on mathematical statistics and probability* (*Vol. 1*, No. 14, pp. 281-297). Academic Press.

Magnusson, M., Vehtari, A., Jonasson, J., & Andersen, M. (2020). Leave-one-out cross-validation for Bayesian model comparison in large data. *International Conference on Artificial Intelligence and Statistics*. 341-351. http://proceedings.mlr.press/v108/magnusson20a.html

Mahajan, A., Sofi, I., & Mansotra, V. (2017). *Machine Learning Techniques used for the Detection and Analysis of Modern Types of DDoS Attacks Framework to Detect and Analyze Compromised Hosts on network View project Machine Learning Techniques used for the Detection and Analysis of Modern Types of DD. International Research Journal of Engineering and Technology.*

Mahdi, D. A., Ant, A., & Singh, A. (2016). Market Guide for User Authentication. *Gartner Reprint*, (November), 1–15.

Mahfouz, A., Muslukhov, I., & Beznosov, K. (2016). Android users in the wild: Their authentication and usage behavior. *Pervasive and Mobile Computing*, *32*, 50–61. doi:10.1016/j.pmcj.2016.06.017

Ma, K. W. F., & McKinnon, T. (2021). COVID-19 and cyber fraud: Emerging threats during the pandemic. *Journal of Financial Crime*, *29*(2), 433–446. doi:10.1108/JFC-01-2021-0016

Makatjane, K. D., & Moroke, N. D. (2016), Comparative study of Holt-Winters Triple Exponential Smoothing and Seasonal ARIMA: Forecasting Short-Term Seasonal Car Sales in South Africa. *Risk Governance and Control: Financial Markets and Institutions, 6*(1), 71–82. https://virtusinterpress. org/-2016-Issue-1-.html

Makatjane, K., & Tsoku, T. (2022). Bootstrapping Time-Varying Uncertainty Intervals for Extreme Daily Return Periods. *International Journal of Financial Studies*, *10*(1), 10. doi:10.3390/ijfs10010010

Manoharan, H., Teekaraman, Y., Kshirsagar, P. R., Sundaramurthy, S., & Manoharan, A. (2020). Examining the effect of aquaculture using sensor-based technology with machine learning algorithm. *Aquaculture Research*, *51*(11), 4748–4758. Advance online publication. doi:10.1111/are.14821

Marcot, B. G. (2012). Metrics for evaluating performance and uncertainty of Bayesian network models. *Ecological Modelling*, *230*, 50–62. doi:10.1016/j.ecolmodel.2012.01.013

Mastoras, R. E., Iakovakis, D., Hadjidimitriou, S., Charisis, V., Kassie, S., Alsaadi, T., Khandoker, A., & Hadjileontiadis, L. J. (2019). Touchscreen typing pattern analysis for remote detection of the depressive tendency. *Scientific Reports*, *9*(1), 13414. doi:10.103841598-019-50002-9 PMID:31527640

Memon, N. (2017). How Biometric Authentication Poses New Challenges to Our Security and Privacy. *IEEE Signal Processing Magazine*, *34*(4), 196–194. doi:10.1109/MSP.2017.2697179

Meng, W., Wong, D. S., Furnell, S., & Zhou, J. (2015). Surveying the development of biometric user authentication on mobile phones. *IEEE Communications Surveys and Tutorials*, *17*(3), 1268–1293. doi:10.1109/COMST.2014.2386915

Milosevic, N., Dehghantanha, A., & Choo, K. K. R. (2017). Machine learning aided Android malware classification. *Computers & Electrical Engineering*, *61*, 266–274. Advance online publication. doi:10.1016/j.compeleceng.2017.02.013

Milton, L. C., & Memon, A. (2016). Intruder detector: A continuous authentication tool to model user behavior. *2016 IEEE Conference on Intelligence and Security Informatics (ISI)*, 286–291. 10.1109/ISI.2016.7745492

Mohd, T. K., Majumdar, S., Mathur, A., & Javaid, A. Y. (2018). Simulation and Analysis of DDoS Attack on Connected Autonomous Vehicular Network using OMNET++. *2018 9th IEEE Annual Ubiquitous Computing, Electronics and Mobile Communication Conference, UEMCON 2018*. 10.1109/UEMCON.2018.8796717

Mokube, I., & Adams, M. (2007). Honeypots: concepts, approaches, and challenges. *Proceedings of the 45th Annual Southeast Regional Conference*, 321–326. 10.1145/1233341.1233399

Morgan, S. (2016, May 13). Top 5 industries at risk of cyber-attacks. Retrieved on February 17, 2018, from https://www.forbes.com/sites/stevemorgan/2016/05/13/list-of-the-5-most-cyber-attacked-industries/#1edfc762715e

Mori, Y., Kuroda, M., & Makino, N. (2016). *Nonlinear Principal Component Analysis and Its Applications*. Springer. www.springer.com/series/13497

Mota, G., Fernandes, J., & Belo, O. (2014). Usage signatures analysis is an alternative method for preventing fraud in E-Commerce applications. *International Conference on Data Science and Advanced Analytics*, 203-208. 10.1109/DSAA.2014.7058074

Mubalaike, A. M., & Adali, E. (2018). Deep Learning Approach for Intelligent Financial Fraud detection system. *2018 3rd International Conference on Computer Science and Engineering (UBMK)*, 598-603. 10.1109/UBMK.2018.8566574

Mulla, D. J. (2013). Twenty five years of remote sensing in precision agriculture: Key advances and remaining knowledge gaps. Biosystems Engineering. doi:10.1016/j.biosystemseng.2012.08.009

Natakarnkitkul, S. (2019). *Evaluation Metrics: Reference Guides*. Retrieved from https://medium.com/@net_satsawat/evaluation-metrics-reference-guides-7c3a2a055351

NCSA. (2019). *Early Estimates of Motor Vehicle Traffic Fatalities for the First 9 Months (Jan–Sep) of 2019*. https://crashstats.nhtsa.dot.gov/#!/PublicationList/51

Newman, L. (2017, July 1) The biggest cybersecurity disasters of 2017 so far. Wired.

Nitzburg, G. C., & Farber, B. A. (2019). Patterns of utilization and a case illustration of an interactive text-based psychotherapy delivery system. *Journal of Clinical Psychology*, *75*(2), 247–259. doi:10.1002/jclp.22718 PMID:30628062

Niyaz, Q., Sun, W., & Javaid, A. (2016). *A Deep Learning Based DDoS Detection System in Software-Defined Networking (SDN)*. Retrieved from https://arxiv.org/abs/1611.07400

Olson, G. A., & Drew, J. (1998). Reenvisioning the dissertation in English studies. College English, 61(1), 56-66.

Ozer, S., Chen, C. H., & Cirpan, H. A. (2011). A set of new Chebyshev kernel functions for support vector machine pattern classification. *Pattern Recognition*, *44*(7), 1435–1447. Advance online publication. doi:10.1016/j.patcog.2010.12.017

Pabarskaite, Z., & Raudys, A. (2007). A process of knowledge discovery from web log data: Systematization and critical review. *Journal of Intelligent Information Systems*, *28*(1), 79–104. doi:10.100710844-006-0004-1

Pande, S., Khamparia, A., Gupta, D., & Thanh, D. N. (2021). DDOS detection using machine learning technique. In *Recent Studies on Computational Intelligence* (pp. 59–68). Springer.

Pang, Z., Zhang, J., Zhou, Q., Gong, S., Qian, X., & Tang, B. (2017). Crossover Ring Oscillator PUF. *Proceedings - International Symposium on Quality Electronic Design, ISQED*. 10.1109/ISQED.2017.7918322

Pannu, A., & Student, M. T. (2008). *Artificial Intelligence and its Application in Different Areas. Certified International Journal of Engineering and Innovative Technology*.

Papadatou-Pastou, M., Ntolka, E., Schmitz, J., Martin, M., Munafo, M. R., Ocklenburg, S., & Paracchini, S. (2020). Human handedness: A meta-analysis. *Psychological Bulletin*, *146*(6), 481–524. doi:10.1037/bul0000229 PMID:32237881

Pappas, J. P., & Jerman, J. (Eds.). (2011). *Meeting adult learner needs through the nontraditional doctoral degree*. Jossey-Bass.

Park, S., & Choi, J. Y. (2020). Malware Detection in Self-Driving Vehicles Using Machine Learning Algorithms. *Journal of Advanced Transportation*, *2020*, 1–9. Advance online publication. doi:10.1155/2020/3035741

Peacock, S. (2017). The PhD by publication. *International Journal of Doctoral Studies, 12,* 123–134. doi:10.28945/3781

Peterson, L. (2009). *K-nearest neighbor.* Retrieved from http://www.scholarpedia.org/article/K-nearest_neighbor

Peters, R. L. (1997). *Getting what you came for: the smart student's guide to earning a master's or a Ph. D.* Farrar, Straus and Giroux.

Pham, B. T., & Prakash, I. (2019). Evaluation and Comparison of LogitBoost Ensemble, Fisher's Linear Discriminant Analysis, Logistic Regression and Support Vector Machines Methods for Landslide Susceptibility Mapping. *Geocarto International, 34*(3), 316–333. doi:10.1080/1010 6049.2017.1404141

Phan, N. H., Wang, Y., Wu, X., & Dou, D. (2016). Differential privacy preservation for deep auto-encoders: An application of human behavior prediction. *30th AAAI Conference on Artificial Intelligence, AAAI 2016.* 10.1609/aaai.v30i1.10165

Pierce, A. O. (2016). *Exploring the cybersecurity hiring gap* (Order No. 10250186). Available from ProQuest Dissertations & Theses Global. (1848667353)

Pisani, P. H., Giot, R., de Carvalho, A. C. P. L. F., & Lorena, A. C. (2016). Enhanced template update: Application to keystroke dynamics. *Computers & Security, 60,* 134–153. doi:10.1016/j.cose.2016.04.004

Pourghasemi, H. R., Gayen, A., Park, S., Lee, C. W., & Lee, S. (2018). 'Assessment of Landslide-prone Areas and their Zonation using Logistic Regression, LogitBoost, and Naïve Bayes Machine-learning Algorithms. *Sustainability, 10*(10), 3697. doi:10.3390u10103697

Pranckevicius, T., & Marcinkevicius, V. (2017). Comparison of Naïve Bayes, Random Forest, Decision Tree, Support Vector Machines, and Logistic Regression Classifiers for Text Reviews Classification'. *Baltic Journal of Modern Computing, 5*(2), 221. doi:10.22364/bjmc.2017.5.2.05

Quellec, G., Lamard, M., Cazuguel, G., Cochener, B., & Roux, C. (2012). Fast wavelet-based image characterization for highly adaptive image retrieval. *IEEE Transactions on Image Processing, 21*(4), 1613–1623. Advance online publication. doi:10.1109/TIP.2011.2180915 PMID:22194244

Quinlan, J. R. (1986). Induction of decision trees. *Machine Learning, 1*(1), 81–106. doi:10.1007/BF00116251

Rachburee, N., & Punlumjeak, W. (2015). A comparison of feature selection approach between greedy, IG-ratio, Chi-square, and mRMR in educational mining. In *Proceedings of 7th International Conference on Information Technology and Electrical Engineering* (pp. 420-424). IEEE. 10.1109/ICITEED.2015.7408983

Rajendran, K., Jayabalan, M., & Ehsan Rana, M. (2017). A Study on k-anonymity, l-diversity, and t-closeness Techniques focusing Medical Data. *International Journal of Computer Science and Network Security, 17*(12), 172–177. http://paper.ijcsns.org/07_book/201712/20171225.pdf

Raul, N., Shankarmani, R., & Joshi, P. (2020). A comprehensive review of keystroke dynamics-based authentication mechanism. In A. Khanna, D. Gupta, S. Bhattacharyya, V. Snasel, J. Platos, & A. Hassanien (Eds), *International Conference on Innovative Computing and Communications. Advances in Intelligent Systems and Computing* (vol. 1059, pp. 149-162). Springer. 10.1007/978-981-15-0324-5_13

Raykar, V. C., & Saha, A. (2015). Data Split Strategiesfor Evolving Predictive Models. In A. Appice, P. P. Rodrigues, V. Santos Costa, C. Soares, J. Gama, & A. Jorge (Eds.), *Machine Learning and Knowledge Discovery in Databases: European Conference, ECML PKDD 2015, Porto, Portugal, September 7-11, 2015, Proceedings, Part I* (pp. 3–19). Springer International Publishing. 10.1007/978-3-319-23528-8_1

Raza, M., Iqbal, M., Sharif, M., & Haider, W. (2012). A survey of password attacks and comparative analysis on methods for secure authentication. *World Applied Sciences Journal, 19*(4), 439–444. doi:10.5829/idosi.wasj.2012.19.04.1837

Realpe-Munoz, P., Collazos, C. A., Hurtado, J., Granollers, T., & Velasco-Medina, J. (2016). An Integration of Usable Security and User Authentication into the ISO 9241-210 and ISO/IEC 25010:2011. In T. Tryfonas (Ed.), Human Aspects of Information Security, Privacy, and Trust (pp. 65–75). Springer International Publishing Switzerland 2016. doi:10.1007/978-3-319-39381-0

Riedmiller, M., & Braun, H. (1993). Direct adaptive method for faster backpropagation learning: The RPROP algorithm. *1993 IEEE International Conference on Neural Networks.* 10.1109/ICNN.1993.298623

Roberts, C. M. (2010). *The dissertation journey: A practical and comprehensive guide to planning, writing, and defending your dissertation.* Corwin Press.

Rodge, J. & Jaiswal, S. (2019). *Comprehensive Overview of Neural Networks and Its Applications in Autonomous Vehicles.* doi:10.4018/978-1-5225-7955-7.ch007

Rodriguez, J. J., Kuncheva, L. I., & Alonso, C. J. (2006). Rotation forest: A new classifier ensemble method. *IEEE Transactions on Pattern Analysis and Machine Intelligence, 28*(10), 1619–1630. doi:10.1109/TPAMI.2006.211 PMID:16986543

Rowe, N. C., & Rrushi, J. (2016). Introduction to cyberdeception. Introduction to Cyberdeception. doi:10.1007/978-3-319-41187-3

Roy, S., Roy, U., & Sinha, D. (2018). Identifying soft biometric traits through typing pattern on touchscreen phone. In J. Mandal & D. Sinha (Eds.), *Social Transformation – Digital Way. Communications in Computer and Information Science* (Vol. 836, pp. 546–561). Springer. doi:10.1007/978-981-13-1343-1_46

Rührmair, U., Sehnke, F., Sölter, J., Dror, G., Devadas, S., & Schmidhuber, J. (2010). Modeling attacks on physical unclonable functions. *Proceedings of the ACM Conference on Computer and Communications Security.* 10.1145/1866307.1866335

Rumelhart, D. E., Hinton, G. E., & Williams, R. J. (1985). *Learning internal representations by error propagation*. California Univ San Diego La Jolla Inst for Cognitive Science. doi:10.21236/ADA164453

Saevanee, H., Clarke, N., & Furnell, S. (2011). *SMS Linguistic Profiling Authentication on Mobile Device*. Academic Press.

Sahil, S. S., Mehmi, S., & Dogra, S. (2015). Artificial intelligence for designing user profiling system for cloud computing security: Experiment. *2015 International Conference on Advances in Computer Engineering and Applications*, 51–58. 10.1109/ICACEA.2015.7164645

Sahin, Y., & Duman, E. (2011). Detecting Credit Card Fraud by Decision Trees and Support Vector Machines. *Lecture Notes in Engineering and Computer Science*, *2188*(1). https://hdl.handle.net/11376/2366

Schwefel, H.-P. P. (1993). *Evolution and optimum seeking: the sixth generation*. John Wiley & Sons, Inc.

Seyedhossein, L., & Hashemi, M. R. (2010), Mining Information from Credit Card Time Series for Timelier Fraud Detection. *5th International Symposium on Telecommunications (IST'2010)*. 10.1109/ISTEL.2010.5734099

Shackelford, R., Lunt, B., McGettrick, A., Sloan, R., Topi, H., Davies, G., & Lunt, B. (2006). Computing curricula 2005: The overview report. *ACM SIGCSE*, *38*(1), 456–457. doi:10.1145/1124706.1121482

Sharma, D. (2017). Challenges Involved in Big Data Processing & Methods to Solve Big Data Processing Problems. *International Journal for Research in Applied Science and Engineering Technology*, *V*(VIII), 841–844. Advance online publication. doi:10.22214/ijraset.2017.8118

Shokri, R., & Shmatikov, V. (2015). Privacy-preserving deep learning. *Proceedings of the ACM Conference on Computer and Communications Security*. 10.1145/2810103.2813687

Shore, Z. (2016). Grad School Essentials. In *Grad School Essentials*. University of California Press. doi:10.1525/9780520963269

Shukla, M., Verma, P. & Scholar, R. (2015). Honeypot: Concepts, Types and Working. *International Journal of Engineering Development and Research*.

Singh, T. & Mishra, J. (2021). Learning with artificial intelligence systems: application, challenges, and opportunities. *Impact of AI Technologies on Teaching, Learning, and Research in Higher Education*, 236–253.

Singh, S., Kumar, N., & Kaur, N. (2014). Design and development of RFID Basedb intelligent security system. *International Journal of Advanced Research in Computer Engineering and Technology*, 3.

Sivasankari, N., & Kumari, R. S. S. (2022). Reliable set of random number generation using Astable Multivibrator PUF. *Analog Integrated Circuits and Signal Processing*, *112*(1), 29–48. doi:10.100710470-022-02027-w

Skračić, K., Pale, P., & Kostanjčar, Z. (2017). Authentication approach using one-time challenge generation based on user behavior patterns captured in transactional data sets. *Computers & Security*, *67*, 107–121. doi:10.1016/j.cose.2017.03.002

Song, Y., Ben Salem, M., Hershkop, S., & Stolfo, S. J. (2013). System Level User Behavior Biometrics using Fisher Features and Gaussian Mixture Models. *2013 IEEE Security and Privacy Workshops*, 52–59. doi:10.1109/SPW.2013.33

South African Banking Risk Information Centre Report. (2019). *Annual Crime Stats 2019*. https://www.sabric.co.za/media-and-news/downloads/

Spitzner, L. (2002). Honeypots: Tracking Hackers. Journal of Management.

Sridhar, B. (2019). Cross-Layered Embedding of Watermark on Image for High Authentication. *Pattern Recognition and Image Analysis*, *29*(1), 194–199. Advance online publication. doi:10.1134/S105466181901022X

Srivastava, A., Kundu, A., Sural, S., & Majumdar, A. (2008). Credit Card Fraud Detection using Hidden Markov Model. *IEEE Transactions on Dependable and Secure Computing*, *5*(1), 37–48. doi:10.1109/TDSC.2007.70228

Stevenson, G. V. (2017). *Cybersecurity implications for industry, academia, and parents: A qualitative case study in NSF STEM education* (Order No. 10624075). Available from ProQuest Dissertations & Theses Global. (1958945736)

Stokes, M. E., Davis, C. S., & Koch, G. G. (2012). *Categorical data analysis using SAS* (3rd ed.). https://www.amazon.com/Categorical-Data-Analysis-Using-Third/dp/1607646641

Sundaramurthy, S., Saravanabhavan, C., & Kshirsagar, P. (2020). Prediction and Classification of Rheumatoid Arthritis using Ensemble Machine Learning Approaches. *2020 International Conference on Decision Aid Sciences and Application, DASA 2020*. 10.1109/DASA51403.2020.9317253

Thippeswamy, G., & Shilpa, B. (2020). Classification of ECG Signal using Artificial Neural Network. *International Journal of Recent Technology and Engineering*. doi:10.35940/ijrte.E6867.038620

Tipton, S. J., Forkey, S., & Choi, Y. B. (2016). Toward Proper Authentication Methods in Electronic Medical Record Access Compliant to HIPAA and C.I.A. Triangle. *Journal of Medical Systems*, *40*(4), 1–8. doi:10.100710916-016-0465-x PMID:26872782

Tong, W., Hussain, A., Bo, W. X., & Maharjan, S. (2019). Artificial Intelligence for Vehicle-To-Everything: A Survey. *IEEE Access: Practical Innovations, Open Solutions*. Advance online publication. doi:10.1109/ACCESS.2019.2891073

Tramèr, F., Zhang, F., Juels, A., Reiter, M. K., & Ristenpart, T. (2016). Stealing machine learning models via prediction APIs. *Proceedings of the 25th USENIX Security Symposium.*

Tsangaratos, P., & Ilia, I. (2016). Comparison of a Logistic Regression and Naïve Bayes Classifier in Landslide Susceptibility Assessments: The Influence of Models Complexity and Training sets Size. *Catena, 145*, 164–179. doi:10.1016/j.catena.2016.06.004

Tsimperidis, I., Peikos, G., & Arampatzis, A. (2021). Classifying users through keystroke dynamics. In T. Chadjipadelis, B. Lausen, A. Markos, T. R. Lee, A. Montanari, & R. Nugent (Eds.), Data Analysis and Rationality in a Complex World. Studies in Classification, Data Analysis, and Knowledge Organization (pp. 311-319). Springer. doi:10.1007/978-3-030-60104-1_34

Tsimperidis, I., Rostami, S., Wilson, K., & Katos, V. (2021). User attribution through keystroke dynamics-based author age estimation. In B. Ghita & S. Shiaeles (Eds.), *Selected Papers from the 12th International Networking Conference. Lecture Notes in Networks and Systems* (vol. 180, pp. 47-61). Springer. 10.1007/978-3-030-64758-2_4

Tucker, A. B., Aiken, R. M., Barker, K., Bruce, K. B., & Cain, J. T. (1991). *Computing curricula 1991: Report of the ACM/IEEE-CS Joint Curriculum Task Force.* Association for Computing Machinery Press/IEEE Press. doi:10.1145/103701.103710

Turgeman, A., & Zelazny, F. (2017). Invisible challenges: The next step in behavioural biometrics? *Biometric Technology Today, 2017*(6), 5–7. doi:10.1016/S0969-4765(17)30114-5

Udandarao, V., Agrawal, M., Kumar, R., & Shah, R. R. (2020). On the inference of soft biometrics from typing patterns collected in a multi-device environment. In *Proceedings of 2020 IEEE Sixth International Conference on Multimedia Big Data* (pp. 76-85), IEEE. 10.1109/BigMM50055.2020.00021

Ulinskasa, M., Damaseviciusa, R., Maskeliunasa, R., & Wozniak, M. (2018). Recognition of human daytime fatigue using keystroke data. *Procedia Computer Science, 130*, 947–952. doi:10.1016/j.procs.2018.04.094

University of New Brunswick. (2022). *DDoS 2019 | Datasets | Research | Canadian Institute for Cybersecurity | UNB.* Retrieved from https://www.unb.ca/cic/datasets/ddos-2019.html

US Federal Bureau of Investigations. (2021). Retrieved from: https://www.fbi.gov/about

Uzun, Y., Bicakci, K., & Uzunay, Y. (2015). *Could we distinguish child users from adults using keystroke dynamics?* https://arxiv.org/abs/1511.05672

Valli, C. (2003). *Honeyd-A OS fingerprinting artifice.* Academic Press.

Van Balen, N., Ball, C. T., & Wang, H. (2016). A Behavioral biometrics based approach to online gender classification. In R. Deng, J. Weng, K. Ren, & V. Yegneswaran (Eds.), *12th International Conference on Security and Privacy in Communication Networks* (pp. 475-495). Springer International Publishing. 10.1007/978-3-319-59608-2_27

Van-Zadelhoff, M. (2016, September). The Biggest Cybersecurity Threats are Inside Your Company. *Harvard Business Review.*

Vasudavan, H., Jayabalan, M., & Ramiah, S. (2016). A preliminary study on designing tour website for older people. *2015 IEEE Student Conference on Research and Development, SCOReD 2015.* 10.1109/SCORED.2015.7449423

Verizon. (2017). 2017 Data Breach Investigations Report Tips on Getting the Most from This Report. *Verizon Business Journal, 1*, 1–48. doi:10.1017/CBO9781107415324.004

Verizon. (2019). *Data Breach Investigations Report.* https://www.ictsecuritymagazine.com/wp-content/uploads/2017-Data-Breach-Investigations-Report.pdf

Vesel, C., Rashidisabet, H., Zulueta, J., Stange, J. P., Duffecy, J., Hussain, F., Piscitello, A., Bark, J., Langenecker, S. A., Young, S., Mounts, E., Omberg, L., Nelson, P. C., Moore, R. C., Koziol, D., Bourne, K., Bennett, C. C., Ajilore, O., Demos, A. P., & Leow, A. (2020). Effects of mood and aging on keystroke dynamics metadata and their diurnal patterns in a large open-science sample: A BiAffect iOS study. *Journal of the American Medical Informatics Association, 27*(7), 1007–1018. doi:10.1093/jamia/ocaa057 PMID:32467973

Vielhauer, C. (2006). *Biometric User Authentication for IT Security* (Vol. 18). Springer-Verlag. doi:10.1007/0-387-28094-4

Vitale, J., Tonkin, M., Ojha, S., Williams, M. A., Wang, X., & Judge, W. (2017). Privacy by design in machine learning data collection: A user experience experimentation. *AAAI Spring Symposium - Technical Report.*

Wagener, G. (2011). *Self-adaptive honeypots coercing and assessing attacker behaviour.* Institut National Polytechnique de Lorraine-INPL.

Walker, G. E., Golde, C. M., Jones, L., Bueschel, A. C., & Hutchings, P. (2008). *The formation of scholars: Rethinking doctoral education for the twenty-first century.* Jossey-Bass.

Wang, H., & Raj, B. (2017). *On the Origin of Deep Learning.* Retrieved from https://arxiv.org/abs/1702.07800

Wang, P., Wu, L., Cunningham, R., & Zou, C. C. (2010). Honeypot detection in advanced botnet attacks. *International Journal of Information and Computer Security, 4*(1), 30. Advance online publication. doi:10.1504/IJICS.2010.031858

Wang, Q., Gao, M., & Qu, G. (2018). A machine learning attack resistant dual-mode PUF. *Proceedings of the ACM Great Lakes Symposium on VLSI, GLSVLSI.* 10.1145/3194554.3194590

Wang, Q., & Jin, H. (2008). Usable Authentication for Electronic Healthcare Systems. *Proceedings of the Symposium On Usable Privacy and Security (SOUPS).*

Wang, Q., Xu, C., & Sun, M. (2012). Protecting privacy by multi-dimensional k-anonymity. *Journal of Software, 7*(8). Advance online publication. doi:10.4304/jsw.7.8.1873-1880

Wen, Y., & Lao, Y. (2017). Enhancing PUF reliability by machine learning. *Proceedings - IEEE International Symposium on Circuits and Systems*. 10.1109/ISCAS.2017.8050672

Wetcher-Hendricks, D. (2011). *Analyzing quantitative data: An introduction for social researchers*. John Wiley & Sons.

White, G. E. (2017). *The dissertation warrior: The ultimate guide to being the kind of person who finishes a doctoral dissertation or thesis*. Triumphant Heart International.

WhiteHatSecurity. (2016). *Web Applications Security Statistics Report 2016*. https://www.whitehatsec.com/resources/web-applications-security-statistics-report-2016/

Widodo, P. P., Handayanto, R. T., & Herlawati, H. (2013). Penerapan Data Mining Dengan Matlab. *Informatika*. https://elibrary.bsi.ac.id/readbook/200622/penerapan-data-mining-dengan-matlab

Wong, T. T., & Yang, N. Y. (2017). Dependency analysis of accuracy estimates in k-fold cross validation. *IEEE Transactions on Knowledge and Data Engineering*, 29(11), 2417–2427. doi:10.1109/TKDE.2017.2740926

Woods, K., Kegelmeyer, W. P. J., & Bowyer, K. (1997). Combination of multiple classifiers using local accuracy estimates. *IEEE Transactions on Pattern Analysis and Machine Intelligence*, 19(4), 405–410. doi:10.1109/34.588027

Xiao, X., Wang, G., & Gehrke, J. (2011). Differential Privacy via Wavelet Transforms. *IEEE Transactions on Knowledge and Data Engineering*, 23(8), 1200–1214. Advance online publication. doi:10.1109/TKDE.2010.247

Xu, Z., & Yi, X. (2011). Classification of Privacy-preserving Distributed Data Mining protocols. *2011 6th International Conference on Digital Information Management, ICDIM 2011*. 10.1109/ICDIM.2011.6093356

Xuan, S., Liu, G., Li, Z., Zheng, L., Wang, S., & Jiang, C. (2018). Random Forest for Credit Card Fraud Detection. In *2018 IEEE 15th International Conference on Networking, Sensing and Control (ICNSC)*. IEEE. 10.1109/ICNSC.2018.8361343

Yonetani, R., Boddeti, V. N., Kitani, K. M., & Sato, Y. (2017). Privacy-Preserving Visual Learning Using Doubly Permuted Homomorphic Encryption. *Proceedings of the IEEE International Conference on Computer Vision*. 10.1109/ICCV.2017.225

Yuan, M., Chen, L., Rao, W., & Mei, H. (2012). A general framework for publishing privacy protected and utility preserved graph. *Proceedings - IEEE International Conference on Data Mining, ICDM*. 10.1109/ICDM.2012.62

Yuan, X., Li, C., & Li, X. (2017, May). DeepDefense: identifying DDoS attack via deep learning. In *2017 IEEE International Conference on Smart Computing (SMARTCOMP)* (pp. 1-8). IEEE.

Yuill, J., Denning, D. & Feer, F. (2006). Using Deception to Hide Things from Hackers: Processes, Principles, and Techniques. *Journal of Information Warfare*.

Compilation of References

Zhang, L., Zhou, W., & Jiao, L. (2004). Wavelet Support Vector Machine. *IEEE Transactions on Systems, Man, and Cybernetics. Part B, Cybernetics*, *34*(1), 34–39. Advance online publication. doi:10.1109/TSMCB.2003.811113 PMID:15369048

Zhang, Z., Zhou, X., Zhang, X., Wang, L., & Wang, P. (2018). A Model-based on Convolutional Neural Network for Online Transaction Fraud Detection. *Security and Communication Networks*, *2018*, 1–9. Advance online publication. doi:10.1155/2018/5680264

Zhao, P., Yan, C., & Jiang, C. (2016). Authenticating Web User's Identity through Browsing Sequences Modeling. *2016 IEEE 16th International Conference on Data Mining Workshops (ICDMW)*, 335–342. 10.1109/ICDMW.2016.0054

Related References

To continue our tradition of advancing information science and technology research, we have compiled a list of recommended IGI Global readings. These references will provide additional information and guidance to further enrich your knowledge and assist you with your own research and future publications.

Abbas, R., Michael, K., & Michael, M. G. (2017). What Can People Do with Your Spatial Data?: Socio-Ethical Scenarios. In A. Marrington, D. Kerr, & J. Gammack (Eds.), *Managing Security Issues and the Hidden Dangers of Wearable Technologies* (pp. 206–237). Hershey, PA: IGI Global. doi:10.4018/978-1-5225-1016-1.ch009

Abulaish, M., & Haldar, N. A. (2018). Advances in Digital Forensics Frameworks and Tools: A Comparative Insight and Ranking. *International Journal of Digital Crime and Forensics*, *10*(2), 95–119. doi:10.4018/IJDCF.2018040106

Ahmad, F. A., Kumar, P., Shrivastava, G., & Bouhlel, M. S. (2018). Bitcoin: Digital Decentralized Cryptocurrency. In G. Shrivastava, P. Kumar, B. Gupta, S. Bala, & N. Dey (Eds.), *Handbook of Research on Network Forensics and Analysis Techniques* (pp. 395–415). Hershey, PA: IGI Global. doi:10.4018/978-1-5225-4100-4.ch021

Ahmed, A. A. (2017). Investigation Approach for Network Attack Intention Recognition. *International Journal of Digital Crime and Forensics*, *9*(1), 17–38. doi:10.4018/IJDCF.2017010102

Akhtar, Z. (2017). Biometric Spoofing and Anti-Spoofing. In M. Dawson, D. Kisku, P. Gupta, J. Sing, & W. Li (Eds.), Developing Next-Generation Countermeasures for Homeland Security Threat Prevention (pp. 121-139). Hershey, PA: IGI Global. doi:10.4018/978-1-5225-0703-1.ch007

Related References

Akowuah, F. E., Land, J., Yuan, X., Yang, L., Xu, J., & Wang, H. (2018). Standards and Guides for Implementing Security and Privacy for Health Information Technology. In Y. Maleh (Ed.), *Security and Privacy Management, Techniques, and Protocols* (pp. 214–236). Hershey, PA: IGI Global. doi:10.4018/978-1-5225-5583-4.ch008

Akremi, A., Sallay, H., & Rouached, M. (2018). Intrusion Detection Systems Alerts Reduction: New Approach for Forensics Readiness. In Y. Maleh (Ed.), *Security and Privacy Management, Techniques, and Protocols* (pp. 255–275). Hershey, PA: IGI Global. doi:10.4018/978-1-5225-5583-4.ch010

Aldwairi, M., Hasan, M., & Balbahaith, Z. (2017). Detection of Drive-by Download Attacks Using Machine Learning Approach. *International Journal of Information Security and Privacy*, *11*(4), 16–28. doi:10.4018/IJISP.2017100102

Alohali, B. (2017). Detection Protocol of Possible Crime Scenes Using Internet of Things (IoT). In M. Moore (Ed.), *Cybersecurity Breaches and Issues Surrounding Online Threat Protection* (pp. 175–196). Hershey, PA: IGI Global. doi:10.4018/978-1-5225-1941-6.ch008

AlShahrani, A. M., Al-Abadi, M. A., Al-Malki, A. S., Ashour, A. S., & Dey, N. (2017). Automated System for Crops Recognition and Classification. In N. Dey, A. Ashour, & S. Acharjee (Eds.), *Applied Video Processing in Surveillance and Monitoring Systems* (pp. 54–69). Hershey, PA: IGI Global. doi:10.4018/978-1-5225-1022-2.ch003

Anand, R., Shrivastava, G., Gupta, S., Peng, S., & Sindhwani, N. (2018). Audio Watermarking With Reduced Number of Random Samples. In G. Shrivastava, P. Kumar, B. Gupta, S. Bala, & N. Dey (Eds.), *Handbook of Research on Network Forensics and Analysis Techniques* (pp. 372–394). Hershey, PA: IGI Global. doi:10.4018/978-1-5225-4100-4.ch020

Anand, R., Sinha, A., Bhardwaj, A., & Sreeraj, A. (2018). Flawed Security of Social Network of Things. In G. Shrivastava, P. Kumar, B. Gupta, S. Bala, & N. Dey (Eds.), *Handbook of Research on Network Forensics and Analysis Techniques* (pp. 65–86). Hershey, PA: IGI Global. doi:10.4018/978-1-5225-4100-4.ch005

Aneja, M. J., Bhatia, T., Sharma, G., & Shrivastava, G. (2018). Artificial Intelligence Based Intrusion Detection System to Detect Flooding Attack in VANETs. In G. Shrivastava, P. Kumar, B. Gupta, S. Bala, & N. Dey (Eds.), *Handbook of Research on Network Forensics and Analysis Techniques* (pp. 87–100). Hershey, PA: IGI Global. doi:10.4018/978-1-5225-4100-4.ch006

Antunes, F., Freire, M., & Costa, J. P. (2018). From Motivation and Self-Structure to a Decision-Support Framework for Online Social Networks. In V. Ahuja & S. Rathore (Eds.), *Multidisciplinary Perspectives on Human Capital and Information Technology Professionals* (pp. 116–136). Hershey, PA: IGI Global. doi:10.4018/978-1-5225-5297-0.ch007

Atli, D. (2017). Cybercrimes via Virtual Currencies in International Business. In M. Moore (Ed.), *Cybersecurity Breaches and Issues Surrounding Online Threat Protection* (pp. 121–143). Hershey, PA: IGI Global. doi:10.4018/978-1-5225-1941-6.ch006

Baazeem, R. M. (2018). The Role of Religiosity in Technology Acceptance: The Case of Privacy in Saudi Arabia. In J. McAlaney, L. Frumkin, & V. Benson (Eds.), *Psychological and Behavioral Examinations in Cyber Security* (pp. 172–193). Hershey, PA: IGI Global. doi:10.4018/978-1-5225-4053-3.ch010

Bailey, W. J. (2017). Protection of Critical Homeland Assets: Using a Proactive, Adaptive Security Management Driven Process. In M. Dawson, D. Kisku, P. Gupta, J. Sing, & W. Li (Eds.), *Developing Next-Generation Countermeasures for Homeland Security Threat Prevention* (pp. 17-50). Hershey, PA: IGI Global. https://doi.org/doi:10.4018/978-1-5225-0703-1.ch002

Bajaj, S. (2018). Current Drift in Energy Efficiency Cloud Computing: New Provocations, Workload Prediction, Consolidation, and Resource Over Commitment. In S. Aljawarneh & M. Malhotra (Eds.), *Critical Research on Scalability and Security Issues in Virtual Cloud Environments* (pp. 283–303). Hershey, PA: IGI Global. doi:10.4018/978-1-5225-3029-9.ch014

Balasubramanian, K. (2018). Hash Functions and Their Applications. In K. Balasubramanian & M. Rajakani (Eds.), *Algorithmic Strategies for Solving Complex Problems in Cryptography* (pp. 66–77). Hershey, PA: IGI Global. doi:10.4018/978-1-5225-2915-6.ch005

Balasubramanian, K. (2018). Recent Developments in Cryptography: A Survey. In K. Balasubramanian & M. Rajakani (Eds.), *Algorithmic Strategies for Solving Complex Problems in Cryptography* (pp. 1–22). Hershey, PA: IGI Global. doi:10.4018/978-1-5225-2915-6.ch001

Balasubramanian, K. (2018). Secure Two Party Computation. In K. Balasubramanian & M. Rajakani (Eds.), *Algorithmic Strategies for Solving Complex Problems in Cryptography* (pp. 145–153). Hershey, PA: IGI Global. doi:10.4018/978-1-5225-2915-6.ch012

Balasubramanian, K. (2018). Securing Public Key Encryption Against Adaptive Chosen Ciphertext Attacks. In K. Balasubramanian & M. Rajakani (Eds.), *Algorithmic Strategies for Solving Complex Problems in Cryptography* (pp. 134–144). Hershey, PA: IGI Global. doi:10.4018/978-1-5225-2915-6.ch011

Balasubramanian, K. (2018). Variants of the Diffie-Hellman Problem. In K. Balasubramanian & M. Rajakani (Eds.), *Algorithmic Strategies for Solving Complex Problems in Cryptography* (pp. 40–54). Hershey, PA: IGI Global. doi:10.4018/978-1-5225-2915-6.ch003

Balasubramanian, K., & K., M. (2018). Secure Group Key Agreement Protocols. In K. Balasubramanian, & M. Rajakani (Eds.), *Algorithmic Strategies for Solving Complex Problems in Cryptography* (pp. 55-65). Hershey, PA: IGI Global. https://doi.org/ doi:10.4018/978-1-5225-2915-6.ch004

Balasubramanian, K., & M., R. (2018). Problems in Cryptography and Cryptanalysis. In K. Balasubramanian, & M. Rajakani (Eds.), *Algorithmic Strategies for Solving Complex Problems in Cryptography* (pp. 23-39). Hershey, PA: IGI Global. https://doi.org/ doi:10.4018/978-1-5225-2915-6.ch002

Balasubramanian, K., & Abbas, A. M. (2018). Integer Factoring Algorithms. In K. Balasubramanian & M. Rajakani (Eds.), *Algorithmic Strategies for Solving Complex Problems in Cryptography* (pp. 228–240). Hershey, PA: IGI Global. doi:10.4018/978-1-5225-2915-6.ch017

Balasubramanian, K., & Abbas, A. M. (2018). Secure Bootstrapping Using the Trusted Platform Module. In K. Balasubramanian & M. Rajakani (Eds.), *Algorithmic Strategies for Solving Complex Problems in Cryptography* (pp. 167–185). Hershey, PA: IGI Global. doi:10.4018/978-1-5225-2915-6.ch014

Balasubramanian, K., & Mathanan, J. (2018). Cryptographic Voting Protocols. In K. Balasubramanian & M. Rajakani (Eds.), *Algorithmic Strategies for Solving Complex Problems in Cryptography* (pp. 124–133). Hershey, PA: IGI Global. doi:10.4018/978-1-5225-2915-6.ch010

Balasubramanian, K., & Rajakani, M. (2018). Secure Multiparty Computation. In K. Balasubramanian & M. Rajakani (Eds.), *Algorithmic Strategies for Solving Complex Problems in Cryptography* (pp. 154–166). Hershey, PA: IGI Global. doi:10.4018/978-1-5225-2915-6.ch013

Balasubramanian, K., & Rajakani, M. (2018). The Quadratic Sieve Algorithm for Integer Factoring. In K. Balasubramanian & M. Rajakani (Eds.), *Algorithmic Strategies for Solving Complex Problems in Cryptography* (pp. 241–252). Hershey, PA: IGI Global. doi:10.4018/978-1-5225-2915-6.ch018

Barone, P. A. (2017). Defining and Understanding the Development of Juvenile Delinquency from an Environmental, Sociological, and Theoretical Perspective. In S. Egharevba (Ed.), *Police Brutality, Racial Profiling, and Discrimination in the Criminal Justice System* (pp. 215–238). Hershey, PA: IGI Global. doi:10.4018/978-1-5225-1088-8.ch010

Beauchere, J. F. (2018). Encouraging Digital Civility: What Companies and Others Can Do. In R. Luppicini (Ed.), *The Changing Scope of Technoethics in Contemporary Society* (pp. 262–274). Hershey, PA: IGI Global. doi:10.4018/978-1-5225-5094-5.ch014

Behera, C. K., & Bhaskari, D. L. (2017). Malware Methodologies and Its Future: A Survey. *International Journal of Information Security and Privacy, 11*(4), 47–64. doi:10.4018/IJISP.2017100104

Benson, V., McAlaney, J., & Frumkin, L. A. (2018). Emerging Threats for the Human Element and Countermeasures in Current Cyber Security Landscape. In J. McAlaney, L. Frumkin, & V. Benson (Eds.), *Psychological and Behavioral Examinations in Cyber Security* (pp. 266–271). Hershey, PA: IGI Global. doi:10.4018/978-1-5225-4053-3.ch016

Berbecaru, D. (2018). On Creating Digital Evidence in IP Networks With NetTrack. In G. Shrivastava, P. Kumar, B. Gupta, S. Bala, & N. Dey (Eds.), *Handbook of Research on Network Forensics and Analysis Techniques* (pp. 225–245). Hershey, PA: IGI Global. doi:10.4018/978-1-5225-4100-4.ch012

Berki, E., Valtanen, J., Chaudhary, S., & Li, L. (2018). The Need for Multi-Disciplinary Approaches and Multi-Level Knowledge for Cybersecurity Professionals. In V. Ahuja & S. Rathore (Eds.), *Multidisciplinary Perspectives on Human Capital and Information Technology Professionals* (pp. 72–94). Hershey, PA: IGI Global. doi:10.4018/978-1-5225-5297-0.ch005

Bhardwaj, A. (2017). Ransomware: A Rising Threat of new age Digital Extortion. In S. Aljawarneh (Ed.), *Online Banking Security Measures and Data Protection* (pp. 189–221). Hershey, PA: IGI Global. doi:10.4018/978-1-5225-0864-9.ch012

Bhattacharjee, J., Sengupta, A., Barik, M. S., & Mazumdar, C. (2018). An Analytical Study of Methodologies and Tools for Enterprise Information Security Risk Management. In M. Gupta, R. Sharman, J. Walp, & P. Mulgund (Eds.), *Information Technology Risk Management and Compliance in Modern Organizations* (pp. 1–20). Hershey, PA: IGI Global. doi:10.4018/978-1-5225-2604-9.ch001

Bruno, G. (2018). Handling the Dataflow in Business Process Models. In V. Ahuja & S. Rathore (Eds.), *Multidisciplinary Perspectives on Human Capital and Information Technology Professionals* (pp. 137–151). Hershey, PA: IGI Global. doi:10.4018/978-1-5225-5297-0.ch008

Bush, C. L. (2021). Policing Strategies and Approaches to Improving Community Relations: Black Citizens' Perceptions of Law Enforcement Efforts to Intentionally Strengthen Relationships. In M. Pittaro (Ed.), *Global Perspectives on Reforming the Criminal Justice System* (pp. 56–75). IGI Global. https://doi.org/10.4018/978-1-7998-6884-2.ch004

Carneiro, A. D. (2017). Defending Information Networks in Cyberspace: Some Notes on Security Needs. In M. Dawson, D. Kisku, P. Gupta, J. Sing, & W. Li (Eds.), Developing Next-Generation Countermeasures for Homeland Security Threat Prevention (pp. 354-375). Hershey, PA: IGI Global. https://doi.org/ doi:10.4018/978-1-5225-0703-1.ch016

Chakraborty, S., Patra, P. K., Maji, P., Ashour, A. S., & Dey, N. (2017). Image Registration Techniques and Frameworks: A Review. In N. Dey, A. Ashour, & S. Acharjee (Eds.), *Applied Video Processing in Surveillance and Monitoring Systems* (pp. 102–114). Hershey, PA: IGI Global. doi:10.4018/978-1-5225-1022-2.ch005

Chaudhari, G., & Mulgund, P. (2018). Strengthening IT Governance With COBIT 5. In M. Gupta, R. Sharman, J. Walp, & P. Mulgund (Eds.), *Information Technology Risk Management and Compliance in Modern Organizations* (pp. 48–69). Hershey, PA: IGI Global. doi:10.4018/978-1-5225-2604-9.ch003

Cheikh, M., Hacini, S., & Boufaida, Z. (2018). Visualization Technique for Intrusion Detection. In Y. Maleh (Ed.), *Security and Privacy Management, Techniques, and Protocols* (pp. 276–290). Hershey, PA: IGI Global. doi:10.4018/978-1-5225-5583-4.ch011

Chen, G., Ding, L., Du, J., Zhou, G., Qin, P., Chen, G., & Liu, Q. (2018). Trust Evaluation Strategy for Single Sign-on Solution in Cloud. *International Journal of Digital Crime and Forensics*, *10*(1), 1–11. doi:10.4018/IJDCF.2018010101

Chen, J., & Peng, F. (2018). A Perceptual Encryption Scheme for HEVC Video with Lossless Compression. *International Journal of Digital Crime and Forensics*, *10*(1), 67–78. doi:10.4018/IJDCF.2018010106

Chen, K., & Xu, D. (2018). An Efficient Reversible Data Hiding Scheme for Encrypted Images. *International Journal of Digital Crime and Forensics*, *10*(2), 1–22. doi:10.4018/IJDCF.2018040101

Chen, Z., Lu, J., Yang, P., & Luo, X. (2017). Recognizing Substitution Steganography of Spatial Domain Based on the Characteristics of Pixels Correlation. *International Journal of Digital Crime and Forensics, 9*(4), 48–61. doi:10.4018/IJDCF.2017100105

Cherkaoui, R., Zbakh, M., Braeken, A., & Touhafi, A. (2018). Anomaly Detection in Cloud Computing and Internet of Things Environments: Latest Technologies. In K. Munir (Ed.), *Cloud Computing Technologies for Green Enterprises* (pp. 251–265). Hershey, PA: IGI Global. doi:10.4018/978-1-5225-3038-1.ch010

Chowdhury, A., Karmakar, G., & Kamruzzaman, J. (2017). Survey of Recent Cyber Security Attacks on Robotic Systems and Their Mitigation Approaches. In R. Kumar, P. Pattnaik, & P. Pandey (Eds.), *Detecting and Mitigating Robotic Cyber Security Risks* (pp. 284–299). Hershey, PA: IGI Global. doi:10.4018/978-1-5225-2154-9.ch019

Cortese, F. A. (2018). The Techoethical Ethos of Technic Self-Determination: Technological Determinism as the Ontic Fundament of Freewill. In R. Luppicini (Ed.), *The Changing Scope of Technoethics in Contemporary Society* (pp. 74–104). Hershey, PA: IGI Global. doi:10.4018/978-1-5225-5094-5.ch005

Crosston, M. D. (2017). The Fight for Cyber Thoreau: Distinguishing Virtual Disobedience from Digital Destruction. In M. Korstanje (Ed.), *Threat Mitigation and Detection of Cyber Warfare and Terrorism Activities* (pp. 198–219). Hershey, PA: IGI Global. doi:10.4018/978-1-5225-1938-6.ch009

da Costa, F., & de Sá-Soares, F. (2017). Authenticity Challenges of Wearable Technologies. In A. Marrington, D. Kerr, & J. Gammack (Eds.), *Managing Security Issues and the Hidden Dangers of Wearable Technologies* (pp. 98–130). Hershey, PA: IGI Global. doi:10.4018/978-1-5225-1016-1.ch005

Dafflon, B., Guériau, M., & Gechter, F. (2017). Using Physics Inspired Wave Agents in a Virtual Environment: Longitudinal Distance Control in Robots Platoon. *International Journal of Monitoring and Surveillance Technologies Research, 5*(2), 15–28. doi:10.4018/IJMSTR.2017040102

Dash, S. R., Sheeraz, A. S., & Samantaray, A. (2018). Filtration and Classification of ECG Signals. In C. Pradhan, H. Das, B. Naik, & N. Dey (Eds.), *Handbook of Research on Information Security in Biomedical Signal Processing* (pp. 72–94). Hershey, PA: IGI Global. doi:10.4018/978-1-5225-5152-2.ch005

Dhavale, S. V. (2018). Insider Attack Analysis in Building Effective Cyber Security for an Organization. In J. McAlaney, L. Frumkin, & V. Benson (Eds.), *Psychological and Behavioral Examinations in Cyber Security* (pp. 222–238). Hershey, PA: IGI Global. doi:10.4018/978-1-5225-4053-3.ch013

Dixit, P. (2018). Security Issues in Web Services. In G. Shrivastava, P. Kumar, B. Gupta, S. Bala, & N. Dey (Eds.), *Handbook of Research on Network Forensics and Analysis Techniques* (pp. 57–64). Hershey, PA: IGI Global. doi:10.4018/978-1-5225-4100-4.ch004

Doraikannan, S. (2018). Efficient Implementation of Digital Signature Algorithms. In K. Balasubramanian & M. Rajakani (Eds.), *Algorithmic Strategies for Solving Complex Problems in Cryptography* (pp. 78–86). Hershey, PA: IGI Global. doi:10.4018/978-1-5225-2915-6.ch006

E., J. V., Mohan, J., & K., A. (2018). Automatic Detection of Tumor and Bleed in Magnetic Resonance Brain Images. In C. Pradhan, H. Das, B. Naik, & N. Dey (Eds.), *Handbook of Research on Information Security in Biomedical Signal Processing* (pp. 291-303). Hershey, PA: IGI Global. https://doi.org/ doi:10.4018/978-1-5225-5152-2.ch015

Escamilla, I., Ruíz, M. T., Ibarra, M. M., Soto, V. L., Quintero, R., & Guzmán, G. (2018). Geocoding Tweets Based on Semantic Web and Ontologies. In M. Lytras, N. Aljohani, E. Damiani, & K. Chui (Eds.), *Innovations, Developments, and Applications of Semantic Web and Information Systems* (pp. 372–392). Hershey, PA: IGI Global. doi:10.4018/978-1-5225-5042-6.ch014

Essefi, E. (2022). Advances in Forensic Geophysics: Magnetic Susceptibility as a Tool for Environmental Forensic Geophysics. In C. Chen, W. Yang, & L. Chen (Eds.), *Technologies to Advance Automation in Forensic Science and Criminal Investigation* (pp. 15-36). IGI Global. https://doi.org/10.4018/978-1-7998-8386-9.ch002

Farhadi, M., Haddad, H. M., & Shahriar, H. (2018). Compliance of Electronic Health Record Applications With HIPAA Security and Privacy Requirements. In Y. Maleh (Ed.), *Security and Privacy Management, Techniques, and Protocols* (pp. 199–213). Hershey, PA: IGI Global. doi:10.4018/978-1-5225-5583-4.ch007

Fatma, S. (2018). Use and Misuse of Technology in Marketing: Cases from India. *International Journal of Technoethics*, 9(1), 27–36. doi:10.4018/IJT.2018010103

Fazlali, M., & Khodamoradi, P. (2018). Metamorphic Malware Detection Using Minimal Opcode Statistical Patterns. In Y. Maleh (Ed.), *Security and Privacy Management, Techniques, and Protocols* (pp. 337–359). Hershey, PA: IGI Global. doi:10.4018/978-1-5225-5583-4.ch014

Filiol, É., & Gallais, C. (2017). Optimization of Operational Large-Scale (Cyber) Attacks by a Combinational Approach. *International Journal of Cyber Warfare & Terrorism*, 7(3), 29–43. doi:10.4018/IJCWT.2017070103

Forge, J. (2018). The Case Against Weapons Research. In R. Luppicini (Ed.), *The Changing Scope of Technoethics in Contemporary Society* (pp. 124–134). Hershey, PA: IGI Global. doi:10.4018/978-1-5225-5094-5.ch007

G., S., & Durai, M. S. (2018). Big Data Analytics: An Expedition Through Rapidly Budding Data Exhaustive Era. In D. Lopez, & M. Durai (Eds.), *HCI Challenges and Privacy Preservation in Big Data Security* (pp. 124-138). Hershey, PA: IGI Global. https://doi.org/ doi:10.4018/978-1-5225-2863-0.ch006

Gammack, J., & Marrington, A. (2017). The Promise and Perils of Wearable Technologies. In A. Marrington, D. Kerr, & J. Gammack (Eds.), *Managing Security Issues and the Hidden Dangers of Wearable Technologies* (pp. 1–17). Hershey, PA: IGI Global. doi:10.4018/978-1-5225-1016-1.ch001

Gamoura, S. C. (2018). A Cloud-Based Approach for Cross-Management of Disaster Plans: Managing Risk in Networked Enterprises. In S. Aljawarneh & M. Malhotra (Eds.), *Critical Research on Scalability and Security Issues in Virtual Cloud Environments* (pp. 240–268). Hershey, PA: IGI Global. doi:10.4018/978-1-5225-3029-9.ch012

Gao, L., Gao, T., Zhao, J., & Liu, Y. (2018). Reversible Watermarking in Digital Image Using PVO and RDWT. *International Journal of Digital Crime and Forensics*, *10*(2), 40–55. doi:10.4018/IJDCF.2018040103

Ghany, K. K., & Zawbaa, H. M. (2017). Hybrid Biometrics and Watermarking Authentication. In S. Zoughbi (Ed.), *Securing Government Information and Data in Developing Countries* (pp. 37–61). Hershey, PA: IGI Global. doi:10.4018/978-1-5225-1703-0.ch003

Ghosh, P., Sarkar, D., Sharma, J., & Phadikar, S. (2021). An Intrusion Detection System Using Modified-Firefly Algorithm in Cloud Environment. *International Journal of Digital Crime and Forensics*, *13*(2), 77–93. https://doi.org/10.4018/IJDCF.2021030105

Grant, B. S. (2022). All the World's a Stage: Achieving Deliberate Practice and Performance Improvement Through Story-Based Learning. In *Research Anthology on Advancements in Cybersecurity Education* (pp. 394-413). IGI Global. https://doi.org/10.4018/978-1-6684-3554-0.ch019

Hacini, S., Guessoum, Z., & Cheikh, M. (2018). False Alarm Reduction: A Profiling Mechanism and New Research Directions. In Y. Maleh (Ed.), *Security and Privacy Management, Techniques, and Protocols* (pp. 291–320). Hershey, PA: IGI Global. doi:10.4018/978-1-5225-5583-4.ch012

Hadlington, L. (2018). The "Human Factor" in Cybersecurity: Exploring the Accidental Insider. In J. McAlaney, L. Frumkin, & V. Benson (Eds.), Psychological and Behavioral Examinations in Cyber Security (pp. 46-63). Hershey, PA: IGI Global. https://doi.org/ doi:10.4018/978-1-5225-4053-3.ch003

Haldorai, A., & Ramu, A. (2018). The Impact of Big Data Analytics and Challenges to Cyber Security. In G. Shrivastava, P. Kumar, B. Gupta, S. Bala, & N. Dey (Eds.), *Handbook of Research on Network Forensics and Analysis Techniques* (pp. 300–314). Hershey, PA: IGI Global. doi:10.4018/978-1-5225-4100-4.ch016

Hariharan, S., Prasanth, V. S., & Saravanan, P. (2018). Role of Bibliographical Databases in Measuring Information: A Conceptual View. In J. Jeyasekar & P. Saravanan (Eds.), *Innovations in Measuring and Evaluating Scientific Information* (pp. 61–71). Hershey, PA: IGI Global. doi:10.4018/978-1-5225-3457-0.ch005

Hore, S., Chatterjee, S., Chakraborty, S., & Shaw, R. K. (2017). Analysis of Different Feature Description Algorithm in object Recognition. In N. Dey, A. Ashour, & P. Patra (Eds.), *Feature Detectors and Motion Detection in Video Processing* (pp. 66–99). Hershey, PA: IGI Global. doi:10.4018/978-1-5225-1025-3.ch004

Hurley, J. S. (2017). Cyberspace: The New Battlefield - An Approach via the Analytics Hierarchy Process. *International Journal of Cyber Warfare & Terrorism*, 7(3), 1–15. doi:10.4018/IJCWT.2017070101

Hussain, M., & Kaliya, N. (2018). An Improvised Framework for Privacy Preservation in IoT. *International Journal of Information Security and Privacy*, 12(2), 46–63. doi:10.4018/IJISP.2018040104

Ilahi-Amri, M., Cheniti-Belcadhi, L., & Braham, R. (2018). Competence E-Assessment Based on Semantic Web: From Modeling to Validation. In V. Ahuja & S. Rathore (Eds.), *Multidisciplinary Perspectives on Human Capital and Information Technology Professionals* (pp. 246–267). Hershey, PA: IGI Global. doi:10.4018/978-1-5225-5297-0.ch013

Jambhekar, N., & Dhawale, C. A. (2018). Cryptography in Big Data Security. In D. Lopez & M. Durai (Eds.), *HCI Challenges and Privacy Preservation in Big Data Security* (pp. 71–94). Hershey, PA: IGI Global. doi:10.4018/978-1-5225-2863-0.ch004

Jansen van Vuuren, J., Leenen, L., Plint, G., Zaaiman, J., & Phahlamohlaka, J. (2017). Formulating the Building Blocks for National Cyberpower. *International Journal of Cyber Warfare & Terrorism*, 7(3), 16–28. doi:10.4018/IJCWT.2017070102

Jaswal, S., & Malhotra, M. (2018). Identification of Various Privacy and Trust Issues in Cloud Computing Environment. In S. Aljawarneh & M. Malhotra (Eds.), *Critical Research on Scalability and Security Issues in Virtual Cloud Environments* (pp. 95–121). Hershey, PA: IGI Global. doi:10.4018/978-1-5225-3029-9.ch005

Jaswal, S., & Singh, G. (2018). A Comprehensive Survey on Trust Issue and Its Deployed Models in Computing Environment. In S. Aljawarneh & M. Malhotra (Eds.), *Critical Research on Scalability and Security Issues in Virtual Cloud Environments* (pp. 150–166). Hershey, PA: IGI Global. doi:10.4018/978-1-5225-3029-9.ch007

Javid, T. (2018). Secure Access to Biomedical Images. In C. Pradhan, H. Das, B. Naik, & N. Dey (Eds.), *Handbook of Research on Information Security in Biomedical Signal Processing* (pp. 38–53). Hershey, PA: IGI Global. doi:10.4018/978-1-5225-5152-2.ch003

Jeyakumar, B., Durai, M. S., & Lopez, D. (2018). Case Studies in Amalgamation of Deep Learning and Big Data. In D. Lopez & M. Durai (Eds.), *HCI Challenges and Privacy Preservation in Big Data Security* (pp. 159–174). Hershey, PA: IGI Global. doi:10.4018/978-1-5225-2863-0.ch008

Jeyaprakash, H. M. K., K., & S., G. (2018). A Comparative Review of Various Machine Learning Approaches for Improving the Performance of Stego Anomaly Detection. In G. Shrivastava, P. Kumar, B. Gupta, S. Bala, & N. Dey (Eds.), Handbook of Research on Network Forensics and Analysis Techniques (pp. 351-371). Hershey, PA: IGI Global. https://doi.org/ doi:10.4018/978-1-5225-4100-4.ch019

Jeyasekar, J. J. (2018). Dynamics of Indian Forensic Science Research. In J. Jeyasekar & P. Saravanan (Eds.), *Innovations in Measuring and Evaluating Scientific Information* (pp. 125–147). Hershey, PA: IGI Global. doi:10.4018/978-1-5225-3457-0.ch009

Jones, H. S., & Moncur, W. (2018). The Role of Psychology in Understanding Online Trust. In J. McAlaney, L. Frumkin, & V. Benson (Eds.), *Psychological and Behavioral Examinations in Cyber Security* (pp. 109–132). Hershey, PA: IGI Global. doi:10.4018/978-1-5225-4053-3.ch007

Jones, H. S., & Towse, J. (2018). Examinations of Email Fraud Susceptibility: Perspectives From Academic Research and Industry Practice. In J. McAlaney, L. Frumkin, & V. Benson (Eds.), *Psychological and Behavioral Examinations in Cyber Security* (pp. 80–97). Hershey, PA: IGI Global. doi:10.4018/978-1-5225-4053-3.ch005

Related References

Joseph, A., & Singh, K. J. (2018). Digital Forensics in Distributed Environment. In G. Shrivastava, P. Kumar, B. Gupta, S. Bala, & N. Dey (Eds.), *Handbook of Research on Network Forensics and Analysis Techniques* (pp. 246–265). Hershey, PA: IGI Global. doi:10.4018/978-1-5225-4100-4.ch013

K., I., & A, V. (2018). Monitoring and Auditing in the Cloud. In K. Munir (Ed.), *Cloud Computing Technologies for Green Enterprises* (pp. 318-350). Hershey, PA: IGI Global. https://doi.org/ doi:10.4018/978-1-5225-3038-1.ch013

Kashyap, R., & Piersson, A. D. (2018). Impact of Big Data on Security. In G. Shrivastava, P. Kumar, B. Gupta, S. Bala, & N. Dey (Eds.), *Handbook of Research on Network Forensics and Analysis Techniques* (pp. 283–299). Hershey, PA: IGI Global. doi:10.4018/978-1-5225-4100-4.ch015

Kastrati, Z., Imran, A. S., & Yayilgan, S. Y. (2018). A Hybrid Concept Learning Approach to Ontology Enrichment. In M. Lytras, N. Aljohani, E. Damiani, & K. Chui (Eds.), *Innovations, Developments, and Applications of Semantic Web and Information Systems* (pp. 85–119). Hershey, PA: IGI Global. doi:10.4018/978-1-5225-5042-6.ch004

Kaur, H., & Saxena, S. (2018). UWDBCSN Analysis During Node Replication Attack in WSN. In C. Pradhan, H. Das, B. Naik, & N. Dey (Eds.), *Handbook of Research on Information Security in Biomedical Signal Processing* (pp. 210–227). Hershey, PA: IGI Global. doi:10.4018/978-1-5225-5152-2.ch011

Kaushal, P. K., & Sobti, R. (2018). Breaching Security of Full Round Tiny Encryption Algorithm. *International Journal of Information Security and Privacy*, *12*(1), 89–98. doi:10.4018/IJISP.2018010108

Kavati, I., Prasad, M. V., & Bhagvati, C. (2017). Search Space Reduction in Biometric Databases: A Review. In M. Dawson, D. Kisku, P. Gupta, J. Sing, & W. Li (Eds.), Developing Next-Generation Countermeasures for Homeland Security Threat Prevention (pp. 236-262). Hershey, PA: IGI Global. doi:10.4018/978-1-5225-0703-1.ch011

Kaye, L. K. (2018). Online Research Methods. In J. McAlaney, L. Frumkin, & V. Benson (Eds.), *Psychological and Behavioral Examinations in Cyber Security* (pp. 253–265). Hershey, PA: IGI Global. doi:10.4018/978-1-5225-4053-3.ch015

Kenekar, T. V., & Dani, A. R. (2017). Privacy Preserving Data Mining on Unstructured Data. In S. Tamane, V. Solanki, & N. Dey (Eds.), *Privacy and Security Policies in Big Data* (pp. 167–190). Hershey, PA: IGI Global. doi:10.4018/978-1-5225-2486-1.ch008

Kenny, P., & Leonard, L. J. (2021). Restorative Justice as an "Informal" Alternative to "Formal" Court Processes. In L. Leonard (Ed.), *Global Perspectives on People, Process, and Practice in Criminal Justice* (pp. 226–244). IGI Global. https://doi.org/10.4018/978-1-7998-6646-6.ch014

Khaire, P. A., & Kotkondawar, R. R. (2017). Measures of Image and Video Segmentation. In N. Dey, A. Ashour, & S. Acharjee (Eds.), *Applied Video Processing in Surveillance and Monitoring Systems* (pp. 28–53). Hershey, PA: IGI Global. doi:10.4018/978-1-5225-1022-2.ch002

Knibbs, C., Goss, S., & Anthony, K. (2017). Counsellors' Phenomenological Experiences of Working with Children or Young People who have been Cyberbullied: Using Thematic Analysis of Semi Structured Interviews. *International Journal of Technoethics*, *8*(1), 68–86. doi:10.4018/IJT.2017010106

Ko, A., & Gillani, S. (2018). Ontology Maintenance Through Semantic Text Mining: An Application for IT Governance Domain. In M. Lytras, N. Aljohani, E. Damiani, & K. Chui (Eds.), *Innovations, Developments, and Applications of Semantic Web and Information Systems* (pp. 350–371). Hershey, PA: IGI Global. doi:10.4018/978-1-5225-5042-6.ch013

Kohler, J., Lorenz, C. R., Gumbel, M., Specht, T., & Simov, K. (2017). A Security-By-Distribution Approach to Manage Big Data in a Federation of Untrustworthy Clouds. In S. Tamane, V. Solanki, & N. Dey (Eds.), *Privacy and Security Policies in Big Data* (pp. 92–123). Hershey, PA: IGI Global. doi:10.4018/978-1-5225-2486-1.ch005

Korstanje, M. E. (2017). English Speaking Countries and the Culture of Fear: Understanding Technology and Terrorism. In M. Korstanje (Ed.), *Threat Mitigation and Detection of Cyber Warfare and Terrorism Activities* (pp. 92–110). Hershey, PA: IGI Global. doi:10.4018/978-1-5225-1938-6.ch005

Korstanje, M. E. (2018). How Can World Leaders Understand the Perverse Core of Terrorism?: Terror in the Global Village. In C. Akrivopoulou (Ed.), *Global Perspectives on Human Migration, Asylum, and Security* (pp. 48–67). Hershey, PA: IGI Global. doi:10.4018/978-1-5225-2817-3.ch003

Krishnamachariar, P. K., & Gupta, M. (2018). Swimming Upstream in Turbulent Waters: Auditing Agile Development. In M. Gupta, R. Sharman, J. Walp, & P. Mulgund (Eds.), *Information Technology Risk Management and Compliance in Modern Organizations* (pp. 268–300). Hershey, PA: IGI Global. doi:10.4018/978-1-5225-2604-9.ch010

Ksiazak, P., Farrelly, W., & Curran, K. (2018). A Lightweight Authentication and Encryption Protocol for Secure Communications Between Resource-Limited Devices Without Hardware Modification: Resource-Limited Device Authentication. In Y. Maleh (Ed.), *Security and Privacy Management, Techniques, and Protocols* (pp. 1–46). Hershey, PA: IGI Global. doi:10.4018/978-1-5225-5583-4.ch001

Kukkuvada, A., & Basavaraju, P. (2018). Mutual Correlation-Based Anonymization for Privacy Preserving Medical Data Publishing. In C. Pradhan, H. Das, B. Naik, & N. Dey (Eds.), *Handbook of Research on Information Security in Biomedical Signal Processing* (pp. 304–319). Hershey, PA: IGI Global. doi:10.4018/978-1-5225-5152-2.ch016

Kumar, G., & Saini, H. (2018). Secure and Robust Telemedicine using ECC on Radix-8 with Formal Verification. *International Journal of Information Security and Privacy*, *12*(1), 13–28. doi:10.4018/IJISP.2018010102

Kumar, M., & Bhandari, A. (2017). Performance Evaluation of Web Server's Request Queue against AL-DDoS Attacks in NS-2. *International Journal of Information Security and Privacy*, *11*(4), 29–46. doi:10.4018/IJISP.2017100103

Kumar, M., & Vardhan, M. (2018). Privacy Preserving and Efficient Outsourcing Algorithm to Public Cloud: A Case of Statistical Analysis. *International Journal of Information Security and Privacy*, *12*(2), 1–25. doi:10.4018/IJISP.2018040101

Kumar, R. (2018). A Robust Biometrics System Using Finger Knuckle Print. In G. Shrivastava, P. Kumar, B. Gupta, S. Bala, & N. Dey (Eds.), *Handbook of Research on Network Forensics and Analysis Techniques* (pp. 416–446). Hershey, PA: IGI Global. doi:10.4018/978-1-5225-4100-4.ch022

Kumar, R. (2018). DOS Attacks on Cloud Platform: Their Solutions and Implications. In S. Aljawarneh & M. Malhotra (Eds.), *Critical Research on Scalability and Security Issues in Virtual Cloud Environments* (pp. 167–184). Hershey, PA: IGI Global. doi:10.4018/978-1-5225-3029-9.ch008

Kumari, R., & Sharma, K. (2018). Cross-Layer Based Intrusion Detection and Prevention for Network. In G. Shrivastava, P. Kumar, B. Gupta, S. Bala, & N. Dey (Eds.), *Handbook of Research on Network Forensics and Analysis Techniques* (pp. 38–56). Hershey, PA: IGI Global. doi:10.4018/978-1-5225-4100-4.ch003

Lapke, M. (2018). A Semiotic Examination of the Security Policy Lifecycle. In Y. Maleh (Ed.), *Security and Privacy Management, Techniques, and Protocols* (pp. 237–253). Hershey, PA: IGI Global. doi:10.4018/978-1-5225-5583-4.ch009

Liang, Z., Feng, B., Xu, X., Wu, X., & Yang, T. (2018). Geometrically Invariant Image Watermarking Using Histogram Adjustment. *International Journal of Digital Crime and Forensics*, *10*(1), 54–66. doi:10.4018/IJDCF.2018010105

Liu, Z. J. (2017). A Cyber Crime Investigation Model Based on Case Characteristics. *International Journal of Digital Crime and Forensics*, *9*(4), 40–47. doi:10.4018/IJDCF.2017100104

Loganathan, S. (2018). A Step-by-Step Procedural Methodology for Improving an Organization's IT Risk Management System. In M. Gupta, R. Sharman, J. Walp, & P. Mulgund (Eds.), *Information Technology Risk Management and Compliance in Modern Organizations* (pp. 21–47). Hershey, PA: IGI Global. doi:10.4018/978-1-5225-2604-9.ch002

Long, M., Peng, F., & Gong, X. (2018). A Format-Compliant Encryption for Secure HEVC Video Sharing in Multimedia Social Network. *International Journal of Digital Crime and Forensics*, *10*(2), 23–39. doi:10.4018/IJDCF.2018040102

M., S., & M., J. (2018). Biosignal Denoising Techniques. In C. Pradhan, H. Das, B. Naik, & N. Dey (Eds.), *Handbook of Research on Information Security in Biomedical Signal Processing* (pp. 26-37). Hershey, PA: IGI Global. https://doi.org/ doi:10.4018/978-1-5225-5152-2.ch002

Mahapatra, C. (2017). Pragmatic Solutions to Cyber Security Threat in Indian Context. In R. Kumar, P. Pattnaik, & P. Pandey (Eds.), *Detecting and Mitigating Robotic Cyber Security Risks* (pp. 172–176). Hershey, PA: IGI Global. doi:10.4018/978-1-5225-2154-9.ch012

Majumder, A., Nath, S., & Das, A. (2018). Data Integrity in Mobile Cloud Computing. In K. Munir (Ed.), *Cloud Computing Technologies for Green Enterprises* (pp. 166–199). Hershey, PA: IGI Global. doi:10.4018/978-1-5225-3038-1.ch007

Maleh, Y., Zaydi, M., Sahid, A., & Ezzati, A. (2018). Building a Maturity Framework for Information Security Governance Through an Empirical Study in Organizations. In Y. Maleh (Ed.), *Security and Privacy Management, Techniques, and Protocols* (pp. 96–127). Hershey, PA: IGI Global. doi:10.4018/978-1-5225-5583-4.ch004

Malhotra, M., & Singh, A. (2018). Role of Agents to Enhance the Security and Scalability in Cloud Environment. In S. Aljawarneh & M. Malhotra (Eds.), *Critical Research on Scalability and Security Issues in Virtual Cloud Environments* (pp. 19–47). Hershey, PA: IGI Global. doi:10.4018/978-1-5225-3029-9.ch002

Mali, A. D. (2017). Recent Advances in Minimally-Obtrusive Monitoring of People's Health. *International Journal of Monitoring and Surveillance Technologies Research*, *5*(2), 44–56. doi:10.4018/IJMSTR.2017040104

Mali, A. D., & Yang, N. (2017). On Automated Generation of Keyboard Layout to Reduce Finger-Travel Distance. *International Journal of Monitoring and Surveillance Technologies Research*, *5*(2), 29–43. doi:10.4018/IJMSTR.2017040103

Mali, P. (2018). Defining Cyber Weapon in Context of Technology and Law. *International Journal of Cyber Warfare & Terrorism*, *8*(1), 43–55. doi:10.4018/IJCWT.2018010104

Malik, A., & Pandey, B. (2018). CIAS: A Comprehensive Identity Authentication Scheme for Providing Security in VANET. *International Journal of Information Security and Privacy*, *12*(1), 29–41. doi:10.4018/IJISP.2018010103

Manikandakumar, M., & Ramanujam, E. (2018). Security and Privacy Challenges in Big Data Environment. In G. Shrivastava, P. Kumar, B. Gupta, S. Bala, & N. Dey (Eds.), *Handbook of Research on Network Forensics and Analysis Techniques* (pp. 315–325). Hershey, PA: IGI Global. doi:10.4018/978-1-5225-4100-4.ch017

Manogaran, G., Thota, C., & Lopez, D. (2018). Human-Computer Interaction With Big Data Analytics. In D. Lopez & M. Durai (Eds.), *HCI Challenges and Privacy Preservation in Big Data Security* (pp. 1–22). Hershey, PA: IGI Global. doi:10.4018/978-1-5225-2863-0.ch001

Mbale, J. (2018). Computer Centres Resource Cloud Elasticity-Scalability (CRECES): Copperbelt University Case Study. In S. Aljawarneh & M. Malhotra (Eds.), *Critical Research on Scalability and Security Issues in Virtual Cloud Environments* (pp. 48–70). Hershey, PA: IGI Global. doi:10.4018/978-1-5225-3029-9.ch003

McAvoy, D. (2017). Institutional Entrepreneurship in Defence Acquisition: What Don't We Understand? In K. Burgess & P. Antill (Eds.), *Emerging Strategies in Defense Acquisitions and Military Procurement* (pp. 222–241). Hershey, PA: IGI Global. doi:10.4018/978-1-5225-0599-0.ch013

McKeague, J., & Curran, K. (2018). Detecting the Use of Anonymous Proxies. *International Journal of Digital Crime and Forensics*, *10*(2), 74–94. doi:10.4018/IJDCF.2018040105

Meitei, T. G., Singh, S. A., & Majumder, S. (2018). PCG-Based Biometrics. In C. Pradhan, H. Das, B. Naik, & N. Dey (Eds.), *Handbook of Research on Information Security in Biomedical Signal Processing* (pp. 1–25). Hershey, PA: IGI Global. doi:10.4018/978-1-5225-5152-2.ch001

Menemencioğlu, O., & Orak, İ. M. (2017). A Simple Solution to Prevent Parameter Tampering in Web Applications. In M. Korstanje (Ed.), *Threat Mitigation and Detection of Cyber Warfare and Terrorism Activities* (pp. 1–20). Hershey, PA: IGI Global. doi:10.4018/978-1-5225-1938-6.ch001

Minto-Coy, I. D., & Henlin, M. G. (2017). The Development of Cybersecurity Policy and Legislative Landscape in Latin America and Caribbean States. In M. Moore (Ed.), *Cybersecurity Breaches and Issues Surrounding Online Threat Protection* (pp. 24–53). Hershey, PA: IGI Global. doi:10.4018/978-1-5225-1941-6.ch002

Mohamed, J. H. (2018). Scientograph-Based Visualization of Computer Forensics Research Literature. In J. Jeyasekar & P. Saravanan (Eds.), *Innovations in Measuring and Evaluating Scientific Information* (pp. 148–162). Hershey, PA: IGI Global. doi:10.4018/978-1-5225-3457-0.ch010

Mohan Murthy, M. K., & Sanjay, H. A. (2018). Scalability for Cloud. In S. Aljawarneh & M. Malhotra (Eds.), *Critical Research on Scalability and Security Issues in Virtual Cloud Environments* (pp. 1–18). Hershey, PA: IGI Global. doi:10.4018/978-1-5225-3029-9.ch001

Moorthy, U., & Gandhi, U. D. (2018). A Survey of Big Data Analytics Using Machine Learning Algorithms. In D. Lopez & M. Durai (Eds.), *HCI Challenges and Privacy Preservation in Big Data Security* (pp. 95–123). Hershey, PA: IGI Global. doi:10.4018/978-1-5225-2863-0.ch005

Mountantonakis, M., Minadakis, N., Marketakis, Y., Fafalios, P., & Tzitzikas, Y. (2018). Connectivity, Value, and Evolution of a Semantic Warehouse. In M. Lytras, N. Aljohani, E. Damiani, & K. Chui (Eds.), *Innovations, Developments, and Applications of Semantic Web and Information Systems* (pp. 1–31). Hershey, PA: IGI Global. doi:10.4018/978-1-5225-5042-6.ch001

Moussa, M., & Demurjian, S. A. (2017). Differential Privacy Approach for Big Data Privacy in Healthcare. In S. Tamane, V. Solanki, & N. Dey (Eds.), *Privacy and Security Policies in Big Data* (pp. 191–213). Hershey, PA: IGI Global. doi:10.4018/978-1-5225-2486-1.ch009

Mugisha, E., Zhang, G., El Abidine, M. Z., & Eugene, M. (2017). A TPM-based Secure Multi-Cloud Storage Architecture grounded on Erasure Codes. *International Journal of Information Security and Privacy*, *11*(1), 52–64. doi:10.4018/IJISP.2017010104

Nachtigall, L. G., Araujo, R. M., & Nachtigall, G. R. (2017). Use of Images of Leaves and Fruits of Apple Trees for Automatic Identification of Symptoms of Diseases and Nutritional Disorders. *International Journal of Monitoring and Surveillance Technologies Research*, *5*(2), 1–14. doi:10.4018/IJMSTR.2017040101

Nagesh, K., Sumathy, R., Devakumar, P., & Sathiyamurthy, K. (2017). A Survey on Denial of Service Attacks and Preclusions. *International Journal of Information Security and Privacy*, *11*(4), 1–15. doi:10.4018/IJISP.2017100101

Nanda, A., Popat, P., & Vimalkumar, D. (2018). Navigating Through Choppy Waters of PCI DSS Compliance. In M. Gupta, R. Sharman, J. Walp, & P. Mulgund (Eds.), *Information Technology Risk Management and Compliance in Modern Organizations* (pp. 99–140). Hershey, PA: IGI Global. doi:10.4018/978-1-5225-2604-9.ch005

Newton, S. (2017). The Determinants of Stock Market Development in Emerging Economies: Examining the Impact of Corporate Governance and Regulatory Reforms (I). In M. Ojo & J. Van Akkeren (Eds.), *Value Relevance of Accounting Information in Capital Markets* (pp. 114–125). Hershey, PA: IGI Global. doi:10.4018/978-1-5225-1900-3.ch008

Nidhyananthan, S. S. A., J. V., & R., S. S. (2018). Wireless Enhanced Security Based on Speech Recognition. In C. Pradhan, H. Das, B. Naik, & N. Dey (Eds.), Handbook of Research on Information Security in Biomedical Signal Processing (pp. 228-253). Hershey, PA: IGI Global. https://doi.org/ doi:10.4018/978-1-5225-5152-2.ch012

Norri-Sederholm, T., Huhtinen, A., & Paakkonen, H. (2018). Ensuring Public Safety Organisations' Information Flow and Situation Picture in Hybrid Environments. *International Journal of Cyber Warfare & Terrorism*, *8*(1), 12–24. doi:10.4018/IJCWT.2018010102

Nunez, S., & Castaño, R. (2017). Building Brands in Emerging Economies: A Consumer-Oriented Approach. In Rajagopal, & R. Behl (Eds.), Business Analytics and Cyber Security Management in Organizations (pp. 183-194). Hershey, PA: IGI Global. doi:10.4018/978-1-5225-0902-8.ch013

Odella, F. (2018). Privacy Awareness and the Networking Generation. *International Journal of Technoethics*, *9*(1), 51–70. doi:10.4018/IJT.2018010105

Ojo, M., & DiGabriele, J. A. (2017). Fundamental or Enhancing Roles?: The Dual Roles of External Auditors and Forensic Accountants. In M. Ojo & J. Van Akkeren (Eds.), *Value Relevance of Accounting Information in Capital Markets* (pp. 59–78). Hershey, PA: IGI Global. doi:10.4018/978-1-5225-1900-3.ch004

Olomojobi, Y., & Omotola, O. T. (2021). Social Media: A Protagonist for Terrorism. *International Journal of Cyber Warfare & Terrorism*, *11*(1), 31–44. https://doi.org/10.4018/IJCWT.2021010103

Pandey, S. (2018). An Empirical Study of the Indian IT Sector on Typologies of Workaholism as Predictors of HR Crisis. In V. Ahuja & S. Rathore (Eds.), *Multidisciplinary Perspectives on Human Capital and Information Technology Professionals* (pp. 202–224). Hershey, PA: IGI Global. doi:10.4018/978-1-5225-5297-0.ch011

Pattabiraman, A., Srinivasan, S., Swaminathan, K., & Gupta, M. (2018). Fortifying Corporate Human Wall: A Literature Review of Security Awareness and Training. In M. Gupta, R. Sharman, J. Walp, & P. Mulgund (Eds.), *Information Technology Risk Management and Compliance in Modern Organizations* (pp. 142–175). Hershey, PA: IGI Global. doi:10.4018/978-1-5225-2604-9.ch006

Prachi. (2018). Detection of Botnet Based Attacks on Network: Using Machine Learning Techniques. In G. Shrivastava, P. Kumar, B. Gupta, S. Bala, & N. Dey (Eds.), *Handbook of Research on Network Forensics and Analysis Techniques* (pp. 101-116). Hershey, PA: IGI Global. https://doi.org/ doi:10.4018/978-1-5225-4100-4.ch007

Pradhan, P. L. (2017). Proposed Round Robin CIA Pattern on RTS for Risk Assessment. *International Journal of Digital Crime and Forensics*, *9*(1), 71–85. doi:10.4018/IJDCF.2017010105

Prentice, S., & Taylor, P. J. (2018). Psychological and Behavioral Examinations of Online Terrorism. In J. McAlaney, L. Frumkin, & V. Benson (Eds.), *Psychological and Behavioral Examinations in Cyber Security* (pp. 151–171). Hershey, PA: IGI Global. doi:10.4018/978-1-5225-4053-3.ch009

Priyadarshini, I. (2017). Cyber Security Risks in Robotics. In R. Kumar, P. Pattnaik, & P. Pandey (Eds.), *Detecting and Mitigating Robotic Cyber Security Risks* (pp. 333–348). Hershey, PA: IGI Global. doi:10.4018/978-1-5225-2154-9.ch022

R., A., & D., E. (2018). Cyber Crime Toolkit Development. In G. Shrivastava, P. Kumar, B. Gupta, S. Bala, & N. Dey (Eds.), *Handbook of Research on Network Forensics and Analysis Techniques* (pp. 184-224). Hershey, PA: IGI Global. https:// doi.org/ doi:10.4018/978-1-5225-4100-4.ch011

Raghunath, R. (2018). Research Trends in Forensic Sciences: A Scientometric Approach. In J. Jeyasekar & P. Saravanan (Eds.), *Innovations in Measuring and Evaluating Scientific Information* (pp. 108–124). Hershey, PA: IGI Global. doi:10.4018/978-1-5225-3457-0.ch008

Ramadhas, G., Sankar, A. S., & Sugathan, N. (2018). The Scientific Communication Process in Homoeopathic Toxicology: An Evaluative Study. In J. Jeyasekar & P. Saravanan (Eds.), *Innovations in Measuring and Evaluating Scientific Information* (pp. 163–179). Hershey, PA: IGI Global. doi:10.4018/978-1-5225-3457-0.ch011

Ramani, K. (2018). Impact of Big Data on Security: Big Data Security Issues and Defense Schemes. In G. Shrivastava, P. Kumar, B. Gupta, S. Bala, & N. Dey (Eds.), *Handbook of Research on Network Forensics and Analysis Techniques* (pp. 326–350). Hershey, PA: IGI Global. doi:10.4018/978-1-5225-4100-4.ch018

Ramos, P., Funderburk, P., & Gebelein, J. (2018). Social Media and Online Gaming: A Masquerading Funding Source. *International Journal of Cyber Warfare & Terrorism, 8*(1), 25–42. doi:10.4018/IJCWT.2018010103

Rao, N., & Srivastava, S., & K.S., S. (2017). PKI Deployment Challenges and Recommendations for ICS Networks. *International Journal of Information Security and Privacy, 11*(2), 38–48. doi:10.4018/IJISP.2017040104

Rath, M., Swain, J., Pati, B., & Pattanayak, B. K. (2018). Network Security: Attacks and Control in MANET. In G. Shrivastava, P. Kumar, B. Gupta, S. Bala, & N. Dey (Eds.), *Handbook of Research on Network Forensics and Analysis Techniques* (pp. 19–37). Hershey, PA: IGI Global. doi:10.4018/978-1-5225-4100-4.ch002

Ricci, J., Baggili, I., & Breitinger, F. (2017). Watch What You Wear: Smartwatches and Sluggish Security. In A. Marrington, D. Kerr, & J. Gammack (Eds.), *Managing Security Issues and the Hidden Dangers of Wearable Technologies* (pp. 47–73). Hershey, PA: IGI Global. doi:10.4018/978-1-5225-1016-1.ch003

Rossi, J. A. (2017). Revisiting the Value Relevance of Accounting Information in the Italian and UK Stock Markets. In M. Ojo & J. Van Akkeren (Eds.), *Value Relevance of Accounting Information in Capital Markets* (pp. 102–113). Hershey, PA: IGI Global. doi:10.4018/978-1-5225-1900-3.ch007

Sabillon, R., Serra-Ruiz, J., Cavaller, V., & Cano, J. J. (2017). Digital Forensic Analysis of Cybercrimes: Best Practices and Methodologies. *International Journal of Information Security and Privacy, 11*(2), 25–37. doi:10.4018/IJISP.2017040103

Sadasivam, U. M., & Ganesan, N. (2021). Detecting Fake News Using Deep Learning and NLP. In S. Misra, C. Arumugam, S. Jaganathan, & S. S. (Ed.), *Confluence of AI, Machine, and Deep Learning in Cyber Forensics* (pp. 117-133). IGI Global. https://doi.org/10.4018/978-1-7998-4900-1.ch007

Sample, C., Cowley, J., & Bakdash, J. Z. (2018). Cyber + Culture: Exploring the Relationship. In J. McAlaney, L. Frumkin, & V. Benson (Eds.), *Psychological and Behavioral Examinations in Cyber Security* (pp. 64–79). Hershey, PA: IGI Global. doi:10.4018/978-1-5225-4053-3.ch004

Sarıgöllü, S. C., Aksakal, E., Koca, M. G., Akten, E., & Aslanbay, Y. (2018). Volunteered Surveillance. In J. McAlaney, L. Frumkin, & V. Benson (Eds.), *Psychological and Behavioral Examinations in Cyber Security* (pp. 133–150). Hershey, PA: IGI Global. doi:10.4018/978-1-5225-4053-3.ch008

Shahriar, H., Clincy, V., & Bond, W. (2018). Classification of Web-Service-Based Attacks and Mitigation Techniques. In Y. Maleh (Ed.), *Security and Privacy Management, Techniques, and Protocols* (pp. 360–378). Hershey, PA: IGI Global. doi:10.4018/978-1-5225-5583-4.ch015

Shet, S., Aswath, A. R., Hanumantharaju, M. C., & Gao, X. (2017). Design of Reconfigurable Architectures for Steganography System. In N. Dey, A. Ashour, & S. Acharjee (Eds.), *Applied Video Processing in Surveillance and Monitoring Systems* (pp. 145–168). Hershey, PA: IGI Global. doi:10.4018/978-1-5225-1022-2.ch007

Shrivastava, G., Sharma, K., Khari, M., & Zohora, S. E. (2018). Role of Cyber Security and Cyber Forensics in India. In G. Shrivastava, P. Kumar, B. Gupta, S. Bala, & N. Dey (Eds.), *Handbook of Research on Network Forensics and Analysis Techniques* (pp. 143–161). Hershey, PA: IGI Global. doi:10.4018/978-1-5225-4100-4.ch009

Singh, N., Mittal, T., & Gupta, M. (2018). A Tale of Policies and Breaches: Analytical Approach to Construct Social Media Policy. In M. Gupta, R. Sharman, J. Walp, & P. Mulgund (Eds.), *Information Technology Risk Management and Compliance in Modern Organizations* (pp. 176–212). Hershey, PA: IGI Global. doi:10.4018/978-1-5225-2604-9.ch007

Singh, R., & Jalota, H. (2018). A Study of Good-Enough Security in the Context of Rural Business Process Outsourcing. In J. McAlaney, L. Frumkin, & V. Benson (Eds.), *Psychological and Behavioral Examinations in Cyber Security* (pp. 239–252). Hershey, PA: IGI Global. doi:10.4018/978-1-5225-4053-3.ch014

Sivasubramanian, K. E. (2018). Authorship Pattern and Collaborative Research Productivity of Asian Journal of Dairy and Food Research During the Year 2011 to 2015. In J. Jeyasekar & P. Saravanan (Eds.), *Innovations in Measuring and Evaluating Scientific Information* (pp. 213–222). Hershey, PA: IGI Global. doi:10.4018/978-1-5225-3457-0.ch014

Somasundaram, R., & Thirugnanam, M. (2017). IoT in Healthcare: Breaching Security Issues. In N. Jeyanthi & R. Thandeeswaran (Eds.), *Security Breaches and Threat Prevention in the Internet of Things* (pp. 174–188). Hershey, PA: IGI Global. doi:10.4018/978-1-5225-2296-6.ch008

Sonam, & Khari, M. (2018). Wireless Sensor Networks: A Technical Survey. In G. Shrivastava, P. Kumar, B. Gupta, S. Bala, & N. Dey (Eds.), *Handbook of Research on Network Forensics and Analysis Techniques* (pp. 1-18). Hershey, PA: IGI Global. https://doi.org/ doi:10.4018/978-1-5225-4100-4.ch001

Soni, P. (2018). Implications of HIPAA and Subsequent Regulations on Information Technology. In M. Gupta, R. Sharman, J. Walp, & P. Mulgund (Eds.), *Information Technology Risk Management and Compliance in Modern Organizations* (pp. 71–98). Hershey, PA: IGI Global. doi:10.4018/978-1-5225-2604-9.ch004

Sönmez, F. Ö., & Günel, B. (2018). Security Visualization Extended Review Issues, Classifications, Validation Methods, Trends, Extensions. In Y. Maleh (Ed.), *Security and Privacy Management, Techniques, and Protocols* (pp. 152–197). Hershey, PA: IGI Global. doi:10.4018/978-1-5225-5583-4.ch006

Srivastava, S. R., & Dube, S. (2018). Cyberattacks, Cybercrime and Cyberterrorism. In G. Shrivastava, P. Kumar, B. Gupta, S. Bala, & N. Dey (Eds.), *Handbook of Research on Network Forensics and Analysis Techniques* (pp. 162–183). Hershey, PA: IGI Global. doi:10.4018/978-1-5225-4100-4.ch010

Stacey, E. (2017). Contemporary Terror on the Net. In *Combating Internet-Enabled Terrorism: Emerging Research and Opportunities* (pp. 16–44). Hershey, PA: IGI Global. doi:10.4018/978-1-5225-2190-7.ch002

Sumana, M., Hareesha, K. S., & Kumar, S. (2018). Semantically Secure Classifiers for Privacy Preserving Data Mining. In Y. Maleh (Ed.), *Security and Privacy Management, Techniques, and Protocols* (pp. 66–95). Hershey, PA: IGI Global. doi:10.4018/978-1-5225-5583-4.ch003

Suresh, N., & Gupta, M. (2018). Impact of Technology Innovation: A Study on Cloud Risk Mitigation. In M. Gupta, R. Sharman, J. Walp, & P. Mulgund (Eds.), *Information Technology Risk Management and Compliance in Modern Organizations* (pp. 229–267). Hershey, PA: IGI Global. doi:10.4018/978-1-5225-2604-9.ch009

Tank, D. M. (2017). Security and Privacy Issues, Solutions, and Tools for MCC. In K. Munir (Ed.), *Security Management in Mobile Cloud Computing* (pp. 121–147). Hershey, PA: IGI Global. doi:10.4018/978-1-5225-0602-7.ch006

Thackray, H., & McAlaney, J. (2018). Groups Online: Hacktivism and Social Protest. In J. McAlaney, L. Frumkin, & V. Benson (Eds.), *Psychological and Behavioral Examinations in Cyber Security* (pp. 194–209). Hershey, PA: IGI Global. doi:10.4018/978-1-5225-4053-3.ch011

Thandeeswaran, R., Pawar, R., & Rai, M. (2017). Security Threats in Autonomous Vehicles. In N. Jeyanthi & R. Thandeeswaran (Eds.), *Security Breaches and Threat Prevention in the Internet of Things* (pp. 117–141). Hershey, PA: IGI Global. doi:10.4018/978-1-5225-2296-6.ch006

Thota, C., Manogaran, G., Lopez, D., & Vijayakumar, V. (2017). Big Data Security Framework for Distributed Cloud Data Centers. In M. Moore (Ed.), *Cybersecurity Breaches and Issues Surrounding Online Threat Protection* (pp. 288–310). Hershey, PA: IGI Global. doi:10.4018/978-1-5225-1941-6.ch012

Thukral, S., & Rodriguez, T. D. (2018). Child Sexual Abuse: Intra- and Extra-Familial Risk Factors, Reactions, and Interventions. In R. Gopalan (Ed.), *Social, Psychological, and Forensic Perspectives on Sexual Abuse* (pp. 229–258). Hershey, PA: IGI Global. doi:10.4018/978-1-5225-3958-2.ch017

Tidke, S. (2017). MonogDB: Data Management in NoSQL. In S. Tamane, V. Solanki, & N. Dey (Eds.), *Privacy and Security Policies in Big Data* (pp. 64–91). Hershey, PA: IGI Global. doi:10.4018/978-1-5225-2486-1.ch004

Tierney, M. (2018). #TerroristFinancing: An Examination of Terrorism Financing via the Internet. *International Journal of Cyber Warfare & Terrorism, 8*(1), 1–11. doi:10.4018/IJCWT.2018010101

Topal, R. (2018). A Cyber-Psychological and Behavioral Approach to Online Radicalization. In J. McAlaney, L. Frumkin, & V. Benson (Eds.), *Psychological and Behavioral Examinations in Cyber Security* (pp. 210–221). Hershey, PA: IGI Global. doi:10.4018/978-1-5225-4053-3.ch012

Tripathy, B. K., & Baktha, K. (2018). Clustering Approaches. In *Security, Privacy, and Anonymization in Social Networks: Emerging Research and Opportunities* (pp. 51–85). Hershey, PA: IGI Global. doi:10.4018/978-1-5225-5158-4.ch004

Tripathy, B. K., & Baktha, K. (2018). De-Anonymization Techniques. In *Security, Privacy, and Anonymization in Social Networks: Emerging Research and Opportunities* (pp. 137–147). Hershey, PA: IGI Global. doi:10.4018/978-1-5225-5158-4.ch007

Tripathy, B. K., & Baktha, K. (2018). Fundamentals of Social Networks. In *Security, Privacy, and Anonymization in Social Networks: Emerging Research and Opportunities* (pp. 1–22). Hershey, PA: IGI Global. doi:10.4018/978-1-5225-5158-4.ch001

Tripathy, B. K., & Baktha, K. (2018). Graph Modification Approaches. In *Security, Privacy, and Anonymization in Social Networks: Emerging Research and Opportunities* (pp. 86–115). Hershey, PA: IGI Global. doi:10.4018/978-1-5225-5158-4.ch005

Tripathy, B. K., & Baktha, K. (2018). Social Network Anonymization Techniques. In *Security, Privacy, and Anonymization in Social Networks: Emerging Research and Opportunities* (pp. 36–50). Hershey, PA: IGI Global. doi:10.4018/978-1-5225-5158-4.ch003

Tsimperidis, I., Rostami, S., & Katos, V. (2017). Age Detection Through Keystroke Dynamics from User Authentication Failures. *International Journal of Digital Crime and Forensics, 9*(1), 1–16. doi:10.4018/IJDCF.2017010101

Wadkar, H. S., Mishra, A., & Dixit, A. M. (2017). Framework to Secure Browser Using Configuration Analysis. *International Journal of Information Security and Privacy, 11*(2), 49–63. doi:10.4018/IJISP.2017040105

Wahlgren, G., & Kowalski, S. J. (2018). IT Security Risk Management Model for Handling IT-Related Security Incidents: The Need for a New Escalation Approach. In Y. Maleh (Ed.), *Security and Privacy Management, Techniques, and Protocols* (pp. 129–151). Hershey, PA: IGI Global. doi:10.4018/978-1-5225-5583-4.ch005

Wall, H. J., & Kaye, L. K. (2018). Online Decision Making: Online Influence and Implications for Cyber Security. In J. McAlaney, L. Frumkin, & V. Benson (Eds.), *Psychological and Behavioral Examinations in Cyber Security* (pp. 1–25). Hershey, PA: IGI Global. doi:10.4018/978-1-5225-4053-3.ch001

Wu, J. B., Zhang, Y., Luo, C. W., Yuan, L. F., & Shen, X. K. (2021). A Modification-Free Steganography Algorithm Based on Image Classification and CNN. *International Journal of Digital Crime and Forensics, 13*(3), 47–58. https://doi.org/10.4018/IJDCF.20210501.oa4

Xylogiannopoulos, K. F., Karampelas, P., & Alhajj, R. (2017). Advanced Network Data Analytics for Large-Scale DDoS Attack Detection. *International Journal of Cyber Warfare & Terrorism, 7*(3), 44–54. doi:10.4018/IJCWT.2017070104

Yan, W. Q., Wu, X., & Liu, F. (2018). Progressive Scrambling for Social Media. *International Journal of Digital Crime and Forensics*, *10*(2), 56–73. doi:10.4018/IJDCF.2018040104

Yassein, M. B., Mardini, W., & Al-Abdi, A. (2018). Security Issues in the Internet of Things: A Review. In S. Aljawarneh & M. Malhotra (Eds.), *Critical Research on Scalability and Security Issues in Virtual Cloud Environments* (pp. 186–200). Hershey, PA: IGI Global. doi:10.4018/978-1-5225-3029-9.ch009

Yassein, M. B., Shatnawi, M., & l-Qasem, N. (2018). A Survey of Probabilistic Broadcast Schemes in Mobile Ad Hoc Networks. In S. Aljawarneh, & M. Malhotra (Eds.), *Critical Research on Scalability and Security Issues in Virtual Cloud Environments* (pp. 269-282). Hershey, PA: IGI Global. https://doi.org/doi:10.4018/978-1-5225-3029-9.ch013

Yue, C., Tianliang, L., Manchun, C., & Jingying, L. (2018). Evaluation of the Attack Effect Based on Improved Grey Clustering Model. *International Journal of Digital Crime and Forensics*, *10*(1), 92–100. doi:10.4018/IJDCF.2018010108

Zhang, P., He, Y., & Chow, K. (2018). Fraud Track on Secure Electronic Check System. *International Journal of Digital Crime and Forensics*, *10*(2), 137–144. doi:10.4018/IJDCF.2018040108

Zhou, L., Yan, W. Q., Shu, Y., & Yu, J. (2018). CVSS: A Cloud-Based Visual Surveillance System. *International Journal of Digital Crime and Forensics*, *10*(1), 79–91. doi:10.4018/IJDCF.2018010107

Zhu, J., Guan, Q., Zhao, X., Cao, Y., & Chen, G. (2017). A Steganalytic Scheme Based on Classifier Selection Using Joint Image Characteristics. *International Journal of Digital Crime and Forensics*, *9*(4), 1–14. doi:10.4018/IJDCF.2017100101

Zoughbi, S. (2017). Major Technology Trends Affecting Government Data in Developing Countries. In S. Zoughbi (Ed.), *Securing Government Information and Data in Developing Countries* (pp. 127–135). Hershey, PA: IGI Global. doi:10.4018/978-1-5225-1703-0.ch008

Zubairu, B. (2018). Security Risks of Biomedical Data Processing in Cloud Computing Environment. In C. Pradhan, H. Das, B. Naik, & N. Dey (Eds.), *Handbook of Research on Information Security in Biomedical Signal Processing* (pp. 177–197). Hershey, PA: IGI Global. doi:10.4018/978-1-5225-5152-2.ch009

About the Contributors

Victor Lobo is an Invited Full Professor, NOVA Information Management School (NOVA IMS).

Anacleto Correia (M) is an Associate Professor and lecturer of Management and Information Systems subjects at the Portuguese Navy Academy. He holds a Ph.D. in Computer Science, an M.Sc. in Statistics and Information Management, a B.Sc. degree in Management, and also a B.Sc. at Portuguese Naval Academy. His research interests are focused on requirements engineering, software engineering, process modeling, data mining, machine learning, and business engineering. He has also more than 20 years of experience in industry-leading projects and architecting large software development projects and is the author of dozens of scientific papers in journals and conference proceedings.

* * *

Avi Arampatzis is a faculty member at the department of Electrical Engineering & Computer Engineering of Democritus University of Thrace, Greece; elected Lecturer in June 2007, hired in November 2009, promoted to Assistant Professor in August 2013, tenured in February 2018, promoted to Associate Professor in July 2019.

Eduardo Barros is a Cyber Security Analyst and Engineer no Centro Nacional de Cibersegurança [Portuguese National Cybersecurity Center].

Darrell Norman Burrell is post graduate student and a 2017 graduate of the National Coalition Building Institute's (NCBI) Leadership Diversity Institute. He is a Certified Diversity Professional. He is an alumnus of the prestigious Presidential Management Fellows Program www.pmf.gov. Dr Burrell has a doctorate degree with majors in Education and Executive Leadership Coaching from A.T. Still University. Dr. Burrell has an Education Specialist (EdS) graduate degree in Higher Education Administration from The George Washington University. He has two graduate degrees one in Human Resources Management/Development and another Organizational Management from National Louis University. He also has a Master of Arts degree in Sales and Marketing Management from Prescott College. He has extensive years of university teaching experience at several universities.

Maurice Dawson is an Assistant Professor of Information Technology and Management within the College of Computing at Illinois Institute of Technology. Additionally, he serves as Director and Distinguished Member of the IIT Center for Cyber Security and Forensics Education (C2SAFE) and responsible for working with the faculty who are members of this center. Before joining academia, he was an engineering manager for unmanned air systems and senior program manager for rotary-wing aircraft. He has a Doctor of Computer Science from Colorado Technical University and a Doctor of Philosophy in Cyber Security from the Intelligent Systems Research Centre at London Metropolitan University. Additionally, he is the co-editor of Developing Next-Generation Countermeasures for Homeland Security Threat Prevention, and New Threats and Countermeasures in Digital Crime and Cyber Terrorism, published by IGI Global in 2017, and 2015 respectively. He has received for Fulbright Scholar Grants.

Chhaya S. Dule is working as an Assistant Professor in the Department of Computer Science and Engineering, Dayanand Sagar University, Bangalore, KARNA-TAKA -State, India. She is pursuing her Ph.D. in Computer Science and Engineering from Visvesvaraya Technological University, Belgaum. She has completed her B.E from Shri Guru Gobind Singhji College of Engineering, Nanded (Dr. Babasaheb Ambedkar Aurangabad University) and M.Tech in Computer Science and Engineering from Samrat Ashok Technological Institute Vidisha (Rajiv Gandhi Proudyogiki Vishwavidhyalaya, Bhopal). She is having 19+ years of teaching experience. Her domain area of research is Cloud Computing - Security Issues. Her other area of interest is Artificial Intelligence and Neural Networks, DBMS, Software Engineering, Software Testing, Big Data Analytics, Data Mining, and Data Warehousing, Neural Network and Fuzzy logic. She has research publications in reputed National and International journals and conferences. She has attended various faculty development programs (FDP) and workshops organized by AICTE and TEQIP. She is a Life Member of CSI and ISTE professional bodies.

Anuja Jadhav has obtained her BE degree in Computer Science and Engineering from Sant Gadge Baba Amravati University, Amravati, M. Tech in Computer Science and Engineering from Rashta Sant Tukdoji Maharaj, Nagpur University, India. She has more than 13 years of experience and currently she is working in the

Department of Information Technology of Pimpri Chinchwad College of Engineering, Pune, India.

Manoj Jayabalan is a post doctorate fellow in the Faculty of Engineering & Technology, Liverpool John Moores University, UK. Manoj obtained his Ph.D. in Computing from Asia Pacific University of Technology & Innovation, Malaysia with research area focusing on health informatics and data science. He has completed his MSc. in Software Engineering from Staffordshire University, UK. He also holds a B.Eng. in Computer Science from Anna University, India. He was previously head of the Asia Pacific Center for Analytics (APCA), Malaysia. Moreover, he has received numerous excellence award for teaching and research in Asia Pacific University of Technology & Innovation, Malaysia. He engaged in research activities focusing in the area of Big Data, Data Mining, Machine Learning, Health Informatics, and Software Engineering. His area of expertise in the data analytics in performing data wrangling, and implementing models. He has supervised many industrial projects, master dissertations and mentored students for National level competitions. He has been invited guest speakers for several talks on Big Data and conducted many workshops.

Eugene J. M. Lewis is the former Assistant Professor of Marketing at Oakwood University from 2005 to 2010. Currently, he still serves as Adjunct Professor teaching courses in the area Logistics/Supply Chain Management, Marketing, and Information Systems. He has worked in Academic for more than 13 years as a part-time and full-time professor. Furthermore, he is the International Program Manager in the Aviation Industry for the United States Army Department of Defense working in the Foreign Military Sales (FMS) arena. He has served DOD for more than 10 years and has had the opportunity to work with many government officials and dignitaries in several foreign countries around the world.

Rajasekharaiah K. M. is working as Principal and Professor, Computer Science and Engineering, Kshatriya College of Engineering, Armoor, Nizamabad Dist. Telangana State. He has done B.E, M.Tech in Computer Science & Engineering, M.Phil in Computer Science and Ph.D. in Computer Science and Engineering from reputed Universities, India. He is having 35+ years of total experience including 18 years of Industrial and remaining Teaching experiences. He is a Life fellow Member of the Indian Society for Technical Education (ISTE), New Delhi. He has completed his Ph.D. in the domain area of Data Mining & Data Warehousing. He has research publications in reputed National and International journals. His other area of interests is DBMS, Software Engineering, Software Architecture, Computer Networks, Data Structures, and Mobile Computing. Further, he has served as Vice

Principal, Director – Academics, Dean – R & D, Coordinator for NBA and NAAC accreditation process. He organized and participated in conferences, Seminars, Workshops and FDPs at various National and International levels.

Katleho Makatjane is a lecturer in the Department of Statistics, University of Botswana. He is a trained quantitative business and risk analyst with more than four years of research experience together with community engagement. His research interest is in data mining methods with applications in business and finance. In particular, he specializes in Statistical methods used for Text mining and Text analysis, quantitative business and risk analysis, social media and digital tools with social network analysis using R. He also specializes in the area of causal inference in business and finance.

Shedden Masupe (SMIEEE) holds a BSc (Maths & Physics) from Mt Allison University, BScEng (Electrical – Communications and Fields) from University of New Brunswick, MSc (Digital Systems) from Cardiff University and a PhD (Electronics Engineering) from Edinburgh University. He is currently the Chief Executive Officer at Botswana Institute For Technology Research and Innovation (BITRI). He was previously a Full Professor of Computer Engineering at BIUST and an Associate Professor of Digital Systems and Computer Engineering at the University of Botswana. His research interests are in the areas of Computer Systems, Microprocessor Architectures, Low Power VLSI Design, Computer Vision and Smart ICT Solutions for Development.

Ntebogang Moroke is a Professor of Statistics at the North West University in South Africa. She has a PHD in Statistics from NWU in South Africa, and she is also a Deputy Dean in the Faculty of Economic and Management Sciences. She has published a large number of articles in the area of statistics and supervised a large number of doctoral students to completion, and she is a senior member of the South African Statistical Association (SASA).

Banyatsang Mphago holds a PhD in Computer Science from Botswana International University of Science and Technology, where his PhD research was on honeypot security. He also holds an MSc in Information Security from Lulea University of Technology (Sweden), a Post Graduate Diploma in Education from University of Botswana, BSc Computer Science from University of Botswana, and a Certified Ethical Hacker (CEHv7). He know works as a lecturer and a researcher in BIUST.

Dimane Mpoeleng currently works at the Computer Science and Information Systems, Botswana International University of Science and Technology (BIUST).

S. Raschid Muller is a Senior Cybersecurity SME with the Department of Defense at Fort Meade, Maryland. Academically, he serves as a Professor at the University of Maryland Global Campus where he teaches undergraduate courses within the School of Cybersecurity and Information Technology. He also teaches graduate Cybersecurity courses at the Ira A. Fulton Schools of Engineering at Arizona State University, The University of the Cumberlands, and Capitol Technology University. Dr. Muller previously served as the DISA Information Operation Faculty Chair from 2017-2019 at National Defense University and continues to serve as a guest lecturer. Dr. Muller was a 2020 Brookings Institute - LEGIS Congressional Fellow and served on the House Committee for Homeland Security on Capitol Hill. He was assigned to the Subcommittee on Cybersecurity, Infrastructure Protection, and Innovation where his portfolio includes; Cybersecurity and Infrastructure Security Agency (CISA) oversight, drafting and introducing cyber legislation, election security, cyber acquisitions, and Historically Black Colleges and Universities (HBCU) and Minority Serving Institutions (MSI) engagement. He is a 2021 University of California - Berkely Fellow in the Goldman School of Public Policy in their Executive Leadership Academy.

Sivasankari Narasimhan graduated her BE degree in Electronics and Communication Engineering from Anna University, Chennai in 2005 and M.E. in Applied Electronics from Anna University, Chennai in 2008. In the year 2021 she obtained her doctorate degree from Kalasalingam University, Tamilnadu. From 2008 to 2014, she worked as Assistant Professor in the department of Electronics and Communication Engineering, Kalasalingam University, Krishnankoil. Since 2015 she is working as Assistant Professor in Mepco Schlenk College of Engineering, Sivakasi, Virudhunagar District, Tamil Nadu, India. Her research areas include security and Image Processing.

Calvin Nobles is a Cybersecurity Professional and Human Factors Engineer with more than 25 years of experience. He is an Associate Professor and Department Chair at the Illinois Institute of Technology. He retired from the Navy and worked in the Financial and Services Industry for several years. He authored a book on the integration of technologically advanced aircraft in general aviation. He serves on the Cybersecurity Advisory Board at Stillman College and the Intelligence and National Security Alliance Cyber Council. He is a Cybersecurity Fellow at Harvard University.

Kevin Richardson currently serves as an Associate Professor of Business & Technology at Edward Waters University. He is a Certified Diversity Professional and a Certified Trainer. Dr. Richardson has two doctoral degrees and three graduate degrees. In 2016, he received his first doctorate degree in Operations and Quality

Management Systems from The National Graduate School (Washington, DC). In 2021, Dr. Richardson received a Philosophy of Doctorate (Ph.D.) in Technology Management of Information Systems from Capitol Technology University (Laurel, MD). He completed a Master of Science in Natural Resources Economics and Corporate Sustainability at Virginia Tech University (Blacksburg, VA). Dr. Richardson has a graduate degree in Information Systems Engineering Management from Harrisburg Science & Technology University (Harrisburg, PA), and his third master's degree in Counseling Psychology from Springfield College (Charleston, SC). Dr. Richardson has over 25 years of management, teaching, and training the trainer experience in academia, government, and private industries. His university teaching experience included teaching at Edward Waters University, Bethune Cookman University, Allen University, The National Graduate School of Quality Management, and Morris College.

Amalisha Sabie Aridi is a highly seasoned and credentialed organizational, leadership, and employee development professional consultant and coach. Experienced and thorough management consultant with a substantial amount of diversified expertise and education in the field of business management and leadership. Hardworking, multitalented, and keen manager who develops strong working relationships and consistently exceeds goals. Proven management skills that are enhanced by MBA/AB.D/Ph.D. credentials, and distinguished leadership skills that conform to the effective leadership matrix.

Ioannis Tsimperidis received Bachelor Degree from Aristotle University of Thessaloniki in 1997, and MSc and PhD Degrees from Democritus University of Thrace in 2002 and 2017, respectively. Currently he is a PostDoc researcher at the Department of Electrical and Computer Engineering of Democritus University of Thrace. He has been working as a Secondary Education teacher since 2006. His main areas of research interest are keystroke analysis, data mining and digital forensics.

Pallavi S. Yevale Assistant Professor Department of Artificial Intelligence and Data Science Dr. D. Y. Patil Institute of Engineering, Management and Research, Akurdi, Pune, India.

Index

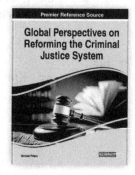

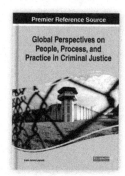

 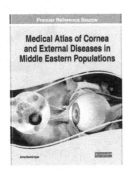 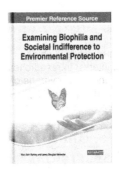 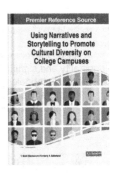

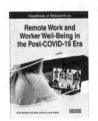

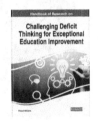

Printed in the United States
by Baker & Taylor Publisher Services